THE GILDED CAGE

The Gilded Cage

TECHNOLOGY, DEVELOPMENT, AND STATE CAPITALISM IN CHINA

YA-WEN LEI

PRINCETON UNIVERSITY PRESS

PRINCETON & OXFORD

Portions of chapter 5 appeared as "Upgrading China through Automation: Manufacturers, Workers and the Techno-Developmental State" in *Work, Employment and Society* (December 2022). Reprinted by permission of SAGE Publications, Inc.

Portions of chapter 7 appeared as "Delivering Solidarity: Platform Architecture and Collective Contention in China's Platform Economy" in *American Sociological Review* (April 2021). Reprinted by permission of SAGE Publications, Inc.

Published by Princeton University Press
41 William Street, Princeton, New Jersey 08540
99 Banbury Road, Oxford OX2 6JX

press.princeton.edu

All Rights Reserved

Library of Congress Cataloging-in-Publication Data

Names: Lei, Ya-Wen, author.
Title: The gilded cage: technology, development, and state capitalism in China / Ya-Wen Lei.
Description: Princeton, NJ: Princeton University Press, 2023 | Includes bibliographical references and index.
Identifiers: LCCN 2023008390 (print) | LCCN 2023008391 (ebook) | ISBN 9780691212821 (paperback) | ISBN 9780691212838 (hardback) | ISBN 9780691249254 (ebook)
Subjects: LCSH: Economic development—China. | Technological innovations—China. | Capitalism—China.
Classification: LCC HC427.95 L475 2023 (print) | LCC HC427.95 (ebook) | DDC 330.951—dc23/eng/20230626
LC record available at https://lccn.loc.gov/2023008390
LC ebook record available at https://lccn.loc.gov/2023008391

British Library Cataloging-in-Publication Data is available

Editorial: Meagan Levinson and Erik Beranek
Production Editorial: Theresa Liu
Jacket/Cover Design: Karl Spurzem
Production: Lauren Reese
Publicity: William Pagdatoon
Copyeditor: Cindy Milstein

Cover image: Krittin Teerawittayaart / Shutterstock

This book has been composed in Classic Arno

10 9 8 7 6 5 4 3 2 1

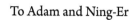

To Adam and Ning-Er

CONTENTS

LIST OF FIGURES AND TABLES

Figures

Tables

ACKNOWLEDGMENTS

ONE MIGHT think book writing would be easier after publishing one's first book. But writing a second book can be just as daunting. Like many other scholars, my first book was based on my PhD project. While developing my dissertation, I received invaluable guidance and feedback from my professors. This helped me feel less overwhelmed while translating my dissertation into my first book manuscript. For my second book, however, there was a new set of pressures. I started to teach, and my tenure clock began to tick. Suddenly, I felt like a first-time writer all over again. I was unsure which ideas to pursue and how much time it would take to finish the project.

My husband, Adam Mestyan, a historian of the modern Middle East, played the most crucial role in helping me move forward. The earliest stirrings of this book started with what has since evolved into chapter 5. I was curious about why some local governments in China were so zealously seeking to replace human workers with robots, despite the potentially enormous social costs and consequences of doing so. I understood the drive toward robotization was only one part of a larger phenomenon, but I struggled at first to identify its contours. It was Adam who suggested I read Gabrielle Hecht's book *The Radiance of France: Nuclear Power and National Identity after World War II*, and it was this exceptional work that guided me to see what really interested me—namely China's profoundly transformative techno-development.

Fortunately, many other scholars also assisted in the writing of this book. They read various iterations of the manuscript and provided invaluable feedback and suggestions. Patrick Heller is my hero—a great mentor, always encouraging, inspiring, and intellectually curious. I first met Patrick when I was invited to give a job talk at Brown University in 2014. I did not get the job, but I got something even more precious: the opportunity to get to know Patrick. Since then, Patrick has followed my work and been a wonderful source of support. Without Patrick's advice, it would have been difficult for me to revise the manuscript. Michael Burawoy and I discussed my manuscript at the 1369 Coffee House in Cambridge, Massachusetts, on June 6, 2022. That was a magical experience for me. I had read a lot of Michael's work, but I did not know him in person—a fact that did nothing to stem his incredible generosity. After our meeting, he sent me a summary of our conversation and his suggestions. I felt extremely grateful and understood how he had educated and inspired so many outstanding sociologists throughout his career. Paul Starr read not only this manuscript but that of my first book too. Neither project would be the same without his sharp insights. We share similar interests in media, law, institutions, and technology. His edited volume *Defining the Age: Daniel Bell, His Time and Ours* greatly helped my research. I also benefited enormously from Ho-fung Hung's detailed and brilliant comments. I thank Craig Calhoun, Bruce Carruthers, Vivek Chibber, and Juliet Schor for their timely and constructive feedback on the manuscript. David Stark and Andreas Wimmer gave me great advice at Bar Boulud, reminding me to develop my own voice and analytic clarity. Julia Adams, Dan Hirschman, Adam Reich, Josh Whitford, and Yun Zhou read and commented on several of the papers that became the building blocks of this book.

My colleagues at Harvard University have contributed tremendously to my intellectual development. I am blessed to have Orlando Patterson as my colleague and mentor in the Department of Sociology. He read my first and second book manuscripts. He always encourages me to think comparatively and historically and pursue ambitious projects. Orlando chaired a four-hour book workshop for me as well. I have benefited immensely from his advice, wisdom, and unwavering support. Michèle Lamont gave me invaluable suggestions on the important literature on valuation and evaluation. Her dedication to scholarship and mentorship was also immensely inspiring to me. David Pedulla read a chapter and provided me with brilliant feedback. I thank all of my colleagues in the department for their collegiality, with special thanks to Paul Chang, Sasha Killewald, Joscha Legewie, and Xiang Zhou. Sasha exemplifies the best of humanity, always taking care of everyone, including students and colleagues. As junior faculty members in my department, Paul, Joscha, Xiang, and I faced challenges together, and I am grateful for their comradeship.

I have also been surrounded by outstanding China scholars at Harvard. The late Ezra Vogel mentored me from 2014 until his death. I learned so much from him and miss him tremendously. The first presentation I gave on this book project was in the living room of his house on Sumner Road in 2017. Susan Greenhalgh's work inspired me greatly. Additionally, she generously shared her edited volume *Can Science and Technology Save China?* with me before its publication. Bill Alford invited me to give a talk in his class and gave me constructive feedback as I developed my project. I feel fortunate to be part of the bright and generous community of colleagues at the Fairbank Center who have taught me so much. I am particularly grateful for the various forms of support and encouragement I have received from Dinda Elliott, Mark Elliott,

Arunabh Ghosh, Liz Perry, Meg Rithmire, Michael Szonyi, Yuhua Wang, Mark Wu, and David Yang.

From time to time, I return to the Society of Fellows to refresh myself and find sources of inspiration. I am grateful to the society for the exciting interdisciplinary environment it provides; indeed, I was exposed to the history of science and technology there. Several of my fellow Fellows encouraged me to pursue this book project.

I am deeply grateful to my informants, interviewees, and numerous friends in China and Taiwan—all of whom went above and beyond to help me with my fieldwork and recruitment. Some accompanied me in my fieldwork and provided me with assistance. I cannot name them due to confidentiality, but their trust and generosity made my research possible. As I hope I have conveyed in these pages, many of my informants and interviewees are struggling with difficult life situations and harsh work conditions. Time is a precious resource for all of them, and I am deeply appreciative for their willingness to share their valuable time and stories with me. While this book focuses on China, I approached the project through a comparative lens. When studying the platform economy in China, I also examined its counterpart in France. I am grateful for the tremendous assistance and support provided by Jean-Daniel Zamor.

I would not have been able to finish the book without various forms of professional, institutional, and research support. I began to work with my editor Kim Greenwell in 2011. Kim edited my dissertation grant proposals, PhD dissertation, articles, first book, and second book for me. She always accommodates my tight writing schedule. Her excellent editing and insightful suggestions have been invaluable to me. I also thank my editors Meagan Levinson and Erik Beranek, production editor Theresa Liu, copyeditor Cindy Milstein, and other members of the production team at Princeton University Press. Their support made the publication of this book possible. In the process of developing this project, I received funding from and am indebted to the Chiang Ching-kuo Foundation for International Scholarly Exchange, Fairbank Center for Chinese Studies, Harvard China Fund, Weatherhead Center for International Affairs, and Dean's Competitive Fund for Promising Scholarship. I want to thank my dear students too—my PhD students, MA students, and many undergraduates who took my Contemporary Chinese Society course. A special thank goes to Fangsheng Zhu, as Fangsheng read several manuscripts for me. My students' support, kindness, and intellectual curiosity have buoyed me throughout this process. I also benefited from presentations at various institutions, including Wellesley College (East Asian Studies), Georgetown University (Department of Sociology), Boston College (Department of Sociology), Duke Law School, Princeton University (Center on Contemporary China), Columbia University (Department of Sociology), Harvard University (Department of Sociology, Harvard Kennedy School, and Harvard Law School), the University of Chicago (Department of Sociology), Brown University (Department of Sociology and the Watson Institute for International and Public Affairs), Heidelberg University (East Asian Studies), Yale University (Department of Sociology), and Cornell University (School of Industrial and Labor Relations).

Most important, this book simply would not have been possible without my dear family. My daily video calls with my mother, Shu-Ling Wu, and my sisters, Ya-Chun and Ya-Ting, have provided me with a constant source of peace, happiness, and stability. I was able to stay calm and steady under immense stress because of their love. I dedicate this book to my husband, Adam, and my daughter, Ning-Er. Much of it was written as we weathered the COVID-19 pandemic together. In fact, one of the silver linings of the pandemic was that it allowed us to enjoy much more of each other's company, even as so many other things about the world seemed to be falling apart. Adam and I cooked and worked on our second books together. I enjoyed our family walks and conversations every day. Due to the pandemic, although I continued to do online interviews and ethnography, I was not able to conduct my fieldwork in China. Ning-Er and I accompanied Adam to France and Turkey for his archival work. We were also able to spend time visiting family members in Hungary. Morning runs with Ning-Er along la Loire, the Danube, and the Bosphorus Strait were some of the best moments I had while writing this book.

When we visited Tihany Abbey in Hungary, Ning-Er noticed that her mother's long work schedule (from 4:30 a.m. to 9:00 p.m.) resembled the daily routines of monks (from 3:30 a.m. to 8:00 p.m.) in the eighteenth century. The analogy felt apt in some ways, as researching and writing a book demands what sometimes feels like an otherworldly level of commitment, endurance, and faith. At the same time, my daughter's observation served as a valuable reminder that in addition to writing about the relentless optimization and instrumental rationality unfolding in China, one must resist their tyranny by reserving time for those priceless things—and people—in life that cannot be quantified.

Budapest, Hungary
May 2023

ABBREVIATIONS

ACFTU	All-China Federation of Trade Unions
AI	artificial intelligence
BRI	Belt and Road Initiative
CAC	Cyberspace Administration of China
CCP	Chinese Communist Party
DSR	Digital Silk Road
FDI	foreign direct investment
FIE	foreign-invested enterprise
FINTECH	financial technology
FSDC	Financial Stability and Development Committee
GPC	gig platform courier
ICT	information and communications technology
IOT	Internet of Things
IPO	initial public offering
IT	information technology
KPI	key performance indicator
PBOC	People's Bank of China
PRC	People's Republic of China
P2P	peer-to-peer
R&D	research and development
RMB	renminbi
ROC	Republic of China
SAMR	State Administration for Market Regulation
S&T	science and technology
SEZ	special economic zone

SME   small and medium-sized enterprise

SOE   state-owned enterprise

SPC   service platform courier

STS   science and technology studies

VIE   variable interest entity

WFOE   wholly foreign-owned enterprise

WTO   World Trade Organization

THE GILDED CAGE

1

Introduction

PRESIDENT BILL CLINTON embarked on a future-looking visit to China in June 1998. The trip was only two years before he pushed the US Congress to approve the US-China trade agreement and China's accession to the World Trade Organization (WTO). Clinton was deeply invested in enhancing US-China relations. The goal was to help US companies sell and distribute products in China made by workers in the United States "without being forced to relocate manufacturing to China, sell through the Chinese government, or transfer valuable technology." The hope, moreover, was that economic and political liberalization would "inevitably go hand in hand" in China.[1]

Clinton's 1998 trip was widely criticized at home because it ended a nine-year hiatus in which US presidents refrained from visiting China after the Chinese government cracked down on the 1989 Tiananmen Square protests. Clinton, however, hailed China's future and sought to use the visit to set the stage for future economic engagement. Joined by First Lady Hillary Clinton, he assembled several "agents of change" for a roundtable discussion with the theme "Shaping China for the 21st Century" at the Shanghai Library on June 20, 1998. These agents of change included a law professor, consumer rights advocate, novelist, scientist, engineer, economist, bishop, and CEO of an internet company.[2]

In the roundtable, science and technology (S&T) emerged as a salient topic that interested both Clinton and the selected agents of change. One partici-pant opined that China would need S&T to support sustainable economic development, and asked about opportunities for China and the United States to cooperate in this area. Clinton pointed to the growing US-China partner-ship in S&T along with the United States' effort to facilitate technology trans-fer and deal with related national security issues. He was particularly excited by the development and dissemination of the internet in China, not least because the visit coincided with the dot-com boom in the United States. Asked by the internet entrepreneur about opportunities for exchange between Chinese and US businesses, Clinton responded that there would be ample ones in the internet sector as it was one of the most rapidly growing areas in the US economy. At one point, when discussion turned to the difficulty faced by Chinese local governments in broadening access to education, Clinton shared his vision of China's future:

> I think what will happen in China—I believe this will happen because of the technological revolution—I think in your economic growth you will almost leap over a whole generation of economic experiences that older European countries and perhaps the United States experienced, where you will essentially be creating an industrialized and a post-industrial society at the same time. And therefore, more quickly, you will have to educate more people at higher levels than we did.[3]

Essentially, Clinton predicted the simultaneous development of an industrial and postindustrial society in China as the result of technological change and the subsequent leap of China's economy.[4]

Reading the news about President Clinton's mention of postindustrial society in Shanghai, sociologist Daniel Bell was surprised. Since the 1960s, Bell had presciently developed the concept of postindustrial society as a "speculative construct" against which "sociological reality could be measured decades hence ... to determine the operative factors in effecting social change." Deeply interested in the futures of both capitalist and Communist worlds, Bell developed the notion of postindustrial society as a framework to guide research and comparative studies. In 1976, he classified China as a preindustrial, collectivist society. Seeing Clinton's comments on China's postindustrial development in 1998, Bell called the National Security Council to ask who had written Clinton's talk. When told that the president's comments were impromptu, Bell was pleased to see how far his ideas had traveled and how influential they had become.[5]

In *The Coming of Post-Industrial Society*, published in 1973, Bell outlines the features of postindustrial society. He forecasts a shift from a goods-producing to a service economy; the rise of a professional and technical class; a reconfigured role for S&T as the source of innovation, economic growth, and policy formulation; planning and control of technological growth by the state; and the substitution of intellectual technologies or algorithms for intuitive judgments in decision-making processes.[6] With its prescient focus on the relationship between economy, society, and S&T, Bell's work has significantly influenced scholarship on information, knowledge, and network societies.[7] Bell predicted that postindustrial society would be the major feature of the twenty-first century. Importantly, his argument was not that one type of society would fully displace the preceding one. As he wrote, "The post-industrial society ... does not *displace* the industrial society, just as an industrial society has not done away with the agrarian sectors of the economy. Like palimpsests, the new developments overlie the previous layers, erasing some features and thickening the texture of society as a whole."[8]

Although scholars and commentators who cite his work often define postindustrial society with primary reference to services, Bell clarified that the novel and central features of postindustrial society were the mutually generative relationship between science, technology, and economy, and "the enhancement of *instrumental* powers based on technology, powers over nature and powers, even, over people." According to Bell, the "design" of industrial society is a "game against fabricated nature" centered on human-machine relationships and the use of energy to transform the natural environment into a technical environment, while the "design" of postindustrial society is a "game between persons" in which intellectual technologies based on information, data, computing, algorithms, and programming rise alongside machine technology.[9] With the rise of intellectual technology, decision makers would be more future oriented, focusing on forecasting and planning as opposed to ad hoc adaptation and experimentation.[10] Bell predicted intellectual technology would play a crucial role in postindustrial society, and along with communication systems, structure and facilitate a new, digitally mediated global economy. Although Bell's work is largely forgotten by sociologists in the United States today, and has certain problems and limitations, I find his emphasis on the rise of instrumental power based on technology over people in postindustrial society profoundly prescient and insightful.

To a large extent, the future projected by both Clinton and Bell has been realized in China. To be sure, some of Clinton's remarks on China's future proved to be wrong.[11] And his strategy of using China to reinvigorate US capitalism created long-term problems for the United States. But Clinton's expectation that China would see simultaneous industrial and postindustrial development exhibited foresight, even if the actual pace of the two forms of development differed. In fact, Clinton's prediction corresponded to the concept of "compressed development" advanced by developmental studies scholars. Countries that develop later, it is argued, tend to be able to grow economically faster than earlier developers thanks to the learning, licensing, and investment of the latter. Also, many rapid developers today experience industrialization and deindustrialization concurrently. Developmental studies scholars further contend that the historical time period in which development takes place matters since the geopolitical, institutional, technological, and ideological context for development changes over time.[12] According to these scholars, what they call the "compressed development era" started around 1990 with the rise of information and communications technology (ICT) and the acceleration of neoliberal globalization.[13] They use China's economic development as an extreme example of compressed development and stage-skipping "catch-up" in the "compressed development era."[14]

Like the developmental states in Japan, South Korea, and Taiwan, the Chinese state plays a critical role in steering its economic development. Whereas South Korea and Taiwan began to develop during what economist Carlota Perez calls the fourth technological revolution (i.e., the age of oil, the automobile, and mass production), China's compressed development took off during the fifth technological revolution (i.e., the age of information and telecommunications) and in an era with a much higher degree of globalization. China benefited tremendously from the learning and investment of earlier developers, including but not limited to its East Asian neighbors as well as international institutions that facilitate the cross-border movement of capital, technology, goods, and services, particularly multilateral trade agreements. China's rural-based, indigenous industrial development burgeoned in the 1980s.[15] Despite the political turmoil in 1989, foreign direct investment (FDI) surged rapidly after Deng Xiaoping promised continued economic reform in 1992. FDI contributed to the rapid rise of labor-intensive, export-oriented manufacturing.[16] In 2001, before China's WTO accession, news media outside China portrayed the country as the soon-to-be "factory of the world."[17] From the early 2000s through the early 2010s, employment in the secondary sector, including both manufacturing and construction, rose steadily and reached a peak in 2012, but the trend reversed after 2012.[18]

The 1980s also saw the emergence of China's information technology (IT)–related sectors. Scientists affiliated with the Chinese Academy of Sciences established IT companies in Beijing's Zhongguancun, where the State Council approved the creation of the Beijing High Technology Industry Development Experimental Zone in 1998. The area soon became an important innovation hub and headquarters to numerous tech firms in China. And Clinton was proven right about the significance and growth of the internet sector in China. His trip to China in 1998 was around the time when many internet companies, such as Sina, Tencent, NetEase, JD, Baidu, and Alibaba, were founded.[19] The post-2008 global financial period marked a new era. As China's major export markets were seriously hit by the financial crisis, the Chinese state doubled down on its attempt to decrease China's reliance on labor-intensive, export-oriented manufacturing and move instead to S&T-oriented socioeconomic development (hereafter *techno-development*), in which domestic consumption plays a greater role alongside international trade.

As part of this effort, the Chinese state deliberately and successfully cultivated the internet sector as a pillar industry of China's economy. The post-2008 period also witnessed the initial public offering (IPO) boom of Chinese internet companies in the United States and their rapid rise on the world stage.[20] As of June 2022, among the top ten internet companies in the world, five were Chinese, while the other five were American.[21] In 2021, China's digital economy was worth US$6.72 trillion, accounting for 39.8 percent of its GDP.[22] China and the United States are arguably the only two countries that currently constitute digital capitalist superpowers. Despite disagreements among social scientists in China about whether China is a postindustrial society now, they all agree that China today has many of the features included in Bell's conception of postindustrial society.[23] Indeed, China's techno-development is simultaneously a process of postindustrial transformation.

Although China was a latecomer in development and has an authoritarian political regime, it has become a world leader whose developmental experiences are now looked to as an inspiring model. Political scientist Yuen Yuen Ang analogizes China's postreform period to the Gilded Age in the United States.[24] Philosopher Slavoj Žižek has gone so far as to declare China "the future of capitalism," noting that the Chinese Communist Party (CCP) "has ironically proved to be a much more efficient manager of capitalism than liberal democracies." The future of capitalism and Western world orders, Žižek argues, will be a mix between free market economic policies and the political and social authoritarianism exemplified by China and Singapore.[25] In *The Age of Surveillance Capitalism*, social psychologist Shoshana Zuboff points out that disappointed by the turmoil of market democracy, some commentators and scholars in liberal democracies now look to emulate China. And political leaders in developing countries are keen to learn from China's state-led economic development.[26] For instance, in 2022, the Mwalimu Julius Nyerere Leadership School—cofounded by the ruling parties of six southern African countries and supported by the CCP—held its inauguration ceremony in Tanzania. At the ceremony, leaders of the six ruling parties expressed their excitement about the opportunity to learn from the CCP—one they hoped would lead to "Africa's development and vitalization."[27] Thanks to the global impact of China in our time, understanding China's techno-development is not only critical in its own right but has far-reaching implications as well.

Behind the Gilded Facade

Despite China's tremendous success in terms of techno-development and postindustrial transformation, there is a dark side behind the gilded facade. To see through it, one has to understand the history and transformation of China's "birdcage economy." In the early 1980s, when Chinese leaders debated how to reform and open up China's economy, Chen Yun, one of the top leaders, advocated a so-called birdcage economy, using the terms *bird* and *cage* to refer to the economy and the state's planning and control, respectively. Chen argued that China should let the bird of the economy fly, but only within a state-managed cage because otherwise the bird would fly away. Chen also emphasized the need for the state to adjust the size of the cage dynamically as the bird developed.[28]

Before the mid-2000s, most discussions on the birdcage economy in Chinese officialdom did not distinguish between different kinds of birds. But as the Chinese state endeavored to shift from labor-intensive, export-oriented manufacturing to techno-development, discourse about the birdcage economy started to change. Local governments began to use birds to refer to industries, businesses, and social groups, and specify different kinds of birds (e.g., "new birds" versus "old birds" or "obsolete birds"). Government officials in coastal China also contended that different kinds of birds deserved different types of cages. According to such discourse, new birds deserve less constrained and better-resourced cages that will facilitate growth, while obsolete birds should be relegated to inferior cages so as not to waste resources or slow techno-development. Whether they described it as identifying and cultivating new birds, "phoenixes," or "beautiful birds that eat less, lay more eggs, and fly high," government leaders increasingly pointed to this task as crucial to the country's future. How the birdcage economy has been conceptualized and evolved over time is thus important in understanding China's process of techno-development, as is specifying the meanings and implications of each term. What I term the *bird question* concerns the process of destroying the old and creating the new, while the *cage question* relates to what Bell called the enhancement of instrumental power over people.

The Bird Question

In *Capitalism, Socialism and Democracy*, economist Joseph Schumpeter coined the concept of "creative destruction," arguing that the "fundamental impulse that sets and keeps the capitalist engine in motion comes from the new consumers' goods, the new methods of production or transportation, the new markets, the new forms of industrial organization that capitalist enterprise creates." Moreover, the process of "industrial mutation . . . incessantly revolutionizes the economic structure from within, incessantly destroying the old one, incessantly creating a new one. This process of Creative Destruction is the essential fact about capitalism."[29]

Although strongly influenced by Schumpeter's view of the role of technology in economic growth and the need for technological forecasting, Bell expected technological advances would bring about material abundance and decrease social inequality.[30] As a result, Bell's work highlights the rise of the professional and technical class, yet it has little to say about how different kinds of capital and laborers would be impacted unevenly by the "gale of creative destruction."[31] Others, however, shared Schumpeter's more pessimistic outlook. Manuel Castells argues that although technological innovation enables unprecedented fluidity, it makes redundant whole areas and populations bypassed by informational networks.[32] Castells further developed the concept of the "fourth world" to refer to marginalized groups in the "black holes of informational capitalism."[33] Indeed, research has shown the devastating consequences of deindustrialization on people left behind by technological changes and globalization, and the widening social inequality in advanced capitalist economies.[34] And it is now factors such as these that many political scientists maintain have fueled rising populism in the United States and Europe today.[35] In 1999, Bell himself reflected on the omissions of his earlier optimism. He looked back and expressed regret that his predictions had not included the persistence of an impoverished "underclass" in the postindustrial society to come.[36]

In China, problems resulting from the process of destroying the old and creating the new are often more complex than similar problems elsewhere for two reasons. As developmental studies scholar argue, China is an extreme case of time-compressed development: changes have happened rapidly and left little time for adjustment. Also, in the Chinese context, the Chinese state has played an instrumental role, wielding its enormous power deliberately to destroy the old and create the new. Under such circumstances, undesirable old birds—including capital and labor—have suffered the impact of not only capricious market forces but state power too.

I began to do fieldwork in Guangdong—a forerunner of China's techno-development—in 2009. When I returned to Shenzhen and nearby cities in the mid-2010s, some small and medium-sized manufacturers pointed to arbitrary and unpredictable law enforcement campaigns as pushing their decision to close altogether. Executives and managers of manufacturers opined a not-so-distant past when they had been welcomed enthusiastically and even courted by local governments. Those governments, however, had since recast manufacturers and their workers as obsolete and "low-end." Businesses and governments now sought to replace low-skilled workers. In 2011, responding to a rise in labor incidents, strikes, and protests, Foxconn—the largest contract electronics manufacturer in the world—declared the company's intention to build a "one-million robot army" to replace low-skilled workers. Two years after Foxconn announced this plan, Zhejiang's government launched its own official agenda of "replacing humans with robots" in order to advance the local economy. Zhejiang's initiative was soon emulated by other local governments, including that of Shenzhen.[37]

Low-skilled workers' prospects within China's plans for techno-development were grim from the start and have remained so. As economist Scott Rozelle shows, despite the country's rise as a technologically savvy economic powerhouse, its labor force has the lowest levels of education of any comparable nation. The danger, Rozelle warns, is that this may leave a considerable proportion of China's laborers unable to find work in the formal workplace as it takes decades for a society to elevate the entire population's level of education. Questions thus arise as to how the Chinese state has dealt and will continue to deal with capital and laborers in the old sectors in its effort to pursue techno-development, and how, for their part, such old birds have responded to these changes, especially considering the country's official socialist ideology.

The Cage Question

The question of how to structure the most appropriate and advantageous cage for the Chinese economy is constantly being reevaluated and fine-tuned, but has taken a particular shape under techno-development. As Bell wrote, postindustrial society is characterized by the enhancement of *instrumental* powers based on technology over people.[38] Bell developed his work when an idealized image of the Keynesian welfare state was predominant. While he recognized that instruments were double-edged swords that could be used to beneficial or ill effect, he did not consider the adverse consequences of an increased reliance on instruments given his own faith in technological rationality along with his tendency to assume a benign state and the supremacy of the state over capital. Bell highlighted the role of the welfare state in the economy and society at large, and saw the state as "the cockpit of politics."[39] In postindustrial society, he asserted, the state would invest more and more in education and S&T in its search for ever more efficient and rational solutions to economic, social, and environmental problems.[40]

The development of postindustrial society in advanced capitalist countries in the post-2008 financial crisis period has revealed both the prescience and limitations of Bell's work. As scholarship on platform capitalism, surveillance capitalism, the metric society, and the society of algorithms demonstrates, postindustrial society today is indeed characterized by the rise of instrumental power and "games between persons," as exemplified by the rise of algorithms and "gamification"—the use of game design in nongame contexts to shape people's behavior—in the digital economy.[41] Yet as Zuboff maintains, instead of having a benign state that exercises control over capital, postindustrial society in the United States has seen the rise of tech companies, their instrumental power in the "politics of lawlessness," and the "secret public-private intelligence collaboration." Bell was right that planning and forecasting are critical in postindustrial society, but Zuboff contends that the key actors doing the planning and forecasting in the United States today are tech companies. In other words, tech companies, not the state, set the rules of the games in the digital economy. According to Zuboff, today's "instrumentarian society" is a planned society produced through tech capital's "total control of [the] means of behavioral modification." Such a society leaves no room for rational deliberation or face-to-face negotiation and compromise; as a result, plans replace politics.[42]

If Bell were alive today, it would be extremely difficult, if not impossible, for him to find a country where intellectual technology and instrument power receive more appreciation and admiration than in China. The Chinese state is an unwavering believer in intellectual technology and instrumental power, and employs both to enhance governance and the economy. Indeed, Bell would likely be fascinated by China's "cockpit of politics," as presented in photos of "digital cockpits" circulated by the state media to showcase the government's state-of-the-art scientific decision-making. In these photos, government officials operate digital platforms and sit in front of multiple oversize monitors that display visualizations of data and statistics about the economy, society, governance, and the environment. China's influential tech entrepreneurs similarly embrace intellectual technology, as illustrated by Alibaba's founder Jack Ma's comments on the planned economy. In 2015 and 2016, Ma told the media and public that the planned economy would expand tremendously and become superior to the market economy by 2030.[43] As he put it, "Big Data will make the market smarter and make it possible to plan and predict market forces so as to allow us to finally achieve a planned economy."[44] According to Ma, although the market economy won over the planned economy, big data and data science will eventually uncover the economy's "invisible hand," thereby contributing to a new type of planned economy.[45] This belief is held not only by Ma but also by some economists in China.[46]

The Chinese state has enacted numerous legal rules and technical instruments, such as metrics, classification systems, and digital platforms, to steer, foster, and control techno-development. Over time and with the Chinese state's support, China's large tech firms became the builders of such instruments. Contrary to Bell's state-centered analysis and Zuboff's tech company–centered narrative, the populace in China is simultaneously subject to the instrumental power of the state and tech capital. Many of my interviewees and informants in China—whether they are workers in new or old sectors, business owners in traditional sectors, or even government officials themselves—describe the struggle of navigating the cage(s) constituted by constantly changing and proliferating legal and technical instruments. Some cages are considered better than others because they afford more freedom and resources, but no one operates outside a cage. Instead, my interviewees and informants work continually to attain better metric values, classification outcomes, and rewards, avoid punishments, and move to a better cage if possible.

The construction and calibration of cages, however, presents its own problems. Although designed to manage old birds, new birds, and techno-development in general, the legal and technical instruments that collectively comprise China's economic cage more broadly are nonetheless limited in their capacity for control precisely because their successful application can generate unruly results. The new birds selected and cultivated by the Chinese state have grown so spectacularly that they now threaten to burst the cage built for their development—prompting the state's crackdown on the tech sector in 2020.

The Gilded Cage aims to uncover the social order and contradictions that have emerged in the process of China's techno-development. It tells the story of birds, cages, and their consequences for those whose lives have been transformed—for better and worse—by China's rapid rise to an economic and technological world leader.

Inquiry into the Techno-Developmental Regime

Borrowing from historian of technology Gabrielle Hecht's concept of "technopolitical regime," I use the term *techno-developmental* regime to refer to the ensemble of state and nonstate actors, institutions, ideas, cultural norms, forms of materiality, and practices that foreground the role of S&T in socio-economic development.[47] Components of the ensemble can be linked and configured in a variety of ways across time and place, comprising different types of techno-developmental regimes. I have chosen the word *regime* because it is more analytically comprehensive than *society* (e.g., postindustrial society), *the state* (e.g., the developmental state), or *model* (e.g., developmental models). Its meaning is broad enough to integrate insights from various scholarly traditions.

One of the thorniest questions I have grappled with while writing this book is what precisely the "gilded cage" is an instance *of*; what category of phenomenon I am describing and theorizing. Some readers might argue the book is about a developmental state, and others might contend it is a story of digital capitalism—capitalism facilitated by the internet—and the most recent phase of postindustrial society.[48] Ultimately, I would characterize the book as examining both a developmental state and digital capitalism, but not fitting squarely or exclusively into either scholarly tradition. Literature on developmental states tends to examine cases before the rise of the internet and digital capitalism (e.g., Japan, South Korea, and Taiwan). In other words, the *material* or technological conditions in the previous studies and the Chinese case differ significantly. As a result, literature on developmental states is inadequate to analyze state-led developmental projects that culminate in a digital capitalist superpower like the Chinese case; neither can this literature help us understand the rise and penetration of instrumental power wielded by both the state and tech capital in China. Meanwhile, scholarship on digital capitalism—including surveillance and platform capitalism—tends to investigate cases in which state actors played a limited role in cultivating and shaping digital capitalism, especially the US case. Therefore, existing studies on digital capitalism cannot fully account for the Chinese case, in which the rise of digital capitalism is an outcome of state-led, time-compressed developmental projects.

As such, the existing scholarship on both developmental states and digital capitalism helps specify and explain China's techno-developmental regime, but neither does so completely. Hence China's techno-developmental regime is ill captured when characterized as an example of only one or the other. In the following section, I will discuss literature on developmental states, digital capitalism, and postindustrial society as well as ideas and beliefs about S&T, authoritarianism, and contradictions, and explain how they contribute to my analysis of China's techno-developmental regime.

Developmental States

A state can play a minimal role in the economy—for example, focusing on contract enforcement and property rights delimitation, but otherwise giving business actors significant autonomy, as advocated by the Washington Consensus.[49] Alternatively, a state can more actively promote techno-development. Influenced by Keynesian economics, Bell expected the state to play a critical role in the planning and control of techno-development in postindustrial society.[50] In fact, Bell's expectations regarding the state aligned with what social scientists would later call the developmental state—one that seeks to advance economic development through state intervention, using measures such as subsidies, interest rates, tax breaks, and state procurement to influence the allocation of material resources and incentivize private actors.[51] Studies of developmental states often focus on successful, newly industrializing countries in East Asia—in particular, South Korea and Taiwan—whose economic growth took off under their respective authoritarian states in the 1960s. As sociologist Peter Evans argues, these developmental states promoted private capital and assisted private businesses to meet ongoing global challenges. Though they also developed close ties with the private sector, these states preserved autonomy for renegotiating goals and policies when national and capital interests were inconsistent.[52]

But scholars also maintain that the developmental state and its associated policies are neither unique to East Asia nor limited to the twentieth century. Rather, they are a recurrent feature of government policy during different historical periods, under different circumstances (e.g., economic crises and wars), and in different geographic locations (e.g., France, Germany, Ireland, the United States, and Latin America).[53] For instance, the United States had a "hidden" or "disguised" developmental state to avoid attacks from market fundamentalists between the 1980s and late 2010s (i.e., after the election of Ronald Reagan and before the increasing US-China rivalry).[54] State planning and subsidies—often in the name of the defense budget—contributed to technological innovations in computers, computer languages, semiconductors, and the internet in the United States.[55]

Literature on developmental states suggests analyzing the rise of China's digital capitalism from the perspective of state-led development. And yet studies of developmental states tend to focus on success in specific sectors, but tell little about whether there is a process of "destroying the old," as theorized by Schumpeter, and whether and how developmental states deal with such a process. Also, the new birds in the cases of classical developmental states (e.g., IT manufacturers) differ from those (e.g., internet companies) in China's techno-development in terms of the extent to which firms have instrumental power over a vast populace. The relationship between the state and new birds is very different in the Chinese case compared with classical developmental states due to the tremendous instrumental and even infrastructural power—the capacity to penetrate society and implement decisions logistically throughout the realm—that internet companies possess.[56]

Instrumentality in Postindustrial Society and Digital Capitalism

Scholarship in postindustrial society and digital capitalism helps analyze the instrumental power of both the state and tech capital, thus speaking to the cage question I framed above. Bell's emphasis on instruments along with the promise of instrumental or technical rationality—the ability to adopt better or more technically efficient means to achieve given ends—was influenced by sociologist Max Weber's writing on rationality and rationalization.[57] Weber uses the concept of rationality in an evaluatively neutral (i.e., "formal") way to define the conjuncture of a capitalist economy, bourgeois private law, and bureaucratic authority in the modern Western social order. Rationalization refers to the process by which rationality becomes increasingly prevalent in the social order, expanding into ever more areas of life.[58] Although each sphere of life has its specific mode of rationality and process of rationalization, common to all is the production of calculability using means or instruments within that sphere. The capitalist production process is rationalized and rendered calculable through techniques of accounting and labor control as well as the use of technology (e.g., machines), while the legal and administrative environment is rationalized and made predictable through formalized rules and procedures. Instrumental or technical rationalization—the development and adoption of more efficient means of achieving given ends—enables bureaucrats and entrepreneurs to exercise control over humans and nature.[59] Bell predicted that technological advancement would speed instrumental rationalization and vice versa.

Indeed, five decades after the publication of *The Coming of Post-Industrial Society*, scholarship on the latest iteration of postindustrial society—the metric society, platform capitalism, the society of algorithms, and surveillance capitalism—shows how digitization, the multitude of data, and the advancement of S&T (e.g., artificial intelligence [AI], data science, and scientific methods of quantification) have expedited and broadened the process of technical rationalization.[60] Research in advanced capitalist countries has shown that the rise of tech companies and their instrumental power has undermined privacy and autonomy and deteriorated work and employment conditions for low-skilled workers.

Although Bell's work and this more recent scholarship all highlight the role and power of instruments—especially ICT—there is inadequate theorization of the intricate entanglements between technology and another critical type of instrument: law.[61] Current scholarship tends to relegate the relationship between law and technology to the background, leading to limited analysis of the role of law in digital capitalism and its interplay with technology. Legal scholars, however, have pointed out the importance of incorporating an analysis of law in order to fully understand the instrumental power of technology.[62] Here, I define technology and law broadly. I use the term *technology* to refer to the application of scientific knowledge (e.g., computer science, data science, and administrative science) for practical purposes.[63] Technology can create sources of power to the extent that it has the capacity to direct or influence the behavior of others or the course of events, as illustrated by the power of algorithms for behavioral modification.[64] I use *law* to refer to a "body of rules of action or conduct prescribed by controlling authority, and having binding legal force." Examples of law include provisions of statutes adopted by legislatures, regulations enacted by administrative agencies, and ordinances adopted by municipalities.[65] Law's binding force and legal consequences make it a powerful instrument.

As Bell wrote, postindustrial society is characterized by the planning and control of techno-development.[66] Law is a critical instrument for such planning and control, especially when one seeks to speed the development and adoption of technology, or (re)construct the social order as new and potentially disruptive technologies are adopted. For its part, law can be used to promote, authorize, and/or restrict technology as well as foster techno-development.[67] Literature on law and development points out that law has become the framework, instrument, and vocabulary for constructing and debating development and industrial policies, including policies on techno-development.[68] The instrumental role of law as a means to foster techno-development can be illustrated by the Chips and Science Act of 2022 in the United States, which aims to "boost American semiconductor research, development, and production, ensuring US leadership in the technology that forms the foundation of everything from automobiles to household appliances to defense systems."[69] Emerging technologies, such as gene editing technologies, tend to spark regulatory challenges from society and governmental agencies. Given its tremendous power, whether and how law authorizes, regulates, or restricts technology has significant consequences for the latter's application and instrumental power.[70] In other words, the instrumental power of law influences that of technology.

Conversely, technology can facilitate legal implementation and enforcement along with the formation of legal relationships, while undermining certain aspects of law. Legal rules are constituted by abstract classifications and categories. The process of applying abstract rules and classifications to specific cases—particularly evaluating specific persons or objects and deciding whether they fall into certain categories—can have significant legal consequences. Technology is now frequently used to assist the application of law. For instance, risk assessment tools are used in legal procedures to decide if an individual possesses certain legal risks (e.g., violence) in many countries. As digital technology becomes a critical medium in economic activities, it facilitates the formation and implementation of legal relationships. In other situations, the application of technology can undermine interests and rights protected by law—for example, digital technologies' encroachment on one's right to privacy.

To the degree that both law and technology can influence behavior or the course of events, both can also constitute or influence the rules of games between persons in many areas of life. Legal scholar Lawrence Lessig argues that code is law in the digital world.[71] Similarly, as John Zysman and Martin Kenney underscore, algorithms and data in the platform economy exist as "regulatory structures" that shape the rules and parameters of action available to platform users.[72] Importantly, both law and technology are also Janus-faced, and can be put to redemptive and/or regressive uses to serve the interests of different groups. Yet there are differences in how law and technology can shape the rules of games. The first major one is that technical rules can be automatically executed, eliminating the need for third-party enforcement and human deliberation.[73] The second difference, noted by Jürgen Habermas in *Between Facts and Norms*, is that law can be more than an instrument for extracting obedience from its subjects under certain political conditions. Specifically, as law derives its validity from the consent of the governed through the process of democratic deliberation, law can serve as the primary medium of social integration and prevent law itself as well as technology from being unduly used as means for control and domination.[74] In the worst-case scenario, however, powerful actors can use law and technology synergistically to undermine the rights and interests of individuals or public interest. An adequate understanding of digital capitalism and postindustrial society in general as an age of enhanced instrumental power must therefore include an analysis of the relations between, and the many potential uses and consequences of, law and technology.

Scholarship in postindustrial society and digital capitalism helps address the bird question too. As suggested by Schumpeter's work on creative destruction, Castells's writing on the "fourth world," and Bell's hindsight regret at not predicting an impoverished underclass, instruments enacted by state and business actors impact various kinds of capital and different social classes differently.[75] Bell predicted the rise of a technical or professional class, yet he also made it clear that it would not be technocrats but rather politicians who would ultimately hold power in postindustrial society.[76] Recently, sociologists Jenna Burrell and Marion Fourcade have fleshed out the class structure in the society of algorithms. They argue that a coding elite comprised of software engineers, tech CEOs, investors, and computer science and engineering professors has consolidated economic power through their "technical control over the digital means of production and by extracting labor from a newly marginalized or unpaid workforce, the cybertariat."[77] The above literature suggests that old birds or the working class are less likely to benefit from techno-development than new birds or the technical class. In addition, the working class is more likely to be subject to harsh instrumental rule in the era of digital capitalism. I want to mention that scholars and media outlets outside China rightly use terms like *digital authoritarianism* and the *surveillance state* to refer to the Chinese state along with its use of technology for political and social control.[78] Unfortunately, most scholarship in this area neglects the class dimension of the Chinese state's instrumental rule.

Ideas and Beliefs about Instruments

As I have mentioned, instruments are Janus-faced, and can be put to redemptive and/or regressive uses to serve the interests of different groups. To further specify China's techno-developmental regime, we need to know more about ideas and beliefs about instruments given their ability to influence how the rules of games between persons are enacted and then play out. Despite Bell's emphasis on culture in his writing on postindustrial society, ironically his cultural analysis did not incorporate ideas and beliefs about technology. In general, ideas and beliefs about technology differ in their degree of optimism or pessimism. The salience of these ideas and beliefs varies across societies, historical periods, and social groups.[79]

Scholars have documented several variants of optimistic views and beliefs about technology, such as techno-utopianism, high modernism, and techno-nationalism. These perspectives tend to connect technology to social or national salvation. Scientific and technological utopianism rose from the eighteenth century through the mid-twentieth century, alongside the Enlightenment and Industrial Revolution, as exemplified by the Saint-Simonian thinking that S&T would solve most of humanity's problems. Techno-dystopianism sees technological advance as depriving people of freedom and dignity, and ultimately bringing destruction to humanity. Skepticism about and apocalyptic views on technology became salient in the mid-twentieth century as the human suffering that could be caused S&T became increasingly evident—from Nazi eugenics to gas chambers, unethical human experimentations, and the use of the atomic bomb.[80] In the 1960s and 1970s, techno-utopianism rose again with the advancement of new ITs and cybernetics amid discussions on postindustrial society, as demonstrated by the writings of futurist Alvin Toffler. This reincarnation of techno-utopianism culminated in the rise of the so-called Californian Ideology in the 1990s.[81] Although Bell considered the counterculture of the 1960s an impediment to the promise of intellectual technology and postindustrial society, the mixing of that counterculture with a profound faith in the emancipatory potential of new ITs, social liberalism of the New Left, and economic liberalism of the New Right gave birth to the Californian Ideology and US high-tech capitalism.[82] Until today, the Californian Ideology, which is characterized by antistatism and liberal individualism, still influences the development of digital capitalism in and beyond the United States, as seen in the antiregulatory tendency of big tech companies.[83]

In *Seeing Like a State*, political scientist James C. Scott documents a high modernist ideology in different parts of the world in the twentieth century, from Germany to France, the Soviet Union, China, and India. It is a strong version of "self-confidence about scientific and technical progress, the expansion of production, the growing satisfaction of human needs, the mastery of nature (including human nature), and, above all, the rational design of social order commensurate with the scientific understanding of natural laws." As such, high modernism puts strong faith in the instrumental power of technology in social and natural engineering. Meanwhile, Scott emphasizes that high modernism is also about "interests" as there is an elective affinity between high modernism and the interests of many state officials.[84]

Ideas about scientific and technological progress are often intermingled with and mobilized alongside ideas and sentiments about national progress, producing forms of techno-nationalism. Here, technology is seen as a means to achieve the goal of national salvation. Harold Wilson's 1963 "white heat" speech is a perfect example of techno-nationalism. The transformative power of technology was central to British Labour Party policy in the 1960s. Just prior to becoming prime minister in 1964, Wilson delivered a renowned speech promising that under the Labour Party, Britain would prosper in the white heat of the scientific and technological revolution. The change was not only inevitable but necessary too; as Wilson warned, "There is no room for Luddites."[85] He argued that the United Kingdom should, through democratic planning, mobilize S&T to revitalize its declining industries—a strategy that would benefit the entire nation, not just a few groups or businesses. Hecht's research on France's nuclear program offers another case in point. Hecht shows that when France lost standing among world leaders after World War II, its technical and scientific experts and government turned to technological prowess to restore "the radiance of France"—the country's national glory and its place as a world leader.[86] Similarly, anthropologist Susan Greenhalgh contends that the idea of using S&T to save and rejuvenate China has been built into the "cultural DNA of the Chinese nation" since the late nineteenth century.[87] Relatedly, science and technology studies (STS) scholars Sheila Jasanoff and Sang-Hyun Kim coined the term *national sociotechnical imaginaries* to refer to "collectively imagined forms of social life and social order reflected in the design and fulfilment of nation-specific scientific and/or technological projects." Such imaginaries, they assert, "describe attainable futures and prescribe futures that states believe ought to be attained."[88] Although various actors—from nation-states to business and civil society actors—can develop their sociotechnical imaginaries, the power of the state to create dominant sociotechnical imaginaries and regulate people's participation therein is unmatched.[89]

Scholars have pointed out the gap between beliefs and reality, and importantly, the consequences of uncritical beliefs in instrumental power. Scott cautions that we should not equate a high modernist ideology with scientific practice as high modernism is a faith that borrows the legitimacy of S&T. He further argues that high modernism can lead to disaster when an authoritarian state is willing and able to use its coercive power to bring high modernist designs into being as well as when a prostrate civil society lacks the capacity to resist those plans.[90] Scott's warning resonates with economic geographer

David Harvey's cautions against the fetishism of technology—"the habit humans have of endowing real or imagined objects or entities with self-contained, mysterious, and even magical powers to move and shape the world in distinct ways."[91] Harvey contends that such fetishism arises when social actors—particularly the state and capitalists—endow technologies with powers they do not have. And while technological fetishism may have an initial grounding in material reality, Harvey asserts that it tends to escape material constraints quickly, as demonstrated by the fantasy of the total domination of nature through technology. He warns of the consequences when social actors from corporations to various branches of government invest in the belief that technology can and will solve all of their problems.

Scholarship that critiques instrumental or technical rationality suggests that beliefs in technology and instrumental power might lead to the unfettered pursuit of instrumental rationality, dissolution of ends and concentration on means alone, justification of inequality, and even the legitimation of domination.[92] Weber's specter of the "iron cage" imagined individuals trapped in systems based on efficiency, rational calculation, and control.[93] Research also indicates that a strong confidence in technology can be linked to meritocracy and used to justify inequality. When technology is considered sacred in society, individuals with technical expertise can be seen as "model citizens," while those lacking technical skills are downgraded to undeserving citizens or "political economic trash."[94]

The most fervent and influential critiques of instrumental rationality came from first-generation Frankfurt school philosophers Herbert Marcuse, Max Horkheimer, and Theodor W. Adorno. Marcuse considered industrial society an exploitative system constituted by means of domination and control. He contended that the increase in comfort and affluency that results from the expansion of instrumental rationality obfuscates the exploitative nature of society.[95] He further maintained that S&T, as a historical-social project, functions simultaneously as a productive force and ideology that legitimates political power. In *Dialectic of Enlightenment* (1947), an intellectual response to rising fascism and totalitarianism, Horkheimer and Adorno argued that the process of progressive rationalization enables human beings to exercise greater power over nature, other human beings, and themselves. In so doing, they related Enlightenment rationality to a will to mastery, control, and domination.[96]

Dialectic of Enlightenment and Bell's *The Coming of Post-Industrial Society* thus present starkly different views on the advance of technology and expansion of instrumental rationality. Although Bell did not engage with *Dialectic of Enlightenment* in *The Coming of Post-Industrial Society*, he read the former when its first English translation was published in 1972—and dismissed it as a wholesale attack on rationality. In notes I found in his personal archive in the

Harvard Library, Bell wrote, "Frankfurt opens the floodgates—the attack on rationality, on objectivity, etc.," and "the underlying theme was a more radical rejection of modernity, a Heideggerian theme of the domination of nature." Moreover, he held that Marcuse, Horkheimer, and Adorno understood neither technology nor democracy. In comparision, Bell highly regarded Habermas—a second-generation Frankfurt school philosopher. As Bell saw it, Habermas corrected Marcuse, Horkheimer, and Adorno's excessive pessimism by developing the ideas of communicative and discursive rationality. For Habermas, first-generation Frankfurt school philosophers reduced rationality to domination by equating instrumental rationality with rationaliy per se, thus undermining the capacity of critical theory to explore possibilities for human emancipation. Although he recognizes the danger of the expansion of instrumental rationality, Habermas argues that the increase in communicative rationality, which aims to reach mutual understanding and consensus, counterbalances the danger.[97]

Bell's dismissive view of Marcuse, Horkheimer, and Adorno reveals how ideas and beliefs about technology and instrumental rationality can vary significantly. Instead of assuming or asserting that any such ideas or beliefs are "irrational," however, I analyze their capacity to influence the ways in which various actors—from the state to business actors and workers—use technology and respond to dissonances resulting from the instrumental rule of technology and law.

Authoritarianism

We also have to consider political regime to further analyze China's techno-developmental regime. Although China and classical developmental states like South Korean and Taiwan share processes of state-led techno-development, South Korea and Taiwan began democratization in the 1970s and 1980s, respectively. According to Freedom in the World reports, South Korea and Taiwan transitioned into a "free" country in 1988–89 and 1996–97, respectively.[98] As a result of democratization, the authoritarian developmental states in South Korea and Taiwan did not need to rely on economic performance as a major source of their legitimacy anymore. Instead, the governments turned to legal-electoral legitimacy. Also, the process of democratization and the building of the rule of law constrained how the governments there could use instruments to foster techno-development as well as structure the relationship between the state, capital, and labor.[99]

China's political regime has several characteristics that have motivated and enabled the state to be *actively* and *dynamically* involved in the planning and control of techno-development. First, China has a one-party authoritarian regime without electoral legitimacy. Sociologist Dingxin Zhou argues that the Chinese state's primary sources of legitimacy come from its economic and ritual performance along with the state's capacity for territorial defense.[100] Promoting techno-development helps sustain the state's legitimacy. And since economic and ritual performance are critical to the Chinese state's legitimacy, upper-level governments often use performance evaluations to ensure that lower-level governments implement techno-development agendas. Second, the CCP prioritizes maintaining its political monopoly, so the Chinese state is sensitive to threats to social stability and national security.[101] Measures to secure the CCP's political monopoly can be in tension, however, with those that promote techno-development.[102] The party-state is therefore likely to pursue the kind of techno-development that does not threaten its political monopoly. Third, the process of techno-development is dynamic. To sustain its legitimacy and political monopoly, the Chinese party-state is likely to recalibrate its planning and control when faced with crises or unacceptable risks. As political scientist Colin Hay asserts, moments of intervention can alter the state from an inertial or reactive status to a dynamic or proactive one. In an inertial status, the state tends to be fragmented, and evolves by iteratively and unreflexively adapting to failure. In other words, the state is involved in mundane, routine managerial practices and follows operational procedures in periods of relative stability. In contrast, in a dynamic status, the state tends to be more unified, at least in relevant policy areas, and evolves through reflexive, strategic, and decisive action conditioned by the intended and unintended consequences of its prior strategies. As the dynamic status itself becomes stabilized, though, the state returns to relative inertia, at least until the next perceived threat.[103] Hay's work resembles sociologist Xueguang Zhou's finding that the Chinese state swings between a mundane, decentralized, and fragmented status, on the one hand, and a mobilized and centralized status, on the other hand.[104] This process can create uncertainty and turmoil.

Furthermore, due to China's authoritarian regime, there are few restrictions on how the state can construct legal and technical instruments to foster techno-development under the rule by law versus the rule of law. Legal scholars have pointed out problems of ruling by law in general. For example, legal scholar Mireille Hildebrandt argues that ruling by law does not include a system of checks and balances that brings the legislator and administration under the reign of the law. Although ruling by law can provide some legal certainty, such certainty remains limited as the law can be easily bent. As a result, law is used as a mere instrument to influence individual behavior in view of policy goals, and can be replaced or used with other policy instruments such as technology.[105] Her criticism of ruling by law in general applies to the Chinese context.

Scholars have also pointed out the importance of public deliberation to socioeconomic development. Economist and philosopher Amartya Sen contends that the viability of development and human flourishing depends on the process of public reasoning.[106] In a similar vein, sociologist Patrick Heller and economist Vijayendra Rao show the significance of deliberation, voice, and collective action to development.[107] But under China's authoritarian regime, there is little external pressure to put the instrumental rationality of the state and tech capital in check, especially since the Chinese state intensified its control of the public sphere and civil society in the mid-2010s.

Contradictions

Contradictions—how they emerge and what implications they have—are central to my analysis of China's techno-development. A contradiction exists "when two seemingly opposed forces are simultaneously present within a particular situation, an entity, a process or an event."[108] Since my analysis centers on the pursuit of instrumental rationality, Weber's work on rationalization in the capitalist economy, legal system, and bureaucracy provides a useful and flexible analytic perspective to examine how contradictions can occur in the process of rationalization.

Although rationalization advances predictability, efficiency, and control, the process can generate antagonism, problems, and disillusion due to the contradiction between formal rationality and substantive rationality and the limits of rational action.[109] As mentioned, Weber uses the term *rationality* in a purely formal or evaluatively neutral way. In comparison, substantive rationality refers to the value of ends or results from certain perspectives. As such, the pursuit of formal rationality (e.g., calculability and efficiency) can be in tension with rationality from the point of view of certain substantive ends, values, or beliefs (e.g., equality, freedom, and human dignity). For example, the Chinese state's pursuit of formal rationality to foster techno-development and its performance legitimacy might contradict its goal to maintain political monopoly under certain conditions.[110] The contradiction between formal and substantive rationality can also occur between social groups with different interests, such as between capital and labor.[111]

Weber also writes about the increasing salience of means-end rational action at the microlevel as rationality became prevalent in the macro social order. He points out the inherent limits of the rationality of individual action, as shown by the distinction between the subjective and objective rationality of action. The subjective rationality of action depends on the point of view of an actor, whereas objective rationality depends on the extent to which action measures up to an objective standard according to scientific knowledge.[112] As such, subjective rational actions can vary in their objective rationality. Scott's work on high modernism and Harvey's work on technological fetishism both highlight the contradiction between appearance and reality.[113]

The existence of contradictions in the process of instrumental rationalization does not necessarily lead to response or resistance. Although dystopian critics of postindustrialism in the 1960s and early 1970s expected postindustrial society to generate new classes of marginal and technologically superfluous people, most anticipated not conflict but instead "stolid order in a new, manipulated world."[114] The comfort, convenience, and affluency afforded by technology and continued participation in games between persons might, as sociologist Michael Burawoy's work suggests, manufacture consent to the rules of the games.[115] On the other hand, Scott's scholarship reminds us of various forms of resistance, whether hidden or overt.[116] Since China's techno-development involves such a wide variety of actors and situations, I examine concretely what contradictions have emerged and how they have unfolded in the process of instrumental rationalization.

The Gilded Cage

I analyze China's techno-development from the mid-2000s to present day—a period marked by the time-compressed process of destroying the old and creating the new, and the enhancement of instrumental power over people. Noting the extraordinary transformation of China's economy and society, political scientist Yuen Yuen Ang has compared China's postreform period to the Gilded Age in the United States.[117] By contrast, I seek to highlight the darker implications of these changes, or as mentioned above, what I refer to collectively as China's gilded cage, but I still include the word *gilded* to acknowledge China's extraordinary success in building a globally leading digital capitalist system.

I argue that a cage constituted by a variety of instruments emerged in the process of techno-development as the Chinese state endeavored to move from an economy relying on labor-intensive, export-oriented manufacturing to "techno-state capitalism"—a digital capitalist system characterized by the rise of tech capital and an *asymmetrically* symbiotic relationship between tech capital and the state. This cage has expanded with the growth of techno-state capitalism as large tech companies began to participate in the making of the cage. As such, China's techno-developmental regime is characterized by: the proliferation of technical and legal instruments established by the state and large tech companies to regulate work and life, and enhance legibility, valuation, efficiency, and behavior modification; the legal, economic, and cultural subordination of work, workers, and forms of capital deemed "obsolete" or "low-end" to those valorized as "high-tech" or "high-end," despite China's official socialist ideology; and the intensified subjection of both "low-end" and "high-end" workers and capital to the precarious and despotic rule by instruments. China's developmental state, an amalgamated ideology of high modernism, techno-nationalism, technological fetishism, and meritocracy, and the country's authoritarian regime explain the above qualities.

Such sweeping, lopsided, and unchecked rule by instruments is novel in China as well as distinctive compared with postindustrial societies in advanced capitalist countries and countries with a classical developmental state in the following ways. Although the Chinese state has always played a critical role in China's postreform socioeconomic development, the Chinese state also left space for state and nonstate actors to improvise, and was previously less equipped and interested in using technical and legal instruments for micromanagement.[118] Furthermore, no enterprises—state owned or otherwise—in the past were able to regulate and influence as many people as do large tech companies today. The scope of instrumental power now possessed by the state and large tech firms is unprecedented in China. In advanced postindustrial societies like the United States and European countries, and in East Asian countries with a classical developmental state, constraints limit the extent to which the state can use law and technology as instruments. In such contexts, it would be difficult, for example, for the state to legally discriminate against a certain type of capital or labor for its perceived inadequate contributions to techno-development.

How did the gilded cage in China come to be? The prototype of the now-fledging techno-developmental regime emerged in coastal, more prosperous provinces in the mid-2000s as a response to the increasing limitations of labor-intensive, export-oriented manufacturing, which were subsequently magnified by the 2008 global financial crisis. Parochial political calculations and an amalgamated ideology of high modernism, techno-nationalism, and meritocracy contributed to local state-led efforts to destroy old birds and cultivate new birds. Such efforts culminated in an emerging instrumental order structurally and ideologically biased against low-end capital and labor, and in favor of their high-end counterparts. Despite criticism from the public and even the central state, this local regime "proved" its efficacy by turning the 2008 global financial crisis into an advantage for China, thereby not only saving but also strengthening the nation. Moreover, Xi Jinping, one of the earliest advocates of such a regime, ascended to the highest leadership in 2012. As a result of these developments, the technical and legal instruments of the prosperous, coastal local regimes and their underlying sociotechnical imaginaries expanded across different parts and levels of the state, although there was little centralized or carefully coordinated effort to disseminate the instruments and logic of such a regime. An increasingly prostrate public sphere and civil society since the mid-2010s along with China's global ascendancy have shielded the techno-developmental regime from criticisms.

The overarching logic of the instrumental apparatus enacted by the state is to foster techno-development by allocating rewards and punishments to different kinds of labor and capital according to their perceived contributions (e.g., skill and technology) and detriments to techno-development as factors of production. The underlying assumption is that with enhanced instruments, the visible hand of the state will help and somehow coordinate with the invisible hand of the market to better allocate factors of production. Technology (e.g., quantification methods) and law are used as instruments for classification, (e)valuation, and (dis)incentivization. Rewards include material and symbolic resources beneficial for production, such as subsidies, land use rights, bank credits, tax breaks, state procurements, state endorsements and promotions, and critically, regulatory toleration and exemptions. In addition, rewards encompass resources for social reproduction, which refers to daily and generational activities that regenerate current laborers, cultivate future laborers, and maintain those who cannot work and the caring infrastructure (e.g., housing).[119] Common rewards for social reproduction include local citizenship, access to public education, access to more affordable housing, and so forth. Punishment is exemplified by harsh and selective law enforcement in the forms of fines, suspension of businesses, and eviction. Punishment also includes hyperactive rule making as law can be made easily.

State and nonstate actors must all follow the state's technical and legal rules that constitute the techno-developmental regime. And yet the very instruments for measuring and classifying the worth and worthiness of everything from capital to labor, technology, and industry according to its perceived contributions to techno-development guarantees that only some can be winners. Among nonstate actors, those considered obsolete are not only deprived of opportunities to receive rewards but also can be subject to harsh state regulation unless they can change their classifications and metric values. In contrast, those considered cutting-edge, especially business actors, prosper and gain resources and power in a friendly regulatory environment. Businesses and labor in labor-intensive manufacturing industries experienced a precipitous drop in status, while large tech firms emerged as the clear favorites in the eyes of the state, at least until the recent state crackdowns.

Importantly, as the internet sector was selected as the prized new bird by the Chinese state to advance techno-development, large tech firms headquartered in China at first enjoyed various significant rewards from the Chinese state: accessing global capital and a protected domestic market, partnering with the Chinese state, and operating in a lax regulatory environment. It is in this context that large tech companies expanded rapidly across sectors, regions, and countries, established and controlled platform infrastructure, and contributed to the second-largest and one of the most successful digital economies in the world. It is also in this context that large tech companies have used technical and legal instruments to design and operate games between persons that influence various actors, from different kind of workers to suppliers and users. Thanks to the state's tolerant regulatory approach, the instrumental rule established by large tech firms has become part of the broader instrumental apparatus that constitutes China's techno-developmental regime. As a result, workers, suppliers, and users are subject to the instrumental rules established by both the state and large tech firms.

The same technical and legal rules that created the gilded cage have nonetheless generated various contradictions too, which in turn have reshaped the cage. The unchecked rule by instruments often ignores the public interest along with the rights of citizens, laborers, and businesses, resulting in contradictions between appearance and reality, the state and capital, the state and citizens, and tech capital and labor. The combination of technological fetishism and authoritarianism frequently leads to the dissolution of ends, a focus solely on means, and the contradiction between appearance and reality. Paradoxically, in the "obsolete" sectors, the techno-developmental regime has generated less visible discontent. Business actors now deemed obsolete have refrained from voicing their grievances precisely because they receive no moral or discursive support in the dominant sociotechnical imaginaries. Despite their many structural disadvantages in the system, most workers in these sectors do not complain about their devalued status or apparent disposability within the ascending techno-nation. Some workers have demanded equal citizenship rights and contested the government's instruments for resource distribution that are biased against their children. But many have internalized the dominant discourse that assesses people's worth and worthiness based on their contribution to techno-development.[120]

The contradictions of the techno-developmental instrumental regime have, quite ironically, become most visible in the "high-end" sectors. Tensions and contradictions have emerged between tech capital and labor. Despite the great promise of technology, those members of the working class who have managed to escape the "backward" sectors and join the ascending tech sectors are belatedly confronted with the bleak realities of labor. They tend to be subject to the harshest instrumental rule in the spheres of both work and life. Rather than seeing itself as a "coding elite," the rising class of technical professionals is acutely aware of the high price for its apparent success, such as the inability to resist working for extremely long hours. Contradictions have emerged between the state and tech capital as well. Ultimately, even the state itself has become a victim of its own success, as it now struggles to curb the unwieldy instrumental and infrastructural power of big tech firms while managing the domestic and transnational risks that have followed in their wake. The state's effort to rewire the state-capital relationship through hyperactive rule making and enforcement has led to an unpredictable domestic regulatory environment and further destabilized the global conditions that earlier fostered China's development.

Despite these contradictions, the gilded cage has not prompted large-scale, overt resistance. The cage's gilded facade glorifying national and technological progress, combined with the necessity for people to engage with instrumental rule in order to improve their own position within the cage, has helped the Chinese state maintain political legitimacy and social stability—so far. But there is no guarantee that the celebrated yet superficial appearance of the cage will hold.

Chapter Outlines

The first part of the book explains the rise of techno-development in China. Chapter 2 establishes the historical context of the Chinese state's turn to techno-development. In chapter 3, I narrate how a local, embryonic techno-developmental regime came to be credited as not only the successful solution to the 2008 financial crisis but also the key to techno-development itself. The second part of the book considers the consequences of this expanding techno-developmental regime for the traditional manufacturing sectors. Chapter 4 examines state campaigns against supposedly obsolete businesses, but also tackles the puzzle of why most businesses and workers in those sectors have chosen not to voice their discontent with their newly devalued status and the government's harsh regulations and crackdowns. In chapter 5, I explain how the instrumental effort to upgrade the traditional sectors through robotization has both reflected and reproduced the fetishization of S&T, leading to a tremendous waste of public funding. Again, I discuss the seeming acceptance and apathy of workers in this sector with their apparent disposability within an otherwise ascending techno-nation. The third part of the book shifts to the internet-related sectors, analyzing the simultaneous expansion of instrumental rule and techno-state capitalism. Chapter 6 details the rise of China's tech companies along with their instrumental and infrastructural power under the state's support. Chapter 7 analyzes how large platform companies use their technical and legal instruments for intense labor control in an unscrutinized regulatory environment, but also how this control has generated growing resistance among platform workers. Chapter 8 focuses on tech professionals—presumably the group most valued within the techno-developmental regime, but increasingly one of the most disillusioned about China's techno-development. Finally, in chapter 9, I look at how the Chinese state has more recently sought to cage large tech companies and tackle the unintended problems generated by its pursuit of techno-state capitalism.

A Note on Methodology

The development of this book has been, in many ways, unexpected. My journey first began with research into the market for *shanzhai* or unbranded/copycat cell phones when I was working on my JSD dissertation between 2009 and 2011. My research at the time was mainly concerned with intellectual property rights, but it gave me the opportunity to interact with various actors participating in the *shanzhai* and regular cell phone markets in Shenzhen, including chip design companies, manufacturers, retailers, wholesalers, merchants from many countries, migrant workers, and local officials. As my research continued after the 2008 financial crisis, I witnessed that event's profound impact on various actors as well as development policy and the regulatory environment in the Chinese context.

At the same time that I was completing my JSD, I was pursuing a PhD in sociology, which ultimately led to the publication of my first monograph, *The Contentious Public Sphere*, in 2018. One of the questions motivating that book was how developments in ICT impacted the emergence of a public sphere in China, particularly in light of narratives, rampant among scholars and other commentators at the time, about the democratizing potential of technology—another example of humans bestowing hope on technology. Guangdong was a good location for this project because important news organizations and internet companies, especially the Nanfang Daily Newspaper Group, NetEase, and Tencent, are there. Although I concentrated more on political development in *The Contentious Public Sphere*, I observed the rapid growth of tech firms like Tencent, their increasingly critical role in the economy, and the rapidly changing socioeconomic landscape in Guangdong. As the laboratory for China's economic reform since the late 1970s and a forerunner of techno-development in China, Guangdong has often been seen as an institutional and policy model by the Chinese state and people.[121] Also, postindustrial development has been a grossly uneven process within China—making Guangdong simultaneously anomalous in some respects, but also the most important province to study in order to analyze the process of destroying the old and creating the new as well as understand how China's gilded cage came to be. Indeed, it was the decade that I spent researching, observing, and talking to people in Guangdong that spurred my decision to write *The Gilded Cage*.

The scope of China's techno-development is massive, so I focus on sectors, areas, and institutions most relevant to the emerging instrumental rule that characterizes China's techno-developmental regime. Although sectors like semiconductor, telecommunications equipment, and many others listed in the Chinese state's "Made in China 2025" plan are critical to China's techno-development, companies in those sectors have less instrumental power over people than large internet companies as the latter can directly reach an enormous population. In other words, I do not aim to study techno-development or technological upgrading per se but instead the emergent instrumental apparatus that marks China's techno-developmental regime. I thus focus on internet-related sectors, but even here, it is important to recognize that these sectors are themselves vast and diverse. As I studied workers' movement from obsolete manufacturing to internet-related sectors, I decided to hone in on food delivery platforms to illustrate how tech companies exercise instrumental and infrastructural power over workers, suppliers, and users. Although different platform companies develop various instruments, the case of food delivery platforms provides a basic understanding of instrumental control. Also, food delivery platforms have absorbed many of China's workers who left the manufacturing sector.

A recurring question I have encountered when giving talks about this book is why I have not included China's social credit system in the discussion. The reason for this is that my goal in *The Gilded Cage* is to explain China's techno-developmental regime and explore the contradictions it has generated. Put another way, I am interested in the origin of the regime and its impact on people's lives. China's social credit system is only a new addition to the already existing instrumental apparatus that constitutes China's techno-developmental regime. As the State Council's guideline on the social credit system shows, the central government sees the system as an essential legal and technical instrument for promoting the optimal allocation of resources, domestic demand, industrial upgrading, and scientific development.[122] As such, the logic of China's social credit system corresponds to the general logic of the instrumental apparatus that I have identified in *The Gilded Cage*. Moreover, perhaps because it is relatively new, although China's social credit system has garnered much attention from media and scholars outside China, it did not figure as particularly impactful in my interviews with various actors within China— from local officials to manufacturers, workers, and tech professionals— between 2016 and 2021. They consider other evaluation systems much more consequential, such as performance evaluation systems for officials and evaluation systems that allocate resources for social reproduction.

In my empirical analysis, I collect, use, and evaluate evidence holistically. I do not restrict myself to specific kinds of evidence in my research. I always collect as much evidence as possible. For the first part of the book, I mostly rely on secondary literature, policy and government documents, news articles, and interviews with a few scholars and technocrats. The second part of the book is based on in-depth interviews and my fieldwork. Starting in 2016, I conducted more than one hundred interviews with executives, managers, engineers, and workers in labor-intensive manufacturing sectors as well as with some local officials in the Pearl River Delta. Initial access was gained through a key informant, Tony, a former high-level employee in an electronics manufacturing company whom I have known since 2007 due to my research on *shanzhai* phones. Tony's reputation and social networks helped me gain research access. Some of my interviewees also put me in contact with their friends.

In addition to formal interviews, I had casual conversations with my interviewees. Thanks to the connections of Tony and some of my interviewees, many executives and managers were generous with their time and invited me to lunch or dinner. I also had lunch with workers in factory cafeterias and talked with them about their work, family, and views on economic transformation in China. They were all informed that these conversations would be part of research data. Since I kept in touch with some of my interviewees and contacted them from time to time, I learned of changes in their work and life trajectories. For example, some of the factory workers I knew eventually moved to the platform sector. They shared their work experiences, hopes, and disappointments with me following this transition. Furthermore, one factory in Shenzhen and another in Dongguan allowed me physical access to observe their daily operations, including their interaction with government officials, such as how they dealt with harsh law enforcement. In addition, I conducted online ethnography by joining a variety of social media groups, including those of managers in big manufacturing companies. Although I conducted most of my interviews and observations in the Pearl River Delta, I interviewed some executives and managers in the labor-intensive manufacturing sectors in the Yangtze River Delta too.

The third part of the book on internet-related sectors is mostly based on in-depth interviews and ethnography. I analyzed secondary literature, policy and government documents, news articles, and public corporate documents to understand the rise of big tech companies and the changing regulatory environment. In order to understand work in the platform sector, I interviewed sixty food delivery workers, six people with management positions, a system development engineer, and an in-house lawyer between 2018 and 2019. I did follow-up phone interviews with some of them in 2021. I also joined ten social media groups formed by platform couriers. In 2018, I conducted on-the-ground ethnography in Chongqing. One platform station allowed me to observe its couriers' and supervisors' routines, and a manager permitted me to visit his office. Finally, I collected interview data to understand the work and life situations of tech professionals. In 2019 and 2020, I conducted in-depth interviews with five informants with management positions in different types of IT and internet companies. These informants had extensive knowledge of the labor market, recruitment process, management system, and demographic backgrounds of software engineers. I also interviewed a labor law attorney to understand the regulatory environment. After this preliminary research, I conducted in-depth interviews with sixty-four software engineers in China's IT and internet companies between 2020 and 2021. In addition, I conducted online ethnography in social media groups formed by software engineers between 2019 and 2021, and reached out to engineers who participated in labor activism. In the methodological appendix, I provide more information about my research methods and data.

The process of accessing interviewees and research sites as well as collecting and analyzing data was challenging, but I did as much as possible to reach a more comprehensive understanding. Many friends, colleagues, and students in China, Taiwan, and the United States generously helped me gain access to informants and interviewees. I also benefited from my position as a faculty member at Harvard University, one of the most well-known US universities in China. As a Taiwanese growing up in Taiwan and having lived in the United States for seventeen years, I am an outsider to China, but I have more than a decade of experience conducting research there. I listened to my informants and interviewees, tried to understand them, and questioned my own assumptions and potential biases as much as I could. Being an outsider, however, came with some advantages. For one thing, my informants and interviewees trusted I would not disclose what they said to people around them. I hold firm the principles of respect and empathy in my research. Fortunately, despite intensifying geopolitical tensions, I did not encounter difficulties or hostility in interacting with my informants and interviewees, and I deeply appreciate their trust and generosity. All interviewee and informant names are anonymized in the book to protect confidentiality.

As a sociologist, I am aware of and acknowledge the limitations of different research methods. In the process of my research, I endeavored to overcome as many constraints as I could and employed a variety of research methods. Given China's increasingly repressive political environment, some might wonder whether my interviewees felt comfortable telling me their genuine views. As my experience doing fieldwork and interviewing grew, I developed some procedures to put my interviewees at ease. It helped, too, that most of my questions were about concrete experiences in their work and life. These questions, except those related to participation in social protests, are not politically sensitive according to local norms. Also, as a former legal professional, I have expertise in evaluating witness statements in judicial procedures. From my interactions with interviewees, I can assess evidence reasonably well and tell if my interviewees are following an "official script" due to political concerns. Overall, I did not sense political concerns among my interviewees. They felt comfortable talking about their experiences and problems. Since an interview usually lasted one to two hours, I had enough time to make sense of what my interviewees told me and ensure I fully understood what they said. I contacted my interviewees again whenever I needed clarification or had further questions.

I hope this book will help readers understand not only the macrolevel economic, social, and political changes in China but also give them a sense of what life is like within the gilded cage for everyday people there—officials, business executives, managers, workers, engineers, parents, and citizens. This book is about their hope, disillusion, and struggle.

2

From Labor to Land
and Technology

THE HISTORY of capitalism shows that in the course of capitalist development, new methods of production, organizational forms, modes of exploitation and dispossession, types of jobs, and markets tend to emerge to create
new modes of capital accumulation.[1] Indeed, in postreform China, as the CCP
turned to capitalist development to rescue and strengthen its legitimacy, the
Chinese party-state actively sought out such new modes of capital accumulation and new engines of economic growth.

China first relied on cheap labor as the major driver of its economic growth
and capitalist development in the postreform period. Then land became another critical source of growth after the 1994 fiscal recentralization reform and
the reform of China's real estate market in 1998.[2] Although using S&T to rejuvenate China has been built into the "cultural DNA of the Chinese nation" since
the nineteenth century, and Deng Xiaoping, China's reform architect, acknowledged S&T as a productive force in 1978, as I will show in chapter 3, provincial
governments in coastal provinces became determined to move to S&T-driven
economic development (i.e., techno-development) only in the mid-2000s.[3]
Because China's techno-development has unfolded—and the gilded cage has
emerged and expanded in China—in the abovementioned context, this chapter
aims to provide a basic contextual background.

I begin by tracking the shift from capitalist development based on cheap
labor to land-driven development. My discussion will include not only production but also social reproduction. Then I will move to the ideational aspect of techno-development or *techno-developmentalism*, which I use as an
umbrella term to refer to ideas and cultural discourses that advocate pursuing national development through a focus on S&T. To be sure, these ideas
and discourses—which are developed and used by political leaders, scholars, and the public alike—have varied over time, with distinct focuses and
even tensions and contradictions. Nonetheless, they share in common an

unwavering faith in the power and potential of S&T to advance the project of national development. The last part of the chapter will look at the impacts of techno-developmentalism on the party-state's statecraft, specifically, how the party-state scientized its own methods of statecraft and with what consequences. An analysis of this historical, institutional, and cultural background will help contextualize the unfolding of techno-development in the mid-2000s and emergence of the instrumental apparatus that would prove so central to that endeavor.

Labor-Driven Development

The rapid economic development and industrialization in China since the 1980s is part of the larger story in which globally mobile capital continues to search for cheap and disciplined labor worldwide. China's development unfolded with the rise of neoliberal globalization, under which international institutions like the WTO were established to remove state-imposed barriers to international trade. But unlike countries in the former Soviet bloc or Latin America, the Chinese state was able to retain its control of the economy as it integrated China into the global division of labor and neoliberal globalization based on China's competitive advantages in supplying cheap labor.[4]

Beginning in the 1980s, the Chinese central state created an incentive system through fiscal reforms that gave local government officials incentives and autonomy to pursue local economic development. Under this decentralized arrangement, local governments acted like a board of directors of a corporation, competing with each other to attract capital investment in their localities by providing cheap labor, land, tax breaks, public infrastructure, and so on.[5] As foreign-invested enterprises (FIEs) rushed to China to establish manufacturing facilities and take advantage of China's vast, underutilized rural labor, China became the "factory of the world" and established its own domestically focused manufacturing industry.[6] Nonetheless, although labor-intensive manufacturing contributed to the tremendous economic growth in China, a huge proportion of profits went to multinational firms at the top of the global value chain. Those firms usually have valuable intellectual property rights like patents and trademarks.[7] For example, at the top of the global value chain, Apple's gross profit margin was 39.3 percent in 2012; in contrast, Foxconn—the largest electronics contract manufacturer in the world that uses China's labor to produce Apple products—only had a 1.5 percent profit margin in the same year.[8] In general, the hierarchical division of labor in the global value chain creates intense competition at the lower value-added stages of production, where low wages and low profit margins prevail for workers and contract manufacturers in low-income countries.[9]

China's cheap and disciplined labor was globally competitive between the 1980s and early 2010s. The ample supply of cheap rural labor contributed to China's rapid economic growth and pushed China beyond low-income countries. In the early years of industrialization between the 1980s and late 1990s, there was little effective increase in the labor-intensive wage rate, thanks to an almost unlimited pool of underutilized workers in the rural population. But the unlimited supply of labor gradually disappeared in the early 2000s as large numbers of rural workers moved into the nonagriculture sectors. The decreasing supply of labor contributed, in turn, to wage growth. Between 2003 and the early 2010s, China enjoyed its fastest period of growth. Employment opportunities were widely available, and wages continued to rise. As a result, China's comparative low-wage advantage began to dwindle in the 2010s.[10] But in 2010, China still had 242.23 million rural migrant workers. Half of them migrated to four coastal provinces, Guangdong, Jiangsu, Zhejiang, and Shandong; also, 36.7, 16.1, and 12.7 percent of the rural migrant workers worked in manufacturing, construction, and the service industries, respectively.[11] As I will show in chapter 3, when these coastal provinces, especially Guangdong, Jiangsu, and Zhejiang, started to encounter problems resulting from the limitation of labor-intensive and export-oriented manufacturing in the mid-2000s, they became determined to pursue techno-development.

One of the most important institutions that contributed to China's relatively low-wage advantage is its household registration (*hukou*) system, which divides the population into urban and rural hukou holders, links people with their place of origin, and produces differential citizenship rights. The latter enable manufacturers to pay much lower wages and social insurance costs when they employ rural migrant workers instead of workers with a local, urban citizenship. Also, local governments in receiving cities only take limited responsibility in providing rural migrant workers with public services and social security, such as education, health care, and social insurance.[12] To reduce fiscal expenditures, local governments in large cities, especially those that receive the most rural migrant workers in the coastal provinces, tend to impose a strict household registration system. As a result, migrant workers often have to leave their children with their family in their hometowns, thereby producing millions of so-called left-behind children. According to data from the 1 percent national population sample, China still had around sixty-nine million children left behind by one or both of their parents due to migration in 2015, and meanwhile, around thirty-four million children moved with their parents to a place where the children did not have a local household registration status and thus had inferior access to public goods than did children with a local citizenship.[13] Although the central government declared its intention to reform the household registration system in 2005, such reform has remained elusive.[14]

In short, low wages and inferior citizenship status make it extremely difficult for migrant workers to raise their children in the places where they live
and work. The household registration system and intergovernmental fiscal
arrangement allow employers and local governments in receiving cities to allocate the costs of social reproduction to migrant workers, their families, and
local governments in migrants' places of origin, although employers and local
governments in receiving cities benefit tremendously from the economic contribution of migrant workers.[15] In chapter 4, I will discuss the continuing difficulties that migrant workers faced in obtaining local citizenship and access
to essential public goods, particularly education, as China turned to techno-
development. In chapter 8, we will see that even tech professionals struggle to
obtain local citizenship in China's megacities—the centers of China's techno-
development and postindustrial transformation.

Land-Driven Development

Following labor, land became another critical source that fueled capital and economic development as the central state sought to recentralize fiscal revenues.
The fiscal reform in 1994 and subsequent tax reforms significantly improved the
fiscal condition of the central state. The ratio of fiscal revenue to GDP rose from
10.8 percent in 1994 to 22.7 percent in 2013; also, the proportion of central fiscal
revenue increased from 22 to 55.7 percent, and has remained around 50 percent
since then.[16] As the central state centralized fiscal revenue, however, China's
fiscal expenditure remains decentralized because the 1994 reform did not significantly change the fiscal expenditure responsibilities between the central and
local governments. After the fiscal reform, local governments still bear most of
the expenditure responsibilities in education, social security, health, environmental protection, and other obligations. It is common for upper-level governments, including the central government, to create unfunded mandates as well.
In such scenarios, upper-level governments set targets and launch new public
projects while leaving localities to pay the costs. Each level of government tries
to pass extra expenses down the bureaucratic hierarchy.[17]

Essentially, the 1994 fiscal reform contributed to a mismatch in the revenue
capacity and expenditure assignments between the central and local governments. For instance, in the 2010s, local governments had to bear over 80 percent
of the fiscal expenditures, whereas the central government controlled more
than 50 percent of the total within-budget revenues.[18] Although the central
government has increased the amount of its fiscal transfers to local governments, such transfers remain insufficient for local governments to close their
fiscal gap.[19] With insufficient tax revenue to meet their expenditure needs, local
governments sought to expand their income through other channels.

Subsequent institutional changes enabled local states to turn to land and urbanization for income. Scholars use the term *land finance* to refer to the mechanism by which local governments increase their income through land transactions. The Land Administrative Law enacted in 1998 endows local governments with the authority to acquire, develop, and transfer rural land; meanwhile, China terminated the distribution of housing in cities and towns in 1998, and established a marked-based housing system, which promoted the development of the real estate market.[20] Furthermore, the central government gave localities a green light to create new backdoor financing institutions, such as local state banks and local government financing vehicles.[21] These financing institutions are crucial for land finance because local governments need capital to acquire land and invest in public infrastructure for land development.[22]

In the context of the abovementioned fiscal conditions, land urbanization occurred rapidly in China. Like China's populace, land is classified into urban and rural. Urban land belongs to the state, while rural land is owned collectively. Land urbanization refers to the expansion of urban land and urban built-up areas as rural land transforms into urban land. In comparison, population urbanization refers to the transfer of the population from rural to urban areas.[23] In the process of China's rapid industrialization, people living in urban areas rose from 17.9 percent in 1978 to 53.7 percent in 2013, as numerous rural migrants moved to work in cities.[24] Land urbanization requires local states to convert collectively owned, rural land to state-owned, urban land. Considerations about fiscal revenue motivate local governments to pursue land urbanization. After acquiring rural land with low costs, local governments transfer the expropriated land to industrial enterprises or real estate developers, and in so doing, obtain a high land transfer fee.[25] In 2014, the revenue from land transfers accounted for 7.25 percent of China's GDP and 31.94 percent of the total government fiscal revenue. The booming construction and real estate industries also increased local governments' tax revenues. Since large cities have imposed strict household registration rules to reduce migration and fiscal expenditures, however, the speed of population urbanization has been slower than that of land urbanization.[26]

Although local governments are the main actors that advance urbanization, the agenda was driven by the central government. In 2005, then president Hu Jintao pointed out the importance of urbanization for the country to increase consumption and domestic demand as well as foster economic growth.[27] The central government further came up with the New Style Urbanization Plan in 2014. As shown in Premier Li Keqiang's 2014 government work report, the central government hoped that land urbanization would drive population urbanization and eventually the conversion of rural citizens to urban ones.[28] As I will show in chapter 7, urbanization is a critical condition for the development of the platform economy in China.

Yet in the process of urbanization, problems arose and intensified after the 2008 financial crisis. Many of them related to land finance and the backdoor financing institutions. First, the rapid state-led land urbanization led to protests against local governments and social instability as peasants became furious with the local states' land grabbing and low compensation. For rural citizens, who lack the same social security system as urban citizens, land is a crucial safety net.[29] But as of 2011, at least sixty million peasants had lost their land due to land urbanization. Even when the affected rural citizens receive urban citizenship along with compensation from local governments in exchange for their land, they still tend to have a lower income than peasants with land and urban, local citizens, given the land-lost peasants' weak position in the labor market and thus limited employment opportunities.[30] Without land or employment security, land-lost peasants live a precarious life.[31] Second, although local governments successfully increased their revenue from land transactions through the auctioning of land, the process contributed to rocketing housing prices.[32] Speculation in the real estate market and rapidly rising housing prices have significantly increased the costs for social reproduction. In chapters 5 and 8, I will discuss how housing prices influence China's techno-development. Third, land finance and the backdoor financing institutions that facilitate land finance led to the accumulation of local government debt with little transparency and central control. The Chinese central state now sees China's growing local government debt as an alarming problem.[33] Finally, although rapid urbanization, the expanding real estate market, and infrastructure-building projects created numerous jobs in the construction sector, those jobs tended to be precarious. In China, informal work is endemic in construction and labor-intensive services.[34] Many construction workers have informal employment with neither a formal labor contract nor access to social insurances. Research shows that construction workers have even had difficulties getting salaries from employers and often worked in slave-like conditions.[35]

The problems emerging from China's urbanization process revealed the unsustainability of state-led land urbanization as a mode of capital accumulation and economic development as well as a solution to local governments' fiscal problems.[36] China's decreasing comparative advantage in labor-intensive, export-oriented manufacturing and the unsustainability of land-driven economic development have combined to make techno-development critical.

Techno-Developmentalism

As I will explore in the next chapter, provincial governments in the most prosperous coastal provinces—those receiving the most rural migrants—decided to turn to technology-driven economic development in the mid-2000s. Then both the central and local governments doubled downed on such efforts after the 2008 financial crisis. Although this shift did not happen until the mid-2000s, it was propelled by a long-standing aspiration to pursue national development through a focus on S&T. Since ideas and discourses about techno-development can vary and even have tensions and contradictions, different ideas can lead to different types and trajectories of techno-development. For example, ideas and discourses about techno-development can emphasize or disregard social equality and valuate people with or without technological skills differently. I therefore examine ideas and discourses about techno-development in this chapter before analyzing how they influenced the unfolding of techno-development in the subsequent chapters.

As theorized by Greenhalgh, using S&T to save and rejuvenate China is a "cultural repertoire" or way of understanding the world in China.[37] This cultural repertoire emerged during a crucial historical period that saw not only China's defeat in the Opium Wars and the onset of the so-called century of humiliation but also the beginning of the country's modernization. At the center of these seemingly paradoxical developments was China's complicated relationship with Western imperialism—a force that on the one hand, China sought to resist, and elements of which, on the other hand, China came to admire and desire for itself. Western imperialism was characterized by military and economic exploitation and produced global inequality between nations, to be sure, but its impact on China forced the recognition of the extent of Western power—and in particular, its grounding in Western S&T.[38] Thus even though some elites in the late Qing dynasty argued against Western S&T, others saw S&T-driven modernization as the key to China's salvation. The latter group prevailed, and in the second half of the nineteenth century, launched the "self-strengthening movement" (*ziqiang yundong*), explicitly prioritizing the adoption of Western S&T in order to resist imperialism and restore China's power.[39]

As such, from its birth, China's techno-developmentalism has been intermingled with national sentiments and existed as a form of techno-nationalism, an ideology that relates technological capabilities to a nation's security and socioeconomic prosperity.[40] After the founding of the Republic of China (ROC) in the early twentieth century, students and intellectuals, including revolutionary socialists, mobilized the notions of science and democracy to strengthen the nation and protect China's sovereignty. The pervasive belief that S&T was essential to building a new China was reflected in the establishment of the Chinese Academy of Sciences in November 1949, just one month after the birth of the People's Republic of China (PRC). The newly socialist state actively set about learning and acquiring as much S&T as it could from the Soviet Union until the Sino-Soviet split in the late 1950s.[41] S&T was considered highly progressive in Marxist philosophy, but Mao Zedong's approach was controversial.

While his "mass line" sought to widen access to scientific and technological knowledge and place S&T in the hands of the people, he famously attacked scientists and intellectuals, and smashed the Chinese Academy of Sciences, State Science and Technology Commission, and China Association for Science and Technology during the Cultural Revolution (1966–76).[42] But despite Mao's persecution of S&T experts, the repertoire of using S&T to save China was resurrected in the aftermath of the Cultural Revolution.

In the following sections, I shift to how top leaders in postreform China—specifically, Deng, Jiang Zemin, and Hu Jintao—talked about and theorized the relationship between S&T and development. Their ideas, to a large extent, overlap and resemble each other because they developed them based on official ideology and discourse, but each leader offered their own unique interpretation with different emphases and/or new components. In reviewing their thoughts, I pay attention to those ideas and discourses that conflicted with the leaders' notions and got sidelined or silenced within the party-state, for it is in these moments of contrast that we can discern the roads not taken.

Deng: S&T as Productive Force

There have been competing conceptions of development in China's official discourse. Deng formulated the most influential one. China's economic reform encountered a serious setback after the 1989 Tiananmen democratic movement. The conservative faction within the CCP saw the movement as a by-product of economic reform and challenged Deng's agenda for development. Deng responded in 1992 with his famous Southern Tour that visited Guangdong, where reform efforts were concentrated, and sought to restore confidence in his plan. During his tour, Deng said, "Our country must develop. If we do not develop, we will be bullied. Development is the only hard truth," thus supplying the slogan that would thereafter be associated with his vision as well as become one of the most renowned and influential slogans in the PRC's history.[43] Notably, Deng's words connected the imperative of national development to the history of imperialism.

From the beginning of economic reform, Deng emphasized the importance of capital and productive forces, particularly labor and S&T, in elevating productivity and thereby achieving economic development. He maintained this stress despite facing both ideological and institutional constraints that obstructed access to capital and the unleashing of productive forces. Deng's solution to this problem was essentially to reinterpret and reinvent socialism in a way that would enable China's access to foreign capital. He also underscored the critical significance of transferring surplus labor from agriculture to nonagricultural activities.[44] What is less discussed about Deng's model of development, however, is his focus on the role of S&T and S&T-related labor in economic development along with the relationship between S&T and politics.

In the aftermath of the Cultural Revolution, connecting S&T and the agenda of development was a challenge faced by Deng and other reform-minded leaders. The issue centered around the contested class status of intellectuals, a group that includes professionals in the S&T fields. Given their association with the ROC regime prior to the Cultural Revolution, the place of intellectuals within China's class structure was already a subject of heated debate.[45] At the Conference on the Issue of the Intellectuals in 1956, Premier Zhou Enlai had announced that intellectuals were part of the working class. Pointing to the contribution of S&T in advancing the military, economy, and culture, Zhou echoed Mao's agenda of "marching for science."[46] Nonetheless, many intellectuals were still classified as rightists during the Anti-Rightist Campaign between 1957 and 1959. It did not help that Mao continued, from time to time, to characterize intellectuals as bourgeoisie.[47] During the Cultural Revolution, professionals in the S&T fields were often classified as counterrevolutionaries, bourgeois experts, or rightists, and hence made targets in class struggles.[48] Along with landlords, rich farmers, antirevolutionaries, bad influences, right-wingers, traitors, spies, and "capitalist roaders," intellectuals were said to belong to the "nine black categories" and dubbed the "stinking old ninth" (chou lao jiu) by the general public.[49] It was only after the end of the Cultural Revolution that leaders in the central government began to rehabilitate those who were persecuted during it, including scientists in S&T.[50]

Cementing the central importance of S&T in development plans moving forward, the CCP's Central Committee and the State Council hosted the National Science Conference in March 1978, arguably one of the most impactful events in the PRC's history of S&T. Two giant red banners hung at the conference venue were emblazoned with messages promoting the party-state's vision: "Raising Chairman Mao's Banner High: Endeavoring to Transform Our Nation into a Modern and Strong Nation under Socialism in This Century" and "Raising Ambition and Aspiration: Marching toward Science and Technology Modernization."[51] The conference ended on a thrilling note with the announcement of the coming "Spring of Science."

Hua Guofeng and Deng were then the CCP's chairman and vice chairman, respectively. Although both recognized the importance of S&T and gave a speech at the conference, the two leaders had different views on the relationship between S&T and development. Wu Mingyu and Lin Zixin, who worked at the State Scientific and Technological Commission's Policy Research Office, drafted Hua's and Deng's speeches in an effort to ensure a coherent political message, but their attempt failed. In the end, Hua decided not to use the drafted speech, while Deng's draft was criticized by a politburo member for failing to cite Mao's thoughts on the need to remold intellectuals. Wu Lengxi, the deputy director of the Office of the Editors and Publications Committee of chairman Mao Zedong, also suggested that Deng revise his comments about the relationship between the working class and intellectuals, but Deng refused.[52] That such contention existed at the highest level of the CCP leadership reveals internal tensions within the state at the time as well as the thorny question of how to think about and value S&T-related labor.

The speech Hua eventually delivered argued that China should pursue not capitalist or imperialist modernization but rather socialist modernization under the direction of the proletariat. According to Hua, four modernizations— that of agriculture, industry, S&T, and defense—were needed to provide a powerful material basis for socialism. To advance S&T, Chinese people should learn about the modern scientific knowledge, labor skills, and management methods required for modern production, along with Marxism-Leninism and Mao's thinking. Following Mao, Hua called for learning from foreign countries. Hua's speech highlighted the role of both *politics* and *expertise* in the development of S&T. He explained, "Politics is the commander and the soul. It's unacceptable to forsake the importance of political thoughts; nonetheless, only doing politics without understanding techniques and having expertise is also unacceptable in the long run." Hua connected the development of S&T to the promise of socialism to reduce disparities between urban and rural, workers and peasants, and manual and mental labor. He further reasoned that raising the nation's scientific achievement in the long term required "workerized intellectuals and intellectualized workers."[53] Essentially, for Hua, China's development should aim to achieve socialist modernization, diminish inequality, and transform intellectuals into the working class. But when Hua lost political power in December 1978, his vision for the future lost influence too.[54]

In his speech at the National Science Conference, Deng said China's goal in the twenty-first century should be to build the country into a modern and strong nation under socialism. He made three historically important assertions in his speech. First, Deng argued that according to Marxist theories, S&T is a productive force. He said, "Many new means of production and methods of production are created in labs. Numerous industries—for example, the polymer synthesis industry, the nuclear energy industry, the computer science industry, the semiconductor industry, the aviation industry, and laser industry—are based on a scientific foundation."[55] In doing so, Deng made an important connection between what Daniel Bell calls theoretical knowledge in science to technology and economy.[56] He highlighted, in particular, how computer science and automation technology could increase the output of human labor. Precisely because S&T is a productive force, Deng contended that the labor associated with advanced scientific knowledge and skills would make a crucial contribution to modern production. Accordingly, most intellectuals should rightly be considered part of the working class. Manual and mental labor, he reasoned, are both socialist labor, differing only in terms of their respective positions in the division of labor. Deng's second key argument concerned the relationship between expertise and politics. In light of Mao's thoughts, intellectuals had to be both "red and professional" (*you hong you zhuan*), with "red" meaning "supportive of socialism." Deng stated that as long as one supports socialism, doing good work on one's job was a form of proletariat politics. Therefore S&T labor should be classified as "red," not "white" or opposed to socialism and/or the party. Third, Deng talked about the division of labor in terms of leadership in S&T-related institutes and organizations. He maintained that party committees should only be in charge of political leadership, steering the political orientation of institutes or organizations; experts, however, were the ones who should direct actual S&T work. Expert opinion and free discussion, he insisted, was needed to reduce mistakes in decision-making. Like Hua, then, Deng prioritized S&T as essential to China's future. But notably, unlike Hua, Deng did not hold that focusing on S&T would also decrease inequality—a difference between the two models of development that would prove to be consequential. Deng then talked about the synergy between technology and the economy. Improving both required China to have talent. And such talent had to be recognized wherever it was; as he put it, "We have talent. We shouldn't bury any talent just because they are not party members or they don't have academic credentials or experiences."[57]

Over time, Deng continuously emphasized the imperative to respect knowledge and talent, while raising the significance of S&T and S&T labor in his plan for economic development. In 1988, he upgraded his argument, now declaring it inadequate to say S&T was a productive force; indeed, it was the *foremost* productive force, and intellectuals, once denigrated as only the "ninth" category during the Cultural Revolution, should be elevated to the *first* of all social categories. He underscored the importance of investing in education to further advance S&T. Later, during his Southern Tour in 1992, Deng reiterated the critical importance of technology and education to economic development. He also began to differentiate technologies, singling out breakthroughs in *high* and *new* technology, in particular, as contributing the most to industrial development. As he aptly summarized, when it came to "doing technology, the higher the better; the newer the better."[58]

Jiang: Rejuvenating the Nation through S&T and Education

Although Deng planned to make Hu Yaobang and Zhao Ziyang his successors, they were both purged due to their liberal-leaning political orientation. Jiang became the CCP's general secretary after the 1989 Tiananmen democratic movement, which led to Zhao Ziyang's step-down. Although there is some degree of continuity between Jiang and Deng in terms of their views on development and its relationship to S&T, Jiang did introduce some new expressions and emphases. A graduate of National Chiao Tung University with a bachelor's degree in electrical engineering and also trained as an S&T professional, Jiang avidly advocated for the importance of S&T. His enthusiasm in this area could be seen as early as his writing and speeches in the mid-1980s, when he served as the head of the Ministry of Electronics Industry.

In the first decade of the economic reform, Jiang weighed in on the debates over the tensions between traditional and high-tech industries as well as between technology and human labor. In the mid-1980s, some officials believed China should focus on cultivating traditional industries and only develop the electronics industry when traditional industries became more established. Others worried about the consequences of automation and high technologies in general on workers' employment. As the head of the Ministry of Electronics Industry, Jiang contended that China should develop high-tech industries and employ advanced electronics technologies to improve traditional industries. He also argued that although China had an abundant supply of labor for labor-intensive industries, it would be a mistake not to acknowledge the indispensability of automation. Jiang reasoned that the primary purpose of automation is not to replace human workers but instead to raise product quality and productivity, increase economic benefits, and create more material wealth without increasing the amount of labor. Increasing wealth, he contended, would meet people's ever-increasing material and cultural needs. In 1984, Jiang wrote,

> Automation will reduce the workforce required for some production processes or positions, but displaced workers can be transferred to new jobs. After achieving a high level of automation, many workers may be needed to monitor technical equipment, write programs, and provide maintenance, repair, and support services. Automation can stimulate the transformation of the workforce from manual to mental labor. The development of new professions in the electronics industry will provide new employment opportunities for more people. For example, the rapid growth of new occupations in software engineering and information processing will require a significant increase in the number of workers and technical services.[59]

As this demonstrates, Jiang leaned toward developing high-tech industries and automation early in China's economic reform, despite other elites' concerns about the potential consequences of technology for workers.

Jiang's attitude toward S&T was evident as well in his view of intellectuals after the 1989 Tiananmen democratic movement, in which intellectuals and students played a crucial role.[60] On May 3, 1990, he gave a talk to commemorate the 1919 May Fourth Movement, an anti-imperialist, political, and cultural movement that highlighted science and democracy to rescue the Chinese nation. Emphasizing the contribution of intellectuals in the movement and the 1949 Chinese Communist Revolution, Jiang asserted that China's modernization and development depended on S&T and thus could not be obtained without intellectuals, especially S&T experts. Although he rebuked intellectuals who participated in the Tiananmen democratic movement, he maintained that those "bad apples" remained minorities not representative of China's twenty million intellectuals. In defending intellectuals as a group, Jiang called on them to fulfill their patriotic obligation and be in solidarity with peasants and workers.[61]

Notably, when discussing development and the central role of S&T, Jiang stressed not only "hard science" and "high technologies" but also "soft science" and techniques of *scientific decision-making*. In his talk on intellectuals in 1990, Jiang said they contribute not only to the making of artificial objects, such as atomic bombs, nuclear submarines, and electron colliders, but the scientific making and implementation of policy too.[62] This attention to scientific decision-making emerged in the 1980s under Zhao Ziyang's leadership.[63] During that period, party leaders, particularly Zhao and Wan Li, and influential scientists promoted scientific decision-making and soft science to correct the "irrational" or politicized decision-making under Mao. For Zhao, scientific decision-making meant incorporating knowledge and research from economics and other professional fields into the decision-making process.[64] Song Jian, an aerospace engineer who significantly shaped China's one-child policy, championed the importance of soft science in decision-making.[65] As he put it, what makes soft science scientific is the *quantitative analysis of data*:

> Quantitative analysis is the scientific basis for correct decision-making. . . .
> In the decision-making process, courage and charisma are important, but decision-making becomes emotional without the support of scientific data. Decision-making based on emotion is fragile and easily susceptible to prejudice.[66]

Song further argued for collaboration between social and natural scientists. In a similar vein, Qian Xuesen, a mathematician, cyberneticist, and aerospace engineer who played a crucial role in building China's nuclear and space projects, also promoted soft science along with the integration of natural and social sciences in decision-making to advance technological and economic development.[67]

Importantly, although Zhao was put under house arrest after Tiananmen due to his leniency toward movement participants, Jiang continued Zhao's insistence on scientific decision-making and appreciation of expertise. Indeed, Jiang highlighted the importance of democratic and scientific decision-making to development on many occasions. His talks and writings suggest that what he meant by "scientific" was integrating input from experts and research institutes, and what he meant by "democratic" was integrating input from the masses.[68] In 1994, the CCP issued a decision that stressed the significance of both these processes.[69] Similar to what happened in Britain in the nineteenth century, the CCP under Jiang's leadership attempted to merge the authority of the state and that of science, while at the same time pointing to the masses as its source of legitimacy.

I interviewed a technocrat, Mr. Wang, who worked for the Development Research Center of the State Council when Jiang was the general secretary, in order to understand how scientific decision-making was understood and practiced in high-level policy circles. As Mr. Wang explained,

> At that time, we thought what makes decision-making scientific is the solid analysis of data. We used modern forecasting methods in our analysis. In our reports, we set the rate of GDP growth and other indicators, such as comprehensive economic benefits, national income distribution, fiscal credit, and so on. We also set concrete goals for technological, educational, and cultural development. The development of these indicators relied on not only experiences but also a lot of quantitative analysis and economic modeling.

Pointing to the importance of numbers, Mr. Wang said, "When making a decision, we relied on data collected by the National Bureau of Statistics, industrial census, various input-output tables, and population census, and so forth. Comprehensive data analysis gave decision-making a solid scientific basis." This prioritization of data, numbers, and quantitative analysis under Jiang's reign resembles what scholars have variously referred to as "governance by indicators," "governance by numbers," and "trust in numbers"—efforts to present the decision-making process as scientific, efficient, consistent, and impartial given its grounding in quantification.[70] My interviews also revealed that technocrats in China at that time were heavily influenced by theories and methods of "social forecasting," which were popular in the Soviet Union, Europe, and North America in the late 1960s and 1970s, as illustrated by the subtitle of Bell's *The Coming of Post-Industrial Society: Venture in Social Forecasting.*[71]

Though more commonly associated with the Soviet Union, ideas about economic or rational planning were prominent in the highest political circles in the United States and United Kingdom in the 1960s as well.[72]

Jiang's S&T-driven conception of development also included specific understandings of how S&T related to economic development, space, and inequality. He was among the first leaders to explicitly embrace the so-called tiered development theory of industrial transfer (*tidu zhuanyi lilun*). Citing scholarship in Europe and the United States, scholars in China, especially those affiliated with the Chinese Academy of Social Sciences, debated China's strategies for development in the 1980s and the applicability of the tiered development theory in the Chinese context.[73] The theory provides developmental strategies for countries or regions with varying levels of economic and technological development. Although the theory was mostly applied at the international level, Chinese scholars applied it in domestic contexts as coastal and inland areas in China had highly uneven development.[74] Proponents of the theory argued that regions with a higher level of economic development, specifically coastal regions, should introduce and adopt advanced or high technologies to upgrade their economy since they have better conditions for industrial upgrading; more developed regions could then transfer technologies to the less developed ones. Proponents of the theory further asserted that the process could decrease developmental inequalities across regions as well as deliver the prosperity and development for all promised by Deng.[75] Opponents of the theory, in contrast, remained concerned about the lagging development in inner and western China. Advancing the so-called antitiered development theory, scholars argued that tiered development would only widen, rather than narrow, the already enormous inequality between regions. As such, they maintained that the government should allow both coastal and inland regions to introduce and absorb advanced technologies according to their respective conditions; in so doing, different regions would be able to develop their own technological and industrial advantages.[76]

Despite the disagreement among scholars, Jiang's talks on several occasions in 1992 and 1994 showed his unwavering support for the tiered development theory as a solution to adjusting China's economic structure. In his report at the Fourteenth National Congress of the CCP in 1992, he said, "The eastern coastal region should vigorously develop an export-oriented economy, focusing on the development of industries and products with high value-added, high foreign exchange earnings, high technology, and low energy and raw material consumption."[77] When visiting Shanghai in 1992, he stated that Shanghai and large cities along the Yangzi River should develop their tertiary industry and upgrade their secondary industry. In addition, government funding should prioritize infrastructure (transportation, energy, and telecommunication) and high-tech industries.[78] His speech in Shenzhen in 1994 offered explicit instructions about how to distribute industries across regions with varying levels of development. Responding to criticism that challenged the necessity for the continuing existence of special economic zones (SEZs), Jiang said that SEZs should stay, but they should develop high- and new-tech industries, and in principle, stop low-tech, labor-intensive industries, especially the so-called export-processing enterprises (i.e., *san lai yi bu* enterprises).[79] Labor-intensive industries, according to Jiang, should be transferred to inland regions, where the level of development was lower. Jiang reasoned that since the development of SEZs was earlier than inland regions, they had better conditions for high-tech industries; meanwhile, the rising labor and production costs prompted SEZs to upgrade industries. He also pointed out that the development of labor-intensive industries in inland regions would help industrial upgrading in SEZs and coastal regions as well as economic development in inland regions, while decreasing the movement of migrant workers from inland to coastal regions and bridging the developmental gap between regions. Jiang further emphasized the critical importance of building multinational conglomerates and cultivating tertiary industries in coastal cities.[80]

In 1995, at the National Science and Technology Conference, Jiang announced a grand strategy of fostering S&T and development. He called it "rejuvenating the nation through S&T and education" (*ke jiao xing guo*). Jiang articulated the difficulty facing China, namely that it still lagged behind many countries in terms of overall technological and economic development. According to Jiang, China's economy had been based on a model of extensive growth—growth premised on the expansion of inputs instead of increasing the productivity of inputs. Certain deep-seated economic problems, such as unreasonable industrial structure and low economic efficiency, had yet to be resolved. Furthermore, problems regarding population, natural resources, and the ecological environment had challenged the sustainability of China's growth model. Building on Deng's notion of S&T as the foremost productive force, Jiang proposed raising the quality of productive forces—technology and labor—through education, while highlighting the role of technology and education in advancing socioeconomic development and national prosperity.

Jiang then came up with specific instructions about how to accelerate technological development. First, businesses, especially large and medium-sized state-owned enterprises (SOEs), should improve their technological innovation capacity and integrate technology and the economy. Second, China should accelerate the upgrading of traditional industries, prioritize high-tech industries, accelerate automation and digitalization, and improve environmental protection and population control. Third, the country should enhance indigenous research and development (R&D) capabilities while continually introducing advanced technology from other countries. While introducing and absorbing foreign technology would help China advance its technological development, Jiang warned against technological dependency. He described innovation as the soul of a nation's progress and the driving force for its prosperity. If a country could not develop indigenous innovation and only relied on foreign technology introduction, it would never escape backwardness. Fourth, China should combine market mechanisms and macromanagement, particularly *scientific management*. The government should consider market demands, solicit input from scientists and experts, and conduct scientific analyses in order to make important decisions. Lastly, China should combine natural and social sciences to uncover as well as guide the inner law of socioeconomic development. Jiang's ideas exemplified a high modernist ideology as he put strong faith in the power of S&T in social engineering.[81]

Education, especially that of S&T labor, was also a crucial component of Jiang's grand strategy. Jiang emphasized that the key to rejuvenating the nation was talent. He said many forms of heavy and repetitive manual labor would be replaced by various automated machines and computers, and the requirements for workers' knowledge and technical proficiency would become higher. As such, it was critical to increase the proportion of S&T talents among laborers and improve the overall quality of the labor force. He also mentioned the importance of selecting and training S&T professionals and experts from workers and farmers. In his later talk on education in 1999, he said the government should broaden vocational and technical schools to educate students who could not attend college, and provide equitable educational opportunities, particularly in disadvantaged areas and for underprivileged populations. In 2002, before stepping down as the party's general secretary, Jiang further formulated the strategy of strengthening the nation through talent (*ren cai qiang guo*). The focus was to create and utilize both domestic and international talent markets as well as recruit "government talents," "business management talents," and "professional and technical talents."[82]

If rejuvenating the nation through S&T and education best represents Jiang's views on the relationship between S&T and development, then his notion of *three represents* (*san ge dai biao*), a term he coined in 2000, best demonstrates his effort to co-opt S&T personnel, management, and entrepreneurs in the advanced private sectors. One component of the three represents is that the CCP represents advanced productive forces. Jiang wanted to broaden the social base of the advanced productive forces. He said that the working class, including intellectuals and the vast number of peasants, had always been the fundamental force driving China's advanced productive forces. Nonetheless, Jiang also argued for the need to accept "outstanding elements" from other strata of the society, as they constituted advanced productive forces too.[83] His talk at the CCP's Sixteenth National Congress in 2002 illustrated certain emerging social strata that he believed should be included in the social base of advanced productive forces: entrepreneurs and technicians of private technology companies, management technicians employed by FIEs, self-employed individuals, private business owners, and freelancers. Moreover, he contended that the country must unite people from all walks of life to contribute to the prosperity of the homeland, encourage their entrepreneurial spirit, protect their legitimate rights and interests, and commend the most outstanding members among them. In so doing, China would invigorate labor, knowledge, technology, management, and capital to create social wealth and welfare for the people.[84] Jiang's view and his decision to allow these new "worthy" strata, especially entrepreneurs, join the party was criticized by some CCP members as betraying the party's interests and being elitist.[85]

In sum, my analysis of Jiang's views and policy reveals the combination of techno-development with meritocracy and high modernism. According to Jiang's plan of social engineering, coastal cities and inland regions should develop into postindustrial society and industrial society, respectively. Talented or worthy workers belong to the coastal, postindustrial society for their contribution to techno-development. In contrast, instead of migrating to coastal cities, rural-origin workers should remain in industrial, inland regions. As we will see in the next chapter, this perspective would profoundly shape the trajectory of China's techno-development along with the instruments created and used by the Chinese state to pursue that process.

Hu: A Scientific Concept of Development

Like Jiang, Hu was trained as an engineer. After receiving a bachelor's degree in water conservancy engineering from Tsinghua University, Hu began his career as an engineer working at a hydropower station. During his term as the CCP's general secretary between 2002 and 2012, Hu continued to highlight some of Jiang's views on S&T and development while systematically linking S&T and development by officially canonizing a *scientific concept of development*. According to Hu, the scientific concept of development is a *people-centered* model that demands comprehensive, coordinated, and sustainable development through what he called *five coordination* (*wu ge tong chou*)— coordination of urban and rural development, regional development, economic and social development, the harmonious development of humans and nature, and domestic development and opening the country to the outside world.[86] During Hu's term as general secretary, the central leadership further coined the term *scientific ruling* (*ke xue zhi zheng*), elevating science—scientific thinking, scientific institution, and scientific methods—to the guiding principle of the CCP's rule.[87]

Research suggests that the scientific concept of development was discussed in party circles in fall 2003.[88] It then became part of China's eleventh five-year plan (2006–10), the CCP's constitution, and the PRC Constitution in 2005, 2007, and 2018, respectively. The concept, however, already existed in the mid-1990s as a critical reflection and reinterpretation of Deng's notion that development is the only hard truth. In fact, before Hu became the general secretary, he had already argued to establish a scientific concept of development. At the second session of the Ninth National People's Congress in 1999, as the PRC's then vice president, Hu exchanged views with congress members from Fujian Province about the impact of the 1997 Asian financial crisis. While reiterating Deng's slogan about development as the only hard truth, Hu told the congress members that people must have a scientific concept of development. Importantly, Hu specified that this must be the kind of development that would deliver real benefits to people, as opposed to development that might only appear to be beneficial. He further asserted that the former kind of development could be achieved only by attending to—and balancing—both the scale and structure, quantity and quality, and speed and efficiency of development.[89]

Hu's 1999 talk had revealed his dissatisfaction with the kind of development that only valued *scale*, *quantity*, and *speed*. This explains why, on becoming the CCP's general secretary, he was so insistent that development had to be multidimensional in terms of its benefits. On many occasions, Hu distinguished economic and social development by asserting that development is by no means just about economic growth; instead, it is the basis to advance comprehensive social development.[90] During his term, the central leadership also prioritized improving China's safety nets and social welfare, and highlighted its will to address education, housing, and health care problems for disadvantaged groups.[91] Hu's notion of five coordination aims to address increasingly salient inequalities between urban and rural areas and across different regions, deteriorating environmental pollution, and growing social conflicts in the process of development to eventually achieve what he called a "harmonious society." Scholars view Hu's conception of development as a correction of Jiang's elitist and urban-centered conception of development, returning the country to a properly "socialist" market economy.[92] As I will show in chapter 3, though, the notion of the scientific concept of development would be used to justify the exclusion of the "unworthy" strata for techno-development.

For Hu, S&T was not only central to this new concept of development but also provided the intellectual and material foundation needed to transform China's economic structure. Considering the crucial role of S&T, Hu formulated the goal of building an innovative nation (*chuan xin xing guojia*) based on Jiang's emphasis on indigenous innovation. In his talk at the National Science and Technology Conference in 2006, Hu remarked, "More than ever, we urgently need a solid scientific foundation and strong technical support to improve the quality, efficiency, and sustainability of development." He asserted that the modernization of a nation depends on S&T.[93] Acknowledging some problems that had emerged in China's developmental process, Hu argued that the country would need to adjust its economic structure, transform its resource-dependent economic growth model into an innovation-driven one, and accelerate industrial upgrading. He saw high-tech industries, innovative businesses, intellectual property rights, and S&T-related talent as critical to an innovation-driven growth model. Soon after the 2006 National Science and Technology Conference, the State Council required the cadres and officials at all levels to take the lead in learning and applying science. It also instructed party leadership to consider cadres' and officials' efforts in promoting indigenous innovation when evaluating the latter's performance.[94]

Crucially, Hu's tenure included both the onset and early aftermath of the 2008 financial crisis. Reflecting in 2010 on the impact of the crisis, Hu contended that it had only accentuated the need to accelerate transforming China's development model. On the one hand, he advocated for the need to upgrade traditional industries and advance new and high-tech industries, service industries, indigenous innovation, and sustainable development. He especially pointed out the importance of IT, flexible manufacturing, intelligent manufacturing, green manufacturing, cloud computing, the Internet of Things (IoT), and automation technology—all buzzwords that I heard repeated by managers, executives, scholars, and officials in my fieldwork between 2016 and 2019. On the other hand, Hu stressed the need to expand domestic demand to maintain economic growth. To that end, he asserted, China would also have to enhance social protection.[95]

Techno-Developmentalism in Society

Thus far, I have described official discourse, but belief in the power of S&T for national salvation has diffused beyond official discourse and practices, taking hold more broadly throughout Chinese society. In their timely edited volume *Can Science and Technology Save China*, Greenhalgh and fellow anthropologist Li Zhang invited their colleagues in medical and environmental anthropology to write about how Chinese people think about the hopes and realities of modern S&T rejuvenating the nation in postreform China. Reflecting on the various empirical studies in the collection, Greenhalgh notes the near total acceptance of and optimism about modern S&T as an ideal solution to all sorts of problems. She suggests that scientism—the faith in science as a panacea for all the nation's ill—and its twin, technicism—the preference for instrumental reasoning and technical efficacy above all—exist not only at the level of official ideology but have now fully penetrated society too. Such near-religious reverence for and worship of S&T, according to Greenhalgh, is in stark contrast with common critiques of the adverse impacts of technologies and encroachment of technological rationality in modern life in the West after World War II.[96]

Greenhalgh's observation corresponds to that of STS scholars Xiaobai Shen and Robin Williams. Shen and Williams argue that although modern S&T arrived in China with enormous opposition in the Qing dynasty, the pendulum swung from resistance to enthusiasm. They point out that the critique of modern S&T has been relatively muted in contemporary China; the expectations for S&T have been overwhelmingly positive, lacking adequate attention to the potential negative outcomes of technological changes and issues related to inequality. According to Shen and Williams, there has also been little attempt among intellectuals in postreform China to engage with scholarly critiques of technology or techniques in other parts of the world. They maintain that such wholesale acceptance is rooted in a utilitarian view of S&T that has endured despite regime changes.[97]

One might question the representativeness of the above observations, but national survey data lend substantial support to Greenhalgh's and Shen and Williams's assertions. The World Value Surveys—a global research project conducted by a worldwide network of social scientists to explore people's values and beliefs—have four S&T-related questions and hence shed light on attitudes toward S&T in China in a comparative context. In table 2.1, I present responses to the four questions from Wave 7 (2017–20), which was conducted in fifty-four countries or territories in the world. The first question asks whether more emphasis on technology in the future is a good thing. Among the respondents in China, 92.5 percent consider such emphasis a good thing. China ranks second among the fifty-four countries/territories in terms of the percentage of respondents with such a positive view. The second question considers whether S&T make our lives healthier, easier, and more comfortable. The scores range from 1 (completely disagree) to 10 (completely agree). The average score in China is 8.63, the third highest among all the countries/territories. The third question asks respondents whether they agree that because of S&T, there will be more opportunities for the next generation. The score is from 1 (completely disagree) to 10 (completely agree). China ranks fourth out of the fifty-four countries/territories, with an average score of 8.52. The last question asks respondents whether "the world is better off, or worse off, because of science and technology." The score ranges from 1 (a lot worse off) to 10 (a lot better off). China ranks first again, with an average score of 8.58.

TABLE 2.1. Attitudes toward S&T

	(1) More emphasis on technology is a good thing		(2) S&T makes lives better		(3) S&T brings more opportunities for the next generation		(4) The world is better off because of S&T	
Rank	Territory	Mean (%)	Territory	Mean	Territory	Mean	Territory	Mean
1	Myanmar	94.0	Bangladesh	8.71	Armenia	9.00	China	**8.58**
2	**China**	**92.5**	Armenia	8.65	Bangladesh	8.69	Kyrgyzstan	8.54
3	Vietnam	90.1	**China**	**8.63**	Kyrgyzstan	8.62	Vietnam	8.35
4	Zimbabwe	90.1	Zimbabwe	8.20	**China**	**8.52**	Bangladesh	8.32
5	Kyrgyzstan	88.2	Vietnam	8.15	Ethiopia	8.46	Tajikistan	8.09
6	Iran	86.2	Iraq	8.13	Myanmar	8.37	Indonesia	7.75
7	Jordan	85.0	Tajikistan	8.13	Vietnam	8.35	Russia	7.72
8	Ecuador	84.5	Kyrgyzstan	8.06	Tajikistan	8.32	Australia	7.69
9	Iraq	84.0	Ethiopia	8.04	Indonesia	8.17	Ethiopia	7.68
10	Nigeria	83.8	Myanmar	8.02	Zimbabwe	8.12	Kazakhstan	7.63
11	Egypt	81.3	Iran	8.01	Germany	8.02	Ukraine	7.63
12	Bangladesh	80.2	Nigeria	7.92	Pakistan	8.01	Germany	7.62
13	Lebanon	80.2	Jordan	7.89	Romania	7.99	New Zealand	7.57
14	Tajikistan	80.2	Indonesia	7.86	Russia	7.99	Zimbabwe	7.54
15	**Taiwan**	79.8	Pakistan	7.78	Iran	7.98	**United States**	7.45
16	Armenia	79.6	Egypt	7.77	Iraq	7.96	Pakistan	7.44
17	Tunisia	77.6	Greece	7.75	Ukraine	7.93	Iraq	7.41

Continued on next page

TABLE 2.1. (*continued*)

	(1) More emphasis on technology is a good thing		(2) S&T makes lives better		(3) S&T brings more opportunities for the next generation		(4) The world is better off because of S&T	
Rank	Territory	Mean (%)	Territory	Mean	Territory	Mean	Territory	Mean
18	Ethiopia	77.5	Romania	7.75	Nigeria	7.74	Greece	7.38
19	Nicaragua	77.0	Russia	7.67	Kazakhstan	7.73	Macau	7.29
20	Kenya	75.8	Ukraine	7.64	Serbia	7.72	Canada	7.20
21	Philippines	74.9	Japan	7.60	Japan	7.67	South Korea	7.20
22	Germany	74.8	Andorra	7.56	Greece	7.61	Hong Kong	7.14
23	Russia	73.9	Malaysia	7.56	Jordan	7.60	Iran	7.14
24	Kazakhstan	72.6	Lebanon	7.55	Puerto Rico	7.59	Armenia	7.13
25	Bolivia	71.3	Tunisia	7.47	Argentina	7.57	Thailand	7.07
26	Hong Kong	70.4	Macau	7.46	Nicaragua	7.57	Lebanon	7.04
27	Colombia	70.1	Kenya	7.44	Egypt	7.55	Nigeria	7.03
28	Pakistan	68.8	Kazakhstan	7.42	Mexico	7.52	Serbia	6.96
29	Japan	68.4	Cyprus	7.38	Malaysia	7.50	Taiwan	6.94
30	Peru	67.9	Singapore	7.38	Turkey	7.44	Cyprus	6.91
31	Indonesia	67.8	Hong Kong	7.35	Canada	7.39	Japan	6.88
32	Macau	67.7	Turkey	7.33	Cyprus	7.35	Turkey	6.87
33	Brazil	66.9	Australia	7.32	Singapore	7.31	Kenya	6.86

34	Greece	65.8	**Taiwan**	7.32	Andorra	7.29	Mongolia	6.86
35	Malaysia	65.3	Serbia	7.31	**Macau**	7.29	Andorra	6.85
36	Cyprus	63.3	Argentina	7.27	Colombia	7.24	Malaysia	6.82
37	**Singapore**	63.3	Canada	7.27	Kenya	7.18	Romania	6.77
38	Puerto Rico	63.1	Germany	7.16	Guatemala	7.14	**Singapore**	6.60
39	Romania	62.5	**South Korea**	7.12	Brazil	7.13	Myanmar	6.47
40	Serbia	62.0	**United States**	7.09	Mongolia	7.13	Mexico	6.46
41	Mongolia	61.2	New Zealand	7.03	**United States**	7.09	Guatemala	6.43
42	Guatemala	60.4	Mongolia	6.88	Bolivia	7.07	Philippines	6.36
43	Ukraine	58.1	Mexico	6.87	Hong Kong	7.06	Brazil	6.23
44	Mexico	56.9	Nicaragua	6.81	Australia	7.04	Jordan	6.23
45	**South Korea**	56.7	Philippines	6.80	Ecuador	7.00	Puerto Rico	6.19
46	Turkey	54.6	Puerto Rico	6.76	Lebanon	6.94	Argentina	6.18
47	**United States**	54.2	Guatemala	6.73	**Taiwan**	6.92	Nicaragua	5.99
48	Chile	51.1	Brazil	6.71	**South Korea**	6.91	Colombia	5.90
49	Canada	50.8	Peru	6.49	Peru	6.90	Egypt	5.81
50	Australia	49.4	Colombia	6.46	Philippines	6.87	Peru	5.77
51	Andorra	47.9	Chile	6.42	Tunisia	6.83	Ecuador	5.72
52	Thailand	46.5	Bolivia	6.40	Chile	6.82	Tunisia	5.65
53	Argentina	43.0	Thailand	6.40	New Zealand	6.81	Chile	5.62
54	New Zealand	40.8	Ecuador	5.92	Thailand	6.33	Bolivia	5.54
	Total	68.9	Total	7.43	Total	7.57	Total	7.04

Source: World Value Surveys, Wave 7, 2017–20.

As a whole, the survey data unambiguously show respondents in China have the most positive and optimistic attitudes toward S&T. The same questions were asked in some of the previous waves of the survey and produced similar responses.

A few countries share similarities with China in terms of their optimistic and positive attitudes toward S&T. These countries tend to have a socialist regime, such as Vietnam, or are part of the former Soviet Union in central or western Asia, such as Armenia, Kyrgyzstan, and Tajikistan. Such a pattern suggests the potential impact of materialism on beliefs in S&T. Shen and Williams point out that the dominant theories in the Soviet bloc articulated overwhelmingly positive expectations surrounding S&T.[98] In addition, all the above countries are either classified as "not free" or "partly free" in terms of political rights and civil liberties in Freedom House's Freedom in the World Reports.[99] In fact, among the top ten countries/territories for the four questions in table 2.1, with the exception of Australia, all are classified as "not free" or "partly free." In comparison, respondents in the places known as the "Four Asian Tigers" (e.g., South Korea, Taiwan, and Singapore) as well as Japan tend to be less overwhelmingly enthusiastic about S&T when compared with their counterparts in China—although the former group do share with the latter a Confucian culture and/or the tradition of emphasizing development.[100]

Beyond the World Value Surveys, research that analyzes attitudes toward the application of specific S&T, particularly biotechnology, reveals a similar pattern: Chinese people are incredibly positive in evaluating the usefulness and moral acceptability of various applications of biotechnology. In contrast, the European public has a broader understanding of the risks involved.[101] Research also shows that certain technologies negatively perceived as "surveillance infrastructure" outside China, such as China's social credit system and censorship technologies, are widely accepted by Chinese people.[102] As I will demonstrate in subsequent chapters, the prevailing belief in the power of S&T for national salvation, combined with an ideology of meritocracy, bolsters people's support for the state's techno-development agenda, despite the negative impacts that agenda might have on their lives.[103]

The Scientization of Statecraft

As the party-state revised—and more specifically, scientized—its conception of development, it sought to apply the same principles to its statecraft so as to ensure the state's capacity to deliver all the promised developmental outcomes.[104] As scholarship on governance and the experience of the United Kingdom's "New Public Management" movement in the 1980s show, the process of governance is itself subject to governance and forms of control.[105]

In China, arguably, party cadres, government officials, and government agencies are critical parts of the party-state machinery as they are responsible for forming and implementing policies and delivering development outcomes. As such, the party-state in the postreform era has endeavored to control its agencies, cadres, and officials in order to ensure they produce desirable outcomes. To do so, it has scientized institutions and techniques for measuring and evaluating performance within the government to align with the changing conception of development.[106]

In some respects, the Chinese government's internal performance evaluation systems are akin to labor control systems in business, which makes sense considering the long-standing, extensive, and deep involvement of the party-state in economic development. Cadres and officials in China often use the metaphor of a conductor's baton to describe performance evaluation systems given that such systems shape their calculation and action.[107] The metaphor resembles what sociologists and historians call "remote control" or "a technology of distance," in the sense that supervisors do not have to directly monitor the supervisees on the spot but instead can monitor through information, numbers, and indicators in performance measurement and evaluation systems.[108] These systems are especially critical in China because of their potential effects on the party-state's ability to secure its legitimacy. As sociologist Dingxin Zhao argues, in postreform China, the major source of the party-state's legitimacy comes from its performance as opposed ideology, as in Mao's period, or democratic elections and the rule of law as in liberal democracies.[109] Presumably, at least from the party-state's perspective, performance evaluation systems help it to monitor and deliver developmental outcomes, while also creating an objective and impartial facade.

The PRC's government performance evaluations systems have their roots in factory management, specifically the so-called target management responsibility system, which was used to implement the planned economy under Mao. To achieve production quotas assigned by the party-state, factories during Mao's era sought to regulate and maximize productivity at every layer, from factories all the way down to workshops, teams, machines, and individual workers. The system sometimes included an element of competition too, generating incentives for workers and work units to compete with each other.[110] With the unfolding of economic reform in the 1980s, SOEs and township and village enterprises emphasized S&T in two ways in their operations. First, enterprises stressed the role of technology in enhancing productivity. Second, they highlighted scientific management. More to the point, they blended the old target management responsibility system with Frederick W. Taylor's concept of scientific management to establish performance evaluation systems. Taylor's *The Principles of Scientific Management*

was translated into Chinese in 1916 by Mu Ouchu, a famous national indus-
trialist in the ROC. Ouchu was trained at the University of Wisconsin at
Madison, University of Illinois at Urbana-Champaign, and Texas A&M University, and deeply influenced by Taylor and Frank Bunker Gilbreth's work
on scientific management.[111] After the beginning of economic reform, enterprises quickly turned to theories of scientific management to seek insights for
management and thus developed performance evaluation systems. Such systems comprised indicators (e.g., outputs and product safety indicators) and
rules for rewards and punishments. Responsibility along with the corresponding rewards and punishments were assigned top-down within an enterprise. Lucrative market revenues that did not exist during Mao's era made
rewards more substantial and effective.[112]

Performance evaluation systems were then disseminated from SOEs and
township and village enterprises to government agencies. Seeing the success
of enterprises in boosting production and revenues, local party-states developed similar systems to evaluate and frequently rank the performance of government agencies, cadres, and officials, mainly in the realms of economic
development and population control—the two most important tasks in the
eyes of the party-state.[113] Sometimes local party-states further contracted out
their own production responsibilities to enterprises. For instance, the Economic Commission in Wuxi City in Jiangsu Province distributed its production quotas for export to local enterprises and asked the latter to ensure the
fulfillment of quotas.[114] Research suggests that the results of cadre performance
evaluations—specifically, GDP growth rates—correlated with the promotion
of provincial-level cadres and officials.[115]

Despite the seeming efficacy of the government's performance evaluation
systems in generating economic growth, criticism of such systems had become
salient during Jiang's tenure as the general secretary in the 1990s. Although
concrete evaluation standards varied across localities, they shared certain core
principles. The predominant criticism was the common practice of using economic growth, especially GDP and GDP growth rates, as the primary indicators for evaluation.[116] Critics argued that this practice wrongly translated
Deng's notion of development as the only hard truth into "economic development is the only hard truth," while further conflating economic development
with GDP.[117] They also pointed out that the focus on GDP and quantitative
evaluations had incentivized officials to fake statistics, and unfairly led to the
promotion of bad apples—cheaters—in the system. Similarly, such evaluation
standards had motivated local officials to invest in the so-called performance
projects (*zheng ji gong cheng*) or image projects (*xing xiang gong cheng* or *mian
zi gong cheng*) that could boost GDP and create an impressive facade in the
short term, despite the expense of piling up government debts and undermin-

ing long-term benefits. Some local governments even imposed arbitrary levies on residents, especially peasants, to collect capital for unnecessary investment projects in order to increase GDP and thus their performance.[118] This vividly illustrates how a state's internal performance evaluation systems can structure interactions between the state and nonstate actors, or so-called state-society relations.

During Jiang's tenure, party theorists, officials, and journalists began to call for the *scientific* restructuring of performance, and amending evaluation standards and methods accordingly. They maintained that performance evaluations should consider not only short-term and sectoral interests but also long-term and overall benefits.[119] Some bottom-up reforms emerged in the 1990s in many provinces.[120] Soon after Hu canonized the notion of the scientific concept of development, the central leadership galvanized efforts to overhaul the cadre performance evaluation system and encourage local party-states to innovate their evaluation systems.[121] Hu wanted to integrate the scientific concept of development and the cadre evaluation system, with the former serving as the guiding principle for the latter.[122] At a symposium on population, resources, and the environment in 2004, Hu pointed out that the cadre evaluation system should include not only economic growth indicators but also "humanistic indicators, resource indicators, environmental indicators, and social development indicators."[123] As such, his solution expanded the application of quantitative indicators to ever more spheres of life. Hu further requested the CCP's Organization Department—the human resource management department of the party—to research and reform the cadre evaluation system. In 2005, Wen Jiabao, then premier, ordered the establishment of a scientific government evaluation system.

Following the central leadership's instructions, both central and local party-states endeavored to improve all kinds of performance evaluation systems. The central party-state aimed to provide a general guideline, while local party-states aspired to develop standards that better fit the heterogeneous local contexts. In the process, public administration experts and professors at the CCP's Central Party School and elite universities played a critical role in introducing evaluation systems from other countries, such as the Government Performance and Results Act of 1993 in the United States. They also helped the central and local party-states to design evaluation standards *scientifically*. Many experts used utility functions to back up their arguments.[124] Some cited research on key performance indicators (KPIs) in business management for designing evaluation systems.[125] Several universities and institutes even established research centers dedicated to research government performance evaluation in general during Hu's term.[126] The Chinese central and local states have generously supported research in this area.

The Organization Department of the CCP's Central Committee began to reform the system in 2004 through a scientific process: extensive experiments at the provincial, city, and county levels, and coordination with the National Bureau of Statistics, National Environmental Bureau, National Population and Family Planning Commission, State Administration of Work Safety, and others to ensure the availability and commensurability of statistics. This scientific process aimed to produce a scientific evaluation system. When the Central Committee was revising the evaluation criteria, many central and local officials expressed their views on how to improve the system. For example, Liu Yunfeng, a member of the standing committee of the Shijiazhuang municipal party committee, wrote to the *People's Daily* that the evaluation standards tended to be too quantitative and economic-centric. He suggested that citizens should be entitled to evaluate cadre performance.[127] In a similar vein, a party theorist suggested that citizen evaluation was important because ultimately development should benefit the masses. He further proposed including not only economic but social, humanistic, and environmental indicators too.[128] Some officials called for stricter implementation of the Statistics Law to prevent cadres and officials from faking statistics. Others complained that despite the existence of various indicators on paper, the significance of "hard" and short-term indicators, such as GDP, always trumped "soft" and long-term ones. They argued that such tendencies needed to be corrected to avoid distorting cadres and officials' behavior.[129] The vice minister of the Organization Department wrote about the difficulty of designing indicators that would reveal not just economic growth but also the quality and structure of socioeconomic development. He emphasized the necessity of having both quantitative and qualitative forms of evaluation.[130]

After two and half years of experiments, discussions, and drafting, the Organization Department eventually enacted a guideline in 2006 to evaluate local leadership (at the above-the-county level) and members of the leadership. The evaluation system drew on both quantitative and qualitative evaluation, and comprised "democratic recommendation, democratic evaluation, public opinion survey, performance analysis, individual interviews, and comprehensive evaluation." The component of performance analysis, one of the most important, was based on a series of indicators, including local per capita GDP and growth, per capita fiscal income and growth, urban and rural residents' income and growth, resource consumption, production safety, basic education, urban employment, social protection, social stability, urban and rural life, population and family planning, resource protection (e.g., cultivated land), environmental protection, investment in S&T, innovation, audit data, and evaluation by the masses.[131] The substance of these indicators perfectly correspond to Hu's scientific concept of development, especially his notion of five coordination.

In 2009, the Organization Department revised the guideline again. Acknowledging heterogeneity across local contexts, the guideline authorized local party-states to develop evaluation standards, indicators, and weights that better fit local contexts. Meanwhile, it reminded evaluators to consider the comparability of evaluation outcomes across localities and the importance of attending to change in performance over time.[132] Crucially, the Organization Department also extended the evaluation system from local party-states to ministries and commissions under the State Council, such as the National Bureau of Statistics, National Environmental Bureau, National Population and Family Planning Commission, and State Administration of Work Safety. These ministries and commissions developed evaluation standards to evaluate their local agencies as well.

Many local party-states also came up with their own solutions to scientize their evaluation standards. Here I use Yunnan's cadre and official performance evaluation system as an example as China's official media highly praised its standards. In 2005, Yunnan's provincial party committee came up with a sixteen-indicator system, in which 70 percent of the indicators were *quantitative* and 30 percent were *qualitative*. Rather than only focusing on economic development, Yunnan's system evaluated leadership according to its performance in economic development (forty points), social harmony (twenty-five points), sustainable development (twenty-five points), and state building (ten points). The system operationalized the four dimensions clearly. In terms of economic development, the system considered not only GDP but also fixed asset investment and its growth rate, the construction and completion of major projects, and the total of retail sales of consumer goods and its growth rate. In terms of social harmony, the system included the growth rate of employment and reemployment, decrease of social protests, and decline in criminal cases. In terms of sustainable development, the evaluation system included the control of population growth, the level of urbanization, environmental protection, and the use of land and resources. Regarding state building, the guideline considered scientific administration, democratic administration, and administration according to the law. Leadership with more than ninety points would be regarded as outstanding and enjoy a priority to be promoted; leadership with a score between sixty-five and seventy-nine would be considered mediocre and asked to reform itself; and leadership with a score below sixty-five would be regarded inferior, and hence subjected to discipline and organizational adjustment.[133]

Although there are spatial and temporal variations in local cadre performance evaluation standards, Yunnan's 2005 guideline remains the basic model for performance evaluation systems. Some components (e.g., public opinion surveys) can be added or removed, and weights can be adjusted. In general, the implementation of a performance evaluation system requires goal setting, which is often based on China's five-year plans for socioeconomic development and the negotiation of goals between two levels of governments. The implementation also requires identifying party-state agencies involved in completing the task, selecting indicators to measure performance, deciding the weight for each indicator, and specifying indicators whose incompletion would lead to unpardonable disciplinary outcomes (i.e., the so-called one-vote veto issues, such as maintaining social stability).[134]

In short, the official canonization of the scientific concept of development galvanized the effort to scientize statecraft and incorporate management science at every level of governance, particularly in the government's many levels of performance evaluation. The process has broadened the scope of evaluation and created much stress for local officials. The process of scientizing performance evaluation systems in China is similar to the so-called social indicators movement in Western countries since the 1970s. The movement was associated with critiques of the dominance of purely economic parameters and the solution of establishing a far-reaching program for measuring society.[135] Scholars find mixed results about the relationship between government evaluation, cadre/official evaluation, and cadre/official promotion. Still, research shows that government evaluation systems, especially the weights of indicators, influence government behavior such as public spending.[136] When I interviewed local officials in Guangdong about their views on performance evaluation, many complained about the various types of evaluation they have to cope with: comprehensive evaluations of a local party-state as a whole, evaluations of a specific department within a local party-state, evaluations of specific projects, and so on. Additionally, now many local governments have digitized performance evaluation systems, storing and administering them through the government cloud. Officials can see and conduct evaluations using personal computer and mobile applications. This is the latest effort to scientize statecraft. All of my interviewees said that they must arrange their work according to the parameters set by various evaluation systems simply to avoid problems and punishments, let alone to seek promotion. We will see such considerations repeatedly throughout the rest of the book along with the impact of such evaluation systems on government officials' action and interaction with other actors.

Conclusion

The aim of this chapter has been to provide historical, institutional, and cultural background to understand and explain China's turn to techno-development in the mid-2000s as well as the emergence of the instrumental apparatus to foster and assess that development. I first described labor-driven capitalist development that started in the late 1970s. As I have shown, the Chinese state successfully integrated China into neoliberal globalization given the country's competitive advantages in cheap labor. As I will discuss in the next chapter, however, local governments began to experience the limitation of labor-driven economic development in the mid-2000s. Also, China's competitive advantages in cheap labor started to decline in the 2010s. I have explained, too, how China's fiscal recentralization in 1994 and the establishment of a marked-based housing system in 1998 led to rapid state-led land urbanization and speculation in the housing market. Labor- and land-driven capitalist development was accompanied by difficulties in social reproduction, particularly access to public education for migrant workers' children due to the differential citizenship rights accorded through the household registration system as well as rocketing housing prices. I foreground these issues in this chapter because, as I will demonstrate in subsequent chapters, they would influence and be influenced by China's techno-development.

I have also analyzed techno-developmentalism in official discourse and society. My purpose is twofold. First, I aim to reveal the debates and tensions within the party-state over the appropriate role of S&T—debates and tensions that several Chinese top leaders attempted to downplay and manage. The fact that countries begin to climb up the "ladder of economic development" or global value chain by turning to techno-development when they lose comparative advantages in cheap labor seems to suggest there is only one type of techno-development. Yet the debates and tensions within the party-state show that there are indeed different visions of techno-development. This is why I coined the term *techno-developmental* regime in chapter 1 to help analyze different types of techno-development.

Indeed, ideas and discourse under the umbrella of techno-development in China are mostly mingled with national sentiments, and as mentioned in chapter 1, reflect what James C. Scott calls a high modernist ideology.[137] Ideas and discourse under the umbrella of techno-development differ, though, in terms of how they perceive the relations between S&T, social inequality, meritocracy, and China's socialist official ideology. Such differences can be illustrated by the different views of Hua and Deng, and Hu's acknowledgment of the pressing issue of inequality after Jiang's term.[138] But as I will look at the next chapter, the 2008 financial crisis created the conditions for political elites to once again promote the use of S&T to save China and downplay issues of domestic inequality. Indeed, as Shen and Williams argue, despite the PRC's official ideology, the party-state has mostly adopted elitist, top-down, instrumental, and uncritical approaches to S&T except for the period when Mao's ideology was prevailing.[139] Nonetheless, I would add to Shen and Williams's observation by noting yet another swing of the pendulum. As the policy shift during Hu's term illustrates, the balance shifted again as top leaders began to sense growing threats to social stability. And as I will show in chapter 9, similar patterns have occurred since 2021. In short, it is crucial to see what issues have been variously downplayed in the shifting official discourse of techno-development and when those issues have reemerged to capture the public's attention as well as demand acknowledgment and action by the state.

My second purpose in analyzing techno-developmentalism is to provide contextual background for understanding how individuals make sense of the promise and peril of techno-development. Unwavering beliefs in the impera-tiveness of national development and overwhelming optimism about S&T as solutions to China's developmental problems in society have provided default public support for the Chinese state's S&T-oriented developmental agendas. Even when concerns about such developmental strategies arise, the party-state can still turn to the repertoire of national salvation to divert criti-cism of domestic problems, especially when China's relations with other countries have worsened in recent years. As I will explore in chapters 4, 5, and 8, many factory workers and software engineers whom I interviewed alluded to the country's developmental imperatives when they consider their own work and life situations.

This chapter has discussed the scientization of statecraft too—the hyper-rationalization of performance evaluation systems—based on scientific man-agement in the postreform era, especially after Hu officially canonized the notion of the scientific concept of development in the mid-2000s. Although performance measurement systems have existed in other countries (e.g., the United States, United Kingdom, Finland, Australia, South Korea, etc.), Chi-nese versions are unique in their scope and consequences (reward/punish-ment) for individual cadres/officials. In other contexts, in general, results of performance measurement are, at worst, linked to budgets for specific projects or agencies or the continuation of projects but not with individuals.[140] In other words, the stakes of performance evaluation systems are much higher for individual officials in China.

In *The Metric Society*, sociologist Steffen Mau begins the book by using China's social credit system as an extreme example of the quantification of the social.[141] China's State Council promulgated the Outline for the Development of a Social Credit System in 2014. The outline proposes using credit scores to measure the integrity of civil servants, the judiciary, business owners, and all individual members of the public; it further links credit scores to various forms of rewards and punishments.[142] Although critics and foreign media were shocked by China's social credit system, its emergence is actually "rational" if we consider the Chinese state's long-standing effort to scientize statecraft as well as its obsession with using performance evaluation systems for control, discipline, and incentivization. Indeed, the State Council views the social credit system as an instrument to optimize resource allocation, expand domestic demand, and facilitate industrial upgrading, and therefore is an indispensable institution for scientific development.[143]

In fact, cadre/official/government performance evaluation systems and the social credit system are just two of the many types of metrics that the Chinese state has developed to pursue scientific development. Reflecting on performance measurement systems broadly conceived, accounting scholar Michael Power suggests that the advent of the so-called knowledge society has intensified demands for metrics to represent and make somehow accountable new knowledge-based categories of value.[144] As I will show in the subsequent chapters, in their effort to pursue techno-development, different levels and parts of the Chinese state have developed various measurement systems to evaluate and classify human as well as economic capital and technology, and accordingly, reward and punish the relevant actors. I will also provide concrete examples of how such behavior-oriented systems shape actions and interactions.

Building on this chapter's analysis of the cultural, historical, and institutional contexts, the next chapter examines how local governments in coastal provinces turned to techno-development and began to develop the instrumental apparatus necessary to that process.

3

The Turn to Techno-Development

ALTHOUGH TECHNO-DEVELOPMENTALISM has existed for a long time in China, the Chinese state was not dedicated to technology-driven development until the mid-2000s. As I mentioned in chapter 2, due to the institutional arrangements between the central and local states, local governments are responsible for—and benefit from—fostering economic development. Under the labor-intensive, export-oriented developmental model, local governments attracted capital investment in their localities by providing cheap labor, land, and public infrastructure.[1] Starting in the mid-2000s, however, local governments in coastal provinces—those receiving most of China's rural-origin migrant workers—began to experience challenges. Although relatively cheap labor was still available, coastal provinces, particularly Jiangsu, Zhejiang, Guangdong, and Shanghai, lacked key resources for further economic development—from water to electricity, and most critically, land. Chen, a former official in Jiangsu, recounted the problem to me:

> In the past, when an investor came, you gave them a piece of land and provided basic infrastructure, and they could build factories to produce goods. But it became increasingly difficult to find extra land for industrial use. The costs of getting land became much more expensive. Also, the government could make more money from real estate development. As a result, we had difficulties bringing in new investment projects to set up factories even though there was capital available. Pollution also became unbearable in some places.

Chen's quote shows the conundrum faced by local governments as the major agents of capital accumulation and economic development.

Indeed, the term *labor-intensive, export-oriented manufacturing* conceals the fact that such a mode of economic development tends to be land extensive. There is a limited supply of land. With the booming real estate market, providing cheap, extensive land to labor-intensive manufacturing with small profit margins meant that local governments would have to forego tremendous revenues. To address this conundrum, local government in prosperous, coastal provinces turned to techno-development as a new mode of capital accumulation and economic development. As demonstrated in the debates and tensions about techno-development within the party-state in chapter 2, though, there are different types and trajectories of techno-development, which can benefit or undermine different social groups in different ways. What kind of techno-development did these coastal, local governments pursue and why?

In this chapter, I will examine the specific form of techno-development that emerged in the coastal provinces and specify its fundamental logic. I will also explain how the logic of this type of techno-development spread nationwide, despite the controversies it engendered. Understanding the logic of such techno-development is crucial because it has shaped everything from resource allocation to the assignment of economic, political, and even moral value to certain industries, technologies, firms, and social groups. Put simply, it both presumes and performs the evaluation of things and humans. And it has effectively extended the party-state's institutions, techniques, and practices of evaluation—previously focused on cadre/official/government performance—to numerous sectors of society. Toward the end of the chapter, I will show how the instrumental apparatus necessary to techno-development gradually emerged and began to take on a life of its own. To better understand China's turn to techno-development comparatively, I will compare the Chinese case with experiences in South Korea and Taiwan as well.

Scientizing the Birdcage Economy

As I mentioned in chapter 1, Chen Yun, one of the top leaders, advocated the so-called birdcage economy in the 1980s, using the terms *bird* and *cage* to refer to the economy and planning/control, respectively. In the mid-2000s, local states in coastal provinces drew on President Hu Jintao's scientific concept of development along with the notion of a birdcage economy to formulate a more specific discourse and logic of "emptying the cage and changing the bird" (hereafter the bird/cage logic). Like Chen's notion of a birdcage economy, the bird/cage logic accentuates the role of the state in managing the economy, but also specifies how exactly the state should do so. According to the bird/cage logic, *birds* refers to industries and businesses, while *cages* refers to resources, especially land. The logic posits an optimal relationship between capital, labor, technology, and land, while highlighting the visible hand of the state in classifying and selecting birds and matching them with appropriate cages. As such, although the notion of a birdcage economy did not distinguish among birds, according to the new bird/cage logic, not all birds are the same or equal.

Local governments in the mid-2000s in Jiangsu, Shanghai, Zhejiang, Guangdong, and Shandong all offered developmental policies based on the bird/cage logic to address the pressing issue of scarce resources. According to this solution, the visible hand of the state should allocate limited resources—in particular, land—to the birds, or industries or businesses, that would yield the largest economic return. Chen, a former official in Jiangsu, explained to me that policies based on the bird/cage logic aimed to address the critical problem of resource distribution and ensure that "an additional unit of input would lead to more return." According to Chen, policies based on the bird/cage logic made intuitive sense to local officials because they seemed to rely on basic principles of economics with which everyone agreed.

Uniting all such policies in the coastal provinces was the invocation of science as supporting the proposed economic relationships. It should be noted that when government officials invoked the language of science, they sought to gain the legitimacy and value that came with it. Though they may have described their policy as "scientific," my interest is less in whether they had an accurate or adequate understanding of science, or even whether they were sincere or purely strategic in their use of such language. Rather, I am interested in the seemingly unanimous understanding that invoking science was beneficial given its association with progress.

The Zhejiang party-state distinguished itself from other coastal provinces with its efforts to formulate systematic theories and policies that focused on industrial upgrading, transfer, and transformation. Zhejiang's developmental policy was heavily shaped by President Xi Jinping, who served as Zhejiang's party secretary between 2002 and 2007. Like his predecessor Hu, Xi was a Tsinghua-trained engineer. He received a bachelor's degree in chemical engineering from Tsinghua University in 1979. And yet unlike Hu, Xi received training in social science as well. While working in Fujian as the deputy party secretary and governor, he was concurrently doing a PhD in Marxist theory and education in ideology and politics at Tsinghua between 1998 and 2001. In 2001, he had three important publications that shed light on his developmental policy in and beyond Zhejiang.

The first publication was a preface written by Xi for an edited volume titled *Science and Patriotism: Rediscovering Yan Fu's Thoughts*. A Fujian-born intellectual, translator, and educator, Yan was well-known for introducing social science, natural science, and Western legal theory and philosophy to China in the late nineteenth century. In his translation of Thomas Henry Huxley's *Evolution and Ethics*, Yan coined the phrase *survival of the fittest (shizhe shengcun)* in Chinese and introduced ideas associated with social Darwinism. He warned China would collapse if it continued to reject reform.[2] In the beginning of the preface to *Science and Patriotism*, Xi expressed his great admiration for Yan. After stating that "technology is the foremost productive force," Xi narrated how China lagged behind the West after the Industrial Revolution. Then Xi described how Yan "raised the two flags of science and patriotism" to save China from the crisis of imperialism. His writing invoked the well-established cultural trope of using S&T to save China, and highlighted the continued relevance of Yan's marriage of scientism and patriotism for contemporary China.[3]

The second publication worthy of discussion is Xi's doctoral dissertation on rural marketization. As media reports outside China and online discussion show, some question exists about whether Xi wrote his own dissertation given his full-time position as the governor of Fujian at the time. There is also some confusion over Xi's academic training because he was awarded the degree of doctor of law.[4] Notwithstanding such questions, I find the dissertation to be valuable because even if written by a ghostwriter, its content had to be reviewed and approved by Xi.

As such, my reading of Xi's dissertation reveals several interesting insights about him. First, his PhD training was in economics, specifically "Marxist political economics," development economics, and agricultural economics, as he listed them in the dissertation's English-language abstract.[5] His education, however superficial, in these fields helps to explain his confidence in formulating developmental and industrial policy as Zhejiang's party secretary. Second, Xi stressed the importance of high and new technologies, especially computers and the internet, in advancing rural marketization and the economy in general. Third, Xi emphasized the visible hand of the government in collecting information, regulating the market, and reducing inequality. He proposed establishing an information monitoring system of the rural economy so that the government could make timely policy decisions and macroadjustments as needed. Xi also advocated using laws to regulate and develop the agriculture commodity market. He further suggested that the government use fiscal, tax, and financial instruments to reduce rural/urban and regional inequalities as well as employ economic, administrative, and legal measures to redistribute incomes in order to realize social fairness and "common prosperity" (*gongtong fuyu*). Yet despite Xi's attention to inequality, his dissertation did not mention institutional discrimination faced by rural citizens as a result of the household registration system or the inferior social welfare system in rural areas. Interestingly, twenty years after submitting his dissertation, Xi invoked the concept of common prosperity again in his speech and writings, and this time, repeatedly. China watchers thus argued that common prosperity emerged as one of the most important concepts guiding China in 2021.[6] I will revisit this theme in chapter 9.

The third important piece of work that Xi published in 2001 was an article in *Qiushi*, the CCP's official theoretical journal. The article proposed local policies to support the implementation of China's tenth five-year plan (2001–5), which aimed to optimize and upgrade China's industrial structure. As Fujian's governor, Xi pointed to the weakness of Fujian's economy and proposed methods to improve Fujian's industrial structure. He prioritized the development of high- and new-tech industries, especially IT, biotechnology, and environmental-related industries. To do so, he said the government should take advantage of China's WTO accession to collaborate with multinational companies so that businesses in Fujian could access foreign capital and advanced technologies.

Meanwhile, he suggested eliminating obsolete businesses in Fujian that wasted resources, had overcapacity problems, used outdated technologies, and/or produced pollution. To allocate resources efficiently, he proposed moving such businesses to other areas in China or other countries. The article also revealed Xi's preference for large enterprises over small and medium-sized enterprises (SMEs) because he thought the former would have the advantage of scale to excel in domestic and international competitions. He specifically pointed out the urgency of cultivating business conglomerates that could operate across regions, industries, or ownership types—a suggestion that now appears ironic juxtaposed with Xi's recent crackdown on big tech companies and his antitrust initiative.[7] Notably, this article made no mention of problems with inequality, or the need to help people who might be adversely impacted by industrial restructuring and relocation.

Taken together, the three publications reveal Xi's long-standing appreciation of the role of S&T in economic development along with his intermingling of S&T and national sentiments. Although Xi expressed some concerns about social inequality, such considerations were ultimately deemed subordinate to the pursuit of S&T-oriented development. Also, Xi saw law and IT as means to help the government's visible hand. His instrumental and zealous view of law and technology would become even more salient with his ascendency to the highest power and the rise of big data and digital technology.

This understanding of Xi's intellectual background helps us understand his policy in Zhejiang in the mid-2000s as Zhejiang's party secretary. Xi argued that the Zhejiang government should cultivate two types of birds in order to "climb the mountain of scientific development." First, Zhejiang should develop phoenixes—a symbol of strength and renewal—by fostering indigenous innovation and developing well-known brand names. Second, Zhejiang should cultivate and attract "beautiful birds that eat less, lay more eggs, and fly high," such as "advanced manufacturing industries and modern service industries." As such, Xi envisioned a postindustrial future in Zhejiang. Xi also said that when matching birds with cages, Zhejiang should think about cages beyond Zhejiang and transfer certain birds—businesses that do not pollute the environment—from

Zhejiang to western China, northeast China, or foreign countries where those old birds could still make an economic contribution.[8] These are the peripheral places that only deserve industrial but not postindustrial development. Essentially, Xi used the bird/cage logic to contend that Zhejiang should overcome the bottleneck of economic development through state-orchestrated industrial upgrading and transfer. His policy in Zhejiang was, in fact, the same as the developmental and industrial policy he proposed as Fujian's governor in 2001. The key difference now, however, was the linking of his proposal to Hu's scientific concept of development after Hu became the top leader.

Techno-developmental policy based on the bird/cage logic was politically and scientifically appealing to provincial officials in coastal areas for two reasons. First, the goal of cultivating good birds, phoenixes, or high-tech industries as well as transferring old birds to less developed areas was, in fact, consistent with top leaders' views. As mentioned in chapter 2, in the early 1990s, despite the debate on the tiered development theory of industrial transfer, Jiang Zemin, then the party's general secretary, had already expressed his support for such a solution to adjusting China's economic structure. Jiang maintained that coastal areas should introduce and adopt high technologies to upgrade their economy since they have better conditions for industrial upgrading; coastal areas could then transfer technologies to less developed regions and benefit the development of the latter. Xi's policy based on the bird/cage logic had much in common with Jiang's view, even though Jiang did not use the metaphors of the bird or cage.

Second, on the surface, the developmental trajectory projected by the bird/cage logic seemed to correspond to the histories of industrial transfer from more industrially developed to less developed countries in East Asia (e.g., from Japan to South Korea and Taiwan, and from South Korea and Taiwan to China) or the so-called flying geese paradigm theorized by Japanese economist Kaname Akamatsu.[9] Japan, South Korea, and Taiwan are well-known for the role of their developmental states in economic development as well as their success in avoiding the so-called middle-income trap—a situation in which a country that attains a certain income gets stuck at that level.[10] Many provincial-level officials believed that although the process of industrial upgrading might slow down economic development, and encounter resistance from businesses and even lower-level officials in the short term, it would have long-term benefits. Meanwhile, around 2007, social scientists, media, and government officials in China began to discuss the issue of the middle-income trap. Industrial upgrading based on the bird/cage logic was seen by officials as a solution to escape the middle-income trap.[11]

To facilitate industrial upgrading, coastal local governments emphasized the need to *select* capital. In the past, local governments competed to attract capital by providing cheap land and other benefits.[12] In 2004, local officials in Jiangsu announced that the province would shift from *attracting* capital (*yinzi*) to *selecting* capital (*xuanzi*). Specifically, high-tech industries such as IT and biotechnology were now seen as more desirable than traditional manufacturing industries, as the former usually invested more and produced more revenue per unit of land. Many local governments also came up with policies that favored Fortune 500 companies and leading domestic and foreign enterprises—firms that local governments saw as more likely to introduce high and new technologies. Some local governments explicitly stated that small businesses tend to lack the capability to address pollution.[13] In 2006, local governments' strategy of selecting capital was further embraced by the central government's Ministry of Commerce, which encouraged foreign investment in "high-tech industries, advanced manufacturing industries, modern service industries, and environmental protection industries." The Ministry of Commerce also lent its support for policies based on the bird/cage logic in coastal areas and industrial transfer from coastal provinces to central and western China.[14]

In addition to selecting capital, local governments endeavored to spare land use. In 2004, Jiangsu began to close down small and scattered businesses or relocate them to industrial parks. In Shanghai, several district governments evicted hundreds of "inferior businesses" (*lieshi qiye*) that consumed too much energy, produced low outputs, or led to severe pollution. Moreover, government officials came up with the strategy of attracting capital without providing land, encouraging existing businesses to expand their capital inputs and transform themselves from labor- to technology- or knowledge-intensive enterprises.[15]

As coastal provinces adopted the bird/cage logic in their developmental policy, local governments in many places and news media increasingly started to use the language of *low-end industries* (*diduan chanye*), *inferior industries* (*lieshi chanye*), and *outdated productive forces* (*luohou shengchanli*). They used these terms in loosely defined, interchangeable, and frequently inconsistent or even contradictory ways. For example, officials and policy documents used the terms to refer to traditional industries, labor-intensive industries, low value-added industries, or overcapacity capital-intensive industries (i.e., steelmaking and construction materials). Local governments also suggested that businesses in these industries tend to have a high level of land occupation, pollution, and energy consumption coupled with a low level of technical capability. Although some officials—for instance, those in the Shenzhen municipal government—stated that the role of the government in the economy should be restricted to maintaining and providing public service instead of actually participating in or attempting to referee the economic "game," it was common for local governments, including district-level ones in Shenzhen, to "select capital" as well as identify and even evict unwanted old birds in their pursuit of industrial upgrading and transformation.[16]

As the bird/cage logic spread, a new category of the population also began to emerge in officialdom and news reports: the "low-end population" (*diduan renkou*). It is instructive to look at an example here—specifically, how the category emerged within and was acted on by district officials in Shenzhen, a city with an excellent and progressive reputation in governance. In April 2008, officials in Shenzhen's Longgang District convened to discuss and study a speech made by Wang Yang after visiting Shenzhen. Wang was then the party secretary of Guangdong and one of the most avid proponents of the bird/cage logic. Elaborating on Wang's talk, Zhang Bei, Longgang District's mayor, spoke of the relationship between population and industrial structure. According to Zhang, although his district was prosperous, the district still had a low-end population since over 70 percent of Longgang's 4.6 million population only had an education level of middle school or less. He vented that the low-end population, which was associated with low-end industries in his district, rendered social management difficult. Zhang believed that industrial upgrading would change not only the industrial structure but the population composition too and thus the population's overall quality. Zhang stated that

> research found that two low-end persons will bring one low-end service provider. We must speed up the pace of industrial transfer. We must eliminate—as soon as possible—labor-intensive industries and industries with a high level of pollution, energy consumption, or a low level of outputs. Industrial transfer will ultimately help to expel the low-quality population.[17]

The Longgang District mayor's words show that he considered employees of labor-intensive industries (i.e., old birds) to be low-quality people. And he rationalized this valuation by drawing on Hu's concept of scientific development and scientific research. In other words, the mayor invoked the language of science to justify evicting labor-intensive industries and the working class in labor-intensive and low-end service industries. Science, Zhang argued, dictated that local officials should seek to attract talent, particularly professional and technical personnel. It should be noted that Zhang invoked science in a superficial and taken-for-granted way, without substantively justifying why what he said or cited was scientific. Other Longgang officials in the meeting said that Longgang would benefit from attracting talent—people with "high quality"—and reducing its low-end population.[18] The fact that these classifications and valuations of industries and people were reported in the *Southern Daily*, the official newspaper of the Guangdong party-state, without controversy reveals the popularity and prevalence of such views among local officials. It also illustrates the extent to which the emerging techno-development regime in Guangdong both relied on and reproduced classifications and valuations biased against the working class in the name of science and development.

Indeed, in my own interactions with local officials in Guangdong, I heard expressions of social Darwinism, which was, as I mentioned above, introduced by Yan to China in the late nineteenth century. Those officials viewed local policies and practices as corresponding to the ideas of survival of the fittest and eliminating the unfit. When asked about how the bird/cage logic and its application to different social groups came to be, one official told me, "We were sympathetic to migrant workers. But since our resources were limited, we could not do charity. We needed talent to help economic transformation and techno-logical upgrading. Those without skills were unfit and could not survive here. They should have studied and worked hard to get a better education." What I found in the news reports and interviews with local officials was an intermingling of techno-developmentalism, an ideology of meritocracy, and some flavor of social Darwinism, used to justify social inequality and exclusion.

But such ideas were not universal. Although local governments in coastal provinces overwhelmingly embraced the bird/cage logic as a scientific solution to their developmental problems, critical voices existed. It should be noted that the political climate during President Hu's term was relatively more liberal than that under Xi. As I have shown previously in *The Contentious Public Sphere*, the 2000s was a decade when people felt public opinion could actually influence government decisions. Liberal-leaning scholars, entrepreneurs, and newspapers were influential actors in China's then rising public sphere.[19] Two prominent economists well-known for their advocacy of market reform, Wu Jinglian and Fan Gang, expressed their criticism publicly. Indeed, the two economists actually worked within the party-state. Wu was a senior research fellow at the Developmental Research Center of the State Council, while Fan was a member of the Central Monetary Policy Committee between 2006 and 2008. Small and medium-sized entrepreneurs in Zhejiang and Guangdong along with their business associations also reached out to journalists and spoke against the rapidly spreading development policy.

Wu and many small and medium-sized entrepreneurs first criticized local governments' preferential treatment of larger domestic enterprises and FIEs. The Wenzhou government, for instance, encouraged local enterprises to collaborate with leading domestic or foreign enterprises in order to help local enterprises obtain advanced technology and managerial expertise, thereby upgrading the industrial structure. Joint or collaborative ventures coestablished by local firms and leading enterprises, according to local policies, received a discount in land use fees, electricity and water fees, and access to bank credits. Small and medium-sized entrepreneurs in Wenzhou complained that only a few local businesses would have opportunities to collaborate with lead-ing domestic or foreign enterprises, and FIEs were the primary beneficiaries of such policies. Commenting on Wenzhou's policies, Wu contended that while FIEs should be welcomed in China, they should not receive preferential treatment as any privileges could lead to complacency and corruption. Wu did not shy away from challenging the bird/cage logic. Emphasizing that industrial clusters tend to emerge spontaneously, Wu questioned the efficacy of govern-ment planning in industrial upgrading and transfer. He further warned that the government's efforts to expel or relocate labor-intensive businesses might be counterproductive because they could disrupt, if not destroy, supply chains. Rather than replacing SMEs with FIEs, the government should help the for-mer with industrial upgrading by providing public service, such as establishing public platforms for enterprises to access information. Finally, Wu argued that by single-mindedly privileging high-tech industries, government policies downplayed the critical process of improving within-industry efficiency and competitiveness.[20]

Fan focused on how local governments treated low-end industries com-pared to high-end ones. He asserted that although China should encourage high-tech industries, it should not discriminate against low-end or traditional manufacturing industries for three related reasons. First, traditional manufac-turing industries provide numerous employment opportunities, especially for the country's rural population. According to Fan, businesses contribute to society by producing not only GDP but employment opportunities too. He lamented,

> Now, most national leaders were trained in science and engineering, so they have a special admiration for "high technology." Spacecrafts are, indeed, fabulous. But many low-tech industries, such as textiles and catering, are obviously much more effective in terms of generating export revenues or absorbing nine-million new job seekers every year.[21]
>
> Labor-intensive industries provide hundreds of millions of peasants with the opportunity to leave the countryside. There are hundreds of mil-lions of farmers in China's countryside. Should they all become computer engineers? Now the government despises labor-intensive low-end indus-tries. Entrepreneurs should not look down on themselves. What's wrong with making leather shoes and socks?[22]

Fan's concern with the rural population's employment security stood in sharp contrast to the stance of many local governments. Considerations about Chi-na's rural population and level of employment rarely appeared in official dis-course or media discussions about industrial upgrading and transformation. Such disinterest in employment issues was related to China's household

registration system, intergovernmental fiscal arrangements, and cadre evaluation systems, under which local governments have hardly political responsibility or incentive to consider migrant workers' unemployment problems.

Second, Fan held that many businesses in China's low-end industries had
global comparative advantages. If businesses are not competitive, they would
withdraw from the market or move to places where they have higher-level
competitiveness, so there is no need for local governments to expel or transfer
them. Moreover, local governments did not have better information than businesses to make economic decisions. Fan was deeply concerned about the government's unconstrained administrative power in expelling businesses. Since
such power is not subject to the rule of law, it could severely impede the competitiveness and innovation of businesses.[23] Fan reasoned, "If 'low-end' industries lose their competitiveness, they will relocate. Local governments should
not artificially discriminate against labor-intensive industries and set up barriers. If these industries are still competitive in the region and can still make
money, why can't they exist?"[24] In fact, due to the rising wages and land use
fees, in the mid-2000s, some firms in labor-intensive sectors, such as garment
and electronics assembly, had spontaneously relocated to or expanded their
facilities in places with lower labor and land costs within the same province,
in other provinces, or other countries, such as those in Southeast Asia.[25]

Fan's third critique was that the one-sided pursuit of industrial upgrading
might exacerbate economic inequality in China. As he put it,

> Considering the country as a whole, I disagree with the notion of "upgrad-
> ing the industrial structure." Instead, I think "expanding the industrial
> structure" may be more appropriate. Whereas we need to develop high-
> end industries for national interests, we cannot give up on "low-end" indus-
> tries. If China does not have a broad industrial structure, the gap between
> rich and poor will be widening, and we will fail to address the problems
> of economic disparity and social conflicts. . . . A region or a city can ignore
> the employment problem of peasants, as long as its local employment is
> OK. But China as a whole cannot ignore the employment of hundreds of
> millions of people.[26]

Essentially, Fan considered the issue of industrial upgrading and techno-
development at the scale of the country, and related the issue to economic
inequality and social conflicts. Indeed, many problems were related to the
scale of governance. Officials I spoke to in Guangdong told me that due to
institutional designs, local governments are only responsible for economic
development and residents in their jurisdictions, not outsiders or problems
beyond their jurisdictions.

Escalating Contestation

As the 2008 financial crisis unfolded and hit China's important export markets, concerns about economic growth and unemployment arose. Many labor-intensive SMEs and their employees in coastal areas were faced with uncertainty and challenges from both local industrial policies and the financial crisis. SMEs also worried about the impacts of China's newly passed Labor Contract Law on labor costs. Amid the crisis, coastal local governments, particularly the Guangdong government, restated their commitment to their developmental policy based on the bird/cage logic. Wang, Guangdong's party secretary, asserted that the government would not bail out "outdated productive forces," although it was unclear how he defined the term.[27] The Guangdong government invested 40 billion renminbi (RMB) in building industrial transfer parks and training labor in less developed areas in Guangdong, so that old birds in the Pearl River Delta could be relocated to less developed areas.[28] Furthermore, to show its political will, the Guangdong provincial government included the implementation of "emptying the cage and changing the birds" in its evaluation of lower-level governments.[29] According to my interviews with local officials there, provincial officials in Guangdong considered this institutional enforcement mechanism necessary due to different views on Guangdong's developmental policy among lower-level officials and close ties between lowest-level officials and labor-intensive businesses. Here we can see that an existing instrument—that is, the government performance evaluation system—was adapted to advance the type of techno-development that the Guangdong government promoted.

Although the Ministry of Commerce lent its support to coastal governments regarding their developmental policies before the financial crisis, surprisingly, the central and Guangdong party-states expressed different views on the policies during the crisis.[30] Both governments acknowledged the need to transform China's industrial structure. But while the central government highlighted employment security, the Guangdong government continued to emphasize industrial upgrading and innovation. Both governments used the CCP's official newspaper, the *People's Daily*, to advance their stances. Such open disagreement between central and local governments is extremely rare. In this case, it related to the fact that the central government's legitimacy depends on its economic and moral performance, whereas provincial governments can pursue economic gain more narrowly without the need to consider political legitimacy.[31] In addition, Guangdong's status as the largest province in China by GDP likely explains why Guangdong's party secretary, Wang, felt able to diverge from the central government.

During his November 2008 visit to Guangdong in the company of Wang, Premier Wen Jiabao stressed the significance of assisting SMEs during the financial crisis.[32] In December 2008, the party and the State Council convened the Central Economic Work Conference. Usually hosted in November or December annually, the conference foreshadows important economic policy for the upcoming year. One of the conclusions of the 2008 conference was that the government should protect employment security in order to assure people's sources of income, thereby helping to expand domestic demand and maintaining economic growth, as China's major export markets were severely hit by the financial crisis. After the conference, an editorial in the People's Daily criticized some provinces as being too hasty in emptying the cage and changing the bird. The editorial argued that labor-intensive SMEs were undeservedly seen by some local governments as obstacles to industrial upgrading. It pointed out that because labor-intensive SMEs absorbed much labor from rural areas, their bankruptcy would force migrant workers to return to the countryside and undermine the country's rural consumption market. Hence, the editorial contended that local governments should not consider labor-intensive SMEs outdated productive forces but rather should treat SMEs fairly. Even if SMEs had problems with production and pollution, local governments should give them time, financial resources, and policy support instead of cracking down on them so brutally. Moreover, the government should take more responsibility for investing in environmental infrastructure and labor protection.[33] The article did not explicitly mention Guangdong, but few readers of the People's Daily would have failed to recognize that the critique was aimed there.

Immediately after the publication of the above editorial, Wang had his defense of the province's developmental model published in the People's Daily. According to Wang, Guangdong's previous development had relied on "low-end productive forces of labor-intensive industries," which depended on cheap land and abundant labor as opposed to technology or innovation. He framed the debate on development as a blatantly obvious choice between a backward "traditional developmental model" and a modern, forward-looking "scientific developmental model." For the sake of scientific development, Wang asserted, Guangdong should continue emptying the cage and changing the bird by insisting on industrial transformation and indigenous innovation. Bailing out outdated or low-end productive forces would only undermine Guangdong's long-term development, although Wang acknowledged the government's responsibility to take care of laid-off workers. He insisted, however, that the key to doing so was to pursue scientific development that situated humans at the center of development—that is, President Hu's conception of development. In doing so, Wang, like so many before him, doubled down on S&T's ability to save China.[34]

Yet Wang's opinion in the *People's Daily* did not provide information about who exactly deserved to be saved in this pursuit of scientific development.[35] Wang's talks with lower-level government officials in Guangdong reveal more details about how he saw the role of humans in development, or put more bluntly, whom he considered as deserving members of the nation. In 2009, Wang had an inspection tour in several townships in Dongguan, a prefectural-level city in Guangdong known as the center of the "world's factory," to discuss Dongguan's industrial upgrading following the severe hit of the financial crisis. Wang stated that in order to transform the current industrial structure, the government had to attract investment from new and emerging industries and leading enterprises, while relocating low-end industries to less developed parts of Guangdong or less developed provinces in China. He argued that only once certain social groups were absent from Dongguan would the quality of the city increase and be capable of attracting the high-end talent needed for industrial upgrading and transformation. As Wang told township officials,

> In recent years, Dongguan has been faced with public security problems from theft to robbery. These problems were caused by the migrant population, especially low-quality migrants who work for labor-intensive business. Therefore we must move low-end industries away from here. These problems impact not only industrial structure but also the quality of the city. Birds of a feather flock together. When there is a large low-end population, the high-end population will not come. When the quality of the city increases, people who can contribute to research and development will eventually move and take root here.[36]

How Wang perceived various social groups is important to understand because he was one of the most fervent and powerful advocates of the bird/cage logic and the party secretary of the largest province by GDP. Wang claimed that human-centered and scientific development was the solution to the financial crisis, but crucially, not everyone was treated equally in his solution. Instead, his developmental model sorted individuals according to human capital and household registration status. The group situated at the top was the high-end population, namely those working in high-end industries. This group was thus equivalent to the technical or professional class in Daniel Bell's writing on postindustrial society.[37] They were to be welcomed and appreciated, regardless of their household registration status. This group also deserved to live in the most developed part of the province, where high and tech industries and modern service industries were located. People with a rural household registration status in Guangdong (in-province peasants) ranked lower, and Wang's model sought to relocate them from agriculture to the secondary and tertiary industries in the less developed parts of Guangdong.

Nevertheless, Wang did encourage businesses to employ in-province peasants because they were at least deemed preferable to migrant workers from other provinces. Migrants working in labor-intensive industries were excluded completely from Wang's developmental model. Unlike peasants from Guangdong, the "low quality" of workers from other provinces was considered irredeemable due to their migrant status.

Faced with such an assertive party secretary, some social groups in Guangdong chose to speak up. Not surprisingly, they were not workers but instead entrepreneurs who relied on workers and were getting uncomfortable with the label of low-end industries along with the state's increasingly interventionist hand. Several entrepreneurs in the Pearl River Delta decided to initiate a collective action by collaborating with the *Southern Metropolitan Daily*, an outspoken newspaper in Guangzhou, and scholars like Wu, Hu Chunli, and Qin Hui. These entrepreneurs criticized the local governments in the region as having contradictory views, policies, and practices regarding emptying the cage and changing the bird, and therefore worsening the already abysmal situation amid the financial crisis. The *Southern Metropolitan Daily* hosted a two-day forum at Dongguan's Songshan Lake in 2008 to discuss economic upgrading and form a consensus in the hope that such consensus would reach provincial government officials and influence their policy making.

The discussion in the forum centered around the meaning of upgrading and the appropriate—and inappropriate—role of government. For the entrepreneurs who attended the meeting, upgrading simply meant improving profitability. Many entrepreneurs argued that when a business model fails to maintain profitability, the failure indicates a need for upgrading. Their definition of upgrading thus differed from the government's more narrow conception, focused on moving from low- to high-end industries. Put another way, entrepreneurs wanted intraindustry upgrading, while the government wanted interindustry upgrading.[38] The forum attendees suggested that the government should focus instead on providing public service—such as building platforms for businesses, especially SMEs—that would help businesses to obtain information, solve technological problems, and access capital. Qin, a prominent economic historian, explicitly argued against the bird/cage logic. He reasoned that it was the market, not the government, that should decide the fate of a bird. After two days of intensive discussion and debates, scholars and entrepreneurs in the forum reached a consensus that industrial upgrading should be directed primarily by market forces rather than the state, although the state did have an important role to play—that is, enhancing the quality of public service.[39]

Amid the financial crisis, some individual economists, particularly Wu, challenged Guangdong's developmental policy too. Wu criticized local governments' designation of labor-intensive industries as low-end ones, and only capital- and knowledge- intensive industries as high-end ones. Such mistaken thinking led local governments to pursue industrial upgrading by using administrative means to force low-end industries to move away, thereby freeing up land for high-end industries. Pursuing industrial upgrading was a move in the right direction, but Wu contended that the process should be initiated by firms rather than implemented by the state using mandatory measures.[40] At the same time, however, other economists supported Guangdong's policy. In some instances, such support was hardly surprising, as was the case for industrial economists at the Institute of Industrial Economics at Jinan University in Guangzhou. The institute was deeply connected with Guangdong government's Provincial Development and Reform Commission, and institute faculty participated in policy making in Guangdong.[41]

Consolidation of the Techno-Development Regime

To maintain economic stability after the global financial crisis, the central government announced a four trillion yuan stimulus package in 2008.[42] In summer 2009, China's economy gradually recovered from the financial crisis. In 2010, as economic statistics improved, Guangdong declared and celebrated victory in handling the financial crisis. Wang proudly announced that he gave the Guangdong provincial government a perfect score in combating the financial crisis.[43] To mitigate the financial crisis, the Guangdong government took a variety of measures, such as providing financial assistance to SMEs as well as helping businesses to expand the domestic market and markets in Africa, Russia, and Southeast Asia. The scope of these measures was broader than those aimed at techno-development. No clear evidence shows the specific actions taken by the Guangdong government for techno-development led to the economic rebound, but the Guangdong party-state unequivocally claimed such a causal relationship.[44] Following Guangdong, the Zhejiang government announced its victory based on a variety of economic indicators—from the rising contribution of the service sector to GDP, to the amount of export and import, number of patent applications, number of patent authorization, usage of electricity, and so on.[45]

The description and causation offered by the Guangdong and Zhejiang governments, and disseminated by the media, resemble each other and have become the dominant narrative. The narrative describes how industrial upgrading and techno-development orchestrated by the governments before the financial crisis, and based on the concept of scientific development, helped resolve the problem of scarce resources, remedy the damages of the financial crisis, and transform the provinces into a glowing phoenix. The rebounding economy served as evidence to support the validity of the bird/cage logic and efficacy of the government's visible hand. Not surprisingly, the causality presented in the narrative did not address potential alternative explanations (e.g., the central government's stimulus package or effort of entrepreneurs) or consider what the situation would have been if local governments had adopted different developmental and industrial policies.

Not everyone was convinced by the dominant narrative and embedded causal stories. When asked about their experiences with the financial crisis, executives and high-level managers in export-oriented enterprises in Guangdong and Zhejiang described the measures they took to overcome the crisis when many of their peers failed to survive. Some emphasized the collaboration among enterprises in participating in international trade shows and getting orders; others said their collective efforts to expand markets in emerging economies played a crucial role. The accounts are similar to what has been documented by sociologist Victor Nee and business scholar Sonja Opper about China's bottom-up entrepreneurship and self-help among entrepreneurs.[46] Importantly, many interviewees believed traditional manufacturers could do well, so did not find the government's assertion about "outdated industries" convincing. Rather than looking down on mid- or low-end markets and cheap, small commodities, these entrepreneurs chose to enhance their competitiveness in such markets. They questioned the effect of industrial upgrading policy in mitigating the financial crisis. Yet they mainly kept these thoughts private, rarely expressing them in the public sphere.

Major academic publications in economics in China have similarly failed to find convicting evidence supporting the validity of the narrative constructed by the Guangdong government. Analyzing data from 2003 to 2012, economists found that the speed of industrial upgrading in the Pearl River Delta slowed down, rather than accelerating, after the Guangdong government implemented its policy of emptying the cage and changing the bird. Their analysis also revealed that most industrial upgrading in the Pearl River Delta resulted not from the government's policy but instead from market considerations.[47] Another study has shown that Guangdong's policy of relocating old birds from the Pearl River Delta to less developed areas in Guangdong did not significantly enhance labor productivity in the less developed areas or decrease the developmental disparities between the Pearl River Delta and the less developed areas.[48] Some economists argue that the government's effort to attract talent to the Pearl River Delta and move low-skilled workers to work in less developed areas might have exacerbated the already unequal development versus helping to combat it.[49] Scholars have also found that policies that encouraged cross-provincial industrial transfer yielded limited success.[50] Ultimately, empirical analyses in economics lend support to economists and entrepreneurs who criticized the emerging techno-developmental policy based on the bird/cage logic in coastal provinces, but such studies did not change the official discourse or narrative.

Asked about the relationship between government policy and expert opinion, two industrial economists in Guangdong told me the provincial government there tends to work with scholars who endorse, as opposed to criticize, the government's policy or initiatives. Scholars who support the government's initiatives tend to have more opportunities to receive research funding from the government or participate in government-sponsored research projects. They are also more likely to get leadership appointments in universities or research institutes as well as expert positions on all kinds of committees in the government. Notably, many scholars have their own companies or sit on the board of directors of a company. With connections with the government, these companies can receive public procurement contracts to develop instruments that aim to advance techno-development. For example, some scholars were developing techniques and big data platforms to help identify new and old birds. My interviewees pointed out that the division of labor within academia ensures that scholars involved in government initiatives focus on only one or a few components of the government's policy rather than considering big-picture questions about the efficacy of the overreaching agendas. One industrial economist, Dr. Chen, shared that the government had asked managerial science and public administration scholars to develop indicators that evaluate investment projects or firms. But even though scholars can design such indicators and evaluation systems, they often have limited knowledge about the efficacy of developmental and industrial policy. According to Chen, scholarly efforts and the government's enormous investment in developing those techniques rests on the shaky assumption that the government's policy will work as intended.

Eventually, China's recovery from the financial crisis, the internal struggles between top elites, and most critically, the ascendance of Xi as the CCP's general secretary in 2012 closed the previous public debates on policy and the emerging type of techno-development based on the bird/cage logic in coastal areas. News media and scholars began to call Guangdong's experience the Guangdong Model. In addition, struggles among China's political elites severely hindered competing developmental models and reduced the space for thinking about alternatives. With the unfolding of the financial crisis, Bo Xilai, Chongqing's party secretary, came up with a series of developmental policies that scholars and media dubbed the Chongqing Model. Unlike Wang's developmental model in Guangdong, centered on high-end populations (i.e., the middle classes), the Chongqing Model highlighted the working class, social welfare, and the incorporation of rural migrants. Wang and Bo along with their respective developmental models were framed as competitors in media reports and scholarly discussions.[51] Enthusiasm for the Chongqing Model not surprisingly waned after Bo was put in jail by the Hu and Wen leadership in spring 2012. In a way, the Guangdong and Chongqing Models show China's compressed development—simultaneous industrial and postindustrial development.[52] The Guangdong Model aimed to transform Guangdong into a postindustrial society, prioritizing the technical and professional class at the expense of excluding the working class without a local citizenship. In contrast, the Chongqing Model aimed to advance an industrial society and prioritized the inclusion of the working class.

Xi's rise to power further cemented the dominance of the bird/cage logic and that type of techno-development in coastal China. As mentioned above, Xi was among the earliest and most enthusiastic proponents of the bird/cage logic.[53] Xi's ascendance suggested that the bird/cage logic and policy based on it could disseminate more broadly and even become part of the national policy. Indeed, in 2013, the Zhejiang party-state added Xi and his scientific theories to the official narrative of Zhejiang's economic success.[54] In 2017, the province celebrated the fifteenth anniversary of the advent of Xi's developmental policy.[55] Xi himself continued to promote his theories and model. Seeing it as an "experimental zone to explore scientific development," Xi chose Guangdong as the first stop to visit after he became the general party secretary. The choice was symbolically significant considering the high-profile promotion of the bird/cage logic in Guangdong during Wang's term. In his talk in Guangdong, Xi emphasized the strategic importance of transforming China's economic structure and developmental model by promoting innovation, developing a high value-added modern industrial system, integrating technology and the economy, supporting less developed and rural areas, and advancing *ecological civilization*—a term that describes the goal of environmental protection. These measures, according to Xi, would help China to escape the middle-income trap.[56] On many important occasions, such as the National People's Congress, Xi reiterated the critical significance of cultivating new and good birds and phoenixes, and thinking about how to deal with old birds and coordinate the relationship between "two hands"—the invisible hand of the market and the visible hand of the government.[57] Per the instructions of the central and provincial party committees, various levels of local party-states hosted numerous meetings to study Xi's thoughts. According to participants, one of the most important themes in these meetings was Xi's views on scientific development, especially techno-development along with his writing, speeches, and policy based on the bird/cage logic.

Xi's views were well integrated into the central party-state's economic reform agendas—the so-called supply-side structure reform and Made in China

2025 plan announced in 2015. One of the major goals of the supply-side structure reform was to enhance the competitiveness of firms and the quality of economic development by reducing excess capacity, restructuring debts, and lowering costs for firms. Most important, the central state wanted to reduce the excess capacity of "outdated" industries or productive forces, exemplified by the steel and coal industries. After steel and coal, overcapacity would be tackled in cement, electric power, nonferrous metals, petroleum refining and petrochemicals, and even labor-intensive export sectors like garments.[58] Essentially, the supply-side structural reforms aimed to address the problem of old birds, allocate resources to innovative sectors, and improve industrial structure. When elaborating on the supply-side reform, Xi accentuated the need to accelerate emptying the cage and changing the bird and cultivating phoenixes. Themes related to industrial upgrading and transformation—from increasing the output rate of factors of production to cultivating emerging industries and modern service industries, upgrading traditional industries, expanding the digital economy, and achieving ecological civilization—were highlighted repeatedly in his speeches.[59]

The "Made in China 2025" document enacted by the State Council begins with a narrative similar to that in Xi's preface to *Science and Patriotism*. Unsurprisingly, the narrative starts with the Industrial Revolution and employs the cultural repertoire of using S&T to rejuvenate China. The essence of the document is to develop cutting-edge and high-end manufacturing industries to realize the "China dream." The document also includes numerical indicators (e.g., innovation capability measured by R&D, expenses, and the number of patents) to evaluate the progress, while pointing out the need to develop systems to evaluate talent, technology, brand names, green manufacturing, and the integrity of businesses.

As the techno-developmental regime in coastal provinces rose to national prominence, an increasing number of local party-states in and beyond coastal areas adopted policies to facilitate techno-development based on the bird/cage logic. In general, local policies focused on four areas: labor, technology, land, and environmental protection. The local policies related to labor emphasized the need for a "high-quality" population, and advocated for turning China's demographic dividend into a "talent dividend" or even "robot dividend."[60] Local party-states also announced policies that gave preferential treatments to high-tech companies and promoted technological innovation and the building of technology incubators. Local policies on land centered on allocating land to economic activities that generate a higher value of outputs. As the central government has highlighted the pursuit of environmental protection, local governments often consider businesses that produce pollution as outdated productive forces or old birds.

Instrumental Apparatus for Techno-Development

The techno-development regime based on the bird/cage logic has further gal-vanized the state's efforts to scientize its statecraft and build ever more expan-sive evaluation systems as the bird/cage logic presumes the role of the state in valuating and evaluating birds, and then allocating resources accordingly. In general, governments at various levels continue to use similar methods of quantification and digitization in their evaluation systems. And yet what is new is that governments have aligned cadre/official/government evaluation systems and other institutions, such as the household registration system, with the new techno-developmental goals and expanded objects of evaluation from cadre/official/government performance to investment projects, industries, firms, laborers, technologies, integrity, and so on. The material manifestations of such governing techniques are tables, quantification rules, databases, and increasingly, platforms based on classification schemes and metrics. When asked about problems with such valuation and evaluation systems (e.g., inac-curacy and doubtful efficacy), two local officials in Guangdong told me that despite their shortcomings, the valuation and evaluation systems are crucial for upper-level governments to collect information, exercise control, and im-plement their goals because the bureaucracy and economy in China are simply too vast.

Furthermore, as I mentioned in chapter 1, we should not neglect the state's use of legal instruments for techno-development. Governments at different levels make numerous regulations that stipulate the allocation of resources, rewards, and punishments according to classification outcomes and metric values. Through using legal and technical instruments, governments aim to not only enhance the legibility of birds and the efficacy of valuation and evalu-ation but shape the behavior of relevant actors too—from government offi-cials to businesses and citizens—with the hope that the enlarging arsenal of instruments would help advance techno-development.

Scholars of industry policy have long criticized the policy and practice of picking winners, but many evaluation systems developed by local govern-ments in China aim to do precisely this for things like investment projects and firms.[61] To be sure, officials are aware of the criticism that the visible hand of the government might distort resource distribution. But their confidence, es-pecially among upper-level officials, is boosted by their perception of quantita-tive analysis and big data. When I interviewed a scholar involved in developing evaluation systems, he told me what China has today is not a planned econ-omy because market participants still make decisions about production, distribution, pricing, and investment. Governments in China do not plan to return to or develop a new form of planned economy; instead, they want to draw on science and data to coordinate the visible hand of the government and the invisible hand of the market, thereby improving market mechanisms. Interestingly, he cited the view of Jack Ma, the former CEO of Alibaba, about the potential of the planned economy in the era of big data and AI. The scholar said that big data would enable the government to uncover the invisible hand of the market and improve planning and prediction. Such belief in data and technology is in stark contrast to the critical view of a few economists with whom I spoke.

In the research process, I was profoundly struck by the enormous number of tables, indicators, and legal and technical instruments in general that different levels and parts of governments in China have produced to facilitate techno-development. The scope of and obsession with valuation, evaluation, and quantification is extraordinary. In my fieldwork, lower-level government officials in Shenzhen and Dongguan frequently complained to me that they felt stifled by the enlarging valuation and evaluation systems, which took away from their time doing more meaningful tasks.

Consider the following examples of how various levels of governments in Guangdong and the central government have upgraded as well as expanded evaluation systems since 2008 to foster techno-development. I focus on Guangdong because many provinces have emulated institutions in Guangdong, and some national agendas have similarly built on experiences and institutions in Guangdong.[62] According to Chen Hongwei, an industrial and regional economist at the Party School of the Guangdong Provincial Committee of the CCP, the Guangdong provincial government saw bringing about economic transformation as a chess game, illustrating yet another popular metaphor used in Chinese officialdom.

Chen pointed out three key chess pieces on the chessboard. The first one was a modern industrial system. Between 2008 and 2012, the Guangdong provincial government invested 40 billion RMB (around US$6.24 billion) in industrial upgrading and transformation. To establish a modern industrial system, the Guangdong provincial government selected the so-called top 502 projects in 2010, including 100 in strategic emerging industries, 100 in advanced manufacturing, 101 in modern service industries, 101 in advantageous traditional manufacturing, and 100 in modern agriculture. According to Guangdong's Development and Reform Committee, the provincial government provided these projects with access to land, while giving projects in strategic emerging industries 2 billion yuan in yearly support.[63] This annual support is around one-fourth of the province's fiscal budget for compulsory education in 2011, and one-third of the provincial expenditure on social insurance and employment assistance in 2010.[64] With assistance from experts and other provincial government agencies, the Development and Reform Committee established many quantitative indicators (e.g., the level of innovation and spill-over effects) along with a committee comprised of seventy-seven experts that selected the top 502 projects from 1,500 projects.[65] This emphasis on quantitative indicators aligns with the guideline published by the Ministry of Commerce at the central government that requires local governments to develop evaluation systems based on scientific principles and quantification.[66]

The second chess piece was the "remolding" of three thousand lower-level cadres/officials in Guangdong to ensure that they would have knowledge about modern industries and be able to interact with business actors properly.[67] The third chess piece was, unsurprisingly, the improvement of the cadre/official evaluation system. The purpose was to incentivize cadres/officials to participate in techno-development.[68] With the emerging techno-developmental regime, governments in Guangdong added several S&T-related indicators for cadre/official evaluations, such as the share of the high- and new-tech industry value added in total GDP, ratio of R&D to GDP, proportion of the value added of modern service industries in the value added of the tertiary industry, and degree of informatization and digitalization.[69] A district-level evaluation table published by the Guangzhou city government in 2008 and translated by me provides a sense of what officials are expected to achieve routinely, keeping in mind that this is just one of many performance evaluations to which cadres/officials are subject.[70] As shown in table 3.1, one-third of the indicators for evaluating economic development aim to advance techno-development. Other local governments use similar tables to evaluate cadre/official/government performance. Some governments include the number of high- and new-tech enterprises along with the number of invention patents per ten thousand people in their evaluation standards.[71]

In addition to investment projects and cadre/official/government performance, governments at various levels have been occupied with evaluating technologies and firms. In the past, the central government gave FIEs a lower corporate income tax rate to attract foreign investment. In 2008, however, the government removed the above tax benefits for FIEs, but began to give high- and new-tech enterprises a 15 percent corporate income tax rate as opposed to 25 percent for ordinary resident enterprises.[72] To do this, the central government established standards to define high and new technologies as well as evaluate the classification of specific firms. State agencies make decisions along with technical and financial experts. Evaluation criteria include the percentage of scientific and technological personnel engaged in R&D among the total number of employees, ratio of R&D expenses to total revenues, ratio of incomes from high- and new-tech products (services) to total incomes, and

TABLE 3.1. 2008 District Socioeconomic Development Evaluation System (Downtown Area) in Guangzhou City

Code	Indicator	Data source	Direction of indicator	Weight
Economic development				**30**
A1	GDP growth speed	Municipal Statistics Bureau	Positive	
A2	Ratio of GDP per capital growth speed to GDP growth speed	Municipal Statistics Bureau	Positive	
A3	Growth speed of fiscal revenue per capita	Municipal Finance Bureau; Municipal Statistics Bureau	Positive	
A4	Proportion of administrative operating costs in general budget expenditures	Municipal Finance Bureau	Negative	
A5	Growth speed of private enterprise value added	Municipal Economic and Trade Commission; Municipal Statistics Bureau	Positive	
A6	Construction land output rate	Municipal Land, Resources, and Housing Management Bureau; Municipal Statistics Bureau	Positive	
A7	**Value added of high- and new tech products as a percentage of GDP**	Municipal Technology Bureau; Municipal Statistics Bureau	Positive	
A8	**R&D expenditures as a percentage of GDP**	Municipal Technology Bureau; Municipal Statistics Bureau	Positive	
A9–1	**Proportion of the value added of modern service industries in the value added of the tertiary industry**	Municipal Statistics Bureau	Positive	
Social development				**22**
B1	Proportion of expenditures on social undertakings and public services in general budget expenditures	Municipal Finance Bureau	Positive	
B2	Area of public cultural facilities per 10,000 people	Municipal Culture Bureau	Positive	
B3	Compliance with fertility rate according to policy	Municipal Population and Family Planning Bureau	Positive	

Continued on next page

TABLE 3.1. (*continued*)

Code	Indicator	Data source	Direction of indicator	Weight
Social development				22
B4	Incidence rate of types A and B infectious diseases and food poisoning per 100,000 people	Municipal Health Bureau; Municipal Food and Drug Administration	Negative	
B5	Social security index	Municipal Public Security Bureau; Municipal Administration of Work Safety; Municipal Statistics Bureau	Positive	
B6	Democracy and the rule of law index	Municipal People's Congress Election Committee; Municipal Proposal Committee for the Chinese People's Political Consultative Conference; Municipal Intermediate People's Court; Municipal Judicial Bureau; Municipal Legal Affairs Office; Municipal Civil Administration Bureau; Municipal Petition Bureau	Positive	
B7–1	**Information development index**	Municipal Information Office; Municipal Investigation Team	Positive	
B8–1	High school graduation rate	Municipal Education Bureau	Positive	
B9–1	Development rate of the community health service system	Municipal Health Bureau	Positive	
B10–1	Key community project completion rate (These projects include a public service center, park, community center, medical care service provider, and surveillance center in charge of security on every street.)	Municipal Development and Reform Commission; Municipal Bureau of Construction; Municipal Civil Administration Bureau; Municipal Health Bureau; Municipal Information Office	Positive	
Quality of life				23
C1	Employment rate of urban unemployed persons	Municipal Labor and Social Security Bureau	Positive	
C2	Basic social security coverage	Municipal Labor and Social Security Bureau	Positive	

C3	Ratio of the growth rate of per capita income of urban and rural residents to the GDP growth rate	Municipal Investigation Team; Municipal Statistics Bureau	Positive
C4	Completion rate of urban environmental management security cases	Municipal Bureau of Construction; Municipal Urban Management Office	Positive
C5–1	Proportion of households with housing difficulties in urban areas to the total number of households	Municipal Land, Resources, and Housing Management Bureau	Negative

Ecological environment

D1	Proportion of environmental protection investment in the general budget expenditures	Municipal Finance Bureau	Positive
D2	Degree of greening	Municipal Forestry Bureau; Municipal Landscape Bureau	Positive
D3	Preservation of agricultural land	Municipal Land, Resources, and Housing Management Bureau	Positive
D4	Completion rate of total emission reduction of major pollutants	Municipal Environmental Protection Bureau	Positive
D5–1	Rain and sewage diversion and the completion rate of septic tank removal	Municipal Water Affairs Bureau; Municipal Bureau of Construction	Positive
D6–1	Completion rate of comprehensive river improvement projects	Municipal Water Affairs Bureau	Positive
D7–1	Rate of road construction and improvement	Municipal Water Affairs Bureau; Municipal Bureau of Construction	Positive
D8–1	Comprehensive evaluation index of urban appearance and environmental sanitation	Municipal Environmental Protection Bureau	Positive

Note: (1) According to the Guangzhou government, positive indicators should continue to grow, whereas negative indicators should continue to decrease. (2) The same table is used to evaluate other parts of Guangzhou City, but the weights are slightly different.

innovation ability.[73] Table 3.2 is designed by the Ministry of Technology for technical experts to evaluate enterprises. The number and quality of intellectual property rights, employment of talent, existence of a talent evaluation and reward system within an enterprise, and so on, are used to quantify and evaluate a company's innovation ability. Local governments at various levels have established their evaluation systems based on the guideline enacted by the central government, and provided high- and new-tech enterprises with other benefits such as monetary awards. Some governments, such as Dongguan City in Guangdong, also offer special admission quotas for children whose parents are deemed to have talent in high- and new-tech enterprises.

With the rise of the techno-developmental regime, governments at various levels have extended the scope of evaluation systems to human capital too, increasingly seen as essential to advance R&D and high- and new-tech enterprises and industries. There have been tremendous governmental efforts to define and evaluate talent and skills. For example, Shenzhen and Guangzhou enacted guidelines to define and attract talent in 2008 and 2010, respectively. Guangzhou's guideline further categorizes different levels of talent and evaluates them based on factors like academic honors, publications, participation in government-funded research projects, and awards in all kinds of competitions, while giving those deemed to have talent health care and housing subsidies and providing their children with access to local public schools.[74] Evaluation of human capital also manifests in the household registration and residence permit systems, which determine local citizenship and access to public services such as public education. In China, people without local household registration status (local citizenship) are usually excluded from public services, but holders of a local residence permit can access public services under certain conditions (e.g., having sufficient human capital).[75]

Point-based human capital evaluation systems emerged first in Guangdong. In 2007, Xiaolan Town in Zhongshan City in Guangzhou developed a point-based school admission system to select migrant workers with a higher level of quality (*suzhi*) so that their children could go to the local elementary school. "Quality" here was measured by a person's skill level, professional training, participation in social insurance, and so on. The government ranked and selected migrant worker applicants based on these points.[76] Building on experiences in Xiaolan Town, the Zhongshan city government developed a point-based household registration system based primarily on the level of education and skill in 2009. Similarly, the city government ranks applicants using points to decide who can obtain local citizenship.[77] Other cities in Guangdong, such as Shenzhen, designed similar point systems in 2010.[78]

In 2010, 15,915 people submitted their household registration applications to the Shenzhen government. Of these, 2,972 received local citizenship, and

Name of the enterprise

- Does the enterprise submit satisfying documents?
- Has the enterprise been registered for more than one year?
- Does the enterprise have qualified intellectual property rights?
- Does the core technology fall into the category of high and/or new technology?
- Does the proportion of scientific and technical personnel meet the requirement?
- R&D expenditures in last three years
- Income from high- and/or new tech products or services this year

1. Intellectual property rights (≤ 30 points)   **Score:**
- Technological advancement (≤ 8 points)   Score:
- Degree to which intellectual property rights play a significant role for   Score:
  major products or services (≤ 8 points)
- Quantity of intellectual property rights (≤ 8 points)   Score:
- How did the enterprise obtain intellectual property rights? (≤ 6 points)   Score:
  A: through indigenous innovation (1–6 points)
  B: through transfer, gift, or merger and acquisition (1–3 points)
- Did the enterprise participate in making national standards, industry   Score:
  standards, testing methods, and technical guidelines?
  (Extra points ≤ 2 points)

2. Ability to commercialize technology (≤ 30 points)   **Score:**
  A: strong, ≥ 5 items (25–30 points)
  B: moderately strong, ≥ 4 items (19–24 points)
  C: normal, ≥ 3 items (13–18 points)
  D: moderately weak, ≥ 2 items (7–12 points)
  E: weak, ≥ 1 items (1–6 points)
  F: none, ≥ 0 items (0 point)

3. R&D and organization management ability (≤ 30 points)   **Score:**
- Established an organizational structure and management system for R&D   Score:
  and an accounting system for R&D expenditure (≤ 6 points)
- Established an in-house R&D institution with sound scientific research   Score:
  conditions; carried out industry-university-research cooperation with
  domestic or foreign R&D institutes (≤ 6 points)
- Established an organizational structure and incentive system to promote   Score:
  the commercialization of technology; launched an open platform to
  encourage entrepreneurship and innovation (≤ 4 points)
- Established a training program for scientific and technological personnel   Score:
  and employees; employed outstanding talent; established a talent
  performance evaluation and reward system (≤ 4 points)

Overall comment on the enterprise's technical innovation ability

Total score

Note: The form was published by the Ministry of Technology.

over 90 percent of these recipients had a college degree or above.[79] Such outcomes reflect the design of the point system. Table 3.3 shows the point-based household registration system developed by the Shenzhen municipal government in 2012. When quantifying a person's value, the Shenzhen government considers things like personal quality, the amount of tax payment, enrollment in social insurance, housing property, age, public service, and whether they have undesirable attributes such as dishonesty and bad personal credits. Here we can already see the relationship between social credits and the household registration system back in 2012. The table also demonstrates that in the eyes of the state, the amorphous category of "personal quality" is a function of education, skill, ability to invent and receive patents, and honor accorded by the state. Clearly, such an evaluation system favors professional and technical personnel and property owners, while discriminating against the working class. Similar point-based systems have been developed across localities, especially in larger cities, to decide local household registration status and evaluate whether residents without local citizenship can access public services. Despite some criticism of the systems and the central government's announcement to reform the household registration system in 2016, larger cities still use similar point-based systems to decide local citizenship and access to public services.[80] In short, the evaluation systems aim to select and reward only those who can contribute to techno-development.

Finally, governments in China have endeavored to upgrade the technologies and infrastructure needed to conduct all of these evaluations. The evaluation systems that I have described have been digitalized. Now local governments have been building more integrated big data platforms to facilitate decision-making. For example, based on the bird/cage logic, local governments in Zhejiang use big data platforms to evaluate the performance of firms based on the land output rate per unit area. Then the governments use the information to make decisions about resource allocations—from land to water, gas, and electricity.[81] Similar big data platforms have been developed and adopted by local governments in other provinces as well.[82]

These big data platforms collect and integrate data from different government agencies in charge of statistics, tax, environmental protection, market regulation, technology, natural resources, and so forth, to calculate indicators (e.g., tax payment per unit of land, revenues per unit of land, and the share of R&D expenditures to total revenues) and evaluate each firm. Firms are then classified into different categories according to the evaluation results. Local governments further implement price discrimination, charging firms in different categories different prices for land, electricity, water, gas, and pollutant emission. Similar to cadres/officials, firms in good categories receive rewards, whereas those in bad categories receive punishment.[83] These big data

TABLE 3.3. 2012 Point-Based Household Registration Scheme in Shenzhen

First-level indicator	Second-level indicator	Third-level indicator	Points
Personal quality	Education and skill	1. Advanced professional technical qualification 2. Professional qualification for senior technicians 3. PhD degree 4. Master's degree with intermediate professional and technical qualification and practicing qualification 5. High-level talent recognized by the Shenzhen municipal government	100 points
		1. Master's degree 2. Bachelor's degree with intermediate professional and technical qualification, practicing qualification, and intermediate or advanced vocational qualification	90 points
		1. Bachelor's degree 2. College degree with professional technical qualification, practicing qualification, and intermediate or senior vocational qualification 3. Technician professional qualification	80 points
		1. Advanced professional qualification	70 points
		1. College degree 2. Intermediate professional and technical qualification	60 points
		1. Intermediate professional qualification 2. Preliminary professional technical qualification	50 points

Continued on next page

TABLE 3.3. (*continued*)

First-level indicator	Second-level indicator	Third-level indicator	Points
		1. High school (including technical secondary school)	30 points
		2. Preliminary professional qualification	
	Skill competition	Awarded in national level-one or level-two vocational skill competitions; awarded in vocational skill competitions held by Guangdong Province and Shenzhen Human Resources Security Department or other vocational skill competitions organized by related industries	40 points for a national level-one award; 30 points for a national level-two award or provincial level-one award; 25 points for a national level-three award, provincial level-two award, or municipal level-one award; 20 points for a provincial level-three award or municipal level-two award; 15 points for a municipal level-three award
	Invention (maximum: 30 points)	Invention patent	20 points for a patent
		Utility model	10 points for a patent
		Design patent	10 points for a patent
	Honor	Obtained honors from the ministries or commissions of the central government, Guangdong provincial party committee and provincial government, Shenzhen municipal party committee and municipal government	30 points for an honor from the central or Guangdong government; 25 points for an honor from the Shenzhen government
Tax payment in last three years	Personal income tax	Above 120,000 yuan	100 points
		Above 60,000 yuan	60 points
		Above 30,000 yuan	30 points
	The applicant is the legal representative of an enterprise registered in Shenzhen. The enterprise has made the following tax payment:	Above 1.5 million yuan	100 points
		Above 800,000 yuan	60 points
		Above 400,000 yuan	30 points

	The applicant is an investor of an enterprise registered in Shenzhen. The applicant has made the following tax payment based on its investment share:	
	Above 300,000 yuan	100 points
	Above 150,000 yuan	60 points
	Above 80,000 yuan	30 points
	The applicant has made the following tax payment as the owner of an individual business:	
	Above 150,000 yuan	100 points
	Above 80,000 yuan	60 points
	Above 40,000 yuan	30 points
Enrollment in social insurance	Social insurance enrollment in Shenzhen (maximum: 40 points)	
	Years of enrolling in social pension insurance in Shenzhen	3 points per year (maximum: 30 points)
	Years of enrolling in other social insurance in Shenzhen	1 point per year (maximum: 20 points)
Residency	Housing in Shenzhen	
	Housing property in Shenzhen	20 points with a mortgage; 30 points without a mortgage
	Time for living in Shenzhen	
	Years of having a Shenzhen residence permit	1 point per year (maximum: 10 points)
Age	Age	
	18–35 years old	5 points
	35–40 years old	1 point
	40–48 years old	−5 points per year old
Bonus points	Social service in Shenzhen in recent five years (maximum: 15 points)	
	Blood donation	2 points per donation (maximum: 10 points)
	Volunteering	2 points every 50 hours (maximum: 10 points)
	Charity donation	2 points per 1,000 yuan (maximum 10 points)
Deduction	Dishonesty record	
	Bad record in personal credits	−20 per record

platforms provide data visualization too, allowing users to see firms and their performance evaluation on a map. Some platforms provide information about how many "outdated" enterprises local governments have evicted and how much land governments have obtained from those firms.[84] The most ambitious ongoing effort is that to build a "smart decision-making platform" in the Guangdong–Hong Kong–Macau Greater Bay Area. According to public procurement documents, the platform will integrate data about strategies, policies, enterprises, and individuals to create a "brain" that will facilitate data-based decision-making about industrial upgrading at the micro-, meso-, and macrolevels. This platform is part of a 240 million RMB (around US$37.5 million) procurement of infrastructure for a big data center.[85]

To understand public procurement, I spoke with two executives of IT companies that specialize in products and services for digital governance (e.g., building digital infrastructure for "smart cities").[86] They both foresee that government spending on digital technologies and platforms for evaluation and governance will only continue to grow as the central government sees data-based quantitative evaluation and decision-making as increasingly crucial for techno-development, high-quality development, and governance in general. The ongoing endeavor is to integrate data and evaluation systems dispersed in different parts and levels of the bureaucratic structure.

Taiwan and South Korea's Turn to Techno-Development

As I was working on my book, several sociologists who generously read my manuscript suggested I compare China's turn to techno-development with the classic developmental state examples of Taiwan and South Korea. Specifically, one scholar asked whether the Taiwanese developmental state was as obsessed as the Chinese state with valuation and evaluation. To answer the question, I interviewed a government official in Taiwan's National Development Council who is knowledgeable about the historical and current role of the Taiwanese state in economic development. He told me that despite the existence of long-term economic planning in Taiwan, the Taiwanese government's effort to foster techno-development sought to help firms in specific sectors (e.g., semiconductors) to obtain what they needed (e.g., technological transfer and expertise building), rather than focusing as near exclusively on building quantitative indicators to measure firms and people as the Chinese government had. Indeed, in their turn to techno-development, both the Taiwanese and Korean governments targeted specific industrial sectors for support and indigenization.[87] Also, according to my interviewee, although there have been internal evaluations of civil servants within the Taiwanese government, the assessment has never been linked to socioeconomic development outcomes.

The government uses the evaluation of specific projects to reflect on and improve government budgeting instead of rewarding or disciplining civil servants. In general, Taiwanese citizens keep the government accountable through elections at various levels. He noted as well that certain practices of the Chinese state, such as allocating access to public services according to human capital, might well be considered unconstitutional or in violation of fundamental legal principles in Taiwan.

Crucially, unlike China, the process of industrialization and economic development in Taiwan and South Korea was accompanied by that of democratization. Taiwan began accelerating its industrial growth in the 1950s. Then the Kuomintang developmental state was effective in steering economic development by nurturing businesses in labor-intensive light manufacturing sectors. The authoritarian developmental state started to plan for techno-development in the 1970s as its economic planners saw the necessity to upgrade and diversify Taiwan's industrial structure.[88] In 1973, the Taiwanese government founded the Industrial Technology Research Institute. Through facilitating R&D and the commercialization of technology, the institute played a crucial role in helping Taiwan transition from an economy relying on labor-intensive manufacturing to an innovation-driven economy. The 1980s was a period when both high-tech industries and the democratization movement grew simultaneously. Taiwan's martial law was lifted in 1987, the same year that the Taiwan Semiconductor Manufacturing Company—arguably one of the most important high-tech companies in Taiwan and the world—was founded. In the past, specific social groups such as the military, bureaucrats, and teachers had enjoyed better social protection systems as they were critical for the state to maintain political stability, but the democratization process and the strengthening of the electoral institution led to an increasingly universal and inclusive welfare state.[89]

South Korea had a similar trajectory. Its authoritarian developmental state under Park Chung-hee jump-started industrialization and economic modernization in the early 1960s by promoting nascent homegrown industries, especially in labor-intensive manufacturing sectors.[90] During the 1970s, the Park regime began to look for a new engine for sustained development and plan for techno-development. In 1973, the authoritarian developmental state established the Daedeok Research Complex, which later became an important innovation hub.[91] Gradually, South Korean firms moved into higher value-added sectors, such as shipbuilding and eventually high-tech manufacturing industries, under the guidance of the state, which utilized a mix of measures (e.g., strategic tariffs, export incentives, and government-subsidized R&D) to facilitate industrial upgrading.[92] Later, in the 1980s, the IT sector started to emerge.[93] Like Taiwan, South Korea's turn to techno-development was accompanied by democratization. In 1987, South Korea's authoritarian leaders initiated the process of democratization as they became aware that the country's continuing economic growth was no longer sufficient to quell citizens' demands for rights. The process of democratization also contributed to the promotion of "growth with equity" and the extension of social welfare (e.g., health care) to a broader range of citizens, such as farmers and rural and urban self-employed workers, because such agendas helped politicians to extend their electoral base.[94]

In sum, Taiwan and South Korea's shift to techno-development unfolded in the context of democratization as their authoritarian developmental states began to seek legal-electoral legitimacy instead of relying solely on performance legitimacy. The democratization process contributed to a more inclusive welfare state that better protects disadvantaged social groups too. Although social policy was subordinated to economic policy, the former became increasingly decoupled from the latter as democratization proceeded.[95] In contrast, in China, the turn to techno-development happened against the backdrop of the Chinese state shoring up its political control as it continued to rely on performance legitimacy. Institutions, such as the legal system, put few constraints on the Chinese state's zealous pursuit of techno-development. As I have shown in this chapter and will continue to demonstrate in subsequent chapters, it is extremely difficult, if not impossible, for people adversely impacted by or critical of China's techno-developmental regime to influence policy making or government decisions through institutional and extrainstitutional channels. China's institutional conditions do not motivate the Chinese state to address the tensions between techno-development and social inequality. The Chinese state tends to either sideline the problem or come up with some ad hoc measures like Xi's common prosperity slogan, with almost no input from the Chinese people.

Conclusion

The debates around the relationship between techno-development and social inequality discussed in chapter 1 as well as the examples of Taiwan and South Korea's shift toward techno-development illustrate that there can be various types and trajectories of techno-development. Therefore it is critical to specify China's techno-development. In this chapter, I explored China's shift to a specific type of techno-development based on the bird/cage logic, despite the criticisms of such techno-development. This turn, which began at the provincial level in coastal provinces in the mid-2000s, was interrupted by the 2008 financial crisis and even questioned by the central government. But the rebound of China's economy, especially in coastal areas, "proved" the superiority and "scientific" nature of this type of techno-development. The coincidence of Xi's ascendance to general secretary in 2012 secured and expanded the bird/cage techno-development as Xi was among its earliest and most enthusiastic proponents. The increasingly shrinking public sphere and civil society under Xi's rule further suppressed criticisms of China's techno-development.

The bird/cage logic, which appeared as a scientific principle, has profoundly shaped the *substance* and *form* of China's techno-developmental regime. Substantively, since the logic accentuates the scarcity of resources, government officials, particularly those at the upper levels, see development problems as issues of matching and maximization—matching limited resources with deserving investment projects, technologies, industries, firms, and laborers that can advance techno-development to maximize the return of resource. By this logic, undeserving firms, industries, and laborers should be excluded from accessing valuable resources, such as land and essential public services. Conversely, firms, industries, and laborers considered valuable to techno-development deserve to exist in the most prosperous parts of China, which have the most expensive land and the best public services. As mentioned, a common criticism of China's techno-developmental regime is its tendency to exacerbate social and spatial inequalities.

Specifically, the institutions and policies that aim to advance techno-development systematically favor professional and technical personnel while discriminating against the working class by design. It is true that not every locality has the same level of exclusionary and discriminatory institutions and practices, as seen in the Chongqing Model. And yet the most prosperous, "developed," or postindustrial parts of China have the most severe class-based exclusionary institutions and practices. Moreover, these places continue to be seen by the Chinese public and various levels of the Chinese government as the forerunners or models of techno-development. In other words, they exist as "prototypes" for the nation's development as a whole.[96]

My findings resonate with sociologist Eli Friedman's study of access to education in China. Studying urbanization and migrant children's access to public school, Friedman astutely points out that as local governments have refined their citizenship regime, their sorting mechanisms have increasingly relied on social class rather than rural or urban household registration status. He develops the concept of "just-in-time urbanization" to contend that this shift is a solution for cities trying to address the need for specific labor power, but also seeking to avoid the costs of "warehousing" a surplus population.[97] I would supplement Friedman's argument, however, by noting that the shift from status to social class is not only about urbanization but is part of the government's effort to pursue techno-development since the mid-2000s as well. The point-based household registration scheme is only one part of a rapidly expanding evaluation system designed to achieve the goal of techno-development.

One might assert that the Chinese central leadership under Hu and Wen did improve rural children's access to free public education, expand pension and medical insurance systems, enact labor and employment laws to increase employment security, and raise the minimum wage.[98] In addition, Xi initiated a process of so-called targeted poverty alleviation in rural China in 2014. And yet scholars of the welfare state have shown that in China, social welfare provisions remain limited and defensive in both ambition and practice. Limited institutional reforms and the poverty alleviation campaign only provide limited social protection, and do not change the increasingly pervasive discriminatory class-based institutions, categories, and practices established to promote techno-development.[99]

The bird/cage logic has also shaped the *form* of China's techno-development, contributing to the emerging and expanding instrumental apparatus that aims to advance techno-development. Sociologists Fred Block and Margaret Somers use the term *market fundamentalism* to refer to a strong belief in the ability of the free market to solve economic and social problems.[100] Chinese governments, especially at the upper levels, exemplify technology fundamentalism—an enduring belief in the ability of S&T, particularly scientific methods along with high and new technologies, to solve socioeconomic, developmental, and political problems—despite simultaneously having an often superficial understanding of S&T. Unlike followers of market fundamentalism, Chinese governments are deeply skeptical about the market. Believing in the mutually empowering relationship between the visible hand of the government and S&T, different levels and parts of the Chinese state have been actively involved in the process of valuating and evaluating the actual or potential contribution of things (e.g., firms, industries, investment projects, and technologies) and humans (e.g., laborers and government officials) to techno-development through expanding data collection, production, and quantification. Government agencies then use the outcomes of valuation and evaluation for classifications and resource distributions.

Despite evidence and opinions that challenge the efficacy of the instrumental apparatus in advancing techno-development, the instrumental apparatus has continued expanding and taken on its own life. Although some scholars were skeptical about the efficacy of the bird/cage logic and instruments built on the logic, others still helped to justify and develop the instruments, due in part to the symbolic capital (e.g., honors accorded by the state), economic capital, and social capital they can receive from being complicit in the state's agendas. In the 1999 forward to *The Coming of the Post-Industrial Society*, Bell uses the example of Fang Lizhi—a former vice president of the Chinese University of Science and Technology exiled to the United States after the 1989 Tiananmen democratic movement—to illustrate the struggle between science and politics. Far from being simply objective or neutral, Bell warned that science can be threatened by bureaucratization, or subordinated to political or corporate ends.[101] As I have demonstrated in this chapter, we see the coexistence of critical voices and subordination of scholars to politics and political elites in China's turn to techno-development, but the increasingly restricted political conditions under Xi's rule have disempowered those critical voices. As a result, we see more and more effort and investment to build instruments, despite private skepticism about the efficacy of the instruments.

Although the emerging instrumental apparatus that aims to foster techno-development builds on existing instruments, such as the cadre/official/government evaluation system, it is novel in China in two ways. First, the instrumental apparatus aligns distinct and separate valuation, evaluation, and classification systems with the new goal of techno-development. In the process, certain long-standing institutions, such as the cadre/official/government evaluation and household registration systems, were redesigned and repurposed for techno-development. Also, the perceived contribution to techno-development became a major criterion in determining the order of worth. Second, the scope of instruments has been expanding as the bird/cage logic dictates that the government must continually valuate, evaluate, and classify an increasing list of objects and humans. The rise of big data and digital technology has further motivated and enabled the Chinese state to develop an even larger arsenal of tools. Although governments in other countries engage in valuation and evaluation too, it would be difficult, if not impossible, to find a government more enthusiastic about and invested in building all-encompassing valuation, evaluation, and classification systems than the Chinese state.[102]

With this understanding of China's turn to techno-development based on the bird/cage logic, we will move to how old birds—businesses and workers deemed obsolete by the Chinese state—have experienced and responded to techno-development.

4

Obsolete Capital and Labor

IN CHAPTER 3, I examined key policy-making processes and debates at the provincial and national levels, and explained how China turned to a specific type of techno-development based on the bird/cage logic. But of course, developmental policies require ongoing institutionalization and implementation at lower levels of the bureaucratic system. In this chapter, I tell the story of what has happened on the ground in industries deemed obsolete by local governments. Specifically, how have lower-level local officials performed their work? How have the businesses and workers now considered obsolete experienced and responded to a techno-developmental regime that seems so intent on replacing them? And how have lower-level officials and businesspeople and workers in the outmoded sectors engaged with the expanding instrumental apparatus that aims to foster techno-development?

First, let me provide some background information about my research sites. Most of my data in this chapter were collected through observations and interviews in cities in the Pearl River Delta in Guangdong Province. I conducted most of my research in Dongguan and Shenzhen, though I also interviewed managers and executives in Zhejiang. Dongguan and Shenzhen are adjacent cities, but they are located differently in the bureaucratic hierarchy. As a prefecture-level city, Dongguan is situated lower than Shenzhen administratively. Famous for its manufacturing industries, Dongguan is sometimes described as the center of the "factory of the world." In comparison, Shenzhen is a major subprovincial city and one of the SEZs of China. Since the beginning of economic reform, Shenzhen has enjoyed a special status and extraordinary resources because the Chinese central government views the city as key to China's policy of opening up. Although primarily famous for IT industries, there are still many labor-intensive manufacturers in Shenzhen's peripheral areas—districts formerly lying outside the Shenzhen SEZ. Firms, people, and goods move between Dongguan and Shenzhen due in part to their geographic proximity.

Demographic information (see table 4.1) also provides a window into the two cities. The size of the regular residential population (*changzhu renkou*)—

TABLE 4.1. Demographic Information for Dongguan and Shenzhen

City	Dongguan		Shenzhen	
Year	2010	2020	2010	2020
Regular residential population (*changzhu renkou*)	8.22 million	10.47 million	10.42 million	17.56 million
People with a local household registration status (*huji renkou*)	1.82 million	2.64 million	2.51 million	4.96 million
The percentage of permanent residents with a local household registration status	22.14%	25.21%	24.09%	28.25%
Males per 100 females	117.81	130.06	118.23	122.43
The number of people with college education or above per 100,000 permanent residents	7,103	13,241	17,545	28,849

Source: Sixth and Seventh National Population Census. *Note*: (1) Permanent residents are those who have lived in a place for at least six months. (2) The gender ratios in 2000 in Dongguan and Shenzhen were 89.02 and 97.74, respectively.

those who have lived there for more than six months regardless of their household registration status—has increased in both cities over time.[1] Both are migrant cities. Less than 30 percent of the regular residential population in both cities had local citizenship in 2020. The education level of permanent residents in Dongguan and Shenzhen has been rising. The most interesting yet largely unstudied demographic change in both cities is the gender ratio of the regular residential population—specifically, the number of males per 100 females. Shifts in this ratio are intriguing because they reveal the gendered dimension of the techno-developmental regime. Due to the preference for sons and China's one-child policy, males have long outnumbered females.[2] For the past two decades, the gender ratio of the general populace has been around 105–106 males per 100 females. Dongguan and Shenzhen were exceptions, however; prior to 2010, both cities had more female than male regular residents (see figure 4.1). In her study of one factory in Shenzhen in 1992–93, sociologist Ching Kwan Lee found that women made up 80 percent of all production employees, and there was a clear division of labor by gender. All assembly-line workers and most line leaders were women, while men occupied positions as repair workers, forepersons, or supervisors.[3] Indeed, as experiences in Taiwan, Singapore, Indonesia, Malaysia, and Mexico have shown, cheap, young, and docile female manual labor often plays a crucial role in the process of industrialization.[4]

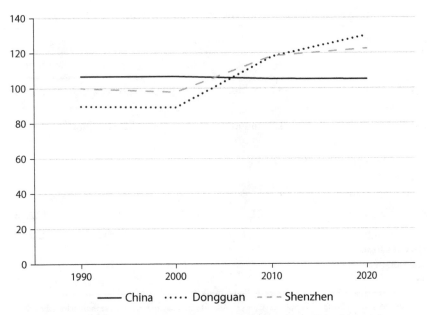

FIGURE 4.1. Population gender ratio in China, Dongguan, and Shenzhen.
Source: The Seventh National Population Census.

And yet the gender ratio rose from 89.02 in 2000 to 130.06 in 2020 in Dongguan, and from 97.74 in 2000 to 122.43 in 2020 in Shenzhen. Among those with local citizenship, however, the gender ratios remain relatively balanced and stable, indicating that the shift has been driven by male migrants. In fact, Guangdong was the province with the highest gender ratio in China in 2020.[5] Such shifts reflect the changing industrial and occupational structures in Dongguan and Shenzhen. In 2020, Dongguan and Shenzhen ranked ninth and second among cities in China, respectively, in terms of the number of high- and new-tech enterprises recognized by the central government.[6] As the industrial structure has been changing, demand for technical and professional personnel has increased in both cities, while unskilled or low-skilled jobs have been increasingly relocated to inland China or other countries—and the skill distinction frequently maps onto the gender categories.

During my research trips, I took Didi (like Uber) while traveling within Dongguan and Shenzhen and between the two cities to visit my informants and interviewees in industries and businesses considered obsolete by local governments. In my conversations with township and street-level officials, executives, and managers, I learned that local officials tend to see labor-intensive manufacturing industries and the businesses therein as outmoded. These businesses rely more on labor input than capital input, and do not invest much in R&D or apply for patents. They also tend to employ a high percentage of unskilled or low-skilled workers for manufacturing (usually above 70 percent) and a small percentage of college graduates. In short, local officials view these businesses as obsolete because they rely on human labor—more specifically, manual, low-skilled labor. Wanting to see what this obsolescence looks like on the ground, I visited businesses that fell into this category. Most produce cell phone cases, silicone rubber buttons, shoes, clothing, electronic components, and so on, or assemble electronic components. It usually takes less than one week for such businesses to train a new unskilled or low-skilled worker. All were located in industrial areas that look old and distinct from high-tech parks or districts.

Interestingly, on my trips between 2016 and 2019, many of the Didi drivers I met were former factory owners or managers of outdated businesses. They became Didi drivers while looking for new opportunities after corporate bankruptcy or layoffs. I had not expected to see such direct connection between the platform and manufacturing sectors. Since traffic was often congested, I had plenty of time to talk to these drivers. Most assumed I worked in the manufacturing sector myself because I was traveling between factories and talking to them about manufacturing and industrial policies. Some of them became my interviewees after learning about my research. My conversations with these drivers gave me valuable insight into the experience of being rendered obsolete, seemingly overnight.

Against the Obsolete

Most of the manufacturers that I visited have ties with the township or street-level governments through local communities. Few are FIEs, and none of the owners or executives of the manufacturers are local people in Dongguan or Shenzhen.[7] The majority of these manufacturers have rented collective land or facilities from local communities (or villages)—a situation that has made some communities with rights to collective land in Dongguan and Shenzhen quite affluent.[8] Many of these communities have formed corporations to manage their land, buildings, and other assets. In some communities in Shenzhen, each community member can receive a large dividend (hundreds of thousands of RMB) every year. In Dongguan, some local communities have built beautiful villas and provided social benefits for their members, such as school buses for children and private health care insurance. Notably, it is common for members of local communities to work as officials in the local government too.

When a manufacturer rents a piece of land or a factory from a local community, the former often hires a few people from the local community. The arrangement is mutually beneficial. On the one hand, the hired individuals receive a handsome salary without the need to work regularly. On the other hand, local people help the manufacturer interact and deal with local governments and the local community when any issues arise. I gained access to township and street-level officials through extensive local networks that span across manufacturers, local communities, and local governments. Only a minority of the manufacturers that I visited have land use rights themselves and do not rent land or facilities from others.

My interviews with township and street-level officials, executives, and managers show that since around 2012, there have been waves of campaigns against obsolete businesses in the form of law enforcement. Local governments police businesses that violate laws or regulations regarding fire and work safety, environmental protection, construction, and so on. In other words, these laws and regulations were repurposed for techno-development and became part of the enlarging instrumental apparatus. The campaigns against outmoded businesses have intensified and become more frequent since the mid-2010s. In such campaigns, local governments describe targeted businesses as scattered (*san*), chaotic (*luan*), polluting (*wu*), low-end (*di*), small (*xiao*), and/or dangerous (*wei*). According to officials I interviewed, the campaigns were initially imposed by the Guangdong provincial government onto the municipal and lower-level governments under the agenda of emptying the cage and changing the bird to accelerate industrial upgrading. After Xi took leadership, the bird and cage agenda has gone hand in hand with an initiative also prioritizing environmental protection.[9]

As mentioned in chapter 3, pollution was one of the problems shaping the nascent techno-developmental regime in coastal provinces. When Xi was the governor in Fujian in 2001, he already suggested eliminating obsolete businesses in Fujian that waste resources, have overcapacity problems, use outdated technologies, or produce pollution; meanwhile, he prioritized the development of high- and new-tech industries, including environmental-related ones. Xi later proposed similar policies as Zhejiang's party secretary in the mid-2000s. As such, combating pollution and developing environmental-related industries have been critical components of China's techno-developmental regime. Bao'an is a district in Shenzhen. In the Bao'an district government's campaign against obsolete businesses in 2018, for example, one of the major goals of policing businesses that violate environmental and other regulations was to spare land for high-end industries as well as high- and new-tech enterprises.[10]

How have lower-level governments perceived and performed their work under the techno-developmental regime? Cai, a township official, shared his thoughts with me:

Those campaigns [against obsolete businesses] are often not good for us because villages and the township government financially benefit from the [outmoded] businesses. Many of us are natives here. We don't want to piss off our relatives and friends. But the upper-level governments have asked us to implement the campaigns. You know we have a lot of [performance evaluation] indicators and targets. The outcomes of those campaigns are part of our performance evaluation.

Cai's words speak to the phenomenon of local protectionism, as connections between businesses and local governments influence the latter's law enforcement against the former.[11] Higher-level governments, though, attempt to curb local protectionism through performance evaluation systems. When I asked Cai how local officials know which indicators and targets are important, given that there are so many, he explained that

there are hard and soft targets. The government above us lets us know which indicators are crucial and asks us to concentrate on important ones because we have limited time and resources. They [ignore] unimportant indicators. When we drink with them [upper-level officials], they tell us directly. Generally speaking, when they ask us to implement a campaign, indicators and targets of the campaign will be important. We have to report how many businesses we police, give fines to, and close down, how much land we spare from evicting businesses, and how many high- and new-tech enterprises we bring to our township. They [upper-level governments] want to see statistics. I want to keep my job. My bosses don't want to lose their posts.

Cai describes significant top-down pressure on lower levels of government, in keeping with what Xueguang Zhou calls the mobilizational mode of governance (*yundong shi zhili*)—top-down bureaucratic efforts to achieve certain goals through resource and political mobilization.[12] The campaigns against obsolete businesses resemble the so-called strike hard against crime campaigns (*yanda yundong*) that emerged in the early 1980s and have periodically reoccurred in China. In the aftermath of the Cultural Revolution (1966–76), the CCP attempted to restore China's legal order. In the early 1980s, the central party-state initiated extremely punitive campaigns to implement the newly enacted Criminal Code and pursue "severe and swift justice."[13] Public shaming and publicizing of the numbers of arrested, sentenced, and executed people are critical characteristics of strike hard campaigns.[14]

In a similar vein, municipal and district governments pursuing campaigns against obsolete businesses initiate media propaganda to publicize statistics, photos, and some names of the targeted businesses as evidence of the campaign's success. For instance, the Dongguan municipal government announced through the media that it would either eliminate or "rectify" five to forty thousand businesses in Dongguan in 2018 and 2019, respectively. Such media reports often include statistics of closed or rectified firms along with tables that rank townships based on their numerical performance.[15] Such publicity imposes tremendous stress on township governments. Asked about whether they worry about the social and economic problems that could arise from the campaigns, such as unemployment, bankruptcy, and substantive and procedural injustice, township and street-level officials told me those issues are not their business. They see themselves as cogs in the machine, responsible only for completing the tasks assigned by upper-level governments. They believe the upper-level governments that made the policy should be responsible for the problems.

Although most campaigns against obsolete businesses result from top-down political pressure, lower-level governments have other motivations to police these businesses in some circumstances. When lower-level governments run out of land quotas to bring in new investment projects that look more high-tech or can bring in more taxes, they sometimes use environmental, safety, and construction regulations to kick out obsolete businesses that lease land or factories from local communities. Tian, a member of a local community in a peripheral district of Shenzhen, shared the experience of his community with me:

> They [street-level officials] told us our tenant was doing outdated business. They thought transforming our buildings into an incubator would be better for us because high-end companies can pay more rent, and we can rent out our place to multiple companies. We told them we had a contract with our tenant. They said the contract wouldn't be a problem because our tenant violated construction and environmental regulations. In the end, our tenant left because of regulatory issues. Local officials were satisfied because there are more high-tech companies in their jurisdiction.

Some executives and managers also told me that lower-level governments use environmental law enforcement to hasten the process of compulsory land acquisition if obsolete businesses have land use rights and disagree on the compensation amount. Some of my interviewees told me of friends who accepted unsatisfying compensation because of the hefty fines imposed by local governments citing environmental laws and regulations.

Campaigns in Action

During my fieldwork, I frequently witnessed the implementation of campaigns against obsolete businesses. I was allowed to conduct research at Diligence—an export-oriented manufacturer with around three hundred employees—for a week in 2019. Although Diligence is located in an old industrial area in Dong-guan, the environment inside the company is clean and tidy. I cannot provide information about what Diligence manufactures to protect the anonymity and confidentiality of my informants and interviewees. At Diligence, I was given free rein to move about, observe, and even talk to anyone I wished, without supervision.

Two incidents occurred while I was there. One day, one of the factories was shut down after a fire safety inspection team from the township government suddenly arrived at its doorstep. The officials said Diligence should have one more exit in one of its workshops, but Diligence's managers pointed out that other safety inspection teams had already inspected and approved the factory several times. Dai, a Diligence employee and native of the local community, communicated with the inspection team about the situation. The team leader requested 2,000 RMB (US$313) in cash for himself and 1,000 RMB (US$157) for each of the other team members.[16] I was surprised because I thought Xi's vast and ruthless anticorruption campaigns had curbed requests for bribes. After receiving what they wanted, the inspection team left and allowed Dili-gence to operate again.

The second incident took place a couple days later. This time, officials from a bureau at the Dongguan Municipal Government showed up to inspect wastewater. After the inspection, the officials announced that they found some leakage in a pipeline connected to a spraying workshop. As a result, the bureau decided to seal the power panel of the spraying workshop for thirty days, ef-fectively shutting the workshop down. I did see some water drops from the pipeline, but the amount of water was less than that of the water leakage pro-duced by a typical air conditioner. Diligence was asked to write a report on how to solve the problem. Due to the shutdown, workers in the spraying work-shop could not work, and managers had to explain the uncertain situation to their clients in other countries because of the potential delay.

As a former legal professional, I was struck by the severity of the adminis-trative measure used by the authority to solve the problem of a minor water leak. In many countries, there is a fundamental legal doctrine called the princi-ple of proportionality. In light of the principle, a public authority shall main-tain a sense of proportion between particular goals and the means that the authority employs to achieve the goals so that the authority's action impinges on individual rights to the minimum extent as it preserves public interests.[17] In China, some administrative guidelines, such as one published by the State Administration of Work Safety, include the principle of proportionality (*bili yuanze*). Legal scholars in China argue that the principle of proportionality is a constitutional principle.[18] In 2018, the Ministry of Ecology and Environment stipulated that local governments are prohibited from using a one-size-fits-all approach to shut down businesses at will in the enforcement of law.[19] And yet proportionality is clearly not a consideration in campaigns against obsolete businesses on the ground. Similar to strike hard campaigns against crime, governments prefer severe and swift legal and administrative outcomes.[20]

Dai, a local employee at Diligence, tried to mobilize his networks, reaching out to friends and classmates in the township government. Although higher-level governments have been attempting to rotate the leadership of bureaus in township governments to reduce any undue influence of local communities, many officials are still native. I asked Diligence's executives and managers whether networks in the township government could help given that it was the municipal government rather than the township one that shut down the workshop. Managers said connections with the township government could still help because due to limited resources, the municipal government must rely on township governments to follow up on cases after the former makes an administrative decision. In order to complete their clients' orders, Diligence temporarily rented a spraying workshop from a tiny factory. The factory owner said he had already paid hundreds of thousands of RMB, so he had not been targeted in the campaigns.

As Diligence's executives and managers were busy solving their crisis, a manager discovered Diligence's name in the local media coverage of the municipal government's latest campaign. The news article, which was disseminated widely on social media, listed Diligence as an example of obsolete businesses along with many others. Executives were extremely worried that this coverage would damage Diligence's reputation. Eventually, the company's short-term crisis was solved through local networks, but it has been challenging for Diligence to cope with the reoccurrence of similar incidents, especially when the frequency of them has increased over time, and as the central government has been restructuring the bureaucratic structure and reshuffling officials. According to Diligence's management, in the past, local officials might perform inspections a few times a year, but starting in 2018, they began to show up monthly or sometimes even weekly. In some of the inspections, local officials directed Diligence to purchase environmental equipment and services from specific companies.

Diligence's experiences are shared by the manufacturers I visited and the Didi drivers I spoke with (i.e., former executives and managers). When I visited Stone, another manufacturing company, an inspection team from the Guangdong provincial government happened to be there as well (see figure 4.2). Wang, a manager in charge of production, told me they have had inspections from the township, municipal, provincial, and even the central government as well as different parts of the government system, such as agencies in charge of fire and rescue, environmental protection, work safety, crimi-

FIGURE 4.2. A Guangdong Province law enforcement team.

nal policing, and so forth. While we were talking, Wang asked if I wanted to see some drones. I said, of course. When we stepped out of the factory building, we saw two drones hovering in the air to collect data for air pollution and then transmit the data to the government. Wang explained that local governments have begun using technology and environment big data platforms to collect and integrate all kinds of data. I asked Wang how he was able to cope with the pressure of constant surveillance from both drones and inspection teams. He told me that Stone would probably be OK this time because it had just purchased a system from an environmental technology company recommended by local officials.

Since the manufacturing process at Stone requires electroplating, the company has an electroplating wastewater treatment system. In one of the previous campaigns against obsolete businesses, the municipal government imposed a huge fine on Stone. Unlike Diligence, Stone did not employ local persons to deal with the government. Although Stone hired a company to fix the water treatment system, the local government did not approve the system. Stone only passed the inspection after it followed an official's suggestion to use a specific environmental equipment company and install a new system.

Following this experience, Stone's CEO asked managers to use water processed and emitted from the system to keep goldfish. When an inspection team came, Stone managers pointed to the goldfish to demonstrate Stone's compliance with environmental protection. Wang confided, "Of course, water from the system cannot keep goldfish alive. Our CEO just tries to please local officials. We have replaced goldfish regularly, especially when there are more inspections." In order to deal with these multiple inspections, Stone has spent 4 million RMB (around US$627,000) for its factory in Dongguan and 3 million RMB (around US$470,000) for its factory in Shenzhen in recent years.

My interviews with executives and managers reveal that the ways in which businesses are "milked" by or transact with local officials have changed with the rise of the techno-developmental regime. Most respondents reported that they now have to pay bribes in cash less frequently than in the past. But more often, local officials require or suggest the purchasing of equipment or services from local high- and new-tech enterprises, especially in environmental-related industries. As the central and provincial governments emphasize the role of technology in administration and surveillance—for instance, using the IoT and big data platforms for pollution monitoring—governments need businesses to have corresponding equipment or systems.[21] Many of my interviewees have struggled between being shut down or punished by the government and buying costly equipment or services from high- and new-tech enterprises suggested by local officials. One Didi driver, whose manufacturing company went bankrupt, told me,

> In the past, I had to give them [local officials] red envelopes [bribes]. But in recent years, they asked me to buy expensive equipment from providers they suggested to pass safety and environmental inspections. I can buy similar equipment from other providers at lower prices, but they specify the providers. I feel the two things [asking for bribes and to purchase equipment] are similarly problematic. No law says I must buy equipment from providers suggested by them. They must get some kickbacks from those providers.

Some of the equipment providers mentioned by my interviewees are SOEs. Two township officials I interviewed said some officials get personal economic benefits, such as kickbacks and dry shares (*gangu*) from the companies they recommend to others. *Dry shares* refer to the corporate shares granted to a third party free of charge. Dry shareholders have the right to dividends. Usually, officials arrange for their family members or reliable friends to be dry shareholders. Also, local governments need to cultivate high- and new-tech enterprises. Asking obsolete businesses to buy things from high- and new-tech enterprises creates a market for the latter.

Businesses in Struggle

Current and former executives and managers all think the political environment has become much more hostile toward obsolete businesses due to increasing regulatory unpredictability and the government's harsh regulatory measures. Similar to businesses studied by sociologist Jieh-min Wu in Guangdong in the 1990s and early 2000s, my interviewees see GDP-centric local governments in the past as corrupt but reasonable and credible. Such conditions allowed businesses to predict and deal with risks.[22] Now, however, my interviewees relate that it has become increasingly difficult for them to predict government behavior and deal with the power of public authority. In particular, they complain about not being able to calculate how much money they will have to spend to satisfy unstable and excessive regulatory requirements. Tao, a manager, angrily described the situation:

> They [local governments] allowed factories to do business here in the beginning. And they told factories their standards and procedures. But the problem is that they have been changing their criteria frequently. Many manufacturers met the standards initially, but the governments have been raising the standards. In a way, they [the governments] don't have standards because they can change standards as they wish anytime. They issue an order in the morning and rescind it in the evening (*zhao ling xi gai*). Whenever they change standards, businesses have to spend millions of RMB to meet their new standards. We can't estimate our costs. In the past, when local officials asked for bribes, we didn't have to spend that much, and they left us alone after they got money. They wanted us to make money, and they cared about GDP and taxes. But now, they come after us again and again, and we don't know what they want. Perhaps they want to extract as much money from us as they can before we go bankrupt and then they can attract high-tech companies here. The problem is we don't have the rule of law. We only have the rule of humans. I think when they can change rules so often and give unnecessarily severe punishment, we only have the rule of humans.

Tao's frustration with the unpredictability of the regulatory environment was widely shared among my interviewees and informants, who brought up the issue of the rule of law frequently. They did not question whether local government decisions were based on laws and regulations but instead criticized the instability of the legal environment due to the government's power to change regulations and exercise discretion at whim.

Cheng and Fang, the owners of a shoe factory and electroplate factory, respectively, provided detailed descriptions of how regulations and standards have changed and impacted them. Each factory has approximately a hundred employees. When Cheng and Fang got permits for their factories, the regulations did not require an environmental evaluation process; now they do. But even when both owners tried to initiate this process, they were prevented from doing so and told by the local government that their specific businesses were now classified as obsolete. Furthermore, local governments have not only raised the exhaust emission standards but also stipulated that they can shut down a factory if a company violates the emission standard more than a couple times in a year. Both Cheng and Fang spent more than one million RMB meeting other regulatory requirements (e.g., installing an online monitoring system) last year. They are both on the brink of bankruptcy. Cheng stated,

> The government does not understand our production process at all. They think all factories should be dust free and look like offices and conference rooms of a publicly listed high-tech company. Otherwise, they label you as a "scattered, chaotic, and polluting" business. We have been suffering from their one-size-fits-all approach. On the one hand, we have to be competitive in the market. Our profit margins are small. On the other hand, we have spent huge [sums of] money satisfying the government's growing and changing standards, but they still don't want to give us certain permits. Without those permits, we are in a precarious situation. Our investment could be in vain anytime.

Managers and executives' depictions of new and revised standards correspond to the government's statistics. Between 2006 and 2016, the Chinese central government planned to make and revise 1,800 environmental protection standards and finished 1,128 of them. During the thirteenth five-year period (2016–20), the government aimed to revise 900 standards and enact 800 new ones.[23] Like other parts of the government, the Ministry of Ecology and Environment has its numerical targets to meet.

Other managers and executives also complained about what they perceive as unrealistically high regulatory standards. For example, Tang, an executive, said,

> The Communist Party is deeply fond of the grandiose (*hao da xi gong*). They want *gao da shang* [high, large, and high-end] things, like high- and new-tech industries and sweeping regulations against traditional manufacturers. The regulatory standards they set are higher than those in developed countries. It's difficult to meet the standards. They wait for firms to violate the standards. Ultimately, they want us to buy equipment from SOEs. They are not honest. Their evaluation system is fake and driving us crazy. There is no rule of law.

Tang's comment is similar to that of manager Wang at Stone. As Wang put it, "The government should be more realistic and shouldn't kill labor-intensive businesses. Businesses do not intend to violate regulations. The government either didn't have regulations in the beginning or suddenly made stringent regulations. Their power over businesses is not restricted at all."

Zhang was a particularly significant interviewee because he worked as a district court judge and lawyer before deciding to do business in Zhejiang. Due to his prior career, he has abundant experience handling economic transactions and legal disputes. Many manufacturers respected him in his city. When we talked, Zhang articulated how the government's industrial and development policies and regulations have led to severe risks for businesses:

> Businesses worry about governmental intervention. As experienced entrepreneurs, we have reasonable expectations and calculations of market risks. We are prepared to deal with those risks and have no complaint about such risks. But governmental intervention is killing us because we simply cannot expect what kind of policy they [governments] will make. You cannot say all of their policies are wrong. But as a rule of thumb, only one or two policies out of ten are correct. The consequences of their mistakes could be deadly because the government has enormous power. They shut down factories, cut your water and electricity, and demolish your factory buildings at will. Many of my friends encountered such situations because of minor violations of regulations. As a result, they lost millions of RMB due to disruption of production and unexpected costs. When the government intervenes so much, entrepreneurs feel exhausted. Many of the government's industrial upgrading and environmental protection policies have severely impacted small businesses, but benefited high-tech industries and big enterprises. Our constitution does not authorize the government to discriminate against small and medium-sized labor-intensive businesses and people who work for those companies.

Because changing policies and regulations introduce so much uncertainty, most of the executives and managers with whom I spoke spend enormous amounts of time and energy—however futilely—trying to track policies and regulations, and even establishing social media groups to exchange information.

How can businesses considered obsolete by the government address their grievances, other than by simply submitting to the instructions of local governments or officials? Grievants in China (e.g., workers and petitioners) often use legal procedures or mobilize public opinion to address their problems, but the executives and managers I talked to were pessimistic about these grievance resolution channels.[24] When a bureau at the municipal government decided to seal the power panel at Diligence's spraying workshop for thirty days, I asked the management if pursuing legal procedures, such as appealing to the municipal or provincial government and filing an administrative lawsuit, would be beneficial. The managers responded that they had never heard of any such efforts resulting in success and noted that the lengthy legal process was ill-suited to resolve the urgent problems of being shuttered. Indeed, the written administrative decision that Diligence received from the bureau indicates that an appeal or lawsuit would not stop the implementation of the decision. Through my conversations with other manufacturers, I discovered that businesses tend to have a more realistic understanding of legal procedures than common petitioners, such as peasants whose land was taken or urban residents whose houses were demolished by local governments, since businesses have stronger ties to local governments and better access to lawyers. Precisely because they know more about how the administrative and legal system works, they do not expect a benevolent higher-level government or impartial court to overturn administrative decisions made by lower-level governments. All of my interviewees—including Zhang, the former judge—consider legal action ineffective and time-consuming.

I asked my interviewees whether they would consider organizing collective action or mobilizing public opinion, as some entrepreneurs did before the consolidation of the techno-developmental regime (as discussed in chapter 3). They all said no because the political environment has become more illiberal under the Xi leadership. They also believed that the public would not sympathize with their predicament. Interestingly, several of my interviewees cited the same popular Chinese saying: when a rat runs across the street, everyone shouts "hit it!" (*guojie laoshu renren handa*). The phrase is used to refer to unpopular or widely hated figures. As such, my interviewees thought the public would side with the government and see businesses as "running rats" that deserve punishment. They observed that the growing inequality in China has led to hatred of the rich (*choufu*) and a preference among media to cover only the unjust experiences of the poor, not the wealthy. In addition, my informants and interviewees felt that government discourse has effectively stigmatized labor-intensive manufacturers as backward, outdated, illegal, polluting, and morally wrong. Zhang shared that one of his friends died by suicide after a local government demolished his factory due to regulatory issues. Still, no media covered the story, even though some manufacturers reached out to journalists.

Some firms do seek to protect themselves from campaigns against obsolete businesses by "gaming" the system—even faking their legal classification if necessary. During my fieldwork in Dongguan, Tong, a factory owner, was beset by reoccurring campaigns against outmoded businesses. One day, Tong contacted me after he heard from Teng, a relative. Tong and Teng operate the same kind of manufacturing business, use the same manufacturing technology, and have the same manufacturing process. Theoretically, they should have the same regulatory problems. And yet a friend of Teng's is a top leader of the township government. The friend suggested that Teng list his company as a high- and new-tech enterprise in order to avoid being targeted as an obsolete businesses, and instead receive land and tax benefits and subsidies. Teng's friend put him in contact with a company that helped him get a high- and new-tech enterprise certificate.

I heard about similar practices from other informants and interviewees as well. In Shenzhen, the executive of Diamond—a manufacturing company—told me,

> There are agency companies that assist businesses to get a high- and new-tech enterprise certificate. People in those companies worked for the government in the past, and of course have friends inside the government. They know the rules of the game and can guarantee people to get a certificate. I paid two hundred thousand RMB. They told me I would have to satisfy several indicators, which include a certain number of patents. This is because the government needs those indicators to boost its scores. I didn't have any invention, but the company filed and got patents for me. Honestly, I'm not fond of this because things are fake and not meaningful. My factory continues to produce the same products using the same methods, but now it is a high- and new-tech company. People are doing this to avoid troubles and get benefits. I don't want to cheat and don't need subsidies, but I don't want to encounter law enforcement again and again.

When I visited Diamond, the executive brought me to a conference room. With my previous training in intellectual property rights, I immediately spotted several patent certificates on the wall. After talking to Diamond's executive, I understood what was going on. Still, given the potential legal consequences, not everyone dares to take the same measures as Teng and Diamond's executive.

Campaigns against obsolete businesses have led to closures and relocations. To be sure, many businesses in coastal China had shuttered or moved elsewhere before such campaigns due to growing labor costs as well as the 2008 financial crisis, but many current and former executives and managers described the intensified campaigns against outdated business as the last straw.[25] Diligence's executive Peng shared his experiences and observations with me:

> Many factory owners here decided to move elsewhere or close down. This is the result of multiple and *accumulative* problems. It's like we are living in a pressure cooker, and the pressure has been building up. If rising labor cost is the only problem, business owners wouldn't want to move elsewhere because relocation is expensive and risky. Relocation can also be difficult for businesses that work with many suppliers because other places don't have similar industrial clusters. The difficulty now is that all kinds of problems have been accumulating—growing labor costs, rising constraints on

capital flow, intensified law enforcement, and so on. Except for this year, it has become more difficult for my company to recruit workers. If you add these things together, it's not surprising that people are either moving or going out of business.

Moreover, Peng explained which kinds of companies would decide to relocate and why:

Only larger companies, especially foreign-invested enterprises, can move to countries in Southeast Asia or elsewhere. They began to move in the mid-2000s. Some electronics manufacturers can move with other companies to inland cities like Zhengzhou or Chongqing if they are suppliers of prominent manufacturers, like Foxconn, because larger manufacturers already set up factories in those cities early on to solve labor shortage problems.[26] But for many small manufacturers, relocation is complicated. That's why many people whom I know chose to end their businesses. Some of them have land. Because of their connections with local officials, they could change land classifications, transform their factories into commercial or residential buildings or fake incubators, and make money from the real estate market. Local governments welcome incubators and the real estate industry because they look high-tech and modern and don't have pollution problems.

Peng's observations are consistent with what I heard from other interviewees and informants.

As I mentioned at the beginning of this chapter, I was surprised that most of the Didi drivers I met in Shenzhen and Dongguan were former factory owners or managers. Without exception, all of them pointed to the government's discrimination and campaigns against labor-intensive businesses as the direct cause of their company's bankruptcy. They also noted that they could not simply raise the price of their products because their competitiveness relied on a low pricing strategy.

Some of my interviewees went bankrupt even after relocating to other provinces due to labor or supply chain issues. For example, after encountering increasing law enforcement, Meng, a Didi driver and former owner of a clothing factory in Dongguan, moved his factory to his hometown, Yulin in Guangxi Province. His workers in Dongguan were all migrants and did not mind working overtime, in part because they were single or did not live with their families. In comparison, his workers in Yulin were mostly local people and lived with their families; more specifically, most were mothers and prioritized family obligations over factory work. Meng complained that instead of following work schedules, his workers decided when they wanted to work. When

Meng did not have orders, workers had nothing to do in the factory. But then when Meng received many orders, workers worked slowly and refused to work overtime, despite a higher overtime pay. In the end, Meng was not able to continue his business and sold his equipment. Leaving his wife and child in Yulin, Meng went back to Dongguan to seek other opportunities. Other interviewees who relocated to inland provinces complained about similar labor issues. Some of their workers worked on their family farmland and could not concentrate on factory work. In general, it is more difficult for factory owners and managers to control and manage labor in inland China, where local workers tend to have family obligations and lower dependence on wages.[27] Some interviewees encountered supply chain issues too. For instance, when Du had a factory in Shenzhen, it took him only three days to get all the electronic components; when he moved to Henan, the same process took twenty days, convincing Du that his business was not viable there. In short, relocation often cannot solve problems caused or worsened by the campaigns against obsolete businesses. And as my interviewees pointed out, similar campaigns have occurred elsewhere, albeit at a smaller scale.

What happens after businesses close and relocate? In Shenzhen and Dongguan, empty factories and buildings have been converted into incubators, high-tech industrial parks, and lucrative real estate projects. The high real estate prices in Shenzhen pushed Huawei to establish a center in Dongguan and move thousands of its engineers there.[28] Several executives and managers told me that the new birds in Dongguan are Huawei and the real estate industry. But in a few relatively remote towns in Dongguan, no new birds have moved in since the old birds left.

Workers

During my weeklong research at two companies—Diligence in Dongguan and Jade in Shenzhen—I was able to talk to workers there, both individually and collectively. The two companies are similar. Both have around three hundred employees, all of whom are migrants (mostly from Hunan, Hubei, Jiangxi, and Guangxi Provinces), except for natives hired to grease the companies' relationships with local communities and governments. Many of the workers in the same companies are relatives or come from the same hometowns. Except for managers and IT personnel, employees have a middle or high school education. In both companies, around twenty clerks work in the offices, while production workers work in factory workshops. Most clerk workers are female, and around half the production workers are female. The salaries of clerks are higher than those of unskilled or low-skilled workers, but similar to or lower than the salaries of skilled workers, who tend to have vocational certificates. Usually, male workers perform work that requires machine operation (i.e., "skilled work"). Although both companies provide dormitories, most workers rent an apartment in the local communities and use dormitories only for napping. To retain workers amid the shortage of labor in coastal China, both companies refrain from imposing the kind of disciplinary rules described in studies of "despotic labor regimes."[29] Notably, both Diligence and Jade allow their employees to bring their children to factories or offices for a few hours each day, provided there are no safety problems. In the late afternoon, I saw some children doing homework in the offices.

Group conversations occurred in workshops and offices. I sat and chatted with workers in the workshops, and performed manual work like packaging and quality inspection. The management in both companies also gave me a seat in an office in order to join clerk workers' conversations. In addition, I conducted individual interviews with fifteen workers in each company. Workers were friendly and enthusiastic. Many of them asked me why I would want to talk to "nobodies" like them.

When asked whether they had ever heard of industrial upgrading, workers told me they heard something at vocational schools and on CCTV—a state-owned broadcaster. They know the big picture of industrial and developmental policy and slogans like Made in China 2025, smart manufacturing, and mass entrepreneurship and innovation. They are aware of governmental efforts to advance high-tech industries too. When we discussed these topics in the workshop, young workers turned our conversation into a playful slogan competition. Teasing each other, some observed that they had all forgotten about the China dream, a slogan coined by Xi. Nonetheless, despite their skepticism regarding official slogans, most workers still see labor-intensive manufacturing industries as sunset industries without a future. Such an understanding diverges starkly from that of migrant workers in the early and mid-2000s. Although migrant workers at that time experienced widespread and severe exploitation, research found that they saw themselves and labor-intensive manufacturing more broadly as making an important contribution to the so-called Chinese economic miracle.[30] One factory owner whom I interviewed had worked at Foxconn as a low-skilled worker in the mid-2000s. He reminisced that people felt proud to be manual workers for large manufacturers like Foxconn in the old days. Such pride in "being a worker," however, has been fading away.[31]

Pride in the Techno-Nation

Similar to the official discourse regarding the techno-developmental regime, the workers I talked to used the dichotomies of high-end versus low-end and modern/developed/advanced versus backward/outdated to classify industries, businesses, places, people, and countries. They view their factories, industries, and even the places where their factories are located as outmoded, retrograde, inferior, and somewhat embarrassing. In sharp contrast, companies like Huawei and Tencent, college-educated professionals working in shiny buildings in IT and finance industries, and places like the Nanshan District in Shenzhen and Songshan Lake Science and Technology Industrial Park in Dongguan are understood to be high-end as well as the nation's pride, hope, and future. Both the Nanshan District and Songshan Lake are within an hour's drive of Diligence and Jade. The Nanshan District is where Tencent and other large tech companies are headquartered. With towering skyscrapers, the district has a futuristic landscape. Many workers told me that the district's GDP is higher than those of many high-income countries. The Songshan Lake Science and Technology Industrial Park is where Huawei built a European-themed research campus. When I was at Jade, two workers showed me photos of Huawei's picturesque campus and Tencent's Seafront Towers on social media, while reminding me I should speak with people at Huawei and Tencent in order to understand China's development. I promised them I would. In their view, Tencent, Huawei, and their employees, workplaces, and technologies represent the best of China—a mighty and ascending country.

Most of the workers support the government's effort to upgrade China's economy through S&T, especially in light of the trade war between the United States and China, the US sanctions against Huawei, and Canada's arrest of Huawei's chief financial officer, Meng Wanzhou. The US government's action was perceived by my interviewees as a shameless endeavor to contain China's rise in technology and the global economy. Most workers consider S&T-oriented developmental strategies and national competitions based on S&T to be inevitable. For China to become an advanced and developed country and keep rising on the global stage, it needs high-tech industries. As Xie, a twenty-six-year-old male production worker, said, "Only when China is stronger and possesses more high-end technologies, we won't be looked down on and bullied by other countries." Xie's words echo the speeches of top Chinese leaders. Other workers share a similar sentiment, linking their fate to that of the nation.[32] As members of the nation, they believe they will benefit from the nation's rise and are deeply proud of its global ascendence. Intriguingly, such nationalist sentiments and expressions were virtually absent in my interviews with managers and executives of obsolete businesses, despite the ongoing US-China trade war, because managers and executives in these sectors see themselves and their businesses as being excluded as well as stigmatized by the Chinese state and techno-nation.

Some of the workers, especially those who had been there longer, had heard about campaigns against businesses that are considered scattered, chaotic, polluting, low-end, and/or small by the government, but they knew few details. For instance, workers at Diligence did not know what happened precisely when the spraying workshop was shut down. Most of the workers I talked to perceived pollution as a severe societal problem, so they appreciated the government's effort to protect the environment and police illegal businesses. They did not generally see harsh punishment and changing standards as problems because they think those are the only ways the government can prevent companies from violating the law and polluting the environment. To wit, most workers have a black-and-white view of law and appreciate harsh legal enforcement.

Despite the seeming similarities among workers in terms of how they think about the government's effort to upgrade the economy and identify themselves with the nation, there are noticeable differences between two groups of workers: those without children and those with them. Since most workers consider labor-intensive manufacturing to be low-end and without a future, I asked them how they plan ahead in such an uncertain context. This prompted them to talk about how they viewed not only the nation or society but themselves and their families too. This is also where workers' views start to diverge. Workers without children tend to be in their early to mid-twenties, while workers with children tend to be in their late twenties or early thirties. At both Diligence and Jade, unskilled or low-skilled production workers are more likely to be younger and single, and they comprise the majority of the workforce. In comparison, clerk workers and skilled production workers tend to be older, and are more likely than unskilled or low-skilled workers to have children.

No Strings Attached

Let me speak first about unskilled or low-skilled workers without children. They were mostly born in the mid- to late 1990s and grew up in an uneasy environment. A large proportion of them were the so-called left-behind children, whose parents went to cities as migrant workers. Some of these workers lived with their grandparents, while others stayed with their siblings or even lived alone as children. As such, they were not migrant children who stayed with their parents in cities for a considerable period of time.[33] In individual conversations, several of them told me their childhood experiences made them feel abandoned and emotionally distant from their parents. They decided to work in Dongguan or Shenzhen in order to experience urban life and explore the cities' opportunities.

Since the majority of unskilled or low-skilled workers without children went to vocational schools, mostly secondary specialized schools (*zhongzhuan*), and several even enrolled in electrical engineering or computing programs,

I was surprised by the fact that they were doing tasks that do not require training or expertise. Consistent with research on vocational education in China, my interviewees complained that they learned little at vocational schools, and confronted an enormous gap between what they were taught and the actual skills recognized or needed at workplaces.[34] Some of my interviewees applied to jobs that aligned better with their programs at vocational schools, but they were told that those jobs require a technical college (*dazhuan*) degree. They said this is because companies could receive benefits from the government by hiring college-educated employees. Indeed, this is related to local governments' performance evaluation systems and indicators that governments use to evaluate and classify firms. For my interviewees, vocational schools are de facto profit-seeking human agency companies. Benefiting from governmental subsidies and commissions from corporations, vocational schools dispatch cheap student interns and graduates to factories, hotels, public security bureaus, and other workplaces.[35] When my interviewees had their first job after graduation, a proportion of their salaries was often deducted by their schools as commissions.

Many of the young workers pursue an urban consumerism lifestyle. Fashion, smartphones, video gaming, cuisine, and gambling are among the most common conversation topics in their daily lives. They told me material consumption makes them feel proud of themselves among their peers. Despite their difficult upbringing, their material condition is better than that of the previous generation of migrant workers. Unlike their parents, these interviewees do not marry young or have children. Also, their parents do not have to rely on their income. As former migrant workers, many of their parents sent remittances home regularly and eventually returned to their hometown after accumulating savings for years. Since their parents have significantly improved the family's financial situation, this younger generation of unskilled or low-skilled workers only needs to feed themselves. Some of them receive financial support from their parents to experience and sustain urban lives. Due to these relatively comfortable material conditions and low family responsibilities, the workers I spoke with feel there is little at stake if and when they quit a job.

In addition, younger and childless workers tend to consider manufacturing jobs undesirable and stigma laden.[36] Although both Diligence and Jade do not have strict disciplinary rules like Foxconn, young workers complain about having limited freedom to arrange their time. Moreover, they dislike the repetitiveness and unskillfulness of jobs. None of my interviewees feel they have learned anything from their jobs. Most interviewees said it took them no more than a few days to master their work, unless they are required to operate a machine—a task that many find daunting. Such perceptions and evaluations of work differ notably from what I heard from several current and former factory owners and managers, who told me they had learned different components and aspects of the manufacturing process and how to do business from being a low-skilled worker and climbing up job ladders in FIEs. Indeed, the mobility from workers to factory owners that I have observed in China was also a salient pattern in the industrialization process in Taiwan.[37] The differences between the two generations of migrant workers in China could be, in part, related to the increasing denunciation of working-class culture. Parents of migrant workers do not want their children to follow in their footsteps by working in factories. Instead, working-class parents want their kids to enter the middle class. Likewise, education at vocational school highlights upward social mobility and emphasizes the notion of being "masters of their own life." Scholars have found a common resistance to working-class jobs, especially manual work, among working-class-origin vocational school students.[38] Given the realities of the labor market, however, many vocational school graduates, like my interviewees, still end up in manual factory jobs, despite their aspirations to pursue something else.

Most of my interviewees have stepwise plans for their future. A manual factory job is merely transitional, and at most, an unimportant stepping stone to their goal. Their ultimate aim is to be their own boss, establishing small businesses like restaurants, beauty salons, supermarkets, and cloth shops (definitely not factories), or pursuing self-employment. This is consistent with research that shows the prevalence of the "middle-class idea of the enterprising self" in China due to the state apparatus, educational and employment systems, and individual and family aspiration.[39]

With manufacturing jobs seen as so undesirable, the turnover rate of unskilled or low-skilled workers is high. The labor shortage in factories also makes my interviewees believe it will be easy to find another factory job. As they see manufacturing only as a transitional job that can help them explore urban life, they are indifferent to the decline of labor-intensive manufacturing industries, relocation or closure of factories, and government's campaigns against obsolete businesses. As Xiao expressed firmly,

I'm not going to stay in the factory. This is just a temporary part of my life, so what has happened in the manufacturing sector is irrelevant to me. My future is not here. I want to do my own business on the internet. Now I use this job to accumulate some capital for my future business. Most of the people I know want to go back to their hometown and establish their own businesses. No matter how difficult it is, everyone wants to try to create their own business.

Several interviewees, especially female workers, think service jobs in supermarkets or beauty salons can probably give them more freedom and social interaction. Yet it is common for them to return to a factory job after finding a service job wanting. But even disappointing experiences in the service sector do not prompt them to commit to or appreciate work in the manufacturing sector. Several female interviewees also pointed out that their mothers expected them to "find a husband before getting old." Many male workers consider quitting their jobs to work as service workers in the rising platform sector. Indeed, Diligence and Jade's managers complained that they have been losing workers to the platform sector, particularly food delivery platforms. Manager Li said,

> Jade has a relatively low turnover rate than many other companies. I talked to every single employee when they left their job here. This year, several female workers quit their job to take care of their children in their hometown. Many male workers, including line leaders, quit their job to work as food delivery workers for Metituan and Ele.me because they believe they would make more money. . . . Those platform companies are not regulated. They don't pay social insurance. I feel it's unfair competition. The government doesn't regulate them, but we have to follow the labor law and other laws. As a result, workers might get higher salaries if they work for platform companies and do not think about social insurance. It [the uneven regulatory environment] makes it challenging to compete with platform companies for workers.

In chapter 7, I turn to the experiences of factory workers who have moved to the platform sector. Ultimately, the general sense I derived from my interviews and observations is that young workers without children have no attachment to manual work or labor-intensive manufacturing industries. As they plan to leave their job and the manufacturing sector sooner or later, they care little about how the government's policies and other factors impact the sector or its future.

Discontent

On the surface, although it seems that most workers agree with the government's techno-developmental policy and are proud of the nation's techno-development, at least one group of workers—those with children—do not wholly support the techno-developmental regime. Against the backdrop of the ongoing US-China trade war and hostile governmental policies, I was curious whether the difficulties experienced by labor-intensive manufacturers would lead to management problems and rising labor contention. But all the executives and managers told me they did not experience strikes or other collective actions, and had not even heard about such instances in recent years in their localities, except for one or two cases in which companies violated the labor law. Some managers told me they only knew of protests for access to public school. For example, manager Fan in Dongguan stated,

> Recent protests here were about school issues because migrant workers' children have difficulties going to local public schools under the point-based school admission system. In the old days, the government gave my company some quotas for employees' children to go to local public schools. The quotas have gradually decreased and then disappeared. Now the government gives quotas to high-tech companies like Huawei because people there are talent and people in my factory are low-end.

The point-based school admission system and quotas are part of the growing instrumental apparatus that aim to foster techno-development.

After hearing similar observations from managers in other companies, I asked around at Diligence. One worker had heard about such protests from her colleague Cheng, who is her sister-in-law as well. The worker kindly brought me to meet with Cheng in Cheng's office. It turned out that Cheng and another clerk, Chang, went to the township government to protest for access to local public schools in 2018. Hearing our discussion, a group of clerks and skilled workers who had not themselves protested but did have children also joined our conversations. Everyone was furious and frustrated.

These workers all brought their children with them, despite the difficulties and expense, because they did not want their kids to become left-behind children. To do well in the point-based household registration and school admission systems, many adopted the same strategy: getting a national-level vocational certificate to boost their points. Usually, female workers get vocational training and certifications in infant care, although infant care has nothing to do with their work, and they do not plan to be infant caregivers. Male workers are more likely to get certificates related to their work, such as skills connected to the molding process. Nonetheless, the consensus among male skilled workers and managers is that the training programs and exams are superficial and pointless. One manager told me his wife participated in an accounting training program. In the end, the training institute arranged for someone to take the exam for her and give her a certificate. All the workers agreed that the training programs and certificates only serve the purpose of point-based household registration and school admission systems. Here we can see that not only officials and businesses but also workers feel they must game systems to survive. When I talked to these workers, I was astounded—and in fact, appalled—by their familiarity with how many points different qualifications are worth in the metric system.

In addition, my interviewees noted that the township government outsources training programs to institutes connected to local officials. Mei shared her experience with me:

> I paid eighteen hundred RMB for the infant care training program, but the institute returned me twenty-two hundred RMB after I got my certificate. I actually earned four hundred RMB. The government has budgets for these training programs, and their own people profit from such programs. I don't understand this. If they have so much money, why don't they use the money to build more public schools for migrant children? They create useless programs to benefit themselves and waste taxpayers' money.

The sad, unexpected, and unacceptable fact for these workers is that getting a household registration status or accumulating points still does not guarantee access to local public schools. For many workers, getting a local household registration status means giving up their right to collective land and other benefits in their hometown. In other words, they pay a high price in exchange for their children's access to local schools. Cheng and Chang told me that the township government promised local public school access to people with household registration status, but their children were denied entry to local schools and instead assigned to faraway ones in another town. As migrants, they have no family members who can transport their children to or from distant schools. And there are no school buses available.

Cheng and Chang told me that after the government announced the admission results in 2018, one parent formed a social media group that eventually attracted more than five hundred parents. Then angry parents went to the township government to demand an explanation. At first the government did not respond to their demands. The second time the parents went to the township offices, the vice mayor eventually came out to speak with them. According to Cheng and Chang, the vice mayor said, "Even people with a housing property here don't have access to school. You guys are propertyless. Why do you think your children deserve a space at local public schools? What is your contribution and qualification?" When the protesting parents refused to leave the government building, the township government compromised and gave them seats in local public schools, although the locations were still quite far away. Meanwhile, the township government detained one of the parents for two days, and information transmitted within and from their social media group was censored.

Hearing what Cheng and Chang said, the workers who joined the conversation all expressed their rage. Wang, a skilled worker, angrily showed me a table that lists the number of students who can go to local public schools in Dongguan through the point-based school admission system. Wang's colleagues presented me with other tables containing metric systems for school access too. I was shocked by the fact that they carried such tables with them, almost as if these tables were precious objects. Indeed, the tables were crucial to the future of their dearest children. In their town, of more than eight hundred thousand residents, only two hundred students could access the local public schools through the point system. Wang commented that "the top 200 kids must have affluent and highly educated parents, not proletariats like us. In the end, poor kids have to go to private schools and pay for expensive tuitions, while children from well-off or talent families can go to public schools and use their money for tutoring services." Although some of my interviewees can get subsidies from the government to pay for part of the tuition fees, the tuition fees remain high for migrant workers.

These workers with children thus see a cruel reality deviating from what they were taught at school and by the government. Growing up, they learned that China is led by the working class and founded on the alliance of workers and peasants. In their own lives, though, they have learned that not only workers and peasants but also the children of workers and peasants are looked down on and sacrificed by the government. This realization strengthens their conviction that their children should not be workers like them. These interviewees compare themselves with two other social groups: wealthy natives from local communities and highly educated talents in high-tech industries. Local people are not highly educated, but they are the rentier class (*shouzu jieji*). Tech talents enjoy all the policy benefits and are the "pillar of the nation." Workers with children are willing to accept their treatment by the state and their position in the social hierarchy, but they have struggled to "change the fate" of their children. They believe their children will have no way to compete with those of the local rentier class and tech talents in an economy based on knowledge and S&T. For example, Tao articulated this grim comparison,

> Inequality between rich and poor is enormous. Tuitions for tutoring services are nothing for local or high-tech people, but the tuitions can be our annual income. Although local people do not have a lot of culture (*wenhua*), they have money to pay for tutoring services. Local families don't interact with our children and us because we are poor and not educated. Talents in high-tech companies are rich and intelligent. The government has built several excellent and beautiful schools for their children around the Songshan Lake. Those people have culture and know how to educate

their children. How can our children compete with theirs? Our children cannot even go to local public schools.

My interviewees also collectively criticized the point-based household registration and school admission systems. On the one hand, they think it is good that there are ways in which their children might get access to public schools. On the other hand, they believe the criteria are unfair and do not guarantee access to school. Cheng reasoned,

> Basically, they [the system] classify people into three, six, or nine categories (*san, liu, jiu deng*). People have different worth in the system depending on whether they belong to the property class and their education level. Under this system, our children already lost the race at the starting point. It's unlikely that they would become talents and work for high-tech companies in the future. . . . Fairness is not an essential criterion in China. To our government, the value of a person depends on their contribution or their parent's contribution to the local economy. . . . Corruption is rampant here, and the government has spent enormous money on unnecessary things. If the government can save money, how many more schools can they build? Now the government talks about industrial upgrading. In the future, our children might not even have factory jobs. Now many manufacturing companies have moved to countries in Southeast Asia and Africa. Our children might eventually become migrant workers there.

Since some of the workers had worked in the area for ten years, I asked them why they did not consider buying a housing property there to get more points. They said the housing prices have kept rising, and they also do not know how long their company and industry can sustain themselves there.

Unexpectedly, although the workers with children whom I spoke to are proud of China's techno-development and the country's rise, they still argued for different priorities—namely that the government should "raise the education first and then work on high technology" (*xian ba jiaoyu tiqilai, zaigao gaokeji*). Otherwise, these workers fear their children will continue to be excluded from the techno-nation and remain outsiders to the China dream. I have not been able to forget the image painted by Jin: "We have so many splendid buildings in Shenzhen and Dongguan. Every company is like Huawei, and everything is high-tech. Our country is doing great. But behind this scene are poor ordinary people like me and my family. We are struggling to survive painfully. We are so close to them, but we are far away." Despite the spatial proximity of Jin's factory and family to high-tech companies along with professionals and their families, she was all too aware of the socially distant and segregated worlds in the techno-nation.

Conclusion

This chapter focuses on old birds—businesses and social groups perceived as obsolete by the state—and their interaction with local states in China's techno-developmental regime. Scholarship on developmental states revolves around the state's role in nurturing new sectors.[40] Similarly, influenced by Keynesian economics, Daniel Bell's work on postindustrial transformation accentuates the role of the state in using instruments to plan for techno-development.[41] Different from the classical examples of developmental states like South Korea and Taiwan, and Bell's expectation about the state's role in postindustrial transformation, the Chinese state developed an arsenal of instruments to not only cultivate new birds but crack down on old birds too. As a result, old birds are subject to both market forces and the unpredictable disciplinary power of the state. In a way, local states were essentially hoping to accelerate the process of creative destruction by disciplining, if not destroying, obsolete businesses.

Despite their different roles in the economy, businesses, local government officials, and workers with children all share similar experiences of struggling with the enlarging instrumental apparatus that constitutes the techno-developmental regime. In chapter 3, I showed that the consolidation of the techno-development regime galvanized the state's efforts to scientize its statecraft and build expansive valuation and evaluation systems. In this chapter, we see legal instruments are also part of the instrumental apparatus. Various kinds of regulations, particularly environmental, safety, and construction regulations, have been reoriented or repurposed by local governments to facilitate techno-development. Furthermore, governments have made numerous new regulations and administrative standards. I have shown how businesses wrestle to survive within this unpredictable regulatory environment, local officials struggle to meet their evaluation standards, and workers with children grapple with various point systems to get access to local public school. Yet I found common efforts to game the systems, as demonstrated by businesses that faked their legal classification, officials who received kickbacks from high- and new-tech businesses by forcing obsolete businesses to purchase equipment from the former, and workers who attended irrelevant vocational trainings to get certificates and more points for their children.

The enactment of the techno-developmental regime through intensified and routinized legal enforcement campaigns and government performance evaluation systems has led to a capricious as well as punitive regulatory environment for industries and businesses deemed outmoded by the government.[42] But obsolete businesses have refrained from voicing their grievances because they receive no moral or discursive support in the dominant sociotechnical imaginaries. Seeing themselves as members of the ascending techno-

nation and having no attachment to manual work, most workers in the up-
dated sectors are not concerned about the uncertain future of them. The only
group that has challenged the techno-developmental regime is migrant workers with children.

In recent years, legal scholars have debated whether China has been turning
toward or away from the law. Some argue that China has been retreating from
legal reform back into unchecked authoritarianism since the mid-2000s,
whereas other assert that Chinese politics have in fact become substantially
more law-oriented under Xi's leadership.[43] The experience of obsolete businesses suggests that how one views this debate depends on what law means.[44]
On the one hand, the regulatory measures taken by local governments against
obsolete businesses are technically based on laws or regulations, despite their
political nature. In fact, I reviewed the legal documents that Diligence received
from the local government, and found the decision and documents adequate
in their form. On the other hand, when public authorities can change regulations easily, and there is no effective channel to hold public authority accountable for its law/regulation making and implementation, the form of law does
not automatically translate into institutional stability, let alone procedural or
substantive justice.

It is thus understandable that my interviewees have two types of reactions
to legal enforcement against obsolete businesses. Most workers view the government's action positively because they approach the issue from the legal/il-
legal binary, without considering institutional stability, or questioning the
procedural or substantive adequacy of law or legal process. They think unlawful
behavior deserves harsh punishment, which in turn can deter illegal behavior.
As legal scholars maintain, launching legal enforcement campaigns—regardless
of their impacts on specific social groups or society as a whole—can benefit the
performance legitimacy of the government because those campaigns signal the
state's commitment to the people, environmental protection, and the legal
order.[45] In contrast, business actors who suffer from the campaigns criticize the
absence of the rule of law based on concerns about institutional stability along
with procedural and substantive justice.

As research has shown, the central government under the Xi leadership has
attempted to curb the power of officials and local governments by launching
anticorruption campaigns, centralizing power, cutting ties between local businesses and officials, and using technology to decrease the discretion of officials.[46] Paradoxically, however, the rise of the techno-developmental regime
has been accompanied by rampant predatory behavior. Although my interviewees pointed out that asking for bribery in cash has become less frequent,
abusing public authority to receive private benefits in other forms is rampant.
The most common type of predatory behavior is using public authority to

specify providers of equipment and service. Also, thanks to the benefits accorded by the government to high-tech enterprises, patent certificate holders, and holders of vocational certificates under the techno-developmental regime's classification and metric systems, local officials profit from brokering businesses and people to receive such certificates. Essentially, despite the central government's effort to curb public power, its extraordinary attempts to build an arsenal of instruments to foster techno-development have created new opportunities for officials to profit from the new metrics of who and what can be counted as "adequate" technology, capital, and labor.

Research on developmental states tends to conceptualize developmental and predatory states as mutually exclusive categories. For instance, Peter Evans wrote that "predatory states extract at the expense of society, undercutting development even in the narrow sense of capital accumulation. Developmental states not only have presided over industrial transformation but can be plausibly argued to have played a role in making it happen."[47] And yet research on China has shown that the Chinese state is simultaneously developmental and predatory. Thanks to certain profit-sharing mechanisms between local governments and businesses, scholars contend that local officials engage in "organized" and relatively restrained corruption so that officials can benefit from businesses' long-term development in the forms of governmental extrabudgetary revenue and personal income. In other words, local governments have incentive to "nurture" their "golden geese."[48] But existing scholarship has not yet examined the changing nature of these golden geese. As I have demonstrated, local governments have been extracting resources from obsolete businesses through legal enforcement campaigns to create a domestic market for high- and new-tech enterprises to prosper. As such, the relationship of local governments to old birds is predatory, but caring to new birds. Meanwhile, it is unclear how long obsolete businesses can sustain themselves under such extraction.

The perceptions and experiences of workers at outmoded businesses under the rising techno-developmental regime differ tremendously from those workers who experienced deindustrialization in China's rust belt in the 1990s and 2000s, when the Chinese state restructured SOEs. With a well-established working-class identity, SOE workers found themselves degraded from masters to losers, and laden with shame and pain, regardless of whether they were laid off or still employed. SOE pensioners and laid-off workers mobilized socialist ideology to protest and fight for their survival.[49] The young migrant workers whom I studied also differ from migrant workers in the early and mid-2000s; back then, they felt proud to be manual workers. Although the rising techno-developmental regime has adversely impacted labor-intensive manufacturing industries, most of the workers to whom I spoke are proud of the nation's technological progress and see the shift to an S&T-oriented developmental model as crucial for the country. As I have shown, the majority of workers—particularly those who are young and without children—are indifferent to the adverse impacts of the techno-developmental regime on labor-intensive manufacturing industries because they view factory jobs as undesirable and transitional. They do not see dignity in or satisfaction with their work. Their view is understandable given that they grew up in an environment when China experienced extraordinary economic growth, had abundant opportunities, produced a whole generation of nouveau riche, and became one of the largest economies and S&T powerhouses in the world. They grew up in a context when the Chinese government doubled down on its patriotic education too.[50]

Interestingly and surprisingly, the only protests that I have observed in the obsolete sectors have been sparked not by unemployment, job security, or working conditions but rather by the state's discriminatory metrics against children of the working class.[51] In *The Coming of Post-Industrial Society*, Bell already foresaw increasing competition over access to education as the importance of S&T in the economy grows.[52] My findings show that as migrant workers recognize the heightened significance of education in techno-development, they have begun to question institutional disparities and the reproduction of inequality within the techno-nation.

Despite the plight of obsolete businesses, there are ways in which these businesses can disassociate themselves from obsolescence. One way is through robotization. In the next chapter, I explain how the Chinese state and labor-intensive manufacturers have endeavored to advance techno-development through robotization.

5

Robotization

IN CHAPTER 4, I described the experiences of businesses and workers deemed obsolete by the Chinese state. In this chapter, I explain what has happened to manufacturers, low-skilled workers, technicians, engineers, and local officials as firms and the state have turned to a common strategy as well as seeming solution to the problem of upgrading businesses and fostering techno-development: robotization. Here I use the term *robots* to refer to mechanical devices that "can be programmed to perform a variety of tasks of manipulation and locomotion under automatic control."[1] Since robots can be manipulated through programming, they are more flexible than other types of automation devices. Daniel Bell used the example of computer programmable and nonprogrammable machines in his work to show the difference between intellectual versus and mechanical technologies. He argued that industrial and postindustrial societies were characterized by mechanical and intellectual technologies, respectively.[2] I am interested in robots because of the simultaneous promise and threat—both material and symbolic—they represent within China's techno-developmental regime.

Before turning to this discussion, let me briefly explain concerns and academic debates about automation, which encompasses robotization. For two centuries, humans have been worried about whether and how automation technology might replace human labor. Concern regarding automation can be traced back to the Luddite movement in Britain in the early nineteenth century.[3] Some four decades later, people's feelings about automation remained just as fraught, leading Karl Marx to write, "In machinery, objectified labour materially confronts living labour as a ruling power and as an active subsumption of the latter under itself."[4]

Politicians in the United States and United Kingdom attempted to take advantage of the opportunities and address the challenges brought about by automation in the 1960s. Dubbed "the automotive age" by British labor politician Harold Wilson at the time, the 1960s saw a growing number of politicians, trade union leaders, and scholars as well as the public at large, in both the

United States and United Kingdom, seeking to reckon with the new levels of automation enabled by computers and program-controlled machines. Indeed, the transformative power of technology was central to British Labour Party policy in that decade. On the other side of the Atlantic, people in the United States similarly sought to understand and respond to a rapidly changing society. In 1964, reacting to concerns about the impact of technological changes, especially automation, on employment against the backdrop of substantial and persistent unemployment since the 1950s, President Lyndon B. Johnson formed the National Commission on Technology, Automation, and Economic Progress. Bell and Robert Solow, the economics Nobel laureate who theorized technological progress as the major driver of economic growth, both served as commission members.[5] According to President Johnson, the commission's purpose was to understand "what is to come" so that the country could take advantage of the opportunities created by technology for greater productivity and progress, while also ensuring that "no working man, no family, must pay an unjust price for progress."[6] Like Wilson, Johnson embraced automation technology on the condition that it would benefit all, not just a select few.[7]

Today, automation manifests most commonly in robots. In recent years, the rapid development of robotics and AI has triggered concerns about unemployment and underemployment.[8] A study in the United States shows that people with less education, nonwhite minorities, and females express the most apprehension about robots, AI, and unemployment.[9] A study of European countries finds that 74 percent of respondents express concern about robots and believe AI would threaten more jobs than it would create, although more educated Europeans are less worried. According to the same survey, respondents who had heard of AI were more likely to have a favorable view of it. An analysis of low- and middle-skilled workers in eleven economically developed and developing countries finds that workers feel more positive than negative about automation. Still, negative perceptions are prevalent among older, poorer, and less educated workers.[10] A study of workers in the United Kingdom complements the above ones by showing that workers support technical change when they see it as progress and investment for longer-term job security.[11] Scholars further compare workers' attitudes across eleven countries and find that workers in economically developing countries tend to be more positive about automation than those in economically developed countries; also, workers in China have the second-least-negative view on automation.[12]

Moreover, technological development in robots and AI has rekindled scholarly debate over the extent to which automation actually displaces human labor. Most studies have been conducted by labor economists. Unfortunately, scholars have no consensus on the issue. In its analysis of the relationship between technology and labor displacement, one group of labor economists focuses on workers' skills because it theorizes that the level of skill influences labor displacement. The group specifically posits that technology favors high-skilled workers and disadvantages low-skilled ones. Since high-skilled workers are capable of using technology to increase production, technological advancement creates demand for them; in contrast, low-skilled workers will be replaced by technology.[13] This view resembles that of sociologists who contend that automation leads to an increase in workers' skills as workers are expected to learn new technologies.[14]

In comparison, another group of economists argues that the first group cannot explain the continued existence of low-skilled jobs and occupational polarization—employment growth in both high- and low-skilled occupations—in economically developed countries. For the second group, it is the nature of tasks, specifically the characteristic of routinization, rather than the skills required that determines whether machines can replace human labor. It maintains that technology can replace human labor in routine tasks—activities that can be expressed in step-by-step procedures—but not nonroutine tasks. Routine tasks are characterized by middle-skilled cognitive and manual activities. Nonroutine tasks encompass high-skilled cognitive and low-skilled manual activities. Nonroutine manual tasks, such as cleaning, make up low-skilled jobs in the service sector. The material constraint of technology in substituting for nonroutine tasks and the movement of people from routine, middle-skilled jobs to nonroutine, low-skilled jobs have led to occupational polarization.[15] Scholarship that specifically analyzes the impact of robotization on employment remains scant, and the results are mixed.[16] While some research shows negative impacts of robotization on employment in general, other work finds positive effects.[17]

Notwithstanding these scholarly debates, research does suggest that low-skilled workers and/or workers who perform routine tasks are more likely to be replaced by robotization or automation, broadly speaking. Also, less educated workers are more likely to feel threatened by technology. Since workers in China's labor-intensive manufacturing tend to be less educated, have low-skilled jobs, and perform routine tasks, business actors and the state's embrace of robotization could threaten such workers. In this chapter, I detail how the state, manufacturers, low-skilled workers, technicians, and engineers have variously perceived and made decisions about robotization under China's techno-developmental regime.

The Chinese State's Robot Dream

As argued in chapter 3, techno-developmental policy in China promotes the transformation of the demographic dividend into a talent, and even a robot dividend. Let us look first at the central state's policy. According to economist

Barry Naughton and his colleagues, starting in 2006, the Chinese central government enacted the Medium- and Long-Term Plan for Science and Technology, and gradually built out a planning and industrial policy process.[18] The central planners invested in knowledge and procedures that gave them the ability to carry out industrial and technological policies, as demonstrated by the creation of information resources and targets or KPIs.[19] As shown in chapter 3, my findings align with those of Naughton and his colleagues. I examined the turn to techno-development in coastal provinces in the mid-2000s and support of that endeavor from the central government, such as the Ministry of Commerce. In 2008, the Ministry of Science and Technology, Ministry of Finance, and State Administration of Taxation jointly issued the Administrative Measures for the Determination of High- and New-Tech Enterprises (hereafter Administrative Measures). The Corporate Income Tax Law, which came into effect on January 1, 2008, provides a reduced 15 percent corporate income tax rate for high- and new-tech enterprises, compared to the regular rate of 25 percent.[20] According to the Administrative Measures, to be qualified as high and new tech, an enterprise's products or services must fall within one of the following eight categories: electronic IT, biological and medical technology, aviation and space technology, new materials technology, high-tech services, new energy and energy conservation technology, environmental technology, or transformation of traditional sectors through high and new technology. Robotics falls into the last category.[21]

Indeed, the Chinese state has perceived robotics as a high-end manufacturing industry. As China imported robots from companies in high-income countries, developing robotics has been one of China's top domestic priorities since the early 2010s.[22] This was evidenced by Made in China 2025.[23] The Chinese state viewed Germany as a model to emulate because of the latter's strength in high-end manufacturing. Accordingly, Germany's "Industrie 4.0" plan served as point of reference for Made in China 2025. On paper, both plans share the same stress on a new round of industrial revolution, featuring such innovations as manufacturing digitization, cyberphysical systems, the IoT, intelligent manufacturing. Nonetheless, one of the key differences between the two plans is that many goals stated in Made in China 2025 remain aspirational in the short term due to the different levels of industrial development in Germany and China.[24] The technological changes promoted under Made in China 2025 do not, in reality, aim to achieve fully "networked" or "digitized" manufacturing. As such, most automation projects in China are at the "industry 3.0" stage, which highlights partial automation using programmable controls and computers, as opposed to the "industry 4.0" stage outlined in the German plan.

China's national policy did not mention human-machine substitution, but by 2013, the province of Zhejiang launched an initiative explicitly focused on replacing humans with robots and other automated machinery in order to facilitate techno-development. As mentioned in chapter 3, Zhejiang was one of the provinces that received the most migrant workers, and one of the earliest provinces to embrace techno-developmental policy based on what I described as the bird/cage logic. In 2013, the Zhejiang provincial government spotlighted four techno-developmental agendas: emptying the cage and changing the bird; replacing humans with robots; allocating land according to outputs per unit of land; and advancing the digital economy.[25] The province announced in 2013 that it would implement five thousand human-machine substitution projects every year in the five-year period and invest 500,000 million RMB (around US$78,414 million) in the projects.[26] For a reference, Zhejiang's expenditure on education was 19,319 million RMB in 2013.[27] Zhejiang's policy considered the robotics industry a promising new bird. Through robotization, labor-intensive manufacturers could avoid being designated as old birds by local states. Zhejiang's agenda was soon disseminated to other provinces. For instance, Guangdong enacted a similar policy in 2014. Across all the localities, the policies sought to both facilitate the upgrading of traditional industries and cultivate China's robotics industry. Subsidies were offered as incentives for businesses to invest in robots.[28] By encouraging businesses to upgrade through robotization, local states created a massive market for domestic robotics firms. The human-machine substitution initiative thus resembles the policing of obsolete businesses through law enforcement campaigns in the sense that both agendas could help domestic high- and new-tech enterprises to prosper.

In general, local policies reveal a symbolic dichotomy of progress and backwardness. Policy documents consistently place human labor—with the exception of workers who can create or use high-end technology—on the backward side of the dichotomy. Such valuation partly explains why the policy documents on human-robot substitution that I collected and reviewed never allude to the potential social consequences of the initiative on workers or the problem of labor shortage faced by manufacturers.[29] Instead, the policy documents emphasize only the imperative to upgrade China's industrial structure as well as cultivate indigenous robotics manufacturers and industry. It is true that scholars expected a looming aging crisis and the gradual disappearance of a "demographic dividend" in the mid-2010s.[30] Yet China still had 268.94 million migrant workers in 2013, among which 84.45 million worked in manufacturing.[31] The absolute silence on the lives of migrant workers in manufacturing reveals the appalling indifference of local governments to their fate.

The national sociotechnical imaginaries both reflected and reproduced by China's robotization policies envision a specific set of state-capital-labor-technology relations, perhaps better described as "state-capital-*talent*-

technology" relations. The state directs businesses and talent—people with high-level human capital—to mobilize technology. Although the British and US national sociotechnical imaginaries in the 1960s along with the current national sociotechnical imaginary in China are all characterized by enthusiasm for technology, the Chinese version is distinct in its proactive and unconditional pursuit of automation as well as its silence on issues of unemployment, labor protection, and social equality.[32] Despite the shortage of young workers in coastal China, millions of low-skilled workers are still employed in the manufacturing sectors and could be exposed to potential risks brought about by technological changes. The United States and United Kingdom had a more cautiously optimistic take on automation in the 1960s, acknowledging potential tensions between technology and labor and the issues of inequality and social mobility. Their national sociotechnical imaginaries include firms, labor unions, workers, schools, R&D personnel, and government agencies as stakeholders, whereas the Chinese version only includes governments, firms, and those high-skilled workers deemed talent as the main stakeholders. This difference can be attributed, in part, to the robust union activism in the United States and United Kingdom during the 1960s, whereas independent labor unions do not exist in China.[33]

Robotization in Electronics Manufacturing

To examine the perceptions and practices of local states, manufacturers, low-skilled workers, technicians, and engineers under China's techno-developmental regime, I visited six electronics manufacturing companies in the Pearl River Delta between 2017 and 2019, and conducted 106 interviews (see table 5.1). Concentrated in Guangdong, electronics manufacturing is the second-largest market for industrial robots in China.[34] The industry employs millions of low-skilled workers who conduct routine, manual work that requires little training or education. Electronics manufacturers emphasize standardization in the production process, eliminating all unnecessary actions in an effort to maximize production efficiency. Some manufacturers even calculate the time in seconds required for various tasks to ensure workers meet production goals in terms of quantity, quality, and speed.

I studied six electronics manufacturers, beginning with Apollo, the largest manufacturer among them. The research was then expanded to examine the other five manufacturers. Since scholars have found a positive correlation between firm size and the probability of robot adoption, I included manufacturers of varying sizes.[35] At the time of research, Apollo had over two hundred thousand employees, Bacchus and Clio had around fifteen and six thousand employees, respectively, and Dike, Eris, and Flora had between two to five

TABLE 5.1. Distribution of Interviewees in Six Electronics Manufacturing Companies

		Count (n = 106)			
	Manufacturer	Executives or managers (n = 27)	Low-skilled workers (n = 65)	Technicians (n = 4)	Engineers (n = 10)
1	Apollo	15	22	2	4
2	Bacchus	3	10	1	1
3	Clio	3	9	0	1
4	Dike	2	8	0	2
5	Eris	2	8	0	1
6	Flora	2	8	1	1

hundred employees. The six manufacturers are similar in that about 83 percent of their respective employees are low-skilled workers performing routine manual tasks. All the manufacturers allowed me to visit their facilities.

I interviewed executives, managers, workers, engineers, and technicians currently or previously employed by one of the six manufacturers. The low-skilled workers I interviewed all conducted routine manual work, mostly on assembly lines. Like the workers I talked to in chapter 4, most of them here had a middle or high school level of education. There were many more interviewees at Apollo as it was the original case study. After gaining plentiful information at Apollo, I needed fewer interviews with employees of the other companies to gather general industry-level information. I also interviewed two government officials with knowledge about industrial policies in two cities in the Pearl River Delta. Most of the interviews were done face-to-face, while some were conducted over the phone. In addition to formal interviews, I had casual conversations with executives, managers, workers, and engineers.

Local Techno-Developmental States

Chen and Huang were two municipal-level government officials whom I interviewed. During the interviews, they both showed me several booklets published by their respective offices that featured successful cases of robotization in their cities. Each case study introduced a company, its robotization project, and the effect of robotization on production and employment. Here is a typical example of the description in such case studies in the booklets:

The project lowered business and production costs and optimized the human resources structure. After robotization, the cost of material was reduced by A percent, and the number of employees decreased from B to C. In terms of human resources structure, the percentage of technical talent grew from D to E percent. Therefore the project transformed the employment structure from operational workers to technical personnel. The project also increased production efficiency and shortened product delivery cycles. The production value per employee rose from F RMB to G RMB. Robotization improved the quality of production too. The product yield rate increased by H percent.

Chen and Huang's offices distributed such booklets to local manufacturers in the hope that the latter would emulate the exemplars.

Consistent with China's national sociotechnical imaginaries, Chen and Huang saw technology and talent as key to upgrading China's economy, and viewed the state as responsible for helping manufacturers obtain technology and talent. Both officials felt that the days of manufacturers relying on low-skilled labor were obsolete. Both were proud of the state's robotization plans, which, they argued, would increase traditional manufacturers' efficiency, make them high tech, and create a market for China's domestic robotics industry to prosper.

Both officials were silent on certain issues until I asked about them. First, the question of robots replacing human workers, as debated by economists, seemed to be of no concern.[36] Neither interviewee worried about evidence of human-robot substitution; indeed, they saw it as the point of the entire program and relied on firms to provide them with statistics that would hopefully show progress in this regard. Secondly, neither Chen nor Huang talked about whether government subsidies for robotization achieved a satisfying investment return rate. They were in fact indifferent about this issue as it was irrelevant to their evaluation by higher-level governments. Their task was to ensure that they spent budgets on human-robot substitution. Third, both officials were uninterested in automation's impact on the lives of low-skilled workers and reasoned that most such workers were migrants anyway, who in the words of Chen, should "go elsewhere or return home when they cannot survive here." Chen and Huang's apathy toward migrant workers was due to China's household registration system, which as noted earlier, denies migrants full access to social welfare benefits in places migrants do not have a household registration status.[37] Also, the life situations of migrant workers were not part of Chen and Huang's performance evaluation. According to Chen and Huang, getting a local household registration status became easier in their cities, but the system prefers granting the status to talent instead of low-skilled workers.

Once again, we see the expanding instrumental apparatus under China's techno-developmental regime. In both Chen and Huang's cities, local states employed performance evaluation to ensure the implementation of the human-robot substitution agenda. As in the campaigns against obsolete businesses, governments set up and assigned numerical targets for lower-level governments. Common targets included the amount of investment in technology upgrades, ratio of industrial added value to labor for enterprises above a designated size, percentage of enterprises above a designated size that implement human-robot substitution, number of model enterprises that implement the policy, number of human-robot substitution projects, and number of replaced outdated equipment.[38] According to Chen and Huang, policy documents outlined rewards and punishments that local governments would receive based on implementation outcomes. They could receive bonuses and state honors with outstanding performance in implementing the human-robot substitution initiative. Chen and Huang had to submit various statistical tables monthly. Similarly, when applying for subsidies or after implementing a human-robot substitution project, businesses were required by local governments to fill in evaluation forms as well as supply statistics about how their project decreased the use of human labor and contributed to technological upgrades. These firm-level statistics then became the inputs of local states' statistical tables. Local states further used media to disseminate information and statistics about the efficacy of the human-robot substitution agenda as well as successful stories of the so-called model businesses. The purpose was to mobilize public and business support. Asked about the validity of statistics and possibility of fraud, Chen and Huang both explained they had neither the resources nor the motivation to scrutinize the statistics. Instead, they simply hoped for good statistics and were satisfied when the statistics indicated that the goals set by higher-level government were being met.

Manufacturers: Promise and Reality of Robot Dreams

All the managers and executives whom I interviewed said they paid attention to and were aware of national industrial policies and policies regarding human-robot substitution. At the same time, despite the Chinese state's ambition and successful media stories of human-robot substitution, most of my interviewees—regardless of whether their companies received subsidies—also criticized the policies.

The first criticism concerned fraud. Although my interviewees believed the various levels of government implemented the policies with good intentions, they thought the policies enabled significant fraud. Andrew, an Apollo manager, commented, "Frankly speaking, 70 to 80 percent of the human-robot substitution projects aim to prey on the government's money." Similarly, Clio's manager, Cheng, said, "Many people cheat the government. In China, one must think through how to make money. You can make money from products, tax benefits, government subsidies, labor, or material costs. Making different kinds of money requires different strategies. As far as I know, many people make money from government subsidies." Asked why people could cheat the government so easily, Cheng answered, "There is little mechanism to oversee policy implementation." This view echoed my interviews with the two local officials discussed above. Eris's CEO, Elton, elaborated on the kind of fraudulent practices that emerged from the policies:

> The government created a resource pool. Businesses that are included in the pool can sell their products or service. T-Robot, the most infamous scammer in our city, is included in the pool due to its CEO's connection with officials. The company makes copycat robots with terrible quality. Last year, T-Robot's CEO, Yang, hosted a huge conference in a luxury hotel. Everything—from food to rooms—was free. The party secretary gave a speech at the opening ceremony to show his support. . . . Manufacturers in the resource pool boost the amount of investment. In our city, it's possible that one can get 80 percent of the investment back. Say, for robots worth a hundred thousand RMB, T-Robots can give you a five hundred thousand RMB invoice. In this way, sellers and buyers of robots can make a lot of money even though those robots are not useful. Many people are doing this. People inside and outside the resource pool collude and make money.

Many interviewees told similar stories. For manufacturers, much of the value attached to robots came from government subsidies rather than contributions to production. Interviewees expressed their belief that the government's return on its huge investment in robotization was minuscule.

The second criticism of the policies concerned the state's fetishization of technology.[39] Interviewees at Apollo, Bacchus, Clio, Eris, and Flora felt that policies overestimated the power of robots. All six companies had already introduced industrial robots in their manufacturing process long before the state's initiative, but differed in their efforts to automate production. The main driving factors of robotization and automation included rising labor costs, high labor turnover, and labor management as well as market pressures to decrease the workforce, increase productivity and quality, and reduce work-related physical strains and injuries. The high labor turnover of low-skilled workers meant that firms rarely needed to resort to layoffs when automation reduced the workforce.[40] Consistent with research that examines robot installation in China, I found that larger manufacturers, such as Apollo, Bacchus, and Clio, tended to invest more in automation since they encountered more problems with labor shortages and management.[41] Similar to local state officials, some of the managers and executives at these companies strongly believed in the potential of robots to alleviate labor-related problems. The most famous example in this regard was Foxconn's plan, as mentioned in chapter 1, to build a one-million robot army. After a series of labor suicides, its CEO announced this plan in 2011 as a solution to its labor control and management problems. The CEO explicitly instructed managers to use robots to replace workers, with the goal of employing as few humans as possible. Foxconn has achieved limited success, however.[42] Despite their initial overwhelming optimism about the potential of robots, the managers and executives I spoke to said that their actual experiences made them increasingly aware of robots' limitations and skeptical of the state's single-minded focus. As Bacchus's manager, Boris, explained,

> Our decision-making is restricted by budgets and the return of investment. When we realized our investment in robots did not lead to a satisfying return, we adjusted and corrected our decisions. I am talking about firms that don't prey on governmental subsidies. That's how we differ from the government. They [governments] can spend a lot of money based on a superficial understanding of technology and production. Yet nothing would happen to them for their policy because they have taxpayers to pay for them, and they can sell land. Even if one official finds the policy problematic, no one would admit the problem because acknowledging problems is not good for anyone. For them [officials], the crucial task is to spend money. Officials in charge of the [human-robot substitution] initiative will be considered incompetent if they don't spend their budgets and finance enough projects.

Boris's quote shows why businesses adjusted their investment strategies when they realized that they were overoptimistic about the potential of robots, but there was no similar self-correcting mechanism on the government's side.

Among the six manufacturers, Apollo had the most ambitious automation goal. When labor costs began to rise in the mid-2000s, Apollo started to explore the potential of robotization. By 2009, the company had developed at least fifteen different models of robots collectively capable of performing more than twenty tasks. Similar to labor economists, Apollo's executives and managers believed that routine, low-skilled manual work could be easily shifted to robots, but later it became clear that the company had overestimated robots' potential after the management and engineers learned more about the materiality of robots and human bodies.[43] The small size of consumer electronics products and their components made precise control extremely challenging. Managers and engineers at Apollo told me that a higher speed or physical fluctuation in operation tended to decrease robots' repeat position accuracy. As a result, robots frequently failed to achieve a sufficient level of repeat position accuracy in action. Also, some human movements remained difficult, if not impossible, to replicate with robots. As several managers and engineers told me, although six-axis articulated robots are more flexible and dexterous than previous models in terms of movement, human hands are still better than the most advanced robot arms. In addition, line supervisors at Apollo studied human fingers, joints, and palms extensively, specifically teaching workers how to move more efficiently to speed the assembly process. Human workers knew how much force and pressure to apply through the sense of touch, and accordingly, could adjust their actions when they assembled parts of an electronic product. And the ideal human workers, young people with good eyesight, could assemble tiny components precisely and skillfully at a high speed. Faced with these issues, Apollo's decision makers found themselves appreciating anew the unique qualities of human workers. According to Andy, a manager at Apollo, "We have tried to make robots assemble components, but robots often break delicate and expensive components. From the process, I have realized that the human body is magic."

Robots' limitations were further exacerbated by the growing delicacy of electronics products, which required ever higher levels of flexibility and precision in assembly. Finally, given the declining life cycle of consumer electronics products and increasing differentiation of products, Apollo needed to produce increasingly diverse lines of products, frequently with a smaller quantity for each line. Manufacturing different products requires distinct production lines. For each new line of products, engineers must redesign and adjust production lines—a complicated and expensive process.

Nevertheless, Apollo still achieved one of the highest ratios of robots to humans among manufacturers in China. Some sociologists expect that automation will lead to an increase in workers' skills.[44] Consistent with such a prediction, Apollo hired a growing number of engineers and technicians. Yet even today, diverging from the forecasts of labor economists who postulate that a low-skilled or routine task can be automated easily, the use of robots in production at Apollo remains surprisingly limited. As Archie, a general manager in charge of robotic automation, explained to me,

> Robots did achieve something, but something much smaller than we expected. Electronic devices have become increasingly delicate and thus require *extra* human labor in assembling. Robots release unskilled workers from certain tasks and allow workers to concentrate on tasks that require more physical dexterity and flexibility.

With a PhD degree in engineering, Archie was the key person who convinced Apollo's CEO to invest heavily in robotization. In the end, most of the automation is limited to jobs described by managers as "3D": dirty, dull, and dangerous.

I conducted my interview with Archie in 2017. In 2019, a manager who had previously worked under Archie told me that Apollo had since dissolved Archie's unit—the very unit charged with accelerating robotization—given robots' limitations, and Archie left his job at Apollo. This result is consistent with research that finds that despite the hype about robots, manual labor has proven better suited to a large range of tasks in electronics assembly.[45]

Bacchus, Clio, and Eris had similarly frustrating experiences, but they did not invest as much as Apollo. One of Clio's managers, Chu, said, "Our CEO has been talking about robots for years. Although we can make some improvement, that does not significantly decrease our demand for workers. It is the economic downturn and relocation of our factories to Vietnam for cheaper labor that largely decreased our demand for workers here." Elton, Eris's CEO, commented on the state-promoted agenda:

> I told district-level officials this is a waste of money, but they said provincial officials believe robotics is an effective way to upgrade our economy. . . . Institutions are invisible "software." It's easier for officials to make sense of "hardware," like robots. They don't know how technology works. You can impress them by showing them a robot that cuts noodles.

Indeed, the disillusion with robots expressed by the managers contrasted sharply with the government's technological fetishism.

Similarly, Andrew, a manager at Apollo, spoke with an official at the Development and Reform Bureau. Since the bureau had extra funding to dispense, the official asked Andrew how the government could help enterprises with upgrading. Andrew emphasized that the official was sincere in asking for advice. Andrew suggested that the government help establish platforms for manufacturers to exchange their experiences and learn from each other. The official, however, said Andrew's suggestion would not work because he could not relate it to the cadre/official/government performance evaluation standards. According to Andrew, "He [the official] said since my suggestion wouldn't show up in KPIs, it's 'empty' [*xu*]. He also thought it would be impossible for the upper-level government to accept the idea. In the end, they [the government] continued to dump money into things that they considered cutting-edge and could see with their eyes."

Apollo, Bacchus, and Dike employed a decoupling strategy to respond to the limits of human-robot substitution under China's techno-developmental regime. Although managers at these companies were aware of these limits, they had various reasons to overstate the productive value of robots in their communications with media and the state. As a large manufacturer, Apollo carefully managed its public image by forbidding managers from talking to the media about the limitations of the company's robotization. Even after it became clear that Apollo's goal was not feasible, company executives continued to publicly endorse human-robot substitution. The company even arranged for some media outlets to cover the company's fully automated production lines, without making it clear that such lines were the exception, not the norm. Government officials similarly visited the automated production lines and pointed to their existence as proof of automation's successful implementation.

Arguably, Apollo's continuing embrace of robots and automation technology was largely based on their symbolic meaning rather than their perceived material properties as well as the material benefits that Apollo might receive from the government by being considered high tech. In this way, the symbolic meaning and value of robots were, to a large extent, shaped by China's national sociotechnical imaginaries. As Apollo's manager, Allen, lamented,

> We know we have to continually rely on workers because robots turned out to be not that helpful, but we are not supposed to say this since it's politically and economically unwise. What can we do as a traditional manufacturer? Recently, Toyota announced it had replaced robots with humans to improve the quality of production, but the broader climate in China does not allow us to say things like this.

As manufacturing relying on low-skilled labor has increasingly become seen as low-end or obsolete, high-tech industries have become prioritized as high-end. Such symbolic classification is powerful in China given the state's critical role in distributing resources. As Allen further explained, "In China, it would be difficult for a large corporation to do well if it deviates from state policy. I wish the government could have a realistic understanding of technology, and acknowledge the contribution of migrant workers and manufactures that employ them." His quote and my interviews with other managers revealed alternative sociotechnical imaginaries that envisioned as well as appreciated a different kind of state-capital-labor-technology relationship.

Bacchus was not as famous as Apollo and did not seek public attention. But due to the company's previous experience in robotization, local officials specifically tasked it with being a model business in the government's initiative. Bai, a manager at Bacchus, described the company's involvement as follows:

> The government tends to give money to manufacturers that are already doing better than others or those with connections with officials. In our case, although we don't think we are successful at using robots to replace humans, our level of automation is higher than many other manufacturers here. They [officials] wanted us to be a model business. It was difficult for us to decline. We received subsidies and free media advertisement. They arranged for journalists to visit our company and published news reports.

During our interview, I showed Bai a news article about Bacchus's achievement in human-robot substitution. When I asked whether I should believe the statistics cited in the report, Bai responded with an embarrassed smile, "Absolutely not. It's an exaggeration."

Dike's CEO, Dong, was well-connected with local officials. Since the local industrial policies helped him to get subsidies, he did not have to worry about the return of Dike's investment in robotic equipment. During our conversation, Dong mentioned that his friend in the government needed his help because the friend was being evaluated according to statistics regarding human-robot substitution. I asked Dike how he came up with such statistics; he replied, "It's a rough calculation. We did what other firms did. Everyone makes the numbers look good." Here we can see the collusion between companies and local officials, and how the techno-developmental regime's metric systems shape state-business relationships.

Not every manufacturer in my study participated in the state-promoted initiative. Flora was too small to be eligible for subsidies, while Clio and Eris's management did not want to receive money from the government. As Eris's CEO, Elton, explained to me, "Our company is small. The government prefers giving money to larger companies. Also, I don't want to get money from them. If one of the government officials is arrested for corruption, we will have problems." In a similar vein, Clio's manager, Cheng, said the company's CEO did not want the problems associated with government engagement and echoed Elton's caution.

Executives and managers generally maintained that the government had wasted enormous amounts of money on the human-robot substitution agenda. They believed manufacturers would make their own investment decisions without the state's intervention. Bacchus's manager, Boris, told me that he felt tired of dealing with various agendas promoted by the government, such as the IoT, intelligent manufacturing, and cloud computing. He said, "Whenever they [officials] hear of some new technologies, they want to do something and want us to collaborate as if they know those technologies. But they even don't know what they are talking about. I hope they can leave us alone and stop coming up with new agendas or slogans." Other managers and executives shared Boris's reaction.

Since my interviewees were critical of the state's effort to upgrade China's industrial structure, I asked them what they wished the government to do. Surprisingly, their answers mainly concerned the rule of law and fair competition. Many interviewees complained that it was difficult for them to get bank loans because banks, controlled primarily by the government, preferred giving bank loans to SOEs or companies with connections to officials. Moreover, they complained that they had to sign many despotic contracts (*bawang hetong*) and despotic clauses (*bawang tiaokuan*) with the government and SOEs. Asked about why they would need to sign contracts with the government and SOEs, Cheng at Clio observed,

> Would it be possible that you don't sign such contracts if you want to buy land from the government to build a facility or if you want to get a bank loan? You must sign those things, and all of them are despotic contracts and despotic clauses. That's very risky because when they [the government] want to find trouble with you, you'll be in a dangerous situation. There is no fairness, and we cannot say no because they control land and bank credit. When we are in a legally precarious situation, how can we invest and upgrade businesses without fear? They [the government] behave inconsistently. Today they can be happy with you and buy many things from you. They issue an order in the morning and rescind it in the evening [*zhao ling xi gai*], however. You don't know what's going to happen tomorrow. They don't know how to improve the economy, but they feel they have to do something. Instead of upgrading the industrial structure or economy, they should upgrade or fix the legal system and stop using it as their political tool.

Cheng's quote is interesting in two ways. First, his harsh criticism of the state's monopolistic power in forcing businesses to sign despotic contracts and accept despotic clauses resembles delivery workers' criticism of platform companies in China—a phenomenon I discuss in chapter 7. Second, the notion of issuing an order in the morning and rescinding it in the evening occurred frequently in my interviews with the management of obsolete businesses, as described in chapter 4. In fact, platform workers also complained about the power of platform companies to change rules arbitrarily and unilaterally (chapter 7). Unexpectedly, my interview data point to many similarities between the state and platform companies in China as these two groups of actors both hold certain monopolistic power.

Cheng's quote also reveals a common criticism of China's unpredictable and politicized legal system as well as the government's monopoly of land and control of banks. The majority of my interviewees felt that if banks could stop privileging SOEs, my interviewees would have better access to bank credit for investment.[46] Although my interviewees in this chapter did not experience the kind of crackdowns imposed on obsolete businesses, they still felt uncertain about their position within China's legal and regulatory framework. They were all too aware of how the government could enact and use regulations as unconstrained instruments. They viewed the techno-developmental state's legal enforcement campaigns along with the changing environmental and other regulatory standards as "laughable" (*kexiao*) and backward. Many pointed out that the government did an excellent job building traditional infrastructures like highways and railroads, but was, as they put it, terrible at building "invisible" or "soft infrastructure."

I had a particularly memorable conversation with CEO Bai in summer 2019. As mentioned earlier, Bacchus was chosen by the government as a model business for robotization. Our dinner was interrupted by a phone call from a government official. Apparently there were some problems between Bacchus and the local government. After finishing the phone call, Bai told me I should study the legal system instead of robots, technology, and industrial policy. He told me in a serious tone,

> The rule of law is the most fundamental issue. We entrepreneurs suffer a lot because there is no rule of law, no fairness, and no predictability. Things are scary and arbitrary. The government has invested a lot in high and new technology, and come up with all kinds of policy, but I'm not sure to what extent its investment pays off and its measures work. What I'm sure is that they [the government] don't understand they are destroying technological and economic development by using laws as their instruments. China cannot become a truly high-tech and innovative country without the rule of law. They don't have laws to protect you and your property or intellectual property rights, but they have laws and regulations to torture you. If I were you, I would study why the legal system remains so backward and how to change it.

Bai's comments reveal an enormous gap between what the government has done to foster techno-development and what entrepreneurs actually want. The legal and technical instruments devised by the state to facilitate techno-development are considered, at best, unhelpful and wasteful, and at worst, detrimental to techno-development. This view was shared among many of my interviewees, but Bai articulated it particularly powerfully. Entrepreneurs greatly appreciated the Chinese state's investment in traditional or "hard" infrastructure (e.g., the road and railroad networks) in the past, but they now felt the government should focus on enhancing what the invisible or soft infrastructure—that is, the legal system, financial institutions, and land use rights market.

Workers: Progress, Anxiety, and Indifference

The workers interviewed in this chapter are different from those I spoke to in chapter 4. Since how workers here perceived human-machine substitution is similar to how workers in chapter 4 viewed the techno-developmental regime, though, I did not repeat the same background information. Workers' perceptions of the human-robot substitution agenda were shaped by their status as not only workers but also nationals, parents, and soon-to-be retirees. The salience of each perspective and its attitude toward robotization varied across life stages. The demographic composition of workers differed across the six manufacturers. The larger the manufacturer, the smaller the average age of its low-skilled workers. Larger manufacturers tended to have stricter restrictions on the maximum age. Most low-skilled workers were in their twenties. Smaller manufacturers did not impose an age limit. They employed workers who ranged in age from their twenties to forties. Younger workers tended to have a slightly higher level of education. Workers in their twenties and thirties were more likely than those in their forties to have learned through social media about the various efforts to replace workers with robots.

As I have mentioned, the rapid development of robotics in recent years has triggered concerns about unemployment in the world.[47] Still, I did not find panic among most of my interviewees. Workers in their twenties—the largest age group across all six manufacturers—were mostly uncritical of the state's human-robot substitution campaign, though they did note it would likely lead to serious unemployment problems. Asked why they generally supported the state's policies, Tang responded, "When robots can replace humans, that means China achieves advanced technological development and can compete with other countries. . . . This is what the government wants to achieve through Made in China 2025." Similar quotes were common in the interviews: human-robot substitution meant technological progress, and such progress and policies were beneficial for the nation. Several workers also told me China should learn from Germany because Germany is famous for its high-end manufacturing and robots. Asked where they learned about Germany, they said from vocational schools and social media. The interviewees revealed the salience of their national identity and the imprint of the dominant national sociotechnical imaginaries.

Interviewees in their twenties were asked whether they were worried about their own job security. Most said not really, as they did not intend to stay in manufacturing jobs for a long time. Indeed, many of the low-skilled workers hoped to eventually work in the service sector, especially the emerging platform sector. Consistent with what I have described in chapter 4, most of workers found manual work in manufacturing industries undesirable and transitional. For the minority of young workers who want to stay in manufacturing, they believe there will still be plenty of time to acquire the skills needed to remain employed in the era of robots. As Tang put it confidently, "I'm not afraid. Robots need humans to operate. I'm still young. I have a lot of opportunity to learn." Literally pointing to his older colleagues in the workshop, however, he noted, "Things could be tough for older generations." Most of the interviewees in their twenties expressed similar ideas: time is with them, but not with their older colleagues.

Workers in their thirties were more critical of the human-robot substitution agenda and more worried robots could take their jobs. This group was similar to those workers in chapter 4 who were concerned about their children's future in the techno-nation, although this group of workers left their children in their hometown. As I mentioned in chapter 4, skilled workers and clerks were more likely to be able to afford to bring their children to the cities where they worked. In comparison, my interviewees here were low-skilled workers who could not afford to bring their kids with them. Many of my interviewees in their thirties in this chapter had already tried but failed to find a better job and thus returned to factories. Yang's story was typical. She quit her jobs several times. After leaving her factory job at Flora, she worked in a women's clothing store and nail salon. Finally, she returned to Flora. She explained these shifts to me:

> I like service jobs better, but sometimes the owners didn't pay you. Factory jobs are boring, but if you work in a better factory, they pay your salary regularly and provide social insurance. Before my daughter was born, I wanted to have fun. Now I need to have a stable job. I'm grateful that my boss let me come back to work. It would be terrible if robots take our jobs.

After switching between bad jobs, many of my interviewees in their thirties realized they did not have enough economic or social capital to create a small business, or sufficient cultural capital to sell things to rich people. Yang and many of my interviewees in their thirties spoke from the perspective of a worker and parent rather than a patriotic national. Workers in this group had young children who were being cared for by grandparents in their hometown. These workers were under much stress, and many complained that their children were unlikely to receive a good education due to the household registration system. As Wang, a mother of two, told me, "Now we all know education is key to good jobs, but our children don't have such opportunity. Look at the children of our managers and local people. They go to great schools or study abroad." Unlike interviewees in their twenties, workers in their thirties cared less about glorious national progress. Their primary focus was job security and their children's mobility.

Finally, workers in their forties were the most indifferent to the human-robot substitution agenda. This group was the numerical minority in the factories at the time of this study. Most were line leaders or forepersons with adult children. Tian's quote illustrates the thinking of workers in this age group: "It would take time for them [manufacturers] to figure out how to use robots to replace humans. When that day comes, I will be retiring and going back to the countryside. My son has grown up. I'm done with my responsibility." Looking forward to their retirement from work and family responsibilities, workers in their forties did not view robots as a significant issue in their lives.

Engineers and Technicians: Climbing up
the Social Mobility Ladder

As I have mentioned, all six companies had already introduced industrial robots in their manufacturing process long before the state's human-machine
substitution initiative. Despite discovering the material limitations of robots,
they continued to enhance the level of robotization. Apollo was the most ambitious and successful among the six manufacturers. In the most recent decade,
it reduced the percentage of unskilled workers by 3 percent. Managers and
executives in the six companies reported that they hired more engineers and
technicians because of robotization, and most of the technical personnel
(around 90 percent) were male. When I visited Apollo's plant, I saw one plant
was full of male engineers, all of whom were either adjusting and testing industrial robots along with other machines in workstations or using software
to draw graphs in their offices.

Engineers in the six manufacturers mostly graduated from second-tier
universities or technical colleges. They are considered talent according to the
metrics of China's techno-developmental regime. The six manufacturers have
three major categories of engineers: mechanical, electrical, and software engineers. Mechanical engineers focus on designing and manufacturing outer
parts of electronic products. They spend much of their time working on
computer-aided design or computer-aided manufacturing. Electrical engineers use application software to design parameters in order to adjust and
stabilize industrial robots and other machines. Software engineers use programming languages to develop customized software. The starting salary of
an engineer is around US$900 per month and can increase to about US$3,000
per month when an engineer gains more experience. Among the three kinds
of engineers, software engineers have the highest salaries. In my interviews,
managers often complained that they could not recruit enough engineers.
Indeed, they had to worry about headhunters approaching their experienced
engineers from time to time. As a result, the companies paid higher and
higher salaries. And yet as I will show in chapter 8, good remuneration packages in the electronics manufacturing industry still could not compete with
those in the internet-related sectors. In comparison with engineers, technicians usually received secondary vocational education. They were tasked with
the operation or maintenance of machines. Their jobs involved little design
or programming.

Tasked with ensuring the constant and smooth operation of industrial robots and other machines, the engineers I talked to described being under a
high level of stress as they had to understand as well as to some extent overcome the material limitations of robots and other machines. When their boss

suggested automating a specific manufacturing process, they had to come up with different solutions and evaluate the efficacy of those solutions within a short time. There was a lot of trial and error in the process. In addition, the degree to which they could complete their task depended on their relations with other engineers, especially whether senior engineers were willing to advise and support them. Such relationships gave them a decreased sense of autonomy. Competition among peers was another source of stress. When a client requested an automation solution, manufacturers often asked different teams of engineers to compete and let the client decide on the winning proposal. Since the outcome of such competitions significantly influenced bonuses, engineers were frequently beset by a feeling of tension and failure in the process. Furthermore, many engineers spent a lot of time on the factory floor as opposed to sitting in their office. Sometimes engineers stood on the floor for six to seven hours in order to ensure that the robots or other machines operated properly. They also felt it was somewhat challenging to interact with line superintendents as the latter could treat engineers like workers and be rude. Compared with engineers, technicians experienced a lower stress level as they could rely on engineers to solve their problems.

Despite their work pressure, the engineers reported feeling fulfilled at work. Many of them mentioned exhilaration at a "eureka moment" when they could fix problems and see their robots and machines move properly. Although they were constantly troubled by all kinds of challenges at work, many engineers saw problem-solving as an excellent learning opportunity. In a similar vein, the technicians I talked to enjoyed the ability to make industrial robots or other machines work. One technician told me, "I feel fulfilled when other people fail, but I succeed in adjusting the machine and making it achieve a stable status. Not everyone can do what I do." In sharp contrast with the low-skilled workers whom I talked to, engineers and technicians had a strong sense of pride and joy in the process of making robots and machines work.

Engineers believed their education and work experience were valued in the labor market too. The engineers I interviewed felt fortunate about their upward social mobility. In general, they thought they fared much better than their parents. They mostly came from rural areas or small towns. Their parents tended to be workers, peasants, and small business owners, frequently with a middle school or lower level of education. A small proportion of the engineers were left-behind children, but the percentage was smaller than the low-skilled workers I interviewed. The engineers also emphasized that the strong demand for engineers in the labor market allowed people like them—those from a disadvantaged family background without social networks—to build a solid career path. In addition, robotization made the difference between engineers and workers more visible. The engineers I talked to felt people in China could not distinguish engineers from workers in the past. One engineer pointed out, "Engineers were always considered as workers in China because the two groups both worked in the factory. People either didn't understand or underestimated the value of engineering in manufacturing. Now people know workers cannot deal with complicated technologies like robots." In short, my engineer interviewees thought their social status and career prospects rose in tandem with robotization. Not only engineers but technicians as well felt they now received more material returns and respect. Unlike low-skilled workers, technicians thought they had good job prospects and could accumulate skills at work.

Although engineers and technicians benefited from China's techno-development in terms of their job prospects, younger engineers and technicians felt they were defeated by a strange new bird produced by China's techno-developmental regime—the real estate industry. As mentioned briefly in chapter 4, owners and managers of obsolete businesses said the real estate industry emerged as a new bird as outmoded businesses shut down or relocated. Several younger engineers and technicians told me they would consider quitting their jobs and moving to cities in inland China despite better career opportunities in coastal cities because they could not afford the soaring housing prices there. Indeed, managers whom I spoke with were beset by the high turnover rate of engineers and technicians. Two of the six manufacturers asked their departing engineers and technicians to fill out a survey in order to understand what happened. The surveys revealed two major reasons for resigning; the first was to have higher remuneration, and the second was not being able to buy a housing property near their workplace, particularly given social norms in China that mandate males purchase a home before marriage.[48] And as shown in chapter 4, housing property is crucially connected to access to local public schools even for people with local citizenship, with priority usually going to the children of property owners. The two reasons for leaving are also related because young engineers and technicians must get a higher remuneration package to buy a housing property near their workplace. Unlike some of the software engineers I study in chapter 8, none of the engineers and technicians I talked to were from a middle-class family. They could not compete in the housing market with middle-class-origin professionals in China's internet companies. Feeling distressed, young engineers and technicians tried but still failed to find solutions that would allow them to have good career opportunities *and* sustain a family.

A decade ago, engineers and technicians in their late thirties were able to purchase an apartment with financial support from their families as the housing prices were more affordable then. They told me they felt super lucky. Younger engineers and technicians are not so fortunate as housing prices have surged rapidly in recent years. Scholars use the house price-to-income ratio to

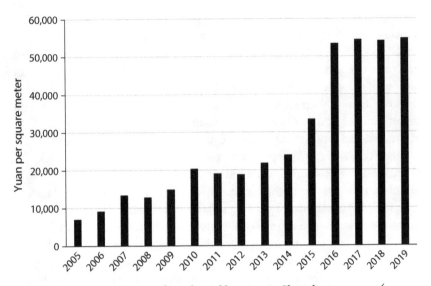

FIGURE 5.1. Average price of residential housing in Shenzhen, 2005–19 (yuan per square meter). *Source*: Shenzhen Statistical Yearbooks.

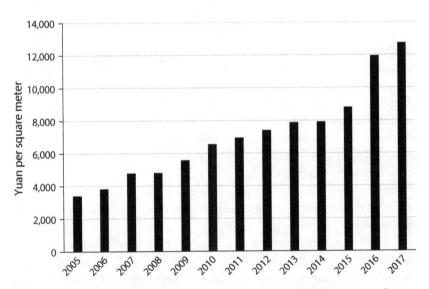

FIGURE 5.2. Average price of residential housing in Dongguan, 2005–17 (yuan per square meter). *Source*: Dongguan Statistical Yearbooks.

measure affordability and consider a house price-to-income ratio of 3 affordable. The first- and second-tier cities along coastal China have an average house price-to-income ratio higher than 10, achieving severe unaffordability. The house price-to-income ratio of Shenzhen and Guangzhou, for example, are 14.5 and 12.9, respectively.[49] Here I show the average price of residential housing in Shenzhen for 2005–19 and Dongguan for 2005–17 to illustrate growing housing prices in the Pearl River Delta cities (see figures 5.1 and 5.2). In interviews, not only younger engineers and technicians but also managers complained about how the real estate boom made their lives and the business environment unsustainable. As I noted in chapter 2, a land-driven economy—and the resulting speculation in the real estate market as well as rapidly rising housing prices—can significantly increase the costs for social reproduction. We see here the adverse impacts of a land-driven economy on techno-development through increasing the costs of social reproduction and manufacturing companies.

A Toxic but Irresistible New Bird

In chapter 2, I briefly introduced labor-, land-, and technology-driven economic development in China. As shown in chapter 3, one of the most important reasons that led coastal provinces, especially Guangdong, Zhejiang, and Jiangsu, to pursue techno-development in the mid-2000s was the lack of land for labor-intensive, export-oriented manufacturing. The proposed solution was to allocate land to "deserving" new birds—businesses and industries that could foster techno-development. Also, in the mid-2000s, both the central and local governments in China were already cognizant of the problems of a land-driven economy. For one thing, rising protests and social conflicts resulting from illegal land grabs in rural areas contributed in part to President Hu Jintao's agenda of building a harmonious society, which was announced in 2004. Ironically, despite the known issues of land-driven economic development and the government's intention to foster techno-development rather than a land-driven economy, the real estate industry emerged as a de facto new bird. Moreover, this new bird was both toxic and irresistible. There is a Chinese saying that refers to "quenching a thirst with poison" (yin zhen zhi ke); it means adopting a remedy that has serious side effects. The Chinese state's reliance on the real estate industry exemplifies such a remedy.

As mentioned in chapter 3, the Chinese state announced a four trillion RMB stimulus plan to combat the fall of GDP growth below its official target amid the 2008 financial crisis. The stimulus plan resulted in a 30 percent growth rate of bank loans and accounted for a 4 percent increase in real GDP growth rate by the end of 2009. Nevertheless, the fiscal stimulus contributed to rising land and housing prices along with difficulties for nonlandholding private businesses to access bank loans.[50] Managers and CEOs whom I interviewed in manufacturing repeatedly complained about the difficulty of getting bank loans as well as the same access to bank credit enjoyed by SOEs and real estate developers.

The misallocation of bank loans from the stimulus package caused a series of problems and vicious cycle. Research has shown that bank credit was allocated disproportionately to finance capital-intensive investment in real estate, infrastructure, and heavy industries. The majority of the loans were channeled to real estate as local governments profited from and relied on land revenues and tax income from real estate–related industries.[51] The increasing capital supply led to an overinvestment in real estate, especially land acquisitions, pushing up land costs and in turn housing prices.[52] Rapidly increasing land prices further induced manufacturing and service firms to participate in speculative buying. They bought more commercial and residential land unrelated to their core businesses, while reducing other investments and innovation activities. Economists found that as banks tended to grant more credit to landholding firms (i.e., those with collateral) in response to an increase in real estate prices, landholding firms (mostly SOEs) speculated in real estate. Such allocation of bank loans then crowded out firms without landholdings, which tended to be private businesses, from getting bank loans.[53] Given the low-interest rate, stock market's volatility, absence of other productive investment vehicles, and speculative motive to gain housing price appreciation, people tended to store their money in real estate in China. The growing capital supply and decreasing capital prices relaxed people's fiscal constraints, increased the demand for housing properties, and ultimately pushed up housing prices.[54]

Although the monetary stimulus led to a short-term GDP growth (about two years), it also contributed to the long-term problems of overinvestment in industries with excess capacity, such as real estate, and rapidly growing debt.[55] The government's action to solve the excess capacity problem paradoxically further increased housing prices because people expected the government would come up with monetary intervention. In fact, the Chinese state had to solve the accumulating excess capacity problem in real estate in the third- and fourth-tier cities in 2015 and 2016 through a political agenda to reduce the volume of unsold new housing under the supply-side structural reform. Nonetheless, the government's one-size-fits-all stimulus measures and the public expectation that housing prices would continue to grow in the first- and second-tier cities under a relaxing monetary policy led to soaring housing prices in those locations. Essentially, people bought housing property in first- and second-tier cities—the frontiers of China's techno-development and postindustrial transformation—to preserve the value of their money and

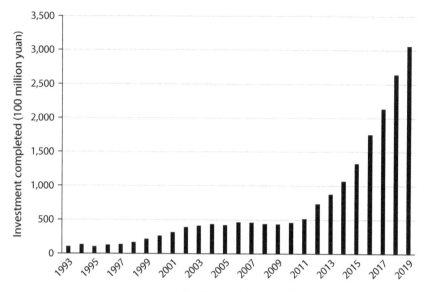

FIGURE 5.3. Investment completed in real estate in Shenzhen, 1993–2019.
Source: Shenzhen Statistical Yearbooks.

speculate on future appreciation. The process thus transferred local government and developers' debt into household debt.[56] The real estate boom has
pressured manufacturers to raise salaries, and made it difficult for engineers
and technicians to purchase a housing property and form a family. In chapter 8,
I will show how the rocketing housing prices and household debt has helped
internet companies to impose overwork norms on China's coding elites.

Here I use statistics from Shenzhen City and the Guangdong and Zhejiang
Provinces to capture the rise of the real estate industry as the Chinese state
endeavored to turn to techno-development. Figures 5.3 and 5.4 depict the continuing growth of investment in real estate and value of land purchased since
2010. After the central state made reducing the volume of unsold new housing
a priority in 2015 and 2016, the investment and value of land purchased in Shenzhen grew even faster. We can also see the resource allocation in real estate
vis-à-vis manufacturing from statistics of fixed-asset investment, which refers
to the amount invested in building, land, machinery and equipment, and infrastructure. Presumably, developing high-end or advanced manufacturing that
relies on high technology requires more significant fixed-asset investment.

Let me begin from the fixed-asset investment in Shenzhen, arguably one of
the few cities with the most advanced manufacturing industries in China. Figure 5.5 shows that fixed-asset investment in real estate in Shenzhen grew enormously since 2010, but that investment in manufacturing only grew slightly. As

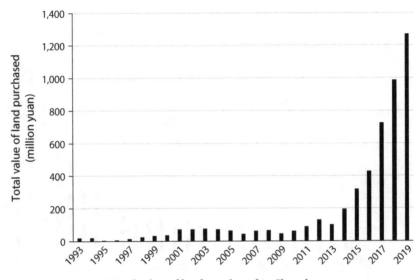

FIGURE 5.4. Total value of land purchased in Shenzhen, 1993–2019.
Source: Shenzhen Statistical Yearbooks.

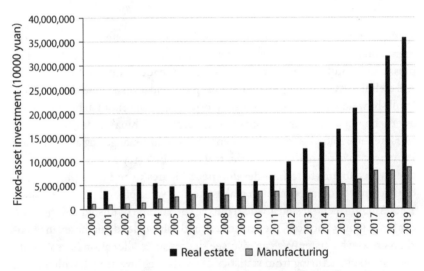

FIGURE 5.5. Fixed-asset investment in real estate and manufacturing in
Shenzhen, 2000–2019. *Source*: Shenzhen Statistical Yearbooks.

figure 5.6 further demonstrates, the ratio of fixed-asset investment in real estate
to total fixed-asset investment rose from 29 percent in 2010 to 51 percent in 2014,
and has remained high, whereas the ratio of fixed-asset investment in manufacturing has remained below 20 percent in the post-2008 period. Now let's move
to the Guangdong Province, which includes Shenzhen and other cities in the

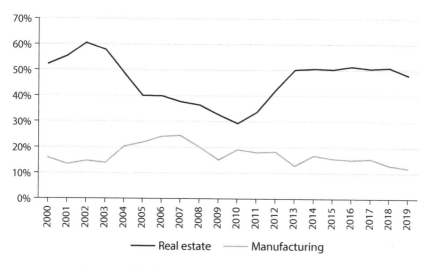

FIGURE 5.6. Ratios of fixed-asset investment in real estate and manufacturing to total fixed-asset investment in Shenzhen, 2000–2019. *Source*: Shenzhen Statistical Yearbooks.

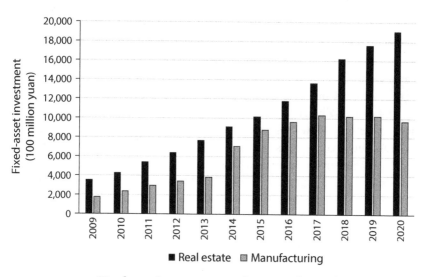

FIGURE 5.7. Fixed-asset investment in real estate and manufacturing in Guangdong, 2009–20. *Source*: Guangdong Statistical Yearbooks.

Pearl River Delta. As I discussed in chapter 3, Guangdong and Zhejiang were among the earliest provinces to pursue techno-development. Figure 5.7 illustrates that fixed-asset investment in real estate has grown consistently since 2010. Although fixed-asset investment in manufacturing increased a lot between 2013 and 2015, it has stopped growing since 2017. The increase between 2013 and 2015

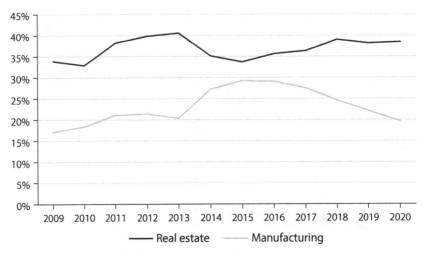

FIGURE 5.8. Ratios of fixed-asset investment in real estate and manufacturing to total fixed-asset investment in Guangdong Province, 2009–20. *Source*: Guangdong Statistical Yearbooks.

may have resulted from the Guangdong provincial government's campaign to speed industrial upgrading, which included the promotion of robotization.[57] Figure 5.8 further shows that the ratio of fixed-asset investment in manufacturing has continued to decline since 2016 in Guangdong—the strongest manufacturing province in China—despite the central government's announcement of the Made in China 2025 agenda in 2015.

The case of Zhejiang—the birthplace of the human-robot substitution agenda—clearly shows the rise of the real estate industry in the post-2008 period. As figure 5.9 portrays, the year 2010 is a critical watershed. Before 2010, fixed-asset investment in manufacturing was higher than that in real estate, but investment in real estate has outpaced that in manufacturing since then. Figure 5.10 further demonstrates that the ratio of fixed-asset investment in manufacturing to total fixed asset declined by 15 percent in the post-2008 period. In short, all the evidence suggests that the real estate industry emerged as a de facto new bird in China's techno-developmental regime, notwithstanding its absence in China's techno-developmental policy, tenuous relationship with high technology, and harmful impact on industrial manufacturers and their employees.

Conclusion

In this chapter, I embed the process of robotization in China's techno-developmental regime, and show how the state, manufacturers, low-skilled workers, technicians, and engineers have perceived and made decisions about

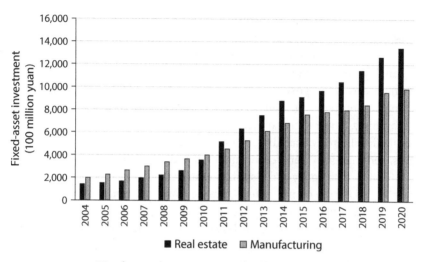

FIGURE 5.9. Fixed-asset investment in real estate and manufacturing in Zhejiang, 2004–20. *Source*: Zhejiang Statistical Yearbooks.

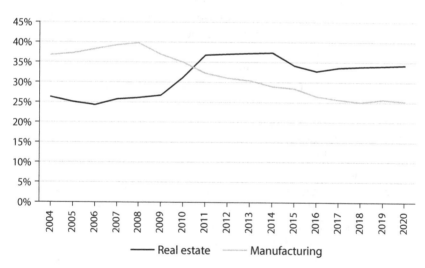

FIGURE 5.10. Ratios of fixed-asset investment in real estate and manufacturing to total fixed-asset investment in Zhejiang Province, 2004–17.
Source: Zhejiang Statistical Yearbooks.

robotization. The Chinese state's effort to advance robotization reveals dominant national sociotechnical imaginaries that foreground abstract notions of national and technological progress along with manufactured statistics over the actual efficacy of automation, protection of labor, and pursuit of economic equality. The imaginaries also prioritize talent and ignore the potential plight of low-skilled workers. The institutional design of the Chinese state contributes to the reproduction of technological fetishism. Economist David Autor argues that journalists and scholars tend to overstate the extent of machine/ technology substitution for human labor.[58] I find the same tendency among manufacturers and government officials. Following implementation, most manufacturers are cognizant of the material limitations of technology, and accordingly, adjust their expectations and decisions about robotization. Yet local officials are evaluated based on whether and how they meet policy targets, and manufacturers receive material and symbolic benefits when they conform to state policy and disseminate success stories. This incentive structure, especially the metric systems, prevents officials from taking the efficacy of policy seriously and thereby sustains technological fetishism.

Although the Chinese state used subsidies to advance robotization, electronics manufacturers tend to consider state subsidies unnecessary and wasteful. Scholars find that the state's policy plays only a minor role in businesses' automation strategies.[59] Indeed, state policy does not change how manufacturers evaluate the productive efficacy of robots. I believe, however, that the value of robots cannot be reduced to their contribution to production under China's techno-developmental regime. Common fraudulent practices among manufacturers with ties to officials mean that manufacturers can get extra material benefits. Participating in local state's initiatives means obtaining media advertising and deepening rapport with officials too. Therefore my finding corresponds to research that shows the influences of the state's policy on robot adoption.[60]

In general, there is a gap between what the state has done to advance techno-development and what manufacturers wish the state to do. The state focuses on providing subsidies and promoting high technologies, but manufacturers want to have the rule of law, or soft or invisible infrastructure. Manufacturers believe that they can fairly compete with other business actors, particularly SOEs when they do not have to sign despotic contracts with the state or SOEs, and when the rule of law exists. I also find that although some officials sincerely intend to help manufacturers, the state's metric systems become obstacles for local officials to adopt manufacturers' suggestions as the latter cannot be translated into points or rewards in those systems.

This chapter helps us to understand the automation of low-skilled, routine, and manual work as well. Although labor economists predict the easy automation of such work, I find that they overestimate the material capacity of robots.[61] Although many manual tasks in electronics manufacturing are routine and require little training or education, such tasks necessitate physical dexterity, which robots still lack. Consequently, several manufacturers have relocated their factories to countries with lower wages. This finding aligns with studies that point to the limited ability of robots to replace routine, manual tasks in a cost-effective manner.[62] Of course, manufacturing processes vary across different industries. Automation or robotization is more straightforward in some industries like the automobile manufacturing industry, but it remains challenging in manufacturing industries that require physical dexterity.

News and scholarly work that discusses public concerns about automation or robotization tends to focus on people's status as workers. Yet I find workers' perceptions of the human-robot substitution agenda are shaped by their status as not just workers but also nationals, parents, and soon-to-be retirees. The positive valuation attached to robots under China's techno-developmental regime influences how workers view robotization. As previous research suggests, media influences perceptions of technology.[63] Younger workers draw on media discourses that link national progress to state policy and technology. They relate automation and robotization to national progress too. Although previous studies have found little concern among Chinese workers regarding automation, I see some variation.[64] Workers consider automation from multiple perspectives, with different life stages influencing the saliency of specific perspectives and degree of anxiety. So while young workers tend to see robotization from the perspective of a member of a rising techno-nation, workers with parenting obligations are more anxious about robotization's impact.

I also find that engineers and technicians face both promises and problems under China's techno-developmental regime. On the one hand, they enjoy excellent career prospects, rising status, and upward social mobility. They are relatively well positioned in the government's metric systems. Unlike the software engineers I study in chapter 8, engineers and technicians here do not feel exploited at work. On the other hand, younger engineers and technicians, who tend to come from working-class families, have encountered insurmountable difficulties in social reproduction as they cannot afford housing properties or establish a family given the ironic rise of real estate as a new bird in China's techno-developmental regime.

Finally, this chapter has shown the negative consequences of the real estate boom on manufacturers that have attempted to upgrade themselves through robotization. Despite the government's effort to advance techno-development, the state-controlled banks prefer distributing bank loans to land developers and SOEs, crowding out bank credit that private manufacturers can receive.[65] Rocketing housing prices make it difficult for manufacturers to retain their talent as well.

Having shown what has happened to old birds in the traditional manufacturing sectors and the rise of a toxic but irresistible new bird as China turned to techno-development, I will move to the emergence of China's glorious and mighty new birds in internet-related sectors in the next chapter.

6

The Rise of Big Tech

HAVING DISCUSSED how the Chinese state dealt with and cracked down on the old birds based on the bird/cage logic to foster techno-development, I will now shift my focus to the privileged new birds under China's techno-developmental regime, especially those in internet-related sectors. Unlike many other high-tech industries, internet-related sectors present the unique promise of creating a variety of digital platforms that can connect and benefit everyone. According to economist Jean Tirole, platforms are intermediaries that bring together different groups of actors to interact, and provide a technological interface to enable or facilitate such interaction.[1] As such, the internet along with the emerging digital and platform services can facilitate not only transactions of goods but also exchanges of different kinds of labor between providers and demanders.[2] This idea was articulated in Premier Li Keqiang's speech in 2014 at the first World Internet Conference, an annual international event hosted by the Chinese government to discuss global internet policies. Li said, "Internet breakthrough is not only a technological revolution but also a social change that guarantees fairness. Regardless of a person's background, wealth, or level of education, everyone can gain a window to understanding the world and a ladder to the market through the internet.[3]" Like Premier Li, many factory workers I talked to viewed the digital and platform economy created by China's tech giants as a land of freedom and opportunity as well as pathway to better jobs. In a similar vein, professionals like software engineers—considered talent under China's techno-developmental regime—saw great prospects for themselves when they looked at the career trajectories of Chinese tech entrepreneurs who rose from engineers to CEOs. Internet-related sectors were seen as generating win-win outcomes for all and by all—from the Chinese state to various kinds of capital and labor and the Chinese nation.

Indeed, the rise of the digital economy and internet companies in China is astonishing. According to data collected by the China Academy of Information

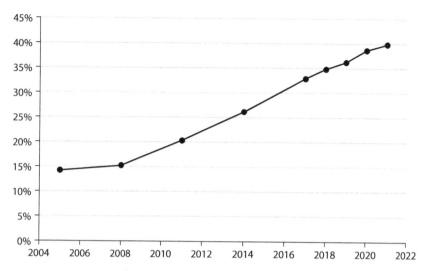

FIGURE 6.1. Digital economy's proportion of China's GDP. *Source*: China
Academy of Information and Communications Technology.

and Communications Technology, a think tank subordinate to the Ministry
of Industry and Information Technology, China's digital economy grew tremendously in the post-2008 global financial crisis period, especially between
2008 and 2017. The China Academy of Information and Communications
Technology defines the digital economy broadly as economic output derived
from the application of digital technology.[4] The digital economy share of GDP
in China has grown from 14.2 percent in 2005 and 15.2 percent in 2008 to
39.8 percent in 2020 (see figure 6.1). Scholars point out that the core of the
digital economy is the digital sector: the IT/ICT sector producing founda-
tional digital goods and services (e.g., software). Also, the emerging digital and
platform services (e.g., e-commerce platforms) created by internet companies
are critical parts of the digital economy.[5]

Despite China's late industrialization, internet companies there developed
around the same time as their US counterparts. The 1980s saw the emergence
of IT/ICT-related sectors in China. Inspired by Silicon Valley experiences,
scientists affiliated with the Chinese Academy of Sciences established IT companies in Beijing. During the dot-com boom in the late 1990s, many internet
companies, such as Sina, Tencent, NetEase, JD, Baidu, and Alibaba, were
founded. Sohu, NetEase, and Sina had their IPOs in the NASDAQ in 2000,
while Tencent went IPO on the Stock Exchange of Hong Kong in 2004. The
post-2008 global financial period marked a new era. As China's major export
markets were seriously hit by the financial crisis, the Chinese state doubled

down on its techno-developmental efforts, hoping domestic consumption would play a greater role alongside international trade. Unlike labor-intensive manufacturing, internet-related sectors were considered cutting-edge and forward-looking by the Chinese state and global financial capital. The post-2008 period also witnessed the IPO boom of Chinese internet companies in the United States and rapid rise of China's internet companies on the world stage.[6] As of 2020, eight of the top twenty internet companies in the world ranked by revenues were headquartered in China, including JD, Tencent, Alibaba, Suning.com, ByteDance, Meituan, Baidu, and NetEase.[7] Among the top ten internet companies in the world ranked by market capitalization, five were Chinese, while the other five were in the United States.[8] To a large extent, the Chinese state, global financial capital, and tech giants in China synergized, collectively advancing techno-development and techno-state capitalism—a digital capitalist system characterized by the rise of tech capital along with an *asymmetrically* symbiotic relationship between tech capital and the state. Only in 2020 did the Chinese state begin to fear that the new birds were out of its control, as I will discuss in chapter 9.

The rise of China's tech giants as key players in and beyond China's economy, and the synergetic relationship between the Chinese state and internet companies, are surprising if we consider the increasingly repressive political climate in China since 2013. From the internet's beginnings in China, scholars and politicians outside China hoped and expected it would foster political liberalization, if not democratization. Indeed, some of the largest Chinese internet companies have provided news services and operated public forums and social media. As I wrote in *The Contentious Public Sphere*, in the late 2000s and early 2010s, many ambitious journalists left liberal-leaning newspaper outlets and instead worked for internet companies to increase their influence within the then-burgeoning public sphere. Internet companies like Tencent, NetEase, and Sina contributed to the rise of China's public sphere. Since 2013, however, President Xi Jinping has significantly elevated the state's scrutiny of internet companies' mediating role in the public sphere.[9] Nonetheless, as I will show in this and subsequent chapters, large internet companies not only became partners of the Chinese state but developed extensive instrumental and infrastructural power of their own as well—eventually alarming the Chinese state, destabilizing state–tech capital synergy, and leading to the Chinese state's efforts to rewire the country's techno-state capitalism. In what follows, I will explain the rise of China's big tech companies, and examine their relationship with the Chinese state and the nature of their power; I will also discuss the rise of China's techno-state capitalism in relation to experiences in South Korea, Taiwan, and the United States.

The Supportive and Tolerant State

While the Chinese state took a harsh regulatory approach to deal with old birds as China turned to techno-development, its relation to new birds was completely the opposite. Here the state endeavored instead to nurture the development of internet companies and internet-related sectors by providing explicit policy support along with a tolerant regulatory environment.

Policy Support

Since the early days of the internet's development, the Chinese state always created a supportive policy environment for internet companies, which only ended with a drastic policy shift in 2020. The state began to give private capital and foreign capital more space in the internet sector in 1996, as China's ninth five-year plan (1996–2000) highlighted the development of IT and the internet.[10] In the aftermath of the 2008 financial crisis, the state selected the internet as a pillar industry, making its development a critical component of the governmental efforts to transform and upgrade China's economy.[11] The twelfth five-year plan (2011–15) included internet-related industries as strategic emerging industries, emphasizing the development of "the next generation" of IT and internet, the IoT, cloud computing, high-end software, and information services. The plan also promoted integrating informatization and industrialization as well as developing a digital economy and digital governance.[12]

In 2015, as China's economic growth rates slowed, the Chinese state doubled down on the role of the internet in the state's domestic and international developmental agendas: as a tool to promote "mass entrepreneurship" and "mass innovation"; generator of new industries, new business forms (*xin yetai*), and new business models; important sector to provide high-quality jobs and absorb surplus labor; stimulator of online and offline consumption; integrator of different industries; and infrastructure of the Chinese state's Belt and Road Initiative (BRI)—a global infrastructure project that seeks to connect Asia with Africa and Europe.[13] In 2015, Premier Li further announced the Internet Plus campaign to use the internet to build a network of banks, financial services, e-commerce, entertainment, other daily services, and modern manufacturing industries.[14] Internet Plus and Made in China 2025, both announced in 2015, are two critical and interconnected components of China's techno-developmental policy.

To be sure, while the Chinese state supported the development of internet companies and internet-related sectors, it kept a watchful eye on issues related to national security and social stability too. As I mentioned in chapter 2,

China's economic development unfolded with the rise of neoliberal globalization. Given amicable global conditions, national security issues resulting from geopolitical tensions were not salient before the onset of the 2018 US-China trade war, although the Chinese state, as I will explain shortly, did restrict foreign capital in certain ways for national security reasons. The Chinese state's concerns were mainly around social stability and threats to the political monopoly of the CCP. Such worries began to be framed as threats to national security in official discourse under Xi.[15] But the regulatory effort before 2020 mainly focused on censorship and ideological control.

Importantly, China's Great Firewall, which aims at censorship and political control, has functioned as a de facto economic shield for the Chinese government to reserve its enormous domestic market for homegrown internet companies, as demonstrated by Google's decision to withdraw from China in 2010 due to censorship-related issues.[16] US-based digital tech giants ultimately are subject to laws and political norms in the United States. As Barry Naughton wrote, "The tripartite combination of party control of information, industrial-policy protectionism, and dynamic and competitive enterprises means that Chinese cyberspace is almost entirely separate from the global, US-dominated internet. All of the largest social media platforms used worldwide are blocked by the Chinese firewall, and their alternatives are owned and operated by Chinese companies."[17] The Chinese state's policies have provided test beds and opportunities for internet companies, but China's homegrown internet companies still have to compete with one another, as illustrated by the heated competition between Alibaba and Tencent in mobile payment and cloud services.[18]

Regulatory Tolerance

The bird/cage logic under China's techno-developmental regime presumes the allocation of rewards and punishments according to the perceived worth of birds. One of the most important ways in which the Chinese state nurtured internet companies and internet-related sectors was through regulatory toleration and exemption. The Chinese state's regulatory toleration is best exemplified by the ambiguous legal environment that has allowed internet companies to access global financial capital. The Chinese central state has developed diverse, sometimes even seemingly contradictory ways to utilize foreign capital. The state allows FDI in nonstrategic sectors (e.g., traditional manufacturing). To a large extent, the rise of China's labor-intensive, export-oriented manufacturing resulted from the alliance between local states and FDI.[19] Yet the Chinese state impedes or even prohibits FDI in strategic sectors, despite China's promise to the WTO to do otherwise.[20] Crucially, the government has maintained an outright ban on foreign investment in China's internet sector to prevent foreign influence or control due to national security concerns as internet companies provide news and information services to a huge populace.[21]

Nonetheless, the Chinese state fully understood that internet companies would need capital to prosper, and the state would need tech firms and global financial capital to advance techno-development, so it has permitted internet companies to access global financial capital in indirect ways. To wit, the Chinese state has allowed internet companies to circumvent its own legal ban, as evidenced by the state's tacit permission for foreign portfolio investment in the form of variable interest entity (VIE).[22] VIE refers to a legal business structure in which a public company has a variable interest not based on having the majority of voting rights.[23] Using this structure, tech giants headquartered in China establish offshore holding companies, often in the Cayman Islands, in order to receive venture capital investment and launch an IPO. In a VIE structure, foreign investors invest in an offshore holding company that channels equity capital into a wholly foreign-owned enterprise (WFOE) in China, while Chinese shareholders own shares at the offshore level. Since a WFOE is not qualified to apply for an operating license in China due to its foreign equity, it nominates Chinese shareholders to own an operating company that possesses a valid license for business in China. Although the WFOE cannot exercise shareholding control over the operating company according to Chinese law, a set of complicated contracts are established between the WFOE, Chinese shareholders, and the operating company to ensure the profits and control of the WFOE. Specifically, the contracts secure that the WFOE and ultimate shareholders of the offshore holding company not only capture the operating company's profits in the form of service fees and royalties but also effectively control how Chinese shareholders vote in the operating company in China.[24] Notwithstanding the Chinese government's tolerance, the VIE structure is legally risky because of the uncertain enforceability of contracts. If Chinese shareholders or the operating company do not respect the contracts they have with the WFOE, the latter will have to enforce the contracts. It is possible that the Chinese authorities could consider a VIE illegal.[25] Therefore Chinese tech companies, such as Alibaba, Tencent, Meituan, and Didi, point out the legal risk of using a VIE structure in their public corporate documents as they do not know whether or when the Chinese state might close this loophole.

Essentially, the Chinese state created and continues to maintain a legally ambiguous environment for the selected new birds to access capital and the state to achieve its developmental goals without relinquishing control. There have been some attempts to close the legal loophole from some parts of the government, but at the time of this writing, the loophole continues to exist.[26]

Such legal ambiguity has led to asymmetrical symbiotic relationships between the Chinese state, internet companies, and global financial capital.[27] At the end of the day, the profits of internet companies and global financial capital depend on the Chinese government's continuing regulatory tolerance.

The Chinese state's regulatory tolerance can also be illustrated by the inertia of China's regulatory authorities in dealing with complaints about monopolistic or anticompetitive practices between 2008 and 2020. China's Antimonopoly Law went into effect in 2008. Since then, some internet companies started to file private, antitrust litigations against other firms (e.g., Baidu, Qihoo 360, and Tencent) in court to ask for compensation, largely because the regulatory authorities in charge of the Antimonopoly Law, particularly the State Administration for Industry and Commerce, failed to respond to or address the complaints in the first place.[28] Legal scholar Angela Zhang argues that due to the central leadership's support for the internet sector and active lobbying from Chinese tech firms, Chinese regulatory authorities before 2020 were averse to regulating Chinese tech giants, despite the latter's legally questionable practices.[29]

Generally, Chinese policy makers see tensions between regulation and development since strict regulation of new technology and business might restrict innovation, thereby undermining economic growth and China's advantage in global competition. The central leadership thus often balances addressing risks and stimulating economic development by strengthening or relaxing regulation. After Li became the premier in 2013, he immediately promoted decentralizing administrative power and enhancing governance to reduce the state's intervention in the economy at the microlevel in order to invigorate market activities.[30] In 2015, as the economy slowed down, he instructed state agencies to "streamline decentralization, enhance governance, and optimize the government's service to businesses and people" (*fang guan fu*).[31]

As I mentioned earlier, the Chinese state kicked off the Internet Plus initiative in 2015 to encourage connections between the internet sector and other sectors, thereby promoting new business forms and models. Since the emerging business forms and models enabled by internet-related technologies have cut across different sectors, regulatory agencies, and geographic areas, however, they have created uncertainties, risks, and tremendous regulation challenges too. Such problems can be illustrated by regulatory issues in the growing ride-hailing market, where Didi became the dominant business actor.

Didi began taxi-hailing services in 2012. In 2014, it commenced ride-hailing services, although the legality of such services remained murky in China. Taxi services were subject to strict regulations, and it was unclear whether ride-hailing services would be subject to similar ones. In fact, a few municipal governments, such as Shanghai, prohibited ride-hailing services in their jurisdic-tions, but eventually the State Council approved the services in 2016. Although it operated in legally gray zones before the state's final approval, Didi aggres-sively acquired its competitors in 2015 and 2016, including Kuaidi and Uber China, to increase its market share.[32] As a result of the acquisition, Uber be-came the second-largest investor of Didi. Didi's business model not only impacted market competition but also triggered social protests. After Didi initiated ride-hailing services in 2014, taxi drivers using Didi's taxi-hailing app complained that ride-hailing services negatively impacted their earnings since the ride-hailing services connected customers to drivers without taxi licenses. To express their grievances, taxi drivers protested in Beijing, Nanjing, Shenyang, Shenzhen, and Xi'an against Didi's ride-hailing services and the government's nonintervention. Protesters even surrounded Didi's headquar-ters in Beijing in 2015.[33] The central government was well aware of the poten-tial problems and risks associated with ride-hailing services. For example, in 2016, the State Council pointed out risks associated with the ride-hailing services, especially customers' personal safety, cyberspace security, sensitive data about national security, drivers' legal rights and interests, unfair market competition, and social stability.[34] Nonetheless, the central state still approved the services in 2016.

In this context, despite the potential risks associated with new technologies as well as business forms and models in general, Premier Li formulated the regulatory principle of being "tolerant and prudent" (*baorong shenshen*) in his Report on the Work of the Government in March 2017.[35] He explained that he was not suggesting a laissez-faire approach because the government would explore necessary "safety valves" and "redlines" to deal with unacceptable risks.[36] Li argued that a tolerant and prudent regulatory approach would create space for new business forms and models to prosper, thereby facilitating in-dustrial upgrading and transformation, generating employment opportunities, and helping the Chinese nation to achieve its developmental goals. The same principle reoccurred in his Report on the Work of the Government in 2018, 2019, and 2020.

With unambivalent signals from the highest leadership, the State Council, National Development and Reform Commission, and other central state agen-cies enacted guidelines and specific policies to encourage the development of the sharing as well as platform economies based on the tolerant and prudent regulatory principle in 2017–19. Like Li, various central state agencies hoped such policies would help solve overcapacity problems in obsolete sectors, gen-erate employment opportunities, accelerate industrial upgrading, and develop globally renowned and competitive platforms. They wanted tech companies to do well in China and then "go out to the world."[37]

The tolerant and encouraging tendency of these policies is illustrated in the fact that the guidelines and policies suggest government agencies specify situations in which platforms can have immunity from legal liability. Furthermore, government agencies are encouraged to relax or even eliminate administrative permissions for market entry except in areas related to personal safety, social stability, financial risks, and national security. The State Council warned that using obsolete methods to regulate new business forms and models would stifle burgeoning business. Corresponding to Li's call to decentralize administrative power, the guideline for developing the platform economy stipulates that state agencies, from the National Development and Reform Commission to Ministry of Industry and Information Technology, Cyberspace Administration of China (CAC), State Administration for Market Regulation (SAMR), Ministry of Public Security, and local governments should be responsible for their regulatory tasks, *respectively*. This shows that the State Council did not intend to closely coordinate or oversee different state agencies but rather authorized them to make individual decisions. The central state also instructed local governments and different state agencies to develop evaluation metrics to incentivize governmental support of the sharing economy.[38] Meanwhile, the central state required media to cover the sharing economy only in positive ways.[39]

The tolerant and prudent guidelines and policies made by the central state nonetheless did point out issues that should be addressed, including but not limited to labor protection, individual data privacy, data sharing between state and businesses as well as between businesses, monopoly and market competition, and the state's technological capacity for oversight. But it was clear that the central state prioritized giving internet companies "adequate space for development," and would only intervene if emerging business forms and models triggered safety valves or crossed redlines, as Li stated.[40] I will explain these safety valves or redlines in chapter 9.

The State and Big Tech Partnership

Over time, the Chinese state and big tech companies in China developed intimate relationships and partnerships under the country's techno-developmental regime. These relationships manifest in many ways. CEOs of tech firms have served as representatives of the National People's Congress and National Committee of the Chinese People's Political Consultative Conference, such as Tencent's Ma Huateng, Baidu's Li Yanhong, Xiaomi's Lei Jun, and JD's Liu Qiangdong.[41] One might question whether these representatives actually have much political influence, but the Chinese state itself acknowledged that Ma's proposal as a National People's Congress representative contributed to the Internet Plus initiative.[42] Executives of China's big tech firms also frequently serve or have served as representatives for local committees of the Chinese People's Political Consultative Conference as well as People's Congresses in Beijing, Shanghai, Guangdong, and Zhejiang—China's postindustrial frontiers.

Tencent and Alibaba, the two largest tech titans, enjoyed informal channels through which they could communicate with and submit reports to the highest leadership, specifically President Xi and Premier Li. With Xi and Li's support, the two giants invited various state agencies to visit their offices and promote their agendas. They obtained support from scholars by funding the latter's projects and conferences too. Those scholars, in turn, provided inputs that supported the positions of tech giants in law- and policy-making processes.[43] The enactment of China's E-Commerce Law shows, for example, that when there were no significant concerns about national security, tech giants were able to successfully shape the law in their favor and lower their legal responsibility in the name of promoting national economic development—even when opposed by some central-level state agencies and other stakeholders.[44]

Additionally, tech firms hired former government officials to influence government policy and grease the wheels of state-business relationships.[45] Alibaba, for instance, hired high-level officials from the Ministry of Industry and Information Technology.[46] And when hiring government affairs professionals, tech firms preferred people with work experience in the government. In their interaction with officials, government affairs professionals focused on helping officials to increase their performance evaluations.[47] Since the state is a powerful market buyer and regulator, a strong state-business relationship helps tech firms obtain public procurement, subsidies, public investment (e.g., investment from the China Investment Corporation—China's sovereign wealth fund), test bed opportunities, honor and recognition, a friendly policy and regulatory environment, and media advertisement opportunities, while avoiding regulatory problems.[48] This symbiotic state-business relationship contributed to the exponential growth of tech giants in China.

The Chinese state and China's leading internet companies gradually formed a partnership in developing digital governance and digital economy. Although the two agendas look distinct and separate, infrastructure building for digital governance is a lucrative market and critical way to advance the digital economy. As I mentioned in chapter 3, the techno-developmental regime based on the bird/cage logic galvanized the state's efforts to scientize its statecraft. Enthusiastic about digital technology, the Chinese state looked to big data technologies to help the government achieve scientific and data-driven decision-making and governance. In the mid-2010s, local governments in many localities began to collaborate with third-party applications, especially

Alibaba's Alipay and Tencent's WeChat Pay, to support delivering public services such as public transportation and health care.[49] As a result, mobile applications developed by numerous local governments embed Alipay or WeChat as payment options. Meanwhile, Alipay and WeChat both have a "city service" module that helps users access public services (e.g., booking a medical or marriage registration appointment, inquiring about traffic violations, and paying utility bills) and get real-time information about transportation. Research finds that the wide user base of apps like Alipay and WeChat along with the technological capacity of large internet companies endow China's tech giants with bargaining power over local governments as well as allow the companies to play a greater role in policy formulation at the local level.[50]

The Chinese state's zeal for digital governance reached a new high in 2014, when the central state announced a national development strategy to promote big data–based decision-making in the government. The plan led to widespread efforts to apply big data, cloud computing, AI, and the IoT to core government activities, thus creating a vast and lucrative public procurement market. The government estimated that there would be a 300 billion RMB (around US$47.8 billion) market between 2014 and 2018.[51] By the end of 2017, over 65 percent of China's provinces had built government cloud platforms.[52] China's state-owned telecom operators and large private tech firms (e.g., Tencent, Alibaba, and Huawei) have played a critical role in such endeavors.

The state's enthusiasm for digital governance manifests in all kinds of "smart city" plans—initiatives that emphasize using digital technologies to improve the operational efficiency of cities—which became popular in the mid-2010. Large internet companies, especially Alibaba, Tencent, Baidu, and JD, have been among the most important players in smart city projects. For instance, the Shanghai municipal government and Alibaba signed a strategic cooperation agreement in 2015. The two parties agreed to cooperate in cloud computing, big data, smart city building, e-commerce, financial technology (fintech), smart health, and the social credit system, thereby helping Shanghai move toward a global technology innovation center. In the same year, Tencent and the Shanghai municipal government signed a similar strategic cooperation agreement, which sought to drive economic transformation and upgrading through technological innovation.[53] One of the most famous smart city projects is Alibaba's City Brain—a pilot project and open AI platform developed in Alibaba's home city of Hangzhou in 2016. The system uses real-time data to provide suggestions about how to use police, medical, and road resources. Thus far, little is known about the efficacy of smart city projects like City Brain in reality.[54] What is known is that City Brain reduced the traffic congestion problems in Hangzhou.[55] As of 2021, there were over five hundred smart cities in China.[56]

In addition to policy about digital governance, the Chinese state's domestic and transnational economic policies deepened and expanded the state–tech capital partnership. Here I provide two examples. The first concerns the state–tech capital partnership in creating flexible employment (*linghuo jiuye*), which means nonstandard employment. With China's old birds now deemed obsolete and the campaign to replace low-skilled workers with robots in full swing, the question of where exactly workers should now work under China's techno-developmental regime moved to center stage. Premier Li began to emphasize the government's support for flexible and new forms of employment in his 2016 Report on the Work of the Government.[57] In 2018, he pointed out the role of the internet, particularly in creating new form of employment.[58] Responding to the central government's policy, China's large tech firms, such as Alibaba, Didi, and Meituan, all stressed their contributions to generating a wide range of employment opportunities while working with local governments to provide employment for migrant workers through their platforms. For instance, in 2016, Alibaba claimed that it created 15 million jobs and 30 million indirect employment opportunities, while Didi said that its company supplied drivers with 13.3 million jobs.[59]

The second example is the state–tech capital partnership in the BRI. Announced in 2013, the BRI is a state-sponsored global infrastructural program designed to tie China with Eurasian and African countries. Scholars argue that BRI is a continuation of China's "going out" strategy that began in the early 2000s, and sought to expand China's global influence and solve its domestic economic challenges, particularly industrial overcapacity (e.g., in steel, cement, optical fiber, and ICT-related products).[60] The BRI has two layers: physical and digital infrastructure. Announced in 2015, the Digital Silk Road (DSR) is a significant part of the BRI.[61] The DSR aims to assist recipient states to create "smart infrastructure," which integrates ubiquitous sensors, telecommunications networks, AI capabilities, cloud computing, e-commerce and mobile payment systems, surveillance technology, and smart cities.[62] Through the DSR, the Chinese state promotes the adoption of the Chinese standards for custom procedures, internet connections, financial transactions, railroads, and highways.[63] China's digital giants like Baidu, Alibaba, and Tencent became the Chinese state's partners in implementing the BRI and DSR. For instance, as of 2019, Alibaba had implemented City Brain in 23 cities across Asia.[64] Through its participation in the BRI and DSR, Alibaba also expanded its e-commerce and logistics services (AliExpress), online payment system (Alipay), and cloud services (Alibaba Cloud) globally.[65] To operate Alibaba Cloud, Alibaba has built data centers in the Middle East, Asia, North America, Europe, and Australia. On its website, Alibaba introduces "Alibaba Cloud's Global Infrastructure" and states that "Alibaba Cloud operates 85 availability zones in 28 regions around the world with more global regions set to follow."[66] Many of Alibaba's data centers are located in BRI countries. The Chinese state would not have been able to implement BRI and DSR projects without its partnerships with China's tech giants.

The Boundary-Spanning New Birds

The supportive and tolerant state and state-tech partnership created boundary-spanning new birds that straddle between different industries and sectors, the private and public, and the local, national, and global. These boundary-spanning properties have made the new birds powerful across different spheres of lives and localities.

Between Industries and Sectors

The Chinese state's long-standing preference for business conglomerates helps explain why, until 2020, it enthusiastically encouraged tech companies to grow across industries and sectors. Since the late 1990s, when the Chinese state began to restructure SOEs, it promoted collaboration between powerful businesses (*qiang qiang lian he*) as well as cultivated business conglomerates capable of operating across regions, industries, sectors, or ownership types.[67] The state reasoned that establishing conglomerates would help businesses become globally competitive and thus speed China's economic development.[68] Furthermore, establishing conglomerates could streamline political control of the businesses involved in information production and dissemination. Since restructuring China's press organizations in the 2000s, the Chinese state now needs to deal with only a few conglomerates instead of numerous organizations in a fragmented market.[69] Indeed, in Zhejiang, where Alibaba is headquartered, the provincial government specifically encouraged platform businesses to operate across regions, industries, and countries.[70] The Internet Plus initiative followed the same logic.

The state's encouragement of cross-industry and sector operation provided a favorable playground for China's tech firms to develop "super platforms" or super apps, which are absent in the United States. Exemplified by Alibaba's Alipay and Tencent's WeChat, super apps are "do-everything apps that bring together an expansive suite of services within a single interface."[71] They have high penetration rates among cell phone users, in part because of network effects and first-mover advantages.[72] China's tech giants embed other platforms within their super platforms that they either invest in or in some manner control, while giving the selected platforms high visibility in their super platforms.[73] Services invested in by the tech giants and included in super apps span a range of industries or sectors, from fintech to news, ride hailing, food delivery, online shopping, entertainment, hospitality, and so forth.

As they grew and absorbed global capital, China's big tech companies became global venture capital investors themselves. For instance, Alibaba has an investment arm, Alibaba Capital Partners; Tencent has the Tencent Industry Win-Win Fund and Tencent Industry Collaboration Fund. The tech giants have created investment portfolios and actively pursued mergers and acquisitions to expand and consolidate their market power and revenues.[74] The big techs and their associated firms constitute largely exclusive app ecosystems or "walled gardens."[75] As of 2020, fourteen and seven, respectively, of the top thirty most popular apps in China belong to Tencent and Alibaba's ecosystems.[76] Through capital investment and mergers and acquisitions, the tech giants can decrease the level of competition in a market and increase the market dominance of their affiliate firms. As media studies scholars astutely point out, China's tech firms build their super apps through the mechanisms of financialization (e.g., providing capital to or acquiring other platforms), conglomeration (e.g., building a multi-industry business group), platformization (e.g., supplying a technological interface that incorporates other platforms), and infrastructuralization (e.g., achieving near-ubiquitous penetration).[77] In so doing, China's leading tech companies have been able to extend their power from one market to another, establish their own app ecosystems, and straddle the boundaries between different industries and sectors.[78]

Between Private and Public

Scholars studying varieties of state capitalism define *state capitalism* as "an economic system in which the state uses various tools for proactive intervention in economic production and the functioning of markets." They argue that state interventions can occur in domestic markets and abroad, in the interests of domestic firms and for diplomatic purposes.[79] China's state capitalism is characterized by the prominent role of SOEs as a tool for state intervention in the economy. Through the State-Owned Assets Supervision and Administration Commission of the State Council, the state maintains direct ownership of assets in strategic sectors of the economy (e.g., telecommunications, energy, transportation, and finance) while engaging in industrial policy to promote priority sectors. The state also has control over personnel appointments for top leadership and managerial positions in SOEs.[80] Due to the critical role of SOEs, scholars consider them the primary vehicles for Chinese state capitalism.[81] As such, leading SOEs exist as China's "national champions" that advance the interests of the nation.[82] As of 2021, 82 Chinese SOEs were among the 2021 Fortune Global 500.[83]

Legal scholars Curtis J. Milhaupt and Wentong Zheng note that scholars and commentators often see Chinese state capitalism as essentially synonymous with SOEs.[84] Indeed, if we only consider ownership types, we might underappreciate the critical role of China's tech companies in the country's state capitalism. But Milhaupt and Zheng assert that due to China's institutional environment, large, successful SOEs, privately owned enterprises, and mixed-ownership enterprises are in reality similar in terms of their market dominance, receipt of state subsidies, proximity to state power, and execution of the state's policy objectives. Irrespective of their ownership types, vast and leading SOEs, privately owned enterprises, and mixed-ownership enterprises obtain special advantages from the state by aligning themselves with the state's interests, goals, and priorities.[85] Therefore the boundary between leading SOEs and privately owned enterprises in terms of their role in China's state capitalism is much more blurred than what is suggested by scholarship and media reports.

China's mammoth internet companies best exemplify the large, successful privately owned enterprises pointed out by Milhaupt and Zheng. In fact, the tech giants could have more "public" functions than typical SOEs. As I have described, the Chinese state has depended on the expertise of China's tech giants to advance both the digital economy and the state's digital governance. Despite their private legal status and intimate connection with global financial capital, tech giants like Alibaba and Tencent are considered national champions too.[86] They have built and provided national infrastructures, such as the online payment system, private and public cloud, and digital governance infrastructure. Moreover, leading tech companies serve as not only the state's contractors that supply digital products and services to the state and public but also the Chinese state's partners in collaborative governance projects, as illustrated by the role of the tech giants in monitoring urban activity and public services as well as participating in urban governance through smart city plans.[87] Arguably, few of China's leading SOEs are directly involved in managing and governing the populace.

Between the Local, National, and Global

In *The Coming of Post-Industry Society*, Daniel Bell wrote that the pace of change and change of scale are "the organizing ideas for the discussion of the central structural components of the post-industrial society, the dimensions of knowledge and technology." Bell added that the revolutions in communication and transportation have "broadened the span of control over the activities of any organization from a center," and "the major social revolution of the latter half of the twentieth century is the attempt to master 'scale' by new technological devises, whether it be 'real time' computer information or new kinds of quantitative programming."[88]

The issue of scale is certainly salient in China's techno-state capitalism. Both the Chinese state and China's tech firms have attempted to "master scale." China's tech giants straddle the boundaries between the local, national, and global, thanks to their technological and market capacity as well as their partnership with different levels of the Chinese government in initiatives of various scales. Leading internet companies often try out their business models in major cities and roll out the models across localities. For example, Meituan has a one-stop platform for food, transportation, travel, shopping, and entertainment. According to its IPO prospectus in 2018, the company served 310 million users and 4.4 million active merchants in over 2,800 cities and counties in China. Presumably it could be difficult for many of the local governments in the 2,800 or so cities and counties to regulate Meituan. Research also shows that when Tencent helped many local governments to build and implement a mobile health care payment system based on WeChat, Tencent had bargaining power vis-à-vis local governments because of its technological capacity and dominant online payment system.[89] Such potentially unequal relationships between China's big tech firms and many local governments are a cause for concern.

Furthermore, as national champions, China's tech giants have participated in the Chinese state's global infrastructure development projects under the BRI and DSR. Whereas the state firmly controls SOEs, tech giants flirt with foreign capital and are subject to the rule of foreign sovereign states. For example, Softbank Group, a Japanese multinational conglomerate holding company, held the largest stake in Alibaba.[90] As I mentioned earlier, many tech firms headquartered in China adopt a VIE structure, and there have been governmental and scholarly concerns about whether these companies are adequately "Chinese" as well as whether the Chinese state should outlaw VIEs.[91] Many tech firms in China, such as Alibaba, also held IPOs in the United States and hence are subject to US laws. The Chinese state wants Chinese companies to be globally influential, but there could be conflicts of interests between the state and tech giants, particularly as geopolitical tensions grow.

The Power of the New Birds

As China's tech giants penetrated different spheres of life and consolidated their market power with support from the Chinese state, they developed instrumental and infrastructure power over a vast number of people, including users, workers, and suppliers in China's techno-state capitalism. Scholarship on platform and surveillance capitalism focuses on the instrumental power of tech companies. The near-ubiquitous penetration of technologies developed by China's tech giants and the state–big tech partnership prompt us to consider the infrastructure power of tech firms as well.[92] Here I will explain instrumental and infrastructure power in turn.

Instrumental Power

Bell argues that postindustrial transformation is characterized by the enhancement of *instrumental* powers based on technology over people. His insights in the 1970s were borne out by scholarship in platform and surveillance capitalism four decades later. Research in these areas shows the capability of internet companies in employing technologies, including but not limited to algorithms, AI, and machine learning, and massive data to shape, influence, and control individual behavior.

There are two common instances of instrumental power. The first is what Shoshana Zuboff calls "instrumentarian power," which Zuboff defines as "the instrumentation and instrumentalization of behavior for the purposes of modification, prediction, monetization, and control."[93] The basic idea is that tech firms know and shape human behavior through their extraction and analysis of massive data about individuals, often with the aid of surveillance devices and technologies such as the IoT. After learning about individual preferences and behavior from massive data, tech firms profit from selling certainty or predictability to advertisers. Zuboff labels this mode of capital accumulation "surveillance capitalism," in which human experience exists as "raw material for hidden commercial practices and extraction, prediction, and sales."[94]

In China, advertisement revenues are essential to all tech giants, like Alibaba, Tencent, JD, Baidu, Meituan, Pinduoduo, Kuaishou, and ByteDance.[95] All leading internet companies emphasize precision microtargeting advertising—the technique of matching ads with audiences efficiently and effectively. According to an engineer at Alibaba whom I interviewed, to take one example, Alibaba uses its own data, third-party data (i.e., data from outside sources), and data from IoT devices for precision microtargeting advertising. Through the company's AI platforms, Alibaba can analyze massive data and establish models to predict audience interests, thereby helping Alibaba's clients observe consumer demand and behavior as well as target a specific audience. The AI platforms further help improve the matching process and achieve a higher degree of precision in microtargeting advertising.

The second common instance of instrumental power is the power to control and manage labor by algorithms and big data. As tech companies have built platforms to facilitate exchanges of different kinds of labor between providers and demanders, they have developed algorithms and platform rules to control and manage workers. Algorithmic control and management entails platform-based rating and reputation systems.[96] Since performance evaluations influence how algorithms match workers and demanders of service, algorithms can influence and control workers' behavior. Although tech companies exercise such instrumental power on a wide range of workers, from low-skilled service workers to high-skilled freelance professionals, low-skilled workers tend to be subject to the most intense control, as exemplified by the harsh punishment of delivery workers by platforms like Meituan and Ele.me (chapter 7). The uneven instrumental power that tech companies have over different kinds of workers is partly due to the fact that the evaluation of low-skilled work can be standardized and conducted relatively easily.[97] Also, compared with middle-class people, low-skilled service workers are more likely to work as full-time platform workers and depend on incomes from platform work.[98] The exercise of instrumental power over labor is consequential in China as millions of workers in the obsolete sectors have moved to internet-related sectors to seek a better future, and as the government cracked down on the old birds and began to emphasize the critical role of internet-related sectors to absorb surplus labor.

In addition to instrumental power based on technology and massive data, internet companies exercise power over users, workers, and suppliers based on legal instruments. They use law-based instrumental power to complement and cement technology and data-based instrumental power. As mentioned earlier, tech giants in China successfully shaped the law in their favor and lowered their legal responsibility in the name of promoting national economic development.[99] In *The Age of Surveillance Capitalism*, Zuboff shows how tech companies in the United States use extremely long privacy documents and abusive contracts to help them extract data from users. Even legal experts familiar with surveillance and privacy issues can struggle to make sense of such documents and agreements.[100] With their unfettered contractual freedom, tech companies can impose unilateral power on users. In China, tech giants adopt similar strategies. In the next chapter, I will show how internet companies employ law-based instrumental power and technology along with data-based instrumental power to manage and control workers and suppliers.

Infrastructural Power

Due to their boundary-spanning property, tech giants in China have developed infrastructural power. Sociologist Michael Mann theorizes two types of state power: despotic and infrastructural power. According to him, the Chinese state has both high despotic and infrastructural power, whereas the US state has low despotic and high infrastructural power. Mann uses the term *despotic power* to refer to "the range of actions which the elite is empowered to undertake without routine, institutionalized negotiation with civil society groups." He defines *infrastructural power* as "the capacity of the state to actually penetrate civil society, and to implement logistically political decisions throughout the realm."[101] The state's infrastructural power can be illustrated by its ability to store and recall a massive amount of information about the populace immediately as well as influence the overall economy. Mann further points out that a common logistical technique that the state uses to advance effective state penetration of social life is the rapid communication of messages and transport of people and resources. Importantly, Mann underscores that no logistical technique belongs necessarily to the state or civil society. So on the one hand, states might not be able to maintain control over their logistical inventions. On the other hand, states often appropriate infrastructural techniques pioneered by civil society groups, such as by capitalist enterprises.

In recent years, scholars in media studies have called attention to the "infrastructuralization of platforms" as certain platforms like Google and Facebook have become large and even ubiquitous, and learned to "exploit the power of platforms . . . to gain footholds as the modern-day equivalents of the railroad, telephone, and electric utility monopolies of the late 19th and the 20th centuries."[102] Arguably, tech giants in China like Alibaba and Tencent could have even more extensive infrastructure power than Google and Facebook as the former pair straddle the boundaries between a wide range of industries and sectors, and have developed partnerships with the Chinese government in the digital economy and governance. Alibaba, for example, has dominated the online payment infrastructure and digital cloud infrastructure as well as developed physical logistic infrastructure in China, and its infrastructures extend to other countries.

Crucially, Chinese tech giants can use their infrastructural power to implement not only their own rules (e.g., platform rules, algorithms, and contractual clauses) but also the government's rules and decisions (e.g., those about censorship, political propaganda, public health policy, and taxation) throughout their respective digital realms, as illustrated by the critical role of Alibaba and Tencent in developing and implementing the Health Code, and the role of Meituan and Ele.me in delivering goods and food in numerous cities and counties after the COVID-19 pandemic erupted in China.[103] Another example is taxation. In recent years, large internet companies such as Alibaba, Byte-Dance, Kuaishou, JD.com, Pinduoduo, and Tencent have developed the business model of livestream shopping, which features lively interactions between consumers and influencers—with many of the latter becoming wealthy and famous in the process.[104] In 2021 and 2022, the State Taxation Administration enacted several regulations and instructions about how to collect taxes from livestream shopping. The government stresses the need to work with internet companies to access and analyze platform data on the cloud for tax assessment.[105] The enormous infrastructural power of China's tech giants begs the questions of how the Chinese state and tech giants can maintain their partnership, and as Mann's work would suggest, to what extent and how the Chinese state might appropriate the infrastructural power of the tech giants.

Comparisons with South Korea, Taiwan, and the United States

How can we understand comparatively the rise of big tech firms and techno-state capitalism in China as the Chinese state endeavored to pursue techno-development? It is meaningful to reflect on the Chinese case in relation to experiences in South Korea, Taiwan, and the United States. I will first compare China with South Korea and Taiwan in terms of their trajectories and the outcomes of techno-development. Then I will compare China with the United States in relation to the development and characteristics of their respective global digital capitalism. My discussion will also highlight the transnational connections between China, South Korea, Taiwan, and the United States.

As development scholar D. Hugh Whittaker and his colleagues convincingly argue in *Compressed Development*, the historical time period in which development takes place matters since the geopolitical, institutional, technological, and ideological context for development changes over time.[106] In *Technological Revolutions and Financial Capital*, economist Carlota Perez identified five successive technological revolutions since the eighteenth century. Each is characterized by a distinct materiality—new technologies and new or redefined industries and infrastructures. What Bell wrote about in *The Coming of Post-Industrial Society* corresponds to what Perez calls the fifth technological revolution (i.e., the age of information and telecommunications), which began in 1971 and is marked by the information revolution, cheap microelectronics, and advancement in computers, software, telecommunications, control instruments, and computer-aided biotechnology and new materials. Perez further pointed out that the internet, with its capacity to profoundly transform the rest of the economy and society, constitutes the central infrastructure of the fifth technological revolution.[107]

Since Silicon Valley is the center of the fifth technological revolution, the development and changes there influenced techno-development in South Korea, Taiwan, and China.[108] In the 1960s and 1970s, the semiconductor industry prospered in Silicon Valley. The growth was in part aided by emergent venture capital in Silicon Valley in the 1970s. US companies, though, lost market and technological dominance to Japanese firms in the 1980s. Then Silicon

Valley gradually moved away from advanced manufacturing, especially chip making, first to software, and then to the internet in the 1990s with the commercialization of the internet.[109] According to digital economy scholar Nick Srnicek, the US government tried to stimulate the economy by inducing low interest rates in the 1990s as the global economy had become saddled by overcapacity and overproduction in the manufacturing sector since the 1970s. The policy resulted in the dot-com bubble in the late 1990s. Although the bubble burst in 2000, the intensification of an easy monetary policy, cash glut of large tech firms, and growing technology fads for automation and the sharing economy led to the rise of platform capitalism in the United States in the post-2008 global crisis period.[110]

As I mentioned in chapter 3, both South Korea and Taiwan started to plan for techno-development in the 1970s, eventually becoming successful in the IT-related sectors. As Silicon Valley moved away from advanced manufacturing, South Korea and Taiwan began to build their semiconductor industries, ultimately becoming world leaders in this regard. Although the big tech firms in the United States successfully developed global digital capitalism focusing on software, the internet, and apps, the United States lost its ability and supply chains to produce the hardware on which all computing depends and its dominance in chip making, which economic historian Chris Miller calls the most critical technology in the world today.[111] But despite their success in IT-related sectors, under US-dominated global digital capitalism, South Korea and Taiwan have not developed world-leading internet companies or the kind of digital capitalism that China has developed. In short, in their pursuit of techno-development, South Korea and Taiwan rose as world leaders in the semiconductor industry, but exist only as players within a US-dominated global digital system.

Unlike South Korea and Taiwan, China's shift to techno-development occurred in the mid-2000s—after the commercialization of the internet. Although the Chinese state has endeavored to develop the semiconductor industry as a new bird under its techno-developmental regime, the progress has remained limited as China has had to rely on other countries for advanced chips. As noted earlier, China's economic development in the postreform era relied heavily on FIEs, including Taiwanese FDI.[112] In the 1990s, as many Taiwanese manufacturers established facilities in or relocated to China, former Taiwanese president Lee Teng-hui declared the policy of "avoid haste, be patient" (*jie ji yong ren*) in 1996, prohibiting Taiwan's semiconductor companies from bringing the most advanced technology to China. Although his policy was criticized by major semiconductor companies in Taiwan at that time, in hindsight, Lee strategically prevented the hollowing out of the Taiwanese semiconductor industry. Ultimately, China's techno-development has not been characterized by the success of the semiconductor industry as in the South Korean and Taiwanese cases but instead was driven by the rise of internet giants and techno-state digital capitalism—the kind of techno-development in which the authoritarian state and tech giants can exercise instrumental and infrastructure power over the populace based on digital technology, massive data, and legal instruments.

China and the United States resemble each other as they both developed global digital capitalism. Big tech firms in both countries possess tremendous instrumental and infrastructural power. The Chinese big internet firms benefited tremendously from US investment. As I have mentioned, China's success to a large extent resulted from a vast, protected domestic market shielded by the Great Firewall, support of the state, and global financial capital.[113] Although many tech entrepreneurs in China were inspired by successful tech giants in the United States and the Silicon Valley legend, the Chinese state and China's internet companies have created their own digital capitalist empire, so to speak. With the rise of China's internet companies, Chinese and US digital capitalism eventually became competing global models. The intercapitalist rivalry has intensified as US-China relations have deteriorated in recent years.

But there are crucial differences between China's digital capitalism, which I call techno-state capitalism, and the US counterpart in terms of the role of the state as well as the relationship between the state, tech capital, and society. Although the US state contributed to the development of the internet and other technologies through the Defense Advanced Research Projects Agency, an R&D agency of the US Department of Defense, the state's involvement was limited to R&D in technology at an early stage. In fact, the national context in the United States between the 1980s and late 2010s (i.e., after the election of Ronald Reagan as president and before the increasing US-China rivalry) was characterized by the dominance of neoliberalism and the so-called Californian Ideology along with a strong separation of powers between the executive, legislature, and judiciary as well as between the federal, state, and local levels, and a weak organized labor force. Such contexts led to several connected consequences in terms of the planning and control of techno-development. First, the US state was not expected to take an active role in planning and regulation. Second, despite the existence of a developmental state, it had to be hidden or disguised to avoid attacks from market fundamentalists. As such, centralized or more visible intervention became less likely, as demonstrated by the declining federal investment in R&D since the early 1990s.[114] Third, after the September 11 attacks in 2001, there has been collaboration between the US state and tech firms, but it is largely restricted to intelligence. Fourth, in a politically and legally fragmented institutional environment, and with support from financial capital, tech companies were able to lobby and use technology and law to construct games between persons that benefit their interests.[115] In recent years, however, workers, trade unions, and community activists have started to challenge the instrumental power of tech firms, although collective action remains restrictive and difficult.[116]

In sharp contrast with the US state, the Chinese state went above and beyond to cultivate its new birds, while helping the birds to grow not only domestically but globally too. As such, the rise of China's digital capitalism is a result of a state-led process and the state–tech capital partnership; in comparison, the development of US digital capitalism was not orchestrated by the US state, notwithstanding the state's investment in R&D in the beginning. Yet the Chinese state has made China's leading internet companies both more and less powerful than US big tech firms. On the one hand, tech giants in China are more powerful than their US counterparts in terms of the former's penetration of society, their crucial role in digital governance, and their participation in the Chinese state's ambitious global expansion projects. On the other hand, tech giants in China are nevertheless still birds in a cage built by the mighty Chinese state and thus still dependent on the mercy of the Chinese state. Although tech giants in China have developed impressive technological and legal instruments and can exercise power over the populace with the permission of the Chinese state, the Chinese state—as the ultimate power holder—can exercise instrumental power over China's tech giants and appropriate the latter's power (chapter 9). Finally, while users and laborers in the US digital capitalist system are mostly subject only to the instrumental power of US tech giants, Chinese users and laborers are subject to the power of both the Chinese state and China's tech giants.

Conclusion

This chapter has detailed the rise of China's tech giants and techno-state capitalism as the Chinese state endeavored to pursue techno-development. Under China's previous developmental model based on export-oriented, labor-intensive manufacturing, alliances existed between local governments and the leading manufacturing FIEs like Foxconn. Such alliances still exist in China today, especially in inland provinces. But with the shift to techno-development, partnerships between the Chinese state—at both the central and local levels—and the leading internet companies became increasingly salient and critical. Some discussions on digital capitalism in China only emphasize the Chinese state's competitive relationships with China's tech firms. For example, Zuboff wrote, "In China the state vies with its surveillance capitalists for control."[117] As I will show in chapter 9, such a description is accurate, but insufficient in capturing the state's effort to cultivate China's leading internet companies, dependency of the state on the technological capacity of the big tech firms, and dynamic state–tech capital partnership. In a supportive policy condition and tolerant regulatory environment, internet companies have developed unprecedented boundary-spanning instrumental and infrastructural power that helps the Chinese state advance the digital economy and governance as well as achieve the goal of techno-development. Arguably, no other types of business conglomerates in the PRC's history have been capable of penetrating so many different spheres of life, connecting with so many types of organizations (e.g., government agencies and various private businesses), and influencing so many individuals in complicated ways as China's leading internet companies.

As they have grown, tech giants in China have become cobuilders of the expanding instrumental apparatus under China's techno-developmental regime. As demonstrated in chapters 2–5, in order to foster techno-development, the Chinese state built an arsenal of technological and legal instruments based on the bird/cage logic to allocate rewards and punishments to individuals, firms, and government agencies. Living in the cage constituted by these instruments, citizens, officials, and businesses struggle for better classification outcomes and metric values. I have also shown the class dimension of the instruments as they tend to assign resources to high-end capital and labor.

China's leading internet companies have participated in building the instrumental apparatus in two ways. First, they have helped the Chinese state build its technological instruments in all kinds of digital governance projects. The Chinese state and tech giants are in fact surprisingly similar in terms of their engagement and obsession with the problem of matching. The Chinese state is involved in matching birds with limited resources or different categories of cages, while the tech giants match ads with audiences and service providers with demanders using big data, algorithms, AI, and machine learning. The Chinese state greatly values the expertise of leading tech firms in scientific matching as it can help the state's goals of scientific planning, decision-making, and ruling.

Second, the Chinese state permitted the large internet firms to freely build and employ their technological and legal instruments in their respective digital kingdoms due in part to their perceived contributions to techno-development. In their digital kingdoms, the tech giants act like sovereigns and can impose rules on users, laborers, and suppliers unilaterally. In some ways, the situation in China resembles what Zuboff refers to, as noted earlier, as a politics of lawlessness and the self-regulation of tech companies in the United States. According to Zuboff, in the US case, "a weakened state in which elected officials depend upon corporate wealth in every election cycle has shown little appetite to contest behavior modification as a market project, let alone to stand for the moral imperatives of the autonomous individual."[118] In other words, the unfettered power of tech giants in the United States resulted from a weakened state. In stark contrast, the almost unconstrained power of China's leading internet companies came not in spite of but rather thanks to the Chinese state's deliberate decisions. As the Chinese state saw the tensions between regulation and the goal of techno-development, it deliberately chose to prioritize the latter and let go of the former.

Having explained the rise of the new birds and techno-state capitalism under China's techno-developmental regime, I will move to workers' lives in the new digital kingdoms in the next chapter. Many workers I talked to in the obsolete sectors viewed the digital and platform economy created by China's tech giants as a land of freedom and opportunity as well as a pathway to less exploitative jobs. In chapter 7, I follow some of them as they move from the obsolete sectors to the realms of the new birds and discuss the new cages some workers have discovered there.

7

From Factories to Platforms

AS CHINA'S techno-development unfolded, the Chinese state and workers saw great promise in the internet-related sectors to provide employment opportunities. On the government side, Premier Li Keqiang began to emphasize the government's support for flexible employment and new forms of employment in 2016.[1] In 2018, he pointed out the role of the internet, in particular, in creating new forms of employment.[2] According to the National Bureau of Statistics, more than two hundred million people (around 15 percent of China's total population) had flexible employment in 2021—nearly three times more than there had been in 2020. The National Bureau of Statistics did not provide information on the actual composition of the statistics, but China's official media portrayed the rapid rise in flexible employment as the successful outcome of China's platform economy.[3]

The penetration of internet or platform companies into hundreds of Chinese cities means that they can create numerous jobs throughout the country—not only in first-tier cities, but in second-, third-, and fourth-tier ones.[4] Many of these cities expanded in the process of rapid state-led land urbanization (chapter 2) as local governments sought to boost economic growth and fiscal revenues. The process led to a substantial amount of new but unsold housing in third- and fourth-tier cities (chapter 5). As discussed in chapter 3, China's techno-developmental regime has a specific spatial logic that excludes what are categorized as undeserving firms and laborers from accessing valuable resources, such as land and essential public services, in the most prosperous parts of China. Jobs created by internet companies in second-, third-, and fourth-tier cities were seen as a potential way to reduce the migration of the "low-end population" to China's postindustrial frontiers. Workers staying in third- and fourth-tier cities might also help absorb unsold housing units there.

On the workers' side, as described in chapter 4, I found that the majority of workers were indifferent to the adverse impacts of the techno-developmental regime on labor-intensive manufacturing industries. Most

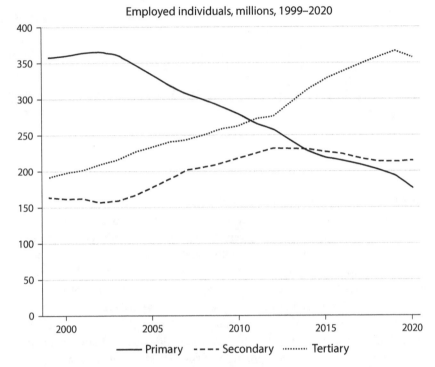

Employed individuals, millions, 1999–2020

FIGURE 7.1. Total employment in China by sector. *Source*: National Bureau of Statistics of China. *Note*: The figure was made by Dr. Ilaria Mazzocco, based on Rozelle et al. 2020.

workers—particularly those who were young and without children—did not express concern about robotization or the government's crackdowns on the old birds, because like the government, they viewed factory jobs as obsolete, undesirable, and transitional. Factory managers complained that they were losing workers to the platform sector, especially the food delivery platforms. In 2017, several of the workers I interviewed told me they quit their factory jobs and started working as food delivery platform workers. Their decisions prompted me to follow their lives from factories to platforms.

The decisions of my interviewees reflect the changing employment patterns in China. Here I present research conducted by Scott Rozelle and his colleagues along with statistics analyzed by Dr. Ilaria Mazzocco.[5] As figure 7.1 shows, although employment in the primary sector (i.e., agriculture) continues to decline, workers no longer flock to the secondary sector (i.e., manufacturing and construction). In fact, employment in the secondary sector has declined somewhat since 2012, whereas employment in the tertiary sector (i.e., services) has grown enormously. Since most nonagricultural jobs are in cities,

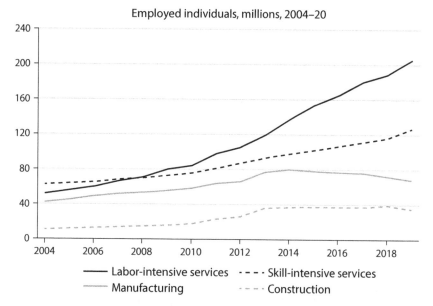

FIGURE 7.2. Urban employment in the secondary and tertiary sectors in China.
Source: National Bureau of Statistics of China. *Note*: The figure was made by
Dr. Ilaria Mazzocco, based on Rozelle et al. 2020.

urban employment statistics provide more information about the growing
employment in services. As figure 7.2 portrays, with China's turn to techno-
development, employment in skill-intensive services (e.g., technology, finance, and education) has grown, but employment in labor-intensive services
has also increased tremendously. Since the overall urban employment has not
grown significantly in recent years, the rising employment in labor-intensive
services and declining employment in manufacturing and construction suggest that labor-intensive services have absorbed many workers who previously
worked in manufacturing and construction. The timing of the rise in labor-
intensive service employment corresponds to the timing of expansion in the
platform economy.

Research further demonstrates that the quality and security of jobs in labor-
intensive services tend to be problematic. A large proportion of such jobs falls
into the category of informal employment, in which workers do not have
secure employment contracts, benefits, or social protection (e.g., pension benefits, urban health insurance, and unemployment insurance).[6] As such, workers with informal employment are not protected by social safety nets. In
addition, real wages in informal employment have, on average, grown more
slowly than in formal employment and GDP.[7] As Figure 7.3 depicts, informal

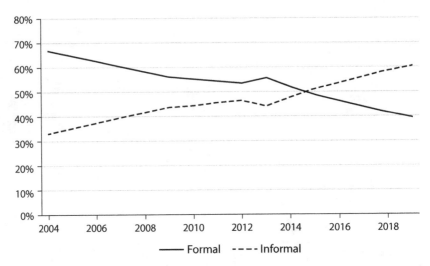

FIGURE 7.3. The share of employment in the formal and informal economy. *Source*: National Bureau of Statistics of China. *Note*: The figure was made by Dr. Ilaria Mazzocco, based on Rozelle et al. 2020.

employment had grown and accounted for almost 60 percent of all nonagricultural workers in cities in 2019, up from around 35 percent in the mid-2000s, when China began to shift to techno-development. Figure 7.4 further shows that most urban informal employment is in labor-intensive services. In 2019, close to two hundred million workers in labor-intensive services did not have formal employment. Although many of my interviewees complained about manufacturing jobs, statistics indicate that manufacturing and construction jobs are more likely to fall into the category of formal employment than labor-intensive service jobs. Overall, research in economics and employment statistics provide valuable information to interpret the announcement of the National Bureau of Statistics that more than two hundred million people had flexible employment in China in 2021. Presumably, most of these people had informal employment in labor-intensive services.

Although the platform economy can generate jobs requiring different skill levels, statistics suggest that most platform jobs are in labor-intensive services in China.[8] Therefore analysis of labor-intensive services mediated by digital platforms can help us understand the nature of China's techno-development. Since food delivery platform jobs are the quintessential form of labor-intensive service employment in China's techno-state capitalism, this chapter focuses on the lives of these workers as they moved from the cages in the obsolete sectors to the rising new digital kingdoms.

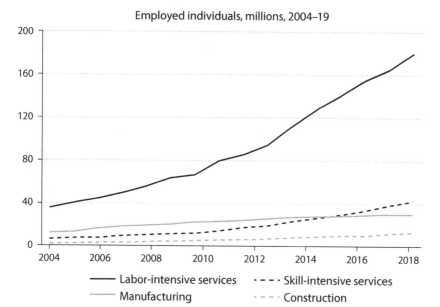

Employed individuals, millions, 2004–19

FIGURE 7.4. Urban employment in China's informal economy.
Source: National Bureau of Statistics of China. *Note*: The figure was made by
Dr. Ilaria Mazzocco, based on Rozelle et al. 2020.

Growing Food Delivery Platforms

China's online food delivery market emerged in 2009 and has expanded vastly
since 2015, when the country had its slowest economic growth in twenty-five
years. As of June 2021, the population that orders food online reached 469
million—that is, 33.5 percent of China's population and 46.4 percent of China's
internet users.[9] According to official statistics, the online food delivery market
and online health care were the fast-growing areas in China's digital economy
in 2021.[10] The two leading food delivery platforms had around six million active couriers in 2020.[11]

Saviors amid the Economic Slowdown

Food delivery platforms are critical due to their vast market values along with
their status in official and popular discourse as "saviors" that have helped to
absorb low-skilled labor. Considering the economic slowdown since 2015 and
COVID-19 pandemic, it is not surprising that the Chinese state has increasingly emphasized flexible employment and looked to food delivery platforms to absorb labor.[12] In 2020, the central state announced sixteen new

occupations, mostly in the emerging industries and service sectors, including platform delivery workers, intelligent manufacturing technicians, industrial internet technicians, AI trainers, and others.[13] According to officials in the Ministry of Human Resources and Social Security, one of the purposes of the central state acknowledging such new occupations is to identify emerging areas where new college graduates, rural-origin workers, and unemployed people can work.[14]

Consistent with what economists have predicted for the platform economy, China's online food delivery market is highly concentrated.[15] As I mentioned in chapter 6, China's tech giants have developed investment portfolios and pursued mergers and acquisitions as a means of expanding and consolidating their market power and revenues. Initially, there were three major players in the food delivery market: Meituan, Ele.me, and Baidu. To enlarge their market shares, the three tech firms burned a vast amount of capital by providing incentives to users and delivery couriers.[16] The competition stabilized in 2017 when Ele.me acquired Baidu. Since then, the market has had a duopoly structure, with Meituan and Ele.me as the two major players. In 2018, Meituan raised $4.2 billion in its IPO on the Stock Exchange of Hong Kong, with Tencent as its largest stockholder. In the same year, Alibaba acquired Ele.me and has independently owned it since then.[17] As such, Meituan and Ele.me now belong to Tencent's and Alibaba's ecosystems, respectively. Tencent and Alibaba embed Meituan and Ele.me in their respective super apps, WeChat and Alipay.[18]

Both platform companies see advantageous conditions for their growth and believe such conditions make them more appealing to global investors than their counterparts in other countries (e.g., Uber Eats and Deliveroo). The first condition is the state's policy support, especially the Internet Plus agenda. The second is the rapid urbanization and growing middle classes. The two companies have operated in hundreds of cities and rapidly expanded to smaller ones. No other countries have so many cities and potential users.[19] The third is labor supply. In stark contrast with the labor-intensive manufacturers discussed in chapters 4, the two companies enjoy abundant labor from agriculture and manufacturing.[20] The fourth is technology. Both companies have developed and improved intelligent dispatch systems powered by big data, machine learning, and AI. For instance, in its IPO prospectus, Meituan reported that the company had improved its dispatching platform to reduce the average dispatch time and labor cost per order, thereby increasing revenues. The two companies have also invested in AI-based autonomous-driving technology to develop driverless delivery vehicles.[21] The last advantageous condition is access to and connection with capital, which allows the two firms to employ talented engineers, advance technology, enlarge market shares, and leverage on Tencent and Alibaba's super platforms.[22]

From Regulation to Cogovernance

Before the central state began to tackle labor and market competition problems in 2020 (chapter 9), regulations about and state intervention into food delivery platforms focused on food safety and traffic safety, and occurred mainly at the local level. Responding to growing public concerns, many local governments demanded that the two platforms supervise restaurants and delivery workers to ensure their compliance with food safety and traffic regulations. Through the efforts of government affair professionals at the two firms, the two platforms and numerous local governments have turned vertical regulatory relationships into horizontal cogovernance and cooperative relationships by forming "government business cogovernance and cooperation agreements" (*zhengqi gongzhi hezuo xieyi*) and "strategic cooperation agreements" (*zhanlue hezuo xieyi*).[23]

Here we can see that the two platform companies straddle the boundaries between the private and public, and that the Chinese state benefits from the infrastructure and instrumental power of the two platform companies. The two tech firms' emphasis on technology and big data aligns well with the state's agenda of scientization (chapter 2) and digital governance, and makes state-business cogovernance and cooperation possible. For example, Meituan's Sky Net System establishes e-archives for merchants operating on its platform and digitizes merchants' licenses and food safety–related data. Its Sky Eye System performs a semantic analysis of consumers' review data in order to quantify and categorize content related to food safety, especially negative reviews. To aid the state's capacity, Meituan connected the two systems to the government's platforms in Shanghai, Shenzhen, Chengdu, Xiamen, and other cities so that corporate data can facilitate the state's law enforcement.[24] Similarly, Ele.me built a platform that shares food safety–related big data with the State Food and Drug Administration agencies.[25] Both Meituan and Ele.me have also participated in "police-business cogovernance" (*jingqi gongzhi*) and shared data about delivery workers with public security agencies in order to enhance riders' compliance with traffic regulations.[26] In short, the two companies have been more than willing to use their platforms and data to improve the state's power as well as strengthen their relationship with local governments. In so doing, tech capital has to some extent transformed itself from a target to a mechanism of state governance at the local level. The digital systems built by the two companies have become part of the enlarging instrumental apparatus under China's techno-developmental regime.

In addition to turning regulatory relationships into opportunities for cogovernance, the two platform companies help local governments increase their performance evaluation metrics under the techno-developmental regime. They assist local governments in poverty reduction, providing job opportunities for rural residents to work in cities. In this regard, Meituan received a national poverty reduction award from the State Council in 2020 as it provided sources of income to 9.31 million delivery workers, including 545,000 workers in poverty, between 2013 and 2020. The company has also offered online courses on developing entrepreneurship in the food delivery business.[27] Furthermore, both companies have established regional headquarters or subsidiary tech companies in multiple cities in order to facilitate the local digital economy, advance industrial upgrading and transformation, and attract talent. These are all critical elements of metrics in performance evaluation systems.

The power and resources of the state and corporations are not commensurable, but state-business interactions offer a window into the level of status and power that the state accords to corporate power and technology. Even for the Shanghai municipal government, which has vast power and resources, collaboration with Meituan meant a tremendous opportunity to the former due to Meituan's status as the third-largest internet company in China and among the top twenty internet companies in the world in terms of market capitalization (i.e., the total value of a company's stock shares).[28] When Meituan established a strategic collaboration agreement with the Shanghai government in 2020, the municipal government publicized the news and hosted a grand ceremony. Shanghai's party secretary, Li Qiang, also a member of the politburo, attended the ceremony and thanked Meituan for its commitment to advancing the digital economy, building a smart city, and bringing talent to Shanghai.[29] Two weeks later, Meituan purchased a piece of land (52,600 square meters) with a reserve price of 6.54 billion yuan from the Shanghai government.[30] When the Shanghai government listed the land for sale, it required that the bidder must be an internationally and nationally renowned internet company that would establish a regional headquarter in Shanghai as well as enhance industrial clusters in the digital economy, big data, and AI there. Not surprisingly, Meituan was the only bidder.[31] Clearly the land was used to woo Meituan's investment. Essentially, although the two platforms are subject to regulations at the local level, their capital and technology give them leverage over local states.

Platform Food Delivery Couriers

According to surveys conducted by Meituan and Ele.me, their couriers are predominantly male (93 percent) since many women, according to my female interviewees, find the work conditions of delivery workers (e.g., exposure to strong sunshine and risk of harassment) unsuitable. Most couriers are in their twenties, with middle or high school education. Around 15 to 20 percent of the couriers have a college-level education, and within this group, most just graduated from college and are in the process of finding a "real" job. Sixty percent of the couriers are married and have at least one child. Spouses of the couriers (60 percent) tend to work outside their families, although some take care of children or elderly family members at home.[32]

Although most of the couriers are migrants (70 percent) and have a rural household registration status (77 percent), over half of them (58 percent) work in their provinces of origin, meaning that they do not have to migrate to faraway cities to find a job as many of them did since the two platforms have expanded rapidly to third- and fourth-tier cities. The Chinese state welcomes such development because it could turn couriers into residents and potential buyers of housing properties in smaller cities, thereby reducing the number of unsold housing properties there; also, the demographic backgrounds of platform workers render them undeserving of residence in larger cities according to the metrics for public resource allocation.[33]

Unlike platform food delivery couriers in advanced capitalist economies, many couriers and their spouses in China have connections with the manufacturing sector. The most common prior occupation among couriers is factory worker (e.g., 35.2 percent of Meituan's couriers in 2020). Among the married couriers, the most frequent current occupation of their spouses is factory work (15 percent). Among Meituan couriers, over 60 percent reported working as a delivery courier because of the freedom and flexibility it affords along with the geographic proximity of the workplace to their hometown; 64 percent of the couriers have food delivery as their only job, and 57.5 percent of them hope to have their own small businesses in the future.[34]

The survey data correspond to my interviews with sixty platform food delivery couriers (see table 7.1). Indeed, many of the couriers I talked to worked in factories previously. None of my interviewees wanted to work as couriers in the long run, but most full-time couriers had no concrete career plans, although they knew they would like to become a small business owner one day. This longing to become a business owner despite lacking a concrete plan of action was common, and it was similar to that of the low-skilled factory workers discussed in chapters 4–5. Many couriers hoped, however, that working as a delivery courier might help them open up a business by providing opportunities to talk to restaurant owners.

In general, the demographic backgrounds of food delivery workers resemble those of factory workers and differ from drivers who work under ride-hailing platforms. Didi drivers tend to be more highly educated and have more financial resources. According to Didi's survey, 51 percent of the Didi drivers have college-level education, and only 0.4 percent of the drivers have less than high school education.[35] For people without much savings or family support,

TABLE 7.1. Distribution of Interviewed Couriers

Type of platform	Service platform ($n = 30$)	Gig platform ($n = 30$)
Gender		
Female	3	2
Male	27	28
Age		
18–25	14	12
26–35	13	14
Over 35	3	4
Educational attainment		
Less than high school	10	11
High school	16	14
Some college	4	5
Full- or part-time		
Full-time	30	21
Part-time	0	9
Migrant status		
Yes	24	24
No	6	6
City		
Chongqing	18	18
Fuzhou	2	2
Harbin	2	2
Linyi	2	2
Nanjing	2	2
Shanghai	2	2
Shenzhen	2	2
Employment history		
Prior experience in the manufacturing or construction sector	18	17
Prior experience as a service platform courier	N/A	3
Prior experience as a gig platform courier	1	N/A
Presence at protests/strikes organized by couriers		
Yes	3	15
No	27	15
Working as a courier at the time of the interview		
Yes	26	26
No	4	4

Note: I collected income information from interviewees, but it is difficult to obtain precise information as neither service platform couriers (SPCs) nor gig platform couriers (GPCs) have fixed earnings. In general, SPCs in my sample made 4,000 to 5,000 RMB (around US$564 to $705) per month. Full-time GPCs in my sample made 6,000 to 7,000 RMB (around US$846 to $987) per month, but they tend to work more hours per day than do SPCs.

being a platform delivery worker is not difficult because it requires relatively less up-front investment. Usually, couriers invest around 4,000–6,000 RMB (around US$590–893), a monthly salary as a factory worker, to get an electronic scooter and other equipment for delivery work.

The Nature of Jobs

Although both Meituan and Ele.me boast that they provide millions of job opportunities, in fact the two companies have only around sixty-nine and fifteen thousand employees, respectively, mostly in Beijing and Shanghai—China's first-tier cities and postindustrial frontiers.[36] Both companies assiduously avoid having formal employment relationships with platform couriers, thus creating millions of informal employment positions throughout the country. Platform companies elsewhere, such as Uber, adopt similar models.[37] Indeed, in its IPO prospectus for global investors, Meituan emphasized, "We do not enter into employment agreements with delivery riders. . . . We require our delivery partners to establish strict recruiting standards and regular training programs for the delivery riders."[38] In other words, the two platform companies sign contracts with delivery partners—local companies—and in turn, these partners form employment or individual contractual relationships with couriers. The two platform companies aim to avoid labor disputes with millions of couriers through such legal arrangements.

From the perspective of employers, the value of labor requires it to be dependable but also disposable.[39] To this end, companies in other industries simultaneously often have standard employment arrangements for core employees and nonstandard employment for other personnel.[40] In a similar vein, Meituan and Ele.me operate two types of platforms through their delivery partners—service and gig platforms—in order to balance the security and flexibility of the workforce.[41] This is specific to Meituan and Ele.me; most food delivery platforms elsewhere, such as Uber Eats and Deliveroo, only have gig platforms. Service platform couriers (SPCs) and gig platform couriers (GPCs) or crowdsourced couriers both pick up food from a restaurant and deliver it to a customer, but they are under different legal arrangements.

The two platforms' delivery partners engage SPCs as full-time employees or contractors.[42] In most cases, SPCs are full-time employees who work for a service station—an actual physical station used to coordinate within a locality—operated by Meituan or Ele.me's delivery partners.[43] In this scenario, there is a labor contract between SPCs and Meituan or Ele.me's partners governed by China's labor law. The delivery partners agree to abide by the operating standards specified by Meituan and Ele.me. The two platforms further require their partners to incentivize and supervise couriers according to the standards set by the platform companies. Importantly, the fact that a labor contract exists between SPCs and Meituan or Ele.me's partners does not mean that Meituan or Ele.me's partners necessarily honor the contract or follow China's labor law. According to my interview data, it is rare that Meituan or Ele.me's partners provide social insurance to SPCs. Many of Meituan or Ele.me's partners also avoid giving SPCs a copy of their labor contract, thereby enabling the companies to better eschew their legal obligations.

GPCs, in contrast, can decide when they want to work and do not share a workplace. Under the gig platform model, Meituan and Ele.me enter into agreements with their delivery partners, which engage couriers as independent contractors. Orders are fulfilled by couriers through a crowd-sourcing platform established by Meituan or Ele.me. GPCs must also abide by the delivery service standards set by the two platform companies' delivery partners. Essentially, the service platform model provides the two companies with a stable workforce, while the gig platform supplies them with a flexible workforce. SPCs and GPCs share similar demographic characteristics and employment histories. The only difference between the two groups is that all the SPCs I talked to, but only 70 percent of GPCs, worked as full-time couriers. Full-time SPCs and GPCs depend wholly on platforms for their livelihood, whereas part-time GPCs use delivery work to supplement their primary source of income.[44]

Couriers themselves decide whether to work as an SPC or GPC. The application processes for SPCs and GPCs are separate. Usually, couriers ask friends or couriers in social media groups how to choose between types of platforms and companies. For people who want a part-time job, being a GPC is the primary option because service stations mostly hire full-time couriers. People who want a full-time job can choose between the two types of platforms. Some interviewees said they just followed their friends. Those who preferred to have a relatively structured life and stable income tended to choose an SPC job. Some thought they could make more money being a GPC. For people who lack familiarity with an area, being an SPC was a good option because supervisors could help the couriers with directions and shortcuts. Prior to actually speaking with my interviewees, three of the thirty GPCs in my sample switched from a service to a gig platform, and only one of the thirty SPCs had switched from a gig to a service platform.

Urban dwellers who order food using a mobile app are familiar with the two major platform companies, but most consumers are unaware of the different types of platforms, let alone which type they are using for a given transaction. Patrons simply choose the restaurant and food. In each transaction, the restaurant selects the type of delivery platform. In general, service platforms offer delivery within a three-kilometer radius, whereas gig platforms do not have such a constraint. For restaurants, the gig platform is the cheaper option, but it is also less reliable because GPCs are not monitored by supervisors.

Dreams of Freedom, Flexibility, and Opportunities

Although the two platforms keep couriers at arm's length legally, they actively promote both SPC and GPC jobs through social media. For instance, the platforms use social media influencers to host live streaming recruitment events and have couriers share experiences using video-sharing mobile apps like Kuaishou and Douyin. A live streaming event can attract more than 1.3 million real-time viewers and 3,000 job applicants.[45] When I asked interviewees what made them decide to work as couriers, many specifically mentioned videos on Kuaishou or Douyin.

Both platforms advertise that SPCs enjoy stable income, promotion, flexible and short work hours, insurance protection, and mentorship. Meituan and Ele.me's advertisements suggest that service platform jobs are superior to factory jobs in several aspects. First, couriers are skilled workers. The companies accentuate that logistical skills are critical and can be further developed at work. Second, SPCs have short and flexible work hours. Couriers only have to work for four hours a day since most of the delivery work occurs during lunch- and dinnertime. Although the workday is longer than four hours, SPCs have freedom when not delivering food. Third, couriers do not have to travel far from home. Lastly, the platform companies advertise that couriers can easily have a monthly salary of 10,000 RMB (around US$1,476). According to the data published by China's National Bureau of Statistics, the average monthly salary of private-sector employees in urban China was 4,467 RMB in 2019.[46]

Meituan and Ele.me's media campaigns note that gig platforms offer a tremendous amount of freedom and flexibility along with a handsome income for everyone who has time for delivery. Couriers can determine their own work hours by logging on and off at will. They have the freedom to choose the task they like. The remuneration is fair because the more one works, the more money one can make. Couriers enjoy a high piece rate and short delivery route thanks to the algorithms the platforms have developed. Furthermore, couriers do not have to wait for monthly or biweekly paychecks; they can get their payment immediately after they complete a task and withdraw cash from their account anytime. Being able to receive remuneration immediately is vital to many of the GPCs I interviewed. Surprisingly, around one-third of my GPC interviewees had to repay microloans that they borrowed using apps. And because many of them borrowed multiple microloans, they had to repay debts every couple of days. I discuss the issues and implications related to microloans in greater depth in chapter 9.

Prior work experiences and demographic backgrounds partly explain why the discourse of freedom and flexibility advanced by the platforms has such strong purchase among couriers in China. To get some sense of how China's food delivery industry relates to those in other countries, I researched food delivery couriers in France too. Compared with couriers in France, those in China are much more likely to mention how much they appreciate freedom and flexibility. Many of my interviewees in China were haunted by experiences or stories of harsh factory conditions, such as night shifts, discipline from supervisors, and the closed environment. Even more than actively wanting to deliver food, these workers sought escape from manufacturing jobs because factories, assembly lines, and dormitories were seen as cages. Those who worked previously at factories where they were frequently prohibited from talking to their coworkers or using cell phones enjoyed being able to chat with other couriers and restaurant people as well as use cell phones regularly. Also, those coming from rural areas appreciated that they could now navigate the city. Freedom, flexibility, and opportunities promised by the platforms enticed many of my interviewees into the food delivery platform sector.

Platform Architecture for Control and Management

As I mentioned in chapter 6, leading internet companies in China have developed instrumental power based on technology, data, and law. Here I show how the two food delivery platform companies exercise their instrumental power over workers. Despite their promises of freedom and flexibility along with the technical absence of an employment relationship between the platforms and couriers, the former have established elaborate systems of what I call *platform architecture*—technological, legal, and organizational control and management in the labor process—in order to ensure a dependable and disposable workforce.[47] *Technological control and management* refers to control and management that uses artifacts or "nonphysical, systematic methods of making or doing things."[48] Many platform companies use algorithms not only to match consumers with service providers but also to manage and control workers' behavior, converting workers' general capacity for work into a specific and quantified amount of labor.[49] Uber, for example, utilizes algorithmic control—characterized by information asymmetries and the opacity of technological design—to shape drivers' behavior.[50] Platform economies also require legal arrangements that govern work as well as delimit the rights and obligations of the various parties involved, such as the classification of workers as independent contractors or employees. In addition, legal scholars note the problems of contractual design in asymmetrical contracts—that is, contract relationships between a dominant business and another market player with unequal bargaining power.[51] Because platforms tend to have enormous market power and resources to make legal arrangements, they can use asymmetrical contracts as a means of labor control and management.[52] The *organizational dimension of control and management* refers to the degree to which management personnel can exercise normative influence and surveillance on platform workers. In traditional workplaces, management personnel tend to have a close supervisory relationship with workers, and influence how workers voice and act on grievances.[53] Platform workers, however, such as Uber drivers, often do not have a human supervisor.[54] The specific form of platform architecture can significantly shape how couriers experience their work, and limit or facilitate their ability to realize their dreams of freedom, flexibility, and opportunities.

Importantly, platform companies enact platform architecture not in a vacuum but rather in concrete political contexts. As mentioned in chapter 6, before its recent crackdown on the tech sector in 2020, the Chinese state made little effort to restrain monopoly power or initiate antitrust investigations.[55] This is understandable since both central and local states rely on tech capital to achieve their developmental goals. China's weak civil society, absence of independent labor unions, and authoritarian context make it difficult for non-state actors to oversee market power too.[56] In such political contexts, platform companies enjoy unbridled contractual power to control labor.

The Service Platform

The architecture of the service platform aims to establish a reliable workforce. As Liu, an in-house lawyer at Meituan, explained, building a dependable workforce necessitates a high level of supervisory power over couriers, but such power also requires bearing the legal responsibilities associated with conventional employment relations. Both Meituan and Ele.me franchise their business to delivery partners to create a reliable workforce. Franchisees (i.e., delivery partners) operate service stations in a local jurisdiction, and employ and supervise district managers, service station supervisors, and delivery couriers. Meituan and Ele.me provide their franchisees with technology—specifically, a platform system for managing delivery orders and couriers. Like the Chinese state, the two platforms are believers in using metrics to shape behavior. Meituan and Ele.me oversee their partners through a series of KPIs. These indicators are aggregated from the performance of individual couriers through the platform system. Cai, a district manager, described how KPIs work, "Platform companies set many KPIs, such as the on-time rate, customer review scores, the number of complaints, and so on. If our KPIs are not good, Meituan can terminate our contract or give us a fine. Therefore we ask everyone to have good KPIs."

Meituan and Ele.me's franchisees use the technology provided by the two franchisors—specifically, the platform system—to assist in managing and controlling the labor process. Technology in this context is a tool used by management personnel rather than something that replaces them, at least currently. On the one hand, franchisees and station supervisors are constrained by the platform system. Station supervisors mostly rely on the platform system and the algorithms embedded in it to dispatch couriers, though they can also dispatch couriers manually. Dispatch algorithms consider couriers' performance metrics when assigning tasks. The platform system incorporates various disciplinary rules, like fines, and sets the maximum time for completing each delivery. Franchisees can change certain parameters in the system such as the amount of fines imposed on couriers.

Meituan and Ele.me's technological control and management includes dimensions of gamification too.[57] Their mobile apps are designed to induce couriers' participation in the "game," with a lively graphic design reminiscent of video games. Similar to popular video games, Meituan and Ele.me's apps classify couriers according to their performance metrics. Higher-level couriers earn certain privileges, such as priority in taking an order. The classification is dynamic, so couriers must maintain their scores to avoid a downgrade. One SPC said, "I was amazed by the fact that working can be like video gaming. I competed with other couriers and tried to raise my level. I shared both my delivery scores and video game scores online with other drivers" (see figure 7.5).

Legally, in most of the cases that I study, it is Meituan and Ele.me's franchisees, as opposed to Meituan or Ele.me, that form a labor contract with SPCs. How franchisees establish a labor contract with couriers varies across service stations, but such contracts must establish a salary structure, both parties' obligations, and the supervisory relationship. All the labor contracts calculate salaries based on piece rates and the number of delivery tasks. Some contracts include a minimum monthly wage, but others do not.[58] In most service stations, supervisors display disciplinary rules on the wall.

The organizational design of the service platform emphasizes the role of management personnel in supervising couriers. Management personnel aim to maximize KPIs through managing couriers. Huang, a service platform supervisor with a high school education, explained, "The platform system is a useful tool because it spares my time from assigning tasks manually, but ultimately my job is to manage people, who have emotion." Cai told me that when hiring supervisors, he considers people with prior experience as couriers to be desirable candidates who can work with SPCs to ensure excellent KPIs.

FIGURE 7.5. WeChat communication between service platform couriers.

Station supervisors and couriers have regular face-to-face interactions. The daily interaction starts with a morning meeting. Yang, an Ele.me station supervisor, described the routines:

> We begin our morning meetings at 10 a.m. Couriers sanitize their delivery boxes. Then we go over statistics. Our company has three service stations in this district. We announce how many orders, good reviews, and bad reviews each station received yesterday. I teach couriers how to behave in a civilized way. We practice how to apologize to customers. I have to do ideology work to better educate couriers, so they would have excellent KPIs. Many customers are crazy, so I often have to lift couriers up.

Note that "ideology work" is the phrase used by the Chinese party-state's propaganda system to indoctrinate people. This quote shows how station supervisors seek to influence how couriers behave, deal with emotion, and generate excellent performance metrics through normative control and emotional labor—in short, by managing workers' feelings and expressions.[59]

The Gig Platform

Meituan and Ele.me contract their partners to operate gig platforms in different cities according to the former's technology and requirements. The technical, legal, and organizational design of the gig platform aims to establish a flexible and disposable workforce. According to Liu, a lawyer at Meituan, gig platforms achieve this goal by surrendering most of the supervisory power of management personnel over couriers: "If management personnel are visibly involved in supervising couriers, the court will consider work relations as employment relations. That means platforms do not have flexibility to adjust workforces. Also, platforms will have to take more legal responsibility."

Consequently, gig platforms automate most management and supervision tasks. Similar to technological control and management under the service platform, Meituan and Ele.me rely on technology to discipline and dispatch GPCs. Disciplinary rules are built into and implemented by the system, such as fines and the deactivation of an app account. Dispatch algorithms incorporate rules that decide which couriers are given priority in choosing assignments. Wong, a system development engineer at Meituan, explained the company's algorithm, "When a consumer makes an order, the system calculates the distances between the consumer and available gig couriers, and the distances between the restaurant and available gig couriers. The algorithm also considers couriers' performance statistics. The system gives priority to gig couriers with better statistics." The two gig platform systems classify couriers into different levels. In addition, the platforms use credit points to measure a courier's credibility— how reliable the courier is—based on their behavior, such as couriers' records of accepting or rejecting dispatch assignments. Similar to the service platform apps, the gig platform apps integrate elements and dynamics of gamification to induce couriers' participation in the game.[60]

The two gig platforms also use algorithms to set remuneration. Under the service platform, piece rates are generally fixed and stated in a contract by Meituan and Ele.me's franchisees. In comparison, Meituan and Ele.me's gig platforms use algorithms that account for several factors (e.g., distance, condition of the destination, and weather) to calculate piece rates. The pricing is similar to Uber Eats' model.[61] Local managers who work for gig platforms' partners can change some parameters in the system that influence remuneration—for instance, the basic rate for a kilometer.

Both Meituan and Ele.me use technology to confirm the identity of gig couriers and monitor couriers' compliance with the rules. Because gig couriers do not have a human supervisor, both platforms require them to scan their face before they can take an order and take a picture of themselves during their work. As Xue, a GPC, described, "Ele.me often asks me to upload a selfie when

I'm on the road. They want to see whether I wear the company's helmets and vests and carry the company's delivery box." Failure to comply with such rules has disciplinary outcomes.

Meituan and Ele.me meticulously design their contracts to maximize the gig platforms' flexibility. Liu, a lawyer at Meituan, sketched out the legal work that the two platforms have done:

> The legal relationship is complicated as there are many parties involved: platforms, couriers, restaurants, consumers, and people on the street. Our task is to minimize the company's liabilities and maximize flexibility. We avoid having an employment relationship with gig couriers. We don't want to be responsible for couriers' traffic negligence. We've left some space for the company to adjust contractual terms, policies, and importantly, technologies.

Indeed, Meituan's clickwrap agreement stipulates that China's Labor Contract Law does *not* apply to the contractual relationship between Meituan or its subcontractors and GPCs. Meituan's clickwrap agreement also stipulates that GPCs must accept every clause in the agreement and any rules published on Meituan's platform, including disciplinary measures. Meituan and Ele.me are similar to conventional companies that employ contingent workers and attempt to avoid liabilities resulting from employment.[62] But unlike conventional companies, Meituan and Ele.me endow themselves with the power to change contractual terms *unilaterally* through a nonnegotiated clickwrap agreement.[63] Asked whether he considered Meituan and Ele.me's contracts to be asymmetrical, Liu—likely influenced by his awareness of my legal training—replied frankly, "The power of platforms and that of couriers are enormously asymmetrical. We only have two major platforms in China. Tencent is the largest stockholder of Meituan, while Alibaba independently owns Ele.me. The two platforms have a lot of capital, political connections, and lawyers. What do couriers have?"

The organizational design of gig platform architecture minimizes the role of management personnel in managing and supervising couriers. Although Meituan's subcontractors and Ele.me set up offices in cities where the two companies' gig platforms operate, Peng, a manager who works for Meituan's gig platform, noted that his office's main focus is monitoring and managing data along with the platform system itself, not overseeing couriers. When I visited Peng's office, I noticed that most of the employees were either analyzing data or identifying irregular patterns in front of their computer screens. Similar to Wong, an engineer whom I interviewed, Peng saw the operation of the delivery platform as a mathematical problem of "multiple goal optimization"—that is, "how to maximize revenues and customer satisfaction through dynamically optimizing the matching of orders and couriers with the best metrics." Couriers' experience was not something Peng, Wong, or the two platform companies sought to optimize.

The number of gig platform offices in a city is much smaller than that of service stations, as the former do not have regular interactions with couriers as service stations do. To activate an app account, both Meituan and Ele.me require couriers to complete online training. They further require offline training as a prerequisite to receive more than a certain amount of delivery tasks or reactivate an app account that was blocked when GPCs violated platform rules. I attended one such offline training, where an instructor talked about the platform company's rules, including fines and other forms of punishment, and ended with an exam that tested whether couriers could memorize the rules. Table 7.2 summarizes the platform architectures of the service and gig platforms.

Since I studied food delivery couriers under Uber Eats and Deliveroo's gig platforms in France too, and GPCs in France and China both ride scooters to deliver food, I was able to compare the labor control and management of GPCs in two countries. I find the two platforms in China have imposed much more intensive and extensive control over couriers. Although Uber Eats and Deliveroo couriers in France are, like their Chinese counterparts, subject to customer reviews and the possibility of app deactivation, most of the disciplinary rules implemented by Meituan and Ele.me, such as all kinds of fines, are absent from Uber Eats and Deliveroo's platform systems. Moreover, neither Uber Eats nor Deliveroo restricts delivery time, meaning GPCs in France do not have to worry so much about being late for delivery—something that makes a huge difference to couriers' safety and quality of life.

In China, the consequences of late deliveries are so feared that they often lead to tragedies. Many Chinese GPCs (as well the SPCs) had traffic incidents because they were speeding in an effort to avoid the steep fines for late delivery. In the WeChat groups I joined, I constantly saw couriers post photos of their injuries or the deaths of other couriers on the road. Some of my interviewees described their traffic accidents, showed their wounds, and complained about the limitation of the work injury insurance they purchased in videos on Kuaishou and Douyin. The necessity of speeding also means that many couriers violated traffic regulations. I saw couriers share videos in which other couriers kneeled to police officers and begged the police not to give them a ticket or confiscate their scooters. In a video, one courier used a knife to harm himself in front of a police officer, while telling the police to let him go because he would be running late for delivery. To avoid violating the rules set by the platform companies, couriers frequently break the traffic regulations enacted by the state. They choose to prioritize the platform rules because the

TABLE 7.2. Platform Architecture

	Service platform	Gig platform
Guiding principle	The purpose is to create a reliable workforce. The design requires a higher level of supervisory power over couriers, at the expense of having legal responsibility based on employment relations.	The purpose is to create a flexible workforce. The design avoids legal responsibility based on employment relations, at the expense of having less supervisory power over couriers.
Technological dimension	Supplementing the task of management personnel • using algorithms that consider performance metrics to dispatch couriers • using algorithms to monitor and discipline couriers • incorporating "gamification"	Automating management and supervision • using algorithms that consider performance metrics to dispatch couriers • using algorithms to monitor and discipline couriers • incorporating "gamification" • using algorithms to set and adjust remuneration • using technologies to confirm couriers' identity and monitor whether couriers wear the company's helmets and vests
Legal dimension	Establishing legal relations based on a conventional employment contract • based on a labor contract that classifies couriers as employees • with a stable salary structure • regulated by labor law	Avoiding legal relations based on a conventional employment contract and maximizing flexibility • based on clickwrap agreements, which are asymmetrical contracts • not classifying couriers as employees • falling outside labor law • endowing the platform with the power to change contractual terms and platform rules unilaterally
Organizational dimension	Management personnel in charge of managing and supervising couriers • emphasizing management of couriers • human supervisors can override certain algorithmic decisions • calculating the KPIs of supervisors and service stations from SPCs' KPIs • imposing normative influences and surveillance on and performing emotional labor vis-à-vis couriers	Management personnel generally *not* in charge of managing and supervising couriers • emphasizing management and monitoring of data and the platform system • testing couriers on whether they can memorize important platform and disciplinary rules in online and limited offline training sessions

enforcement is automated; the digital system automatically knows whether couriers are late and imposes a fine on them. In comparison, there is a much larger chance that the police might not catch the violation of traffic rules, at least until they begin to systematically use AI for policing.

When I described the platform rules in China and showed photos and videos of injured Chinese GPCs to GPCs in France, including undocumented immigrants, GPCs in France expressed shock with big eyes and dropped jaws. They asked how such work conditions were allowed in China and why Chinese couriers accepted the conditions. They told me that kind of control would be impossible in France as couriers would not accept it, and the platforms would be boycotted immediately. I still vividly remember a part-time French courier, who was also an intern journalist, asking me in confusion why a socialist and Communist country like China is so capitalist. This book is, in many ways, my answer to his question.

From Dreams to Dissatisfaction and Disillusionment

Despite their dreams about freedom, flexibility, and opportunities, some couriers in China begin to feel dissatisfied with or even disillusioned about their jobs after working as couriers for a while. With the expansion of the food delivery platform economy, strikes and protests organized by couriers in numerous Chinese cities have emerged (see figure 7.6).[64] I found eighty-seven cases of strikes or protests organized by food delivery couriers between 2017 and 2018. I use the term *strike* to mean a period of time during which people refuse to work; *protest* refers to the expression of opposition to something. All the cases were both strikes and protests, as couriers not only refused to work but expressed their opposition to employers or platforms on banners or signs too. Among the eighty-seven collective actions, 39 percent were organized by SPCs, and 61 percent were organized by GPCs. Why did SPCs and GPCs become discontent with their jobs? And why did GPCs go on strikes and protests more frequently than SPCs, considering GPCs seem to enjoy a higher level of freedom and flexibility as well as work in an atomized condition?[65]

Grievances about the Service Platform

SPCs complained a lot about their work, especially the KPIs and disciplinary measures built into the platform system. Several SPCs expressed that one customer complaint can cost 150 RMB (around US$22.30). On average, SPCs made 5 RMB (around US$0.74) for each delivery, and the most productive couriers completed fifty to sixty delivery tasks each day. Thus a fine could be a considerable proportion of an SPC's daily earnings. Many SPCs complained

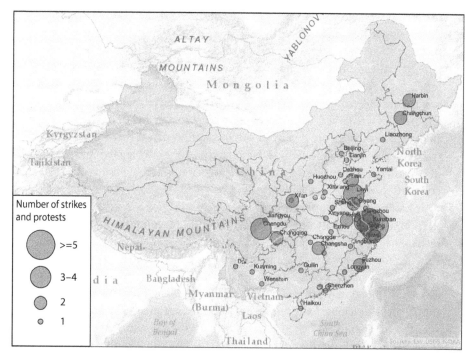

FIGURE 7.6. Geographic distribution of strikes and protests, 2017–18.

about the stress resulting from disciplinary measures built into the app. They talked about speeding in chaotic traffic and severe weather conditions to deliver food on time. Similar to platform workers in the United States who are stressed by performing emotional labor to please customers, SPCs described feeling immense pressure to get excellent reviews.[66]

Although Meituan and Ele.me boasted about the technological sophistication of the dispatch algorithms built by their talented engineers, SPCs complained about the unfairness and stupidity of the algorithms. Chen, a twenty-six-year-old SPC, explained why he thought Meituan's algorithm was unfair: "It's clear that I am closer to the restaurant, but the system does not assign the order to me. Instead, the system assigns the order to a courier with a higher KPIs. Top five couriers keep getting orders, but others do not get many orders. This is unfair." Wang, a twenty-seven-year-old SPC, had similar complaints: "The algorithm is stupid. When I am delivering an order, it always assigns me another within short delivery time. That decreases my on-time rate." Dissatisfaction with algorithmic control and management was prevalent among interviewees.

Despite SPCs' complaints about technological control and management, I found that their dissatisfaction seldom evolved into a grievance due in part to their understanding of the legal relationship. SPCs believed their work conditions were expected based on their labor contracts. Several SPCs mentioned that they knew the salary structure and disciplinary rules from the beginning, and the rates and rules remained the same. As Dong put it, "You know how much you are going to get and what the service station expects you to do. If you are unhappy, don't take the job. You can leave the job anytime." Similarly, another SPC remarked, "The disciplinary rules are harsh, but the service station needs to ensure the quality of service. And we know that from the contract and rules on the wall." These quotes show that the legal design of the platform architecture—specifically, the concrete and stable terms in a labor contract—helps stabilize labor relations.

In addition, SPCs distinguished between dissatisfying and unacceptable aspects of work. They saw salary as the most important component of their contracts. As long as their employers paid their salaries, they did not have serious issues. Wang's view was typical among SPCs: "I'm dissatisfied with the dispatching algorithm, but it's not the most important issue. As long as my boss pays my salary, I'm fine. I got my contract down in black and white. If my employer does not pay me, I'll have evidence to prove his violation of the contract and labor law. I can talk to supervisors. If they don't respond, I will go to court." Asked whether going to the labor bureau or court was difficult, Wang said, "Couriers on WeChat say there are free templates available. We only need to fill out a form to file a complaint. You don't need a lawyer. Some couriers got money back successfully." Wang also told me that in rare cases, he had heard of irresponsible employers trying to deny the existence of a labor contract, but SPCs were able to prove the employment relationship with their payrolls. When I asked Wang whether he would consider a strike or protest if he did not receive his salary, he said he would not do so unless no other methods worked.

SPCs' focus on one contractual element—wages—was reflected in how they thought about social insurance too. Even though service stations did not entirely follow the Labor Contract Law, few SPCs were angry about this. Due to the weak enforcement of labor law, SPCs had low expectations regarding social protection. In fact, only one SPC said his employer bought social insurance for him. The SPCs and supervisors I interviewed, however, said that because the turnover rate of SPCs is high, it is difficult for service stations to provide SPCs with social insurance. In most cases, it was only when a grievance about salary emerged that other issues, such as social insurance and disciplinary measures, were incorporated into the discussion.

SPCs told me they communicate with their supervisors when problems arise, and this makes them feel more informed about the situation even when their complaints are not solved. Many couriers understood that supervisors themselves are constrained by the platform system and Meituan or Ele.me. For example, although Chen and Wang complained about dispatch algorithms, they told me it would be unreasonable to blame their supervisors because their supervisors are obligated to use the algorithms. Chen explained, "I told my supervisor the platform system assigns orders unfairly. I received fewer orders than people with good KPIs. He told me he couldn't change the system, but he manually assigned me some orders from time to time after I talked to him. That made me feel better." This quote also shows that even when a complaint occurs—in Chen's case, from dissatisfaction with algorithmic control—supervisors' intervention could prevent problems from worsening.

Most SPCs told me they had no serious problems with their supervisors, although two complained about supervisors' unfair manual assignment of tasks. I wondered why the supervisory relationship was not more tension ridden. Chen noted that his supervisor's and the station's KPIs are the aggregation of SPCs' KPIs. He and his colleagues can retaliate against their supervisor by lowering their KPIs and then leaving their job if their supervisor is mean to them. Chen also said it is easy for SPCs to transfer their work to another service station.

In interviews with management, I found organizational constraints on supervisors' behavior. Huang, a station supervisor, said, "It's better to educate and communicate with couriers nicely. We are in the service industry, not manufacturing. I need their smile, politeness, and good attitudes to make a living." Similarly, Cai told me that as a district manager, the key is "managing the hearts and minds of both customers and couriers" to get good KPIs. Cai pointed out that according to the franchise contract, the platform could terminate his company's right to operate the delivery business if a strike or protest occurs; franchisees have obligations to oversee SPCs' behavior on social media as well. Essentially, the organizational constraints through KPIs and franchise contracts motivate supervisors to perform emotional labor and exercise normative influence—and surveillance—on SPCs.

Indeed, supervisor Huang said it is not difficult for management to discern what is going on among SPCs as he sees SPCs every day and is in their social media groups. "You know who is doing what. . . . I do extra ideological work on unruly couriers." One aspect of ideological work, according to Huang, is telling SPCs that protests or strikes are illegal. Huang's quote corresponds with how Wu, an SPC, described his supervisor's surveillance: "He knew what we were discussing. It's quite difficult for us to discuss things. Also, couriers with a closer relationship with the supervisor might betray us." Huang's and Wu's quotes reveal that couriers' workspace is not free but instead monitored by management.

Despite organizational control and management, collective contention still arises on rare occasions. For SPCs, the most salient concerns were disciplinary

FIGURE 7.7. A protest organized by service platform couriers.

measures and not receiving their salary. Common phrases used by SPCs on banners included "Pay us salaries according to the contract and the law," and "The employer maliciously withholds our salaries. We need to eat!" (see figure 7.7). SPCs' collective actions typically targeted their employer—Meituan or Ele.me's franchisee. Couriers communicated online and offline to prepare for collective action. They gathered outside their service station, raising banners and chanting their demands. There were typically fewer than thirty participants, as these actions only included SPCs at the same service station. Three SPCs who reported participating in collective action provided similar accounts of why it happened. Ming illustrated one situation, "We were supposed to receive our salaries. Our supervisors didn't know why the company [franchisee] hadn't paid us, but he agreed the company violated its obligation. Since some couriers said the company would go bankrupt soon, we decided to take action [a strike]. We didn't have time for court." After the strike, Ming's company told the SPCs that the company had financial problems. The SPCs eventually received around 80 percent of their salaries.

I also interviewed station supervisors and a district manager about collective action. Yang, a service station supervisor, stated,

> Couriers rarely initiate a strike or protest as supervisors already solve most of the problems. Strikes occur only when franchisees have problems with Meituan or Ele.me, or when there is an internal dispute among investors. These problems create financial difficulty for franchisees and cannot be solved by supervisors. Under such circumstances, franchisees try to pay less.

Yang's quote corresponds to something Cai, a district manager, told me: that it would be difficult for franchisees to deny their obligation to pay salaries. The focus of negotiation from the perspective of franchisees, Cai explained, is to "let couriers know the company's difficulty and accept what the company can afford." Together, my interviews with SPCs and management suggest that even when a collective action arises, couriers and employers do not have fundamentally different views on contractual terms and law. Rather than challenging the legitimacy of contracts, SPCs were demanding that employers honor the contracts. This is consistent with prior research that shows Chinese workers understand and respond to their work grievances according to labor law.[67] In sum, although SPCs were subjected to instrumental power based on technology and data, labor law and human supervision can, to some extent, ameliorate the harshness of instrumental power.

Grievances about the Gig Platform

In comparison, GPCs were subject to instrumental power based on technology, data, and asymmetrical contracts without any protection of law or human intervention. GPCs' work is the quintessential form of employment in China's platform economy. Similar to SPCs, GPCs were critical of the dispatch algorithms and disciplinary rules built into the platform system, but they also had problems with the calculation of remuneration, decreasing remuneration, and changing dispatch and disciplinary rules. Several GPCs accused the gig platforms of "stealing money" from them. Qiang, a twenty-nine-year-old GPC, maintained that "Meituan is scamming us. They know the real delivery distance, but use the linear distance between two points to calculate remuneration. We are not flying an airplane!"

Like gig workers in Europe, GPCs overwhelmingly criticized how platforms have decreased remuneration.[68] They believed platforms change algorithms to reduce remuneration, although the two platform companies have never openly acknowledged that they lower the piece rate. Similar to research on Uber in the United States, gig platforms and couriers in China have asymmetrical information about the platform system.[69] The actual practice of algorithmic pricing remains a "black box," hidden from workers' view, so GPCs complain about the decreasing rate based on their observations. Although gig platforms use algorithms that consider many factors to calculate piece rates, couriers said it is evident that piece rates under similar circumstances have decreased over time.

GPCs often take screenshots of their tasks and share them online, so they believe they have evidence of the decreasing piece rates. There was consensus among my interviewees that Meituan and Ele.me had changed their algorithms, stealthily lowering the piece rate and hoping couriers would not notice. GPCs complained that decreasing piece rates had a significant effect on their lives. According to Shi, a twenty-two-year-old GPC, "I was able to make

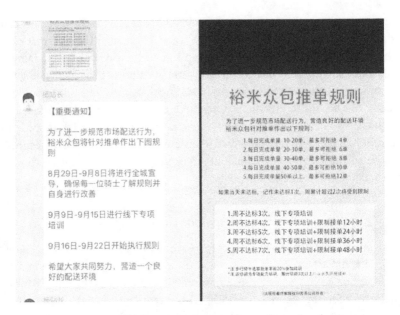

FIGURE 7.8. An announcement of new dispatch rules.

9,000–10,000 yuan [around US$1,278–1,420] per month. Now I make around 6,000 yuan [around US$852] a month." Many GPCs reported having to work two more hours every day to maintain the same level of income.

GPC interviewees emphasized that along with decreasing piece rates, the platforms have been changing the dispatch and disciplinary rules within the system to restrict GPCs' freedom to decline a dispatch assignment.[70] When a GPC declines a dispatch assignment, Meituan's platform system deducts the courier's credit points. Couriers with low credit points are less likely to be assigned orders with higher remuneration. In some cities, Meituan's delivery partners have even made new dispatch rules that require offline training and restrict a courier's eligibility to take an order after they decline a certain number of dispatch assignments (see figure 7.8).

In online communities, I saw a lot of criticism: "Given that couriers do not have freedom, Meituan should stop using freedom in its advertisement to recruit gig couriers"; "The platforms promise to give us freedom, but now they treat us like their slaves. We are forced to take orders with low pay." These comments critiqued the contradiction between gig platforms' promise of freedom at work and how dispatch rules and algorithms negate such freedom. When GPCs realized gig platforms increase technological control to reduce the promised freedom, they saw the platform-courier relationship as adversarial and exploitative, and felt betrayed.

Certain updates of dispatch and disciplinary rules in the gig platform system require corresponding legal arrangements, thus leading to the overlap of technological and legal control and management. Unlike changes in pricing practices, changes to dispatch and disciplinary rules are frequently transparent. Before implementing new dispatch and disciplinary rules in the platform system, local offices notify GPCs and justify the changes by stating their purpose is to "better regulate delivery behavior." I collected several such notices, which were written in ways that resemble how local governments communicated with obsolete businesses.

Local offices further affirm that they have the "ultimate legal rights" to change platform rules according to contracts between the platform and couriers by pointing to the clickwrap agreement that couriers accept when installing the delivery app. None of my gig platform interviewees, though, reported reading the legal texts when they installed the app and accepted the clickwrap agreement, and none knew that platforms had the right to change the content of the agreement and platform rules unilaterally. They all expressed anger about such clauses and other rules enacted one-sidedly by platforms. GPCs called such contractual terms and platform rules despotic clauses, and said they were evidence of exploitation.

I was curious as to why the companies were so secretive when it came to changing pricing practices, but open about changes to dispatching and discipline rules. Manager Peng explained the companies have to announce the latter to shape GPCs' behavior: "We use the carrot-and-stick approach. If the new rules remain unknown to couriers, couriers will not change their behavior even after we incorporate the rules into the platform system." He emphasized the need to adjust platform rules dynamically:

> The purpose is to enhance the efficiency of dispatch assignments and customers' experience. Under the service platform, couriers must accept every order assigned by their station. Under the gig platform, couriers don't have such obligation, but the company wants every order to be taken by an excellent courier. Achieving this goal necessitates the continuing improvement of dispatch and disciplinary rules. Now our platform system is powered by AI and machine learning. It learns from the big data it collects and gives us feedback. These tools help us improve the system's efficiency by changing the rules dynamically.

Peng's remark reminded me of my observations of offline training sections, in which GPCs were required to memorize platform rules and then tested on their content. Gig platforms, I realized, seek to turn couriers into a part of the platform system that automatically implements the rules. When companies change the rules, new rules have to be installed not only in the platform system but in the minds of couriers themselves as well. When this can be done successfully, human workers effectively become part of the platform technology. Such effort resembles that of managers to turn factory workers into part of assembly lines. I vividly remember many manufacturing workers telling me that they worked and were treated like robots. In chapter 5, I discussed the efforts of the Chinese state and businesses to replace human workers with robots. Similarly, Meituan and Ele.me have been developing driverless delivery vehicles. But until they can fully displace human workers, companies must seek instead to integrate humans into platform technology.

Unlike SPCs, however, GPCs do not internalize the rules through normative influence or emotional labor. Gig platforms just announce the changes in platform rules and corresponding disciplinary measures, assert their ultimate legal rights, and test GPCs on the rules. In these moments, technological and legal control overlaps, and the platforms' power becomes salient. As Deng portrayed it,

> When I saw the platform's notice about the new dispatch and disciplinary rules in the system [the platform system] and the company's legal rights, I felt furious. Then I understand why couriers complained about despotic rules on WeChat. Couriers were saying everything—from platform rules to legal clauses—is determined by the platform but not us.

Deng's quote underscores that the revelation of platforms' unbridled legal and technological power turns moments of change into moments of escalation.[71] Although previous literature has focused on the legal classification of platform workers as employees or individual contractors, GPCs are most concerned about platform companies' unilateral and unconstrained legal and technological power.[72] In the interviews, many GPCs emphasized that the platforms' exploitation is blatant. For example, one GPC remarked, "Now the platforms implement all kinds of despotic clauses. If you don't follow their rules or terms, they deduct money from you. They force you to accept their dispatch assignments with low pay. If you don't take their order, they deactivate your account. It is unfair. Platforms blatantly exploit couriers." In general, gig couriers believed platforms used unfair legal arrangements, making the inputs and return of labor totally disproportional. They understood that the two platforms may not technically violate any existing law, but they felt there were unfair loopholes in the legal system. Here we can see how the legal dimension of the gig platform architecture generates grievances.

Asked whether they can address their grievances through the labor bureau or court, most GPCs said no because they simply do not know which law platform companies are violating. Importantly, they understood that their legal situation differed from conventional employment relations, but they could not use legal terms to describe their status. As Zeng said, "We don't have a contract.

I mean a labor contract. I don't know what kind of status we have. I only know we're not their employees. I don't think we can go to court or the labor bureau. That's for people with a labor contract. We don't know what kind of law the platforms have violated. We just feel they are wrong and things are unfair." In social media group discussions, most GPCs shared the same legal understanding as Zeng. As one GPC shared with a social media group composed of other GPCs, when he went to a labor bureau for legal advice, he was told the bureau could not help because it could only assist people with a labor contract.

The organizational design of the gig platform further intensifies grievances and increases the appeal of collective contention. As the gig platform largely automates control and management, GPCs do not develop social relationships with management personnel. Rather, they interact with the "cold" technological interface. GPCs use the apps to interact with platform companies. Similar to Uber drivers in the United States, GPCs encounter difficulties trying to speak to platform representatives.[73] As Shi told me, "I tried many times, but they'd never responded to me. Last time when they changed platform rules, I contacted them to complain. I was not the only one. In the end, couriers became angrier and angrier. We had to do something else to get our voices heard." Indeed, GPCs shared similar frustrations about not being able to solve their problems through apps or local offices. Frustration and anger escalated grievances.

The disengagement of platform companies also means GPCs have relatively free spaces to mobilize solidarity and organize collective action, mostly online but also offline.[74] GPCs expressed their anger in social media groups. I saw GPCs rename their social media groups as a "labor union" even though they could not form formal labor unions according to Chinese law (see figure 7.9). Many couriers discussed the importance of solidarity with online statements like "We must have solidarity to defend our interests, brothers. Otherwise, we'll continue to be exploited by the platform." Some couriers began to organize collective action offline. To be sure, the platforms try to undermine online organizing. In some cases, after local offices found GPCs were organizing a protest via social media groups, they deactivated organizers' app accounts and asked social media companies to block those groups. Nonetheless, GPCs were still able to form new groups.

For GPCs, the most salient concerns were decreasing piece rates along with the unilateral change of contract terms or platform rules. Collective action occurred mostly when GPCs believed gig platforms had drastically decreased remuneration by changing algorithms, or when platform offices notified GPCs of new platform rules and simply cited the platform's contractual right to do so. Usually a core group of GPCs—those with existing interpersonal relationships—initiated a strike or protest. They did so in the absence of assistance from grassroots, labor nongovernmental organizations or government-organized trade unions. Here we see again an important connection between

FIGURE 7.9. WeChat communication between gig platform couriers.

the manufacturing and platform sectors. GPCs with experience working in the manufacturing sector played a crucial role in organizing such collective actions. Core organizers tended to be those who completed a huge amount of orders every day. Decreasing rates and changing rules cost such workers hundreds of RMB daily. Core organizers' attempts to improve their work situation was understandable given that so many did not want to return to the manufacturing sector and did not have a feasible alternative career plan.

GPCs organized action through social media and offline meetings. Because GPCs did not have a conventional workplace, they stood or sat in public space, such as plazas or the sidewalks outside restaurants. They attached signs to their scooters and held banners on the sidewalk so that the public could see their grievances (see figure 7.10). GPCs also organized "flying pickets," in which they honked and rode scooters with strike/protest signs while patrolling outside restaurants or on the street to prevent nonparticipating GPCs from delivering food. The number of participants in a collective action organized by GPCs tended to be larger—often with more than fifty participants—than those organized by SPCs. Common slogans used by GPCs included "Ele.me reduces the rate maliciously, shortens delivery time, deceives couriers, and ignores lives"; "Meituan reduces the rate crazily. Brothers, stop taking orders. Resist Meituan!"; "Resist monopoly!"; "Despotic clauses!"; "Who can make the most despotic contracts? Ele.me!"; and "Ele.me exploits couriers. We need to feed our families. We want justice."

FIGURE 7.10. A protest sign.

Here I use a series of strikes and protests in Chongqing in 2018 to illustrate a typical mobilization process in "free spaces" online and offline. The core organizers belonged to a close-knit group. Tang, a twenty-three-year-old GPC, recounted how his group organized a strike after Meituan announced a change in dispatch and disciplinary rules:

> We only had four people in the beginning. We became friends through a WeChat group. Four of us hang out after work twice to three times a week. When we saw that couriers got angry in social media groups, we discussed [it] in a BBQ place and decided to organize a strike. . . . I saw how people in my factory went on strikes. They got what they wanted. . . . A lot of couriers had already expressed their discontent to Meituan, but Meituan didn't respond. No one knows how to file a legal complaint under such circumstances.

Tang and his friends made banners and signs featuring messages such as "despotic clauses," "resist exploitation," and "stop taking orders." They chose these terms because other GPCs had used them in WeChat groups, where Tang and his friends recruited participants. They then visited several restaurants because restaurant owners suffered from asymmetrical contractual relations with Meituan too. Many restaurants complained that Meituan increased commission fees and forced restaurants not to work with Ele.me. In other words, Meituan used its dominant position in the market to force restaurants owners to accept contractual terms that the latter considered despotic. Three restaurant owners lent their support, not only by hanging banners saying "resist monopoly, resist Meituan" and "resist despotic clauses," but by providing GPCs with free meals to show solidarity. The core group sent out a message warning couriers that if non-striking gig couriers were seen delivering food during a strike, their tires would be slashed. One core member organized a ten-person patrol team to this end.

After the strike and protest began in a plaza, GPCs uploaded screenshots of their delivery app to social media groups to further mobilize participation. They proclaimed their own "offline" status with comments like "Hundreds of brother couriers are offline. Don't be a bad apple. Our patrolling team is sanctioning bad apples on the street," and "We've determined not to be exploited by evil capital-ists. Long live the working people!" GPCs often join multiple social media groups, so information spread quickly online and among GPCs who worked for different companies. Some nonparticipants encountered violence for disregard-ing warnings. Faced with potential sanctions, several GPCs decided not to work and instead went to protest sites as bystanders. Tang was surprised by what hap-pened: "Initially we had a strike in our district and drew about a hundred couri-ers, but it soon spread to five other districts and lasted for a week. In each of the subsequent strikes, I saw fifty to eighty couriers. We initiated a strike against Meituan, but the strikes also attracted Ele.me couriers." Most participants were full-time GPCs, who are more dependent on platforms. One part-time GPC with a job as a professional photographer told me, "[The protest] isn't my busi-ness because I have a real job." He also said that he was not as angry as full-time couriers as his stake was low. This finding resonates with literature that shows how economic dependency influences work experiences.[75]

Eventually, GPCs sieged one of Meituan's local offices in Chongqing for a number of hours, and the core members shared their specific demands con-cerning platform rules and remuneration. Zhang, a twenty-year-old GPC with a high school education, recalled that moment:

> Finally we saw those people [the management] who've never responded to us. Four to five people came out from the office. They were all in their twen-ties, just like us. You could tell they were college graduates. The manager was a woman. They were so scared and could not say anything to the couri-ers. Although they did not tell us, we found they increased the rate. They also sent out a notice to withdraw the new platform rules. . . . After the pro-test, Meituan did not decrease the rate for eight months, but it deactivated a few participants' accounts.

Zhang's quote reveals class and gender boundaries between management and couriers along with the awkward absence of interaction when GPCs ultimately encountered management.

Their singular focus on optimization of the platform system made gig plat-forms' local offices ill-equipped to address grievances and resistance. This tendency was evidenced by Meituan's attempt, in September 2019, to install more restrictive dispatching rules in Chongqing, despite the strikes in 2018. When many GPCs threatened to initiate another strike, Meituan finally gave up trying to install the new rules. GPCs were happy to see Meituan change its plan under such pressure, but they also recognized their inability to oversee the platform and actualize such threats regularly.

I was interested in why GPCs joined a collective action, particularly considering potential police suppression, rather than simply finding another job. Several GPCs told me they joined the collective action because the platform companies are so despotic and their rules are so unfair. Rage and a strong sense of unfairness, as opposed to an instrumental calculation about the potential pros and cons of collective action, prompted some GPCs who were not core organizers to join a collective action. Fang told me how such sentiment drew him into a protest: "I went there because the relationship is so unfair. I didn't know if we can change the situation, but I had to go because I was so angry." In fact, several GPCs were puzzled when I asked why they protested instead of finding another job. They said that they might find a job sooner or later because they did not plan to be a GPC for a long time, but they still wanted to teach platform companies a lesson.

A few couriers told me they were just bystanders. One GPC remarked, "When other couriers and I knew some gig couriers went on a strike in a plaza from social media groups, many of us immediately dashed to the site. We felt curious and wanted to see what happened." Interviewees who described themselves as bystanders shared the same sentiment as other GPCs, but they emphasized their need to make money to sustain their lives. Nonetheless, the presence of bystanders did escalate collective action. Not surprisingly, GPCs who decided not to join a collective action talked about needing to make money and thought such collective action would not work.

Asked why they were not afraid of police suppression, many GPCs said they were just bystanders or pretended to be bystanders; they did not think the police would arrest them because a lot of people were there. Participants who joined the protests in Chongqing in 2018 said the police took away only a few participants, and told them organizing a strike or protest was illegal. Most interviewees did not seem intimidated by the police.

Ambivalent Upgrading

After working as SPCs or GPCs for a while, many of my interviewees, such as Pan, developed contradictory feelings about their jobs and became perplexed about the future. I got to know Pan in a factory in Shenzhen when I did my research for chapter 4. Originally from a rural county in Chongqing, Pan worked in several factories in Shenzhen, including Foxconn. When he returned to Chongqing and worked first as an SPC and then a GPC, I met him again in Chongqing. Pan had a group of friends with similar employment trajectories. Because of Pan, I was able to join their gatherings.

Pan and his friends were unsure if their lives had been upgraded after leaving the most, as they put it, backward jobs and joining the growing internet sector. When I first met him in Shenzhen, Pan complained that few aspects of his factory jobs touched on what makes humans human—according to him, social interaction and "some freedom from not following instructions." He disliked his line supervisors and unfreedom in the factories. Having seen Tencent's magnificent Seafront Towers in Shenzhen, Pan believed in the power of internet companies and technology in improving people's lives. He also saw tech entrepreneurs like Alibaba's Jack Ma and Tencent's Ma Huateng as idols. As he later reflected on his views, he said, "I thought technology would liberate us from tedious and exploitative jobs, and I thought tech entrepreneurs would be different from sweatshop bosses. Tech companies became successful because of innovation and technology. Sweatshop factories made money by exploiting workers."

Indeed, as a platform courier, Pan felt he had more freedom—the freedom to ride a scooter on the street as well as see his wife and son once a week. Since he worked in the urban core of Chongqing, he still had to rent a place in the city and could only go back home on the weekends, but the situation was an improvement over his time in Shenzhen, where he could only see his family about three times a year. Also, in Chongqing, his son did not have problems going to school, unlike migrant children in Shenzhen. In this respect, Pan and his friends felt their lives were upgraded by technology and platform companies.

Yet they felt less free because technology and platform companies did upgrade how along with the degree to which they were monitored and controlled at work. SPCs not only had supervisors but also algorithms and metrics to discipline them. Although GPCs did not have supervisors, they were managed by the platform system and despotic rules unilaterally imposed by the platform companies. Rather than feeling they had freedom, GPCs felt they were coerced by the platform companies. They described themselves as wandering on the street (liu lang jie tou) without purpose, like driverless vehicles. After working as couriers, they began to feel disciplinary measures in the factories were nothing compared to those in the platform sector. Pan and his friends became unsure about the differences between sweatshop factories and tech firms. Reflecting on his experiences, Pan said he moved from an old cage with a visible fence to a new one with an invisible fence, from feeling like a robot to feeling like a driverless vehicle. Despite the exploitative work conditions, though, Pan and his friends believed platform companies could still quickly recruit new couriers through deception and media campaigns in Kuaishou and Douyin due to the vast population as well as the absence of good jobs for people like them.

Ultimately Pan and his friends realized that notwithstanding techno-development, they remained at the bottom of the social ladder—lower than the consumers who ordered food, the security guards who prohibited them from entering buildings to deliver food, and even people on the street. Still, they did not want to return to factories because working on assembly lines was too tedious and the wage of factory workers was fixed. They seriously questioned what they should do for a living, but had no easy answers. Although many of them wanted to operate a restaurant, they realized that even restaurant owners are subject to the monopolistic power of the platforms. Pan mused that perhaps he should work as an apprentice and learn some skills, but this would mean he would not have enough money to feed his son, support his wife, and repay the mortgage loan and microloans. As I mentioned, one-third of my GPC interviewees had multiple microloan debts. They would not have been able to repay their debts if they had stopped working as delivery workers.

Couriers also had contradictory and ambiguous feelings about the state and nation. I interviewed them before the central state's crackdown on the tech sector in 2020. Couriers believed the government was aware of their problems, but that the state still failed to regulate the platform companies. Pan's friend Tao said, "The government should upgrade the law, but it doesn't want to do so." Some told me that because of the absence of independent trade unions and the government's support of tech firms, the platform companies could do whatever they wanted and make despotic clauses. Others said that the government looked down on people at the bottom of society like couriers and thus would do nothing to assist them. According to Pan and his friends, when the government did intervene, it only punished restaurants for food safety issues, and couriers for violating traffic rules and organizing collective action. Nothing was ever done to discipline Meituan or Ele.me. Pan and his friends' perception corresponds to my interview with an official in charge of market regulation in one city. He said that the food delivery platform economy was supported by the central state and benefited the local economy. Moreover, Pan and his friends believed the government only cared about housing prices, and spent most of its time and energy speculating on the real estate market. As strikes and protests grew, the All-China Federation of Trade Unions (ACFTU), a subordinate organ of the party-state, announced in 2018 that it would accelerate building trade unions for platform workers—yet none of my interviewees saw the implementation of the plan.

Paradoxically, despite their criticism of the state and tech capital along with their low position on the social ladder, many couriers still appreciated the Chinese state given its contribution to building a strong nation. Pan and his friends said that because of the government's support of business and China's diligent people, the country had developed much faster than other countries, and was more politically and socially stable than other countries. Pan commented that "decades of development in China equates to hundreds of years of development in other countries. China began to develop only decades ago. Now we have big high-tech companies like Huawei, Alibaba, and Tencent. TikTok is popular in other countries. Other places are in turmoil, but China is always stable." Pan and his friends agreed that although China's development sacrificed many people, including themselves, it contributed to a geopolitically and technologically powerful nation. They were proud of the exponential growth of China's tech giants, although they acknowledged that those same tech companies exploited them. A friend of Pan told me, "There are benefits to having a strong nation. Other countries won't bully you when your country is strong. When we were weak in the past, other countries bullied us. The situation is different now, and we all benefit from a strong nation. But there are some problems as well. It's difficult to say."

Some readers might find it difficult to make sense of such contradictory and ambiguous feelings. It is important to situate platform workers' simultaneous criticism and appreciation of the Chinese government and big tech companies in a historical and comparative context. These workers and their parents experienced improving material conditions over the course of their lives. In interviews, they mentioned how poor their families were in the past, and noted their ability now to buy many things and enjoy online shopping. They also saw China's infrastructure (like high-speed rail and futuristic-looking cities) as evidence of the country's remarkable progress. Despite their complaints about work conditions, they felt the Chinese government had improved living conditions tremendously in the past four decades. My interviewees believed fervently in the "rise of the East and decline of the West" too—an official narrative widely disseminated in China. They thought US-China tensions were simply the result of the United States' jealousy of the rise of China and its tech firms. Some of my interviewes referenced the arrest of Huawei finance chief Meng Wanzhou in Canada and the resulting geopolitial tensions as demonstrating the Chinese people's continued need for a strong nation, powerful government, and advanced technology. In short, materialism, consumerism, and techno-nationalism have influenced how platform workers make sense of their work and life conditions as well as allocate blame and acclaim to the government and tech companies. In the end, my interviewees reasoned, work is only one aspect of life.

Conclusion

This chapter has analyzed the reality versus the promise of work in the platform economy as well as the dreams and actual conditions of workers who left the obsolete sectors for the new digital kingdoms. As China's economic growth has slowed since 2015, the central state's view of the platform economy, including food delivery platform companies, as a new engine of growth and vast sponge of surplus labor has only intensified. Indeed, food delivery platform companies have created millions of jobs throughout the country, but most of this employment is informal, labor-intensive service jobs that provide little or no social protection. Food delivery companies help local governments increase performance metrics. In addition, the companies' platforms, data, and technology have helped local governments enhance the latter's infrastructural power and state capacity, thus contributing to the cogovernance relationships between the two platforms and numerous local governments. The state–tech capital relationships are in stark contrast to the disciplinary one between the state and obsolete capital (chapter 4).

The cozy state–tech capital relationship means that prior to the central state's crackdown on the tech sector in 2020, the two major food delivery platforms had a favorable regulatory environment. Under such conditions, the two platform companies were like sovereigns, able to use legal and technological instruments to create rules and order in their realms without much interference from the state. The symbiotic state–tech capital relationship, duopoly market structure, weak civil society, and absence of independent trade unions made platforms much more powerful vis-à-vis couriers and restaurants.[76] In this context, the actors subject to strict regulation tended to be couriers and restaurants instead of the platforms, as the latter used big data and technology to help local governments enforce traffic and food safety regulations. Many similarities exist in how gig platforms exercise technological, legal, and organizational control and management across contexts—in China, the United States, and Europe. Based on my research in the French context and existing literature on gig platforms, however, Meituan and Ele.me impose much more intensive and extensive technological and legal control on couriers than do their counterparts in other countries. For one thing, food delivery platforms in other contexts do not use so many metrics and KPIs as surveillance and disciplinary tools as do Meituan and Ele.me.

As mentioned in the book's introduction, Daniel Bell argued that postindustrial society would be an age of enhanced instrumental power over people, and he expected the state to use enhanced instruments for planning and control.[77] In the Chinese context, with the rise of techno-state capitalism, we can see expanding instrumental apparatuses, as illustrated in the case of the food delivery platform economy. Both the state and the two platform companies are the builders of the instrumental apparatuses or cages. Under the cogovernance relationship, the platform companies established digital systems to help the state regulate couriers and restaurants. The systems thus became part of the state's digital governance infrastructure. Furthermore, with the freedom to rein in their respective digital kingdoms, the two platforms built legal and technological instruments to control and manage restaurants along with millions of workers. As one worker put it, he felt stifled by the harsh rule of both the government and platform companies, but often found it difficult to obey both sets of rules. I also want to emphasize that the expanding instrumental apparatuses have a class dimension because most of the employment created by the internet companies consists of labor-intensive service jobs—meaning that the working class is more likely to be subject to the rule of the expanding instrumental apparatuses.

The Chinese state and China's two major food delivery platforms share many similarities in their love of using technology and law for control. They share a belief in the power of big data, machine learning, and AI, and are enthusiastic about using metrics and KPIs to shape actors' behavior. They can both impose rules unilaterally. Also, as shown in chapter 4, the Chinese state frequently changes regulations arbitrarily and abruptly. How the platform companies change disciplinary and platform rules as well as contractual terms shows a similar tendency. This similarity is related to the state and the two platforms' respective monopolistic power. The Chinese state has political monopoly over other actors in China. In comparison, the two platforms have monopolistic market power over couriers and restaurants, which was made possible by the state's supportive regulatory environment.

Many workers left factories to pursue their dreams of freedom, flexibility, and opportunities in the platform sector. Yet their dreams have been undermined by the platform companies' technological, legal, and organizational control along with the synergetic relationship between the authoritarian, techno-developmental state, internet companies, and global financial capital. The "blatant" exploitation, as many of my interviewees pointed out, allows couriers to see how law and technology are used by the platform to control workers and small businesses, leading to resistance and some cross-cutting solidarities. On the one hand, gig couriers working for one platform company can mobilize support and solidarity from restaurant owners and couriers working for the other company. On the other hand, couriers understand the limitation of their resistance, considering the power of the internet companies and their relationship with the state. Workers nevertheless still have dreams. Unhappy as they are at not realizing their individual dreams, they do find comfort in the realization of the national techno-development dreams and give credit to the Chinese state in this respect. Having explored the lives of delivery workers in China's techno-state capitalism, I move to the lives of the so-called coding elites in the next chapter.

8

Coding Elites

AS INTERNET-RELATED sectors have grown into important new birds under China's techno-developmental regime, software engineers have arguably become the most valued and necessary talent shaping the techno-nation's future. Software engineers build the digital infrastructure and instruments needed to develop as well as connect the digital economy and digital governance. As mentioned in chapter 3, in its effort to scientize governance techniques and achieve techno-developmental goals, the Chinese state has created big data platforms to enhance its evaluation and surveillance of everything from cadres and officials to investment projects, industries, firms, human capital, social credit, and more. The state outsources such projects to internet and IT companies through public procurement. Building these platforms requires a tremendous amount of labor from software engineers. Similarly, the exponential growth of China's digital and platform economy depends on the labor and expertise of software engineers. Twenty-two percent of Meituan's employees work on R&D, for example, continually improving the company's dispatch algorithms.[1] Software engineers help the Chinese state and tech companies to create and expand instrumental and infrastructural power.

It is thus not surprising that software engineers are highly valued and sought after by both the state and tech capital. China's tech giants view recruiting and retaining top talent as key to their success. Among students who graduated from colleges or postgraduate programs between 2009–17, those who entered IT-related occupations have the highest starting salary and salary raises.[2] Moreover, software engineers are highly valued in local governments' metric systems that allocate scarce public resources since local governments must now compete to attract not only high- and new-tech firms but also the talent they employ. In chapter 7, I mentioned that Meituan established a strategic collaboration with the Shanghai government in 2020 to build a regional headquarter there. In addition to providing land, the government promised to assist Meituan's software engineers in obtaining household registration status, rental subsidies, and so-called talent apartments or housing dedicated to high-value employees.[3] The status of software engineers in the labor market and official metric systems suggests their privileged positions in the social hierarchy. Many software engineers told me about their dream of joining the billionaire club when their firms go for an IPO. If there are clear winners in China's techno-developmental regime, software engineers would certainly seem to belong to this group.

Indeed, scholars have already noted the rise of software engineers in postindustrial society, surveillance capitalism, and the society of algorithms. Daniel Bell, for one, predicted that if the dominant figures in industrial society were "the entrepreneurs, the businessman, and the industrial executive," the "new men" in postindustrial society would be "the scientists, the mathematicians, the economists, and the engineers of the new intellectual technology."[4] In *The Age of Surveillance Capitalism*, Shoshana Zuboff points out that surveillance capitalists employ relatively few people compared to their unprecedented computational resources. This small, highly educated workforce helps build the infrastructure of surveillance capitalism.[5] Similarly, Jenna Burrell and Marion Fourcade have described the rise of what they call the coding elite in today's society of algorithms. They contend that thanks to their mastery of computational techniques, the coding elite possesses cultural, political, and economic power.[6]

Although scholars agree on the critical role of software engineers in postindustrial society, surveillance capitalism, digital capitalism, and the society of algorithms, I see two inadequacies in the scholarship. First, we know little about software engineers in and beyond China. In *The Age of Surveillance Capitalism*, Zuboff focuses on the strategies of tech CEOs and entrepreneurs without providing much information about engineers.[7] As sociologist Robert Dorschel observed, existing empirical studies of labor in digital capitalism have revolved around highly precarious laborers like platform delivery workers, but neglect the growing ranks of affluent "tech workers" or tech professionals.[8] Indeed, there are two quintessential types of employment in China's techno-state capitalism. The first is informal, labor-intensive service employment. As noted in chapter 7, internet-related sectors in China have generated numerous such jobs. Workers with these jobs are subject to intensive instrumental control by both tech firms and the state. The second type is skill-intensive jobs, as exemplified by software engineers. But we know little about the work and life of these coding elites. Are they free from the instrumental rule of the Chinese state and tech companies? What are the relationships between tech capital, the state, and software engineers? How do they perceive the suffering of precarious workers, considering the role of coding elites in building digital instruments and infrastructure?

The second problem is that existing scholarship tends not to distinguish the differences and potential conflicts between surveillance capitalists or tech CEO and rank-and-file software engineers. As described in chapter 6, tech CEOs in China, many of whom began as software engineers, are powerful economic and political elites under China's techno-developmental regime. Several CEOs of China's biggest tech giants are also representatives in the National People's Congress and National Committee of the Chinese People's Political Consultative Conference.[9] And their cultural influence had soared before the Chinese state's crackdown on the tech sector in 2020, as evidenced by the high number of my interviewees who cited tech CEOs as their idols and national heroes. Tech CEOs' upwardly mobile trajectories have reinforced "the middle-class idea of the enterprising self" promoted by the Chinese state as well as the educational and employment systems (chapter 4).[10]

Nonetheless, differences exist between tech CEOs and rank-and-file software engineers in terms of their economic and political capital and cultural influence. Despite their computational skills and central role in facilitating platform, digital, and surveillance capitalism and the surveillance state, rank-and-file software engineers remain laborers employed by tech capital.[11] Analyzing tech CEOs and software engineers in the same category risks overlooking still-significant differences and tensions between capital and labor. In fact, coding elites in China are deeply embedded within and serve as one of the most vivid examples of the normalization of overwork. Scholars define *overwork* as working fifty or more hours per week.[12] Stories about software engineers getting sick or dying from overwork circulate widely on social media. As platform workers began to organize strikes and protests against the technological and legal control of tech companies, some software engineers also started to organize online protests against the exploitation of tech firms—despite the fact that software engineers, by designing and maintaining platforms, possess relatively more control over the digital means of production. In March 2019, an anonymous user created a repository named 996.ICU on GitHub, a code-hosting platform, to protest long working hours. The "996" refers to working from 9 a.m. to 9 p.m. for six days a week; "996.ICU" portends the risk that working such hours will send employees to intensive care units. Some IT companies have imposed regular, mandatory 996 work schedules, but even in those that have not, overwork is common. The 996.ICU protest received public attention and support in and beyond China, including from software engineers at Microsoft, Google, and Facebook in North America.[13]

Considering potential tensions between tech capital and software engineers along with the role of the latter in facilitating exploitation of the cyber-tariat, this chapter examines the experiences of software engineers in realizing their internet dreams as well as their relationships with tech capital, the state,

TABLE 8.1. Distribution of Interviewed Software Engineers

	Count ($n = 64$)	Percentage
Gender		
Female	6	9.38
Male	58	90.63
Education		
College	41	64.06
Master's or above	23	35.94
Marital status		
Married	33	51.56
Not married	31	48.44
Rural origin		
Yes	35	54.69
No	29	45.31
Class origin		
Working class	39	60.94
Middle class	22	34.37
Upper class	3	4.69
Type of firms		
Top firms	37	57.82
Nontop firms	27	42.19
Annual remuneration package (RMB)		
Below 100,000	13	20.31
100,000–200,000	14	21.88
200,000–300,000	8	12.50
300,000–599,000	13	20.31
600,000 and above	16	25.00
Number of housing property		
0	29	45.31
1	32	50.00
2 and above	3	4.69
Working hours		
Less than 50 hours	3	4.69
50–59 hours	15	23.44
60–69 hours	36	56.25
70 and above	10	15.63
City		
Beijing	13	20.31
Chongqing	3	4.69
Guangzhou	6	9.38
Hangzhou	9	14.06
Nanjing	2	3.13
Tianjin	3	4.69
Shanghai	5	7.81
Shenzhen	14	21.88
Suzhou	3	4.69
Xi'an	6	9.38

the nation, and other workers within China's techno-developmental regime and techno-state capitalism. The data for this chapter come from in-depth interviews and online ethnography. I interviewed five informants with management positions in different types of internet and IT companies between 2019 and 2020, a labor law lawyer in 2020, and sixty-four software engineers without managerial positions in China's internet and IT companies between 2020 and 2021 (see table 8.1). Scheduling interviews was tremendously difficult because software engineers usually worked for a long time in their offices. In addition to interviewing, I joined social media group and online forums organized and participated in by software engineers to observe their discussions and interactions between 2019 and 2021. I further reached out to participants in labor activism on GitHub, WeChat, Discord, and Telegram. These data provide a window into the work and life of engineers who contribute to the building of China's techno-state capitalism.

Software Engineers and Their Difficulty in Social Reproduction

Software engineers in China are highly educated in computer science–related disciplines. Some have a three-year technical college or four-year college degree; others have master's or doctoral degrees. They are also more often men than women, as are internet and IT companies' employees in general. For instance, 71.34 percent of all Tencent's employees were male in 2020.[14] Females tend to work in administration, sales, and marketing, while males work in the areas that require skills in computer science. The male-to-female ratio among software engineers is frequently higher than nine to one in the teams in which my interviewees work, except in the case of foreign firms.[15] In foreign firms, the male-to-female ratio is around three to one because those firms tend to attend more to the gender ratio in recruitment. According to my informants, most software engineers without managerial positions are between twenty-five and thirty-five years old—a stage of life when many people consider getting married and starting a family.

Studies of professionals in the United Kingdom show differences in class origin between "traditional" professions (e.g., law, medicine, and finance) and technical and other emerging high-status occupations, particularly those related to IT. Whereas the former is dominated by the children of higher-level managers and professionals, the technical professions recruit more widely.[16] Research finds parallels in China. Compared with occupations in finance, IT-related occupations have fewer barriers to entry for students with a science, technology, engineering, and mathematics background. There are also more working-class-origin professionals in IT-related occupations than in finance. As such, IT-related occupations serve as channels for upward mobility in China.[17]

Indeed, the most intriguing characteristic of software engineers in China's internet and IT companies is the significant heterogeneity in terms of class origin. In previous chapters, I have looked at several occupational groups in China's techno-developmental regime—factory workers, engineers and technicians in manufacturing, and platform delivery workers. Individuals in these groups mostly come from working-class families and rural areas or small towns, and are homogeneous in their class origin. In comparison, while some software engineers come from working-class families, others come from middle- and upper-class ones. Among my interviewees, most of the working-class-origin engineers grew up in rural areas or small towns. Their parents were/are primarily peasants, routine/semiroutine workers, or small shop owners. In comparison, most engineers from middle- and upper-class backgrounds grew up in urban areas. Their parents were/are predominantly professionals (e.g., government officials, teachers, etc.), managers, and business owners. Importantly, although scholars consider software engineers to be elites within digital capitalism, many Chinese software engineers call themselves "coding peasants" (*manong*). This self-deprecation is partly related to the fact that many software engineers come from rural areas and peasant/worker families, and still see similarities between their jobs and those of their parents. As I will show later, software engineers' class and family origins influence tech capital–labor relations along with the strategies that software engineers use to deal with work problems.

Michael Burawoy argues that the capital-labor relationship should be analyzed not only in relation to the labor process and labor market but in relation to social reproduction and the state's regulation too.[18] I have discussed the social reproduction difficulties faced by two groups in previous chapters. In chapter 4, I showed that the household registration and metric systems that local governments use to allocate public resources make it difficult for the children of migrant workers to go to public school. In chapter 5, I explained that despite the government's intention to foster techno-development rather than a land-driven economy, the real estate industry emerged as a de facto new bird. Engineers who work on robotization have encountered insurmountable difficulties in social reproduction as they cannot afford housing properties or establish a family in coastal cities. Notwithstanding their mastery of computational techniques as well as their relatively privileged positions in the social hierarchy and official metric systems, software engineers in internet and IT companies are not free from difficulties in social reproduction. Their greatest challenge comes from housing problems.

Housing issues are further intertwined with difficulties in local citizenship, marriage, and childbearing and/or child-rearing in large cities in China, where most internet and IT companies' offices are located. In recent years, several municipal governments used household registration status as a prerequisite for purchasing housing property in an effort to control skyrocketing housing prices.[19] As a result, local citizenship can influence not only access to public school for migrants' children but also the eligibility to buy housing properties. Beijing, Shanghai, and Shenzhen are where migrants have the most difficulty obtaining local citizenship. But while many studies have examined the difficulties for low-skilled migrant workers in obtaining household registration status, highly educated migrants, including many of my interviewees who work in Beijing, Shanghai, and Shenzhen, face similar issues regardless of their higher status in official metric systems.[20] Furthermore, like London and San Francisco, large Chinese cities have the most expensive housing in the world. Since gender norms in China mandate that men be responsible for gaining home-ownership before marriage, housing issues have created intense pressure on young software engineers, who are predominantly male, and their families.[21] Considerations about child-rearing, especially access to good public schools through homeownership, further amplify the stakes of housing.

Like members of the middle and upper-middle classes in the United States, my interviewees have a consensus about what it means to do well in China.[22] Specifically, one must have local citizenship, a high-paying job, a marriage, at least one child, at least one housing property, and the ability to provide one's child(ren) with a top-notch education. These conditions, however, are extremely challenging to fulfill for most software engineers who reside in the large coastal cities of China. Of course the challenges to social reproduction in such cities are not faced exclusively by software engineers, and are even more prohibitive for the factory and food delivery platform workers who also work there. The difference, however, is that the latter simply recognize that it is impossible for them and their families to live in China's largest cities in the long term, so they plan their lives accordingly. Ironically, the challenge for software engineers is unique because as talent in the techno-nation, only they can even attempt to sustain their lives and families in the most high-end, postindustrial, and prosperous cities. This shows the spatial dimension of China's deep-seated inequality.

Labor Market

My interviewees see a clear hierarchy in the labor market. On the demand side, China's largest tech giants, such as Alibaba, Baidu, ByteDance, Huawei, JD, and Tencent, supply the highest-paying and prestigious jobs. A few foreign multinational firms belong to the top echelon too, although the numbers of their employees are much smaller. Before the early 2010s, foreign firms like

Microsoft and Google were top options for software engineers. But it has become increasingly challenging for foreign firms to compete for the best and brightest talent, as China's tech giants can now offer more competitive remuneration packages. Thanks to supportive state policy, China's tech giants provide unparalleled opportunities for software engineers to develop businesses in the Chinese market, which is mostly protected from foreign competition. Below these nationally and world-renowned tech firms are start-up companies—some of which could eventually rise to the top, while others will fail by, for example, depleting their capital reserves. The offices of tech giants and start-ups are concentrated in Beijing, Shanghai, Shenzhen, Guangzhou, and Hangzhou.

In the lower echelon of the labor market are a variety of IT service, product, and outsourcing companies of varying sizes. Such firms operate in first- and second-tier cities.[23] According to my interviewees, these internet and IT companies prospered between the early 2010s and 2018, but have declined since then. Two conditions facilitated the growth of these firms. The first was the central state's policy support, including for fintech. Also, many local states provided subsidies to support industrial upgrading and transformation as well as the central state's mass innovation and mass entrepreneurship initiative and the Internet Plus agenda. Since these internet and IT companies were often classified as high- and new-tech companies, they were eligible for various subsidies, such as leasing office space in tech incubators. The second condition was the space for small and medium-sized internet and IT firms to develop. During the early stage of the digital economy, small and medium-sized firms had space to explore new areas of business not yet touched by tech giants. Many created apps used in different spheres of life, such as online education.

Both of these conditions have changed over time. Despite its initial support of fintech, the central state eventually tightened its regulation given the financial risk and social instability that fintech companies generated. Many internet and IT companies were involved in fintech, building and operating peer-to-peer (P2P) lending platforms, which enabled and facilitated individuals and businesses to borrow and lend money to each other. Due to widespread fraud and mismanagement coupled with the state's subsequent crackdown, many P2P platform companies collapsed in 2018.[24] Furthermore, the space for small and medium-sized firms to grow and even exist shrunk enormously as tech giants began to compete with smaller firms in emerging areas, such as education technology and health tech technology. As global investors themselves, tech giants have much more capital and powerful platforms to win the competition. As mentioned in chapter 6, China's tech giants embed apps in their super platforms, thus giving leverage to companies within their own ecosystems. Therefore it became difficult for small and medium-sized internet and

IT firms to compete with tech giants and their affiliates. Several of my interviewees had experiences creating and working for small and medium-sized firms that eventually went bankrupt. The fall of many small and medium-sized internet and IT firms means fewer stable job opportunities in second-tier cities, where living costs are lower than in first-tier ones.

In the end, only one type of internet and IT firm in the lower echelon of the labor market has prospered: companies connected to local governments and SOEs, and ones that mostly operate at a local level. According to my interviewees, such firms have survived because government procurement is such a major source of business for local firms. Successful internet and IT firm companies work on government projects, such as apps and platforms for official/cadre/government evaluations, big data platforms, and other types of digital governance projects. Companies without governmental connections face a higher risk of failing. To be sure, China's tech giants participate in public procurement projects too, but they focus on more fundamental infrastructure, such as government cloud infrastructure services. Despite the dominance of tech giants in larger public procurement markets, then, local internet and IT firms with connections to local governments and SOEs still have a niche in certain digital governance service markets. In fact, tech giants also outsource part of their projects to these successful local firms.

Essentially, powerful tech and state capital greatly influence the labor market for software engineers. As employers, tech giants provide the best jobs in first-tier cities—Beijing, Shanghai, Shenzhen, and Guangzhou, and a few second-tier ones like Hangzhou. As influential buyers of services and goods, state capital indirectly creates job opportunities in top tech giants and lower-echelon firms. In most of the second-tier cities across the country, such as Nanjing and Tianjin, internet and IT firms connected to state capital offer the most stable jobs for software engineers. In line with literature on intraoccupational inequalities, my data show the base salary of an entry-level job in a top internet or IT firm could be around three times that of a counterpart in a lower-echelon firm.[25] The level of inequality is even higher when we consider bonuses, stocks, stock options, benefits, career opportunities, and prestige.

On the supply side, software engineers graduating from selective universities—the so-called 211 and 985 universities—are the most sought-after employees.[26] Universities are hierarchically situated in the field of higher education in China. To improve research in critical disciplines and advance socioeconomic development, the Ministry of Education initiated Project 211 in 1995 and selected a group of universities to invest. Then in 1998, the central state launched Project 985 to cultivate world-class universities. Since then, the Chinese government has poured enormous resources into the universities involved in the two projects. The 985 universities are the most prestigious, followed by the 211 ones. Most of my interviewees from these universities had internships with leading tech firms and received multiple offers before graduation. With work experience at one top firm, software engineers can find a job in another top firm for higher remunerations. In comparison, it has become difficult for students without a 211 or 985 background to even get an internship or job offer from top firms. Elton, a human resources manager at a top firm, explained to me, "There are too many applications, so we need some thresholds to sift through applications." To be sure, after accumulating experience, engineers without an elite degree can still be hired by top tech firms, but their chances are much lower than those with elite backgrounds.

Labor Control and Management
as well as Overwork Norms

Tech firms in China use remuneration, performance evaluation, and promotion to control and manage labor.[27] Most tech firms classify software engineers into various ranks. A remuneration package includes a base salary and bonuses as well as stocks or stock options in the case of top firms. Like platform workers and government officials, software engineers feel anxious about performance evaluation, which varies across companies. When asked about where their work stress came from, most software engineers pointed to KPIs. David described such stress to me:

> They [the company] set very high KPIs and ask you to PK [have one-on-one competition] with all kinds of people. Everyone is doing a rat race crazily. If you win, you will get money. If you lose, your life will be painful. I am working on online videos. They give us all kinds of KPIs, such as the growth rate of users and the growth rate of video views. We must achieve the goals by all means. Otherwise, our bonuses will be miserable. Such KPIs are set from top to down, layer by layer. There was more freedom when I first began to work in internet companies, but we only have rat racing now.

Software engineers in some top firms, especially Alibaba and Huawei, have the most complaints about their evaluation systems as their systems are more stringent. Dong, an engineer at Alibaba, shared his bleak perspective:

> I feel terribly stressed by performance evaluation because we have the so-called 361 system. Thirty, 60, and 10 percent of the employees are evaluated as outstanding, OK, or underperforming. If I get 3.25 points out of 5 this year, I will be at the bottom 10 percent. That means I will lose my entire annual bonus this year and could be laid off next year.

Indeed, performance evaluation influences bonuses, stocks, stock options, and promotion. Tech firms ask engineers who receive an unsatisfying performance evaluation to improve. The results of promotion further impact remunerations and job security. Many engineers worry that if they are not promoted to a certain rank before they turn thirty-five years old, they will be "optimized" (*youhua*) by their companies. The word *optimize* refers to the optimization of human resources costs. In other words, engineers will be laid off or asked to leave their jobs voluntarily. Ironically, the same software engineers who help internet firms optimize the efficiency of and revenues generated by platforms are also subject to the same processes of optimization. My interviewees, both engineers and human resources managers, told me that the stringent evaluation standards in companies like Alibaba have been disseminated to many other companies, including firms in the lower echelon, via two routes. First, human resources professionals who left Alibaba brought Alibaba's evaluation standards elsewhere. Second, management at other companies saw Alibaba's evaluation system as a factor that contributed to its success. Other companies thus emulated Alibaba's system. The only interviewees who did not express serious concern about their evaluation, promotion, and job security beyond thirty-five years of age were engineers who work for foreign companies.

Performance evaluation and promotion systems interact with overwork norms in China's tech companies. Despite media attention to mandatory 996 schedules, only four interviewees reported having the experience of working on a regular, mandatory 996 schedule. But the absence of mandatory 996 schedules does not mean engineers do not work for long hours. Except for a few interviewees in foreign multinational firms, all interviewees reported the existence of overwork norms in their companies. Only three of them reported working fewer than fifty hours a week; most reported between fifty-five and sixty-five hours a week in offices. Although scholars consider internet-related industries technology or knowledge intensive, surprisingly, my interviewees described their work as *labor* intensive and emphasized the physical rather than intellectual dimension of labor, noting, for example, that their work requires staying in the workplace for long hours.[28] Although I conducted my interviews with engineers after the COVID-19 pandemic began, my interviewees still worked in offices because the pandemic situation was under control. Most engineers spoke of feeling chronically exhausted for years thanks to long work hours.

Many of my interviewees believe overwork norms and practices violate China's labor law. Yet as Dr. Chen, a labor law lawyer, told me, there are many ways in which employers can avoid violating labor law while still having employees work long hours. For instance, companies can argue that they do not force engineers to stay in offices and work for long hours; instead, engineers overwork voluntarily. But even as interviewees believe tech firms violate the labor law, they also consider the law to be essentially useless. Adam, whose view was typical, reasoned, "According to the labor law, laborers should only work for eight hours a day, but all software engineers work more than that. This violates the labor law. Since such phenomenon is so common, however, it is impossible to enforce the law. Also, the government has no incentives to implement the law. The law is useless." Several interviewees mentioned that tech firms have excellent legal support to find legal loopholes as well, so it is meaningless to appeal to the law. Indeed, many engineers thought noncompliance with the norm to overwork voluntarily could influence their performance evaluation and promotion. Therefore even when their bosses do not tell them explicitly to work long hours, they feel pressured to follow the overwork norms.

I was curious to understand the intensity of labor control and management along with overwork norms in China comparatively, so I interviewed several software engineers who work in major internet and IT firms in the United States and India. They all thought the labor conditions for software engineers in China were much worse, and reported not having to work as much as their Chinese counterparts. Some even wondered aloud why people could continue to work under such conditions without resistance. It is to this question that I now turn.

Class Origins and Capital-Labor Relations

As mentioned above, although they share the same elite occupation, software engineers in China are heterogeneous in terms of their class origin. When I talked to my interviewees, it was easy for me to guess their class origin because the ways they spoke differed considerably. Middle-class-origin engineers talked confidently and articulately, while working-class-origin engineers did not have that kind of assurance, even though a number of them graduated from 985 universities and worked in top tech firms. Sociologist Annette Lareau argues that class origin casts a long shadow on experiences in different yet connected spheres of life.[29] Indeed, in keeping with existing research on the impact of class origin, I found that class origin influences not only software engineers' education and in turn their position in the labor market, but also their position in the sphere of social reproduction.[30] Different class origins led to different understandings of and responses to overwork norms and varying capital-labor relations. From my interviews, I identified four types of software engineers: optimalists, strivers, minimalists, and the disillusioned.

Optimalists

Optimalists mostly come from middle-class families and grew up in cities. Their parents were active participants in their education. For example, Eric's mother mobilized social networks to collect information about the labor market when Eric was deciding on colleges and majors. Not surprisingly, most optimalists graduated from 211 or 985 universities; many of them have an advanced degree, and in some cases, their parents financed their postgraduate studies abroad. Optimalists have a smooth school-to-labor market transition. Most began their career in top tech firms. With excellent institutional cultural capital, work experiences, and social capital accumulated through schooling and work, optimalists have plentiful opportunities to move between top tech firms.

They are winners in the sphere of social reproduction, even though their privileged backgrounds lead them to subscribe to high social reproduction aspirations.[31] Most are married or soon-to-be married to partners with similar family backgrounds, as many met their partners at school.[32] They tend to be strategic, paying great attention to government policies on housing properties and mortgage loans. Many carefully decide the timing and order of marriage and property purchases in order to circumvent policy restrictions, obtain better mortgage loans, and accumulate properties.

Optimalists receive generous support from their parents for housing down payments while remaining responsible for the monthly mortgage payment. Adam's case is emblematic. Adam and his wife bought a 645-square-feet apartment in Beijing's Haidian District—an area well-known for its excellent public schools—at the price of 6 million RMB (US$938,200). His wife, also a single child growing up in a city, is a product manager in another top tech firm. Asked how they could purchase an apartment after less than one year of work, Adam replied,

> We are *kenlaozu* [meaning adult children who spend their parents' savings]. Due to government policy, the down payment and fees were 45 percent of the price. We didn't have enough money, but my parents said we should buy an apartment as soon as possible because housing prices would keep rising. We got 3 million RMB (US$469,100) from both sides of [our] parents. The monthly mortgage payment is 20,000 RMB (US$3,127), which is not a problem for us if we are not fired. . . . [My parents] are just high school teachers, but they saved a lot for us.

Adam's parents not only provided him with money. They advised him on where and when to buy an apartment. Not every optimalist is as fortunate as

Adam to have purchased their first apartment in an excellent school district. Since optimalists either have or plan to have a child and are committed to providing their children with an excellent education, many plan on eventually moving to a second apartment—a plan that is often a source of stress.

Another advantage enjoyed by optimalists is their parents' help—unsurprisingly, mostly from their mothers—with child-rearing. Research shows parental support explains how some women are able to balance work and childbearing and child-rearing, given the gender norms for women to be the primary provider of housework and childcare labor.[33] Eric's case illustrates such help and reveals its quality. Eric's wife, Amy, works for a top accounting firm. Graduating from an elite university, the couple aims high in career development and needs two salaries to achieve their desired level of security. When I asked Eric how they both could work for long hours with a toddler, Eric responded,

> Amy's and my parents take turns to take care of our daughter. After retiring from their jobs as teachers and government officials, our parents have handsome pensions. They also have time and expertise. We are super lucky that they can take great care of and educate our daughter, especially our mothers. . . . If we have any accomplishments, it's because of their parenting. They always plan for our success.

Building on the foundation laid by—and resources from—their families, optimalists are well positioned to optimize their social reproduction decisions.

Consistent with their emphasis on making good choices about marriage, housing, and childbearing and child-rearing, optimalists view accepting a job offer as an informed and calculated decision. On the one hand, they emphasize that engineers agree to long work hours when they accept a job offer. As Mina put it,

> When you accept an offer from a top firm, you give tacit consent to long work hours. Although your contract doesn't require you to stay in the company for eleven or twelve hours, everyone knows top tech firms have such work time. This resembles the situation faced by salespersons. Their contracts don't require them to drink with clients, but they must do so.

Optimalists accentuate the notion of "two-way choice" too. As Tim explains, "Companies and workers choose each other, so employment is a two-way choice. You aren't forced to work by a company. The fact that you work there means you chose it." Framing something as a choice implies actors can freely choose among options, commit themselves to a certain path of action, and should be responsible for their choices.[34] My interviewees reason that because engineers are cognizant of the kind of employees each type of tech firm is seeking, engineers should be responsible for their own decisions.

On the other hand, optimalists do complain about long working hours even as they endeavor to optimize their choices as well as comply with workplace rules and norms. Many of them expressed worries about the effect of overwork on their health. Fred, for example, articulated his anxieties about this:

> I would like my job more if I didn't have to work so much. I enjoy working with my brilliant colleagues on cool projects. But if I didn't have to repay my mortgage, I wouldn't work for such crazy hours. I'd rather spend more time with my family. . . . I overdraft my health in exchange for money. Living in Beijing requires tens of millions. The problem is you can find tech jobs only in places like Beijing. . . . Housing and education are super expensive. If any of my family gets sick, I'd need a lot of money. Whenever I hear someone bought an apartment in a great school district, invests a lot in their children, or has a parent who gets ill, I feel insecure.

Research in the United States suggests that professionals with a middle-class upbringing are more likely to underscore the intrinsic values of work than are working-class-origin professionals.[35] Due to growing social reproduction costs, optimalists in China emphasize not only work's intrinsic values but also its material returns. Many optimalists described feeling exploited by their companies, and being expected to sacrifice their health and family lives for their job.

But then precisely because they feel they are paying a high price, optimalists respond to overwork norms and stress from KPIs by optimizing choices. They calculate the "price-performance ratio" of a job. Tim remarked,

> I consider the price-performance ratio of a job, evaluating what I get and the price I pay. I know one must work for a long time in Huawei, and the remuneration is not exceptionally high, so I won't work there because the price-performance ratio is low. In comparison, work hours are long in Byte-Dance, but the remuneration is very high, so I feel OK with ByteDance. Pinduoduo offers very competitive packages, but since its work hours are insane, I won't consider it.

When considering and comparing jobs, optimalists calculate the value of local citizenship. Here we can see how the government's metric systems influence engineers' calculations and decisions. Local governments assign different quotas to top tech firms for household registration according to the perceived contributions of the firms. Many interviewees chose to work for top tech firms that were more likely to provide household registration. For example, after graduating from an elite university in Beijing, Nancy decided to work for Microsoft instead of a domestic firm because the former offered a higher chance to get local citizenship. She explained her calculation:

> The values of a Beijing hukou [household registration status] include access to public education and housing. Since Baidu and Alibaba hired many people, it's much more likely for me to get a Beijing hukou through Microsoft. Although Baidu and Alibaba gave me more competitive remuneration packages, the value of Microsoft's offer was higher when I added the value of Beijing hukou.

Optimalists also improve their choices by hopping from one top firm to another. As Mike related, "Given that we are exploited, it's better to be exploited by firms that can pay more. They exploit us, and we exploit opportunities. . . . Both my wife and I got a 30 percent raise when we changed our jobs. Now our remuneration packages are both around 1 million RMB (US$156,600)." Other optimalists share Mike's view and calculate the timing of changing jobs in order to avoid losing their bonuses, stocks, and stock options.

Finally, optimalists calculate how their work will contribute to the market value of their human capital. Josh, for instance, told me he moved to a more time-demanding job: "My previous job was less time demanding. I worried I'd lose my competitiveness and earn less if I continued to work there. As a software engineer, you need to have a crisis awareness and invest in yourself."

Since most optimalists acknowledge the exploitative aspects of work, they are not critical of people who participate in labor activism, but they do distinguish themselves from the latter. Mike observed, I'm sympathetic to people involved in the anti-996 movement, but we are not as powerless as them. We make rational decisions that benefit ourselves, and we aren't easily incited by others." As I will show later, most engineers involved in the anti-996 movement come from working-class families.

Although some optimalists expressed sympathy for labor activism, most of them had no time for or interest in activism, and did not believe labor activism could change the situation given the government's developmental goals. Nonetheless, optimalists do see space for individual agency under structural constraints. Although engineers in top firms all work for long hours, optimalists emphasized variations in working hours as well as remunerations across and within firms. They believe engineers can work fewer hours in foreign tech firms or as part of certain teams in domestic firms, although those jobs might not yield the highest remunerations. But ultimately, optimalists reason that people who are unhappy with overwork should make a better choice by matching themselves with the right firms and teams.

What struck me the most about optimalists was their repetitive stress in interviews on optimization, calculation, matching, and rationalization in making their work and life decisions. As demonstrated in previous chapters, these strategies and logics are embraced by the Chinese state and tech giants too, and applied to the pursuit of techno-development and corporate revenues. But optimalists apply such logics to almost every aspect of their life. I was also amazed by their ability to master the game of playing with the metric systems and rules set by the government (e.g., household registration rules and quotas) and tech firms (e.g., KPIs).

Strivers

Generally from rural areas or small towns, strivers come from working-class families. Their parents are mostly peasants, factory workers, and small shopkeepers who believe in education's ability to improve one's life chances. Like factory and platform workers, some strivers were left-behind children. Despite the enormous rural-urban and regional disparities along with the adverse impacts of rural labor migration on left-behind children, strivers beat the odds to enter 211 or 985 universities.[36] Some received a master's or doctoral degree, although none had the opportunity to study abroad. With these impressive forms of institutional cultural capital, strivers now work in top firms and benefit from the techno-developmental regime.

Strivers have worked hard since their childhood and believe firmly that through hard work, a person can change their fate and improve their life. Reflecting on his childhood, Dan recalled, "When I was a kid, I knew I could only change my fate through studying. My teachers and parents told me I could find a good job if I do well on the college entrance exam and graduate from a top university. For people from the countryside, we have to eat bitterness to have a better life." Dan's thoughts correspond with research on the ethos of striving for a better life in rural-origin families in China.[37] Strivers' success on college entrance exams and in the labor market affirmed their belief that hard work pays off. Indeed, strivers are partial winners. Unlike optimalists, strivers cannot completely achieve mainstream social reproduction standards, but as we will see, they fare much better than minimalists and most of the disillusioned.

Strivers do well in the marriage market in terms of having a partner with high institutional cultural capital. Like optimalists, most strivers met their spouses or partners at school. They usually marry spouses with similar family origins due to cultural and social proximity, with only a few strivers, mostly female engineers, marrying up in terms of class origin.[38] Due to marital homogamy, strivers and their spouses have fewer family resources than optimalist couples.[39]

Like optimalists, strivers receive parental help with housing down payments, but the support tends to be much less, with the exception of those strivers who married up. Many strivers expressed guilt about accepting monetary help from their parents. As Steve explained, "My parents work under harsh conditions as construction workers. I feel terrible about taking their money." For strivers who live in Beijing and Shenzhen, their savings and family support are usually inadequate for their down payments, so they often borrow money from relatives or have small personal loans to collect enough capital. Compared with optimalists, strivers are less likely to purchase apartments in excellent school districts, yet they still aim to do so in the long term.

Strivers encounter steeper challenges than optimalists in child-rearing due to inadequate family support. Whereas literature focuses on left-behind children from working-class families, some strivers also leave their children with their parents.[40] Tom, a Tsinghua graduate, described his son as a "second-generation left-behind child." He and his wife, a software engineer too, both work from 10 a.m. to 9 p.m., leaving no time to care for their son. And because Tom's parents and in-laws could not move to Beijing due to their own work, Tom and his wife had to leave their three-year-old son with his parents. Tom wept in the interview because he misses his son so much. As a left-behind child himself, he felt heartbroken when he thought of his son. But he told me that he and his wife had no other choice due to long work hours and mortgage loans. Coping with their sense of guilt, Tom and his wife convinced themselves that "children only need physical care when they are young."

Child-rearing can remain a problem, however, even when strivers' parents stay with them. Both sets of parents helped Peter and his wife with caring for their daughter in Hangzhou, but intergenerational frictions resulted, as Peter recounted, "Our parents stayed with us, but Linda didn't like their rural parenting style. Also, our apartment is too small to accommodate four adults and one child. In the end, Linda had quarrels with my mother and mother-in-law, and everyone felt exhausted. Linda eventually quit her job and stayed at home so our parents didn't have to stay with us." Strivers and their rural-origin, working-class parents (again, mostly mothers) sometimes have conflicting views on child-rearing. As such, strivers negotiate between achieving parenting aspirations and pursuing professional and financial goals. As frequently happens to working couples, when strivers and their spouses choose to prioritize parenting, it is the female partners who end up sacrificing their careers. Still, despite the difficulties they encounter in pursuing social reproduction goals, strivers tend not to complain. They always express gratitude for their opportunities to move up the social ladder, and all of them believe they have a much better life than their parents.

Like optimalists, strivers consider overwork norms widely accepted in their profession. They view working for long hours as a personal choice too. Yet they differ from optimalists in how they understand and make choices. Strivers make sense of work through the lens of striving for a better life and changing one's fate. Rather than making a detailed cost-benefit analysis of different jobs, strivers consider the value of jobs in relation to their class and family origins. High-paying jobs in top firms may be demanding of one's time, but for strivers, the life transformation they can achieve is worth it. As Todd observed,

> Overwork is a personal choice. Everyone has different life situations. Some of my former colleagues moved to less time-demanding jobs in foreign tech companies or state-owned enterprises. Because of their family background, they don't need as much money for housing as I do. If I were them, I wouldn't work for twelve hours a day. But for people like me, we don't have problems working for twelve or thirteen hours. My salaries and bonuses allow me to buy an apartment in Hangzhou. I live a much better life than my parents and my hometown friends. I feel lucky and grateful.

In fact, Todd only has thirty minutes interacting with his son every day except for Sunday, but he still feels he has made the best choice for his family.

Whereas optimalists feel they pay a high cost for overwork and acknowledge the exploitative aspects of work, strivers feel that software engineers exaggerate the situation. Interestingly, strivers think like hardworking students, often analogizing work to study. For example, Dan drew a direct comparison between work and school: "Didn't everyone study from 6 a.m. to 10 p.m. every day at school? They [software engineers] didn't complain about study time when they were students. Why do they complain about work? Our work time is shorter than study time at school, so those complaints don't make sense." I was surprised to discover that some strivers fiercely opposed the 996.ICU slogan. Steve rejected the idea that long workdays could harm one's health: "If you work from 9 a.m. to 9 p.m., you can still go to sleep around 11 p.m. and wake up at 7 a.m. Why would people be sent to an ICU with eight-hours sleep? They must have stayed up late and played video games." Although Steve has a two-year-old son in his hometown, he only considered the time for work and sleep. It is thus not surprising that strivers do not think of long workdays as exploitation. For them, long work hours are simply the necessary input to gain high remuneration and secure upward mobility.

Because work is seen as the means to transform one's life, strivers devote themselves to it wholeheartedly. Strivers work longer than optimalists. Rather than complaining about workplace rules, strivers take performance evaluations and promotion opportunities seriously.[41] When unsatisfied with their work performance, they critique themselves instead of others or the rules. As Tina reflected, "When I worked on the online payment project, I was too slow and delayed the entire team's progress. If I can improve my problem-solving skills, I will be able to finish my task faster and improve work efficiency."

Strivers are also more loyal to their companies than optimalists. Only a small number of strivers in my sample had ever changed their jobs. They frequently expressed gratitude to their companies during the interviews.

Indeed, recruiters notice strivers' dedication to work and loyalty. According to two informants in charge of recruitment, human resource managers in some top tech firms see rural-origin, high-achieving students in top universities as excellent candidates. As one informer told me, "Human resource people know that they [rural-origin engineers] work hard and don't complain because they need hukou. They also need money to buy an apartment and pay mortgage loans since their parents don't have money. They are the best employees because they devote all of their time to work." This quote shows that employers are aware of the enormous dependence of rural-origin, high-achieving software engineers on wages, so they exploit the disadvantaged family backgrounds of the latter.

Unsurprisingly, strivers' dedication to work makes them unlikely participants in labor activism. Rather than blaming employers for exploitation, many strivers criticize engineers involved in activism for their "laziness," "selfishness," and "incompetence." As Peter commented, "If [engineers] want to talk about the labor law, they should think about whether they work for eight hours a day. They might stay in companies for twelve hours, but they spend more than four hours on lunch, dinner, naps, video games, and their personal things." All strivers emphasized a positive relationship between inputs and remunerations. According to Tom, "If you want to make more money, you shouldn't be lazy. Numerous peasant workers, like my parents, are willing to work for twenty-four hours if they can receive high pay. They don't have such opportunities, however." Similarly, Dan considered people involved in activism as selfish because they do not consider that time-demanding, high-paying jobs provide engineers from the countryside with great opportunities to transform their lives.

In strivers' opinion, people who complain about long working hours should "vote with their feet." They believe capable engineers will always be able to find other opportunities. If one cannot find a satisfying job, it can only be because they are incapable, and "incapable people shouldn't complain," as Finn starkly put it. Precisely because strivers rose to top universities and firms from disadvantaged backgrounds, they believe others should be able to do the same.

Minimalists

Like strivers, minimalists mostly come from working-class families in rural areas or small towns, but they did not attend top universities. As research shows, disadvantaged family backgrounds lower the likelihood of getting into a selective university.[42] Whereas no optimalists or strivers attended "coding boot camps," some minimalists had. Like coding boot camp students in Canada and the United States, minimalists without a major related to computer science attended boot camps in order to build technical and interview skills.[43] Some computer science students also joined boot camps because their universities did not prepare them for the labor market.

Lacking the institutional capital from a top school, minimalists' school-to-work transitions were less smooth than those of optimalists and strivers.[44] Minimalists complained about not having internship opportunities that could lead to a satisfying job. On graduation, they often spent a couple of months in their first jobs and struggled with job stability because they were more likely to work for small and medium-sized internet or IT companies that go out of business easily. Minimalists mostly work for lower-ranking companies in second-tier cities such as Chongqing and Xi'an. These cities are among the most economically developed in China, yet less expensive than the first-tier cities. Getting local citizenship tends not to be a problem in less expensive cities. Some minimalists work for nontop firms in the most expensive cities. As natives from working-class families in those cities, they do not have household registration problems.

A small proportion of minimalists graduated from selective universities, work in top firms, and live in the most expensive cities. This group has less luck than strivers in three respects, despite their demographic similarities. First, some minimalists have difficulty getting local household registration status because of inadequate quotas in their companies. Tony's company, for example, uses a lottery system to allocate quotas, but he did not win the lottery. Second, some minimalists broke up with their girlfriends at school and remain single, while most strivers married their girlfriends at school and have augmented resources collectively.[45] Third, this group of minimalists tends to have more siblings, thereby having fewer family resources available.[46] These conditions make minimalists with 211 or 985 backgrounds less resourceful than strivers in terms of social reproduction.

Whereas most optimalists and strivers are married or soon-to-be married, most minimalists are not in a relationship due to their relative disadvantages in the dating and marriage market. Mark's situation is typical:

There weren't many girls in STEM majors. The few girls whom I knew at school disdained rural and small-town bumpkins. After I began to work, I didn't have enough time for dating because of long work hours. Neither do I have an apartment to attract girls. . . . [As for dating apps,] we programmers know how dating platforms work. A lot of information and photos are fake. Even when the platforms aren't completely fake, they are for rich, confident, and stylish people. Those people smile like sunshine and go to the gym to build muscle.

Like Mark, many minimalists recognize that their origins, long working hours, and inadequate economic, cultural, and even body capital constitute barriers to relationships.[47]

Not surprisingly, minimalists are unenthusiastic about dating, although their parents worry about their marital prospects. When minimalists go on a date, they usually meet people with similar origins introduced by relatives or colleagues. Minimalists complained that they could not find "pure love" from such arrangements. Peter said, "Women at this stage want to find a man who already has a housing property." Minimalists also pointed out that women introduced to them frequently expect men to pay for the wedding, gifts, and bride prices.[48] Paul, who works in Xi'an, estimated he would need 500,000 RMB (US$73,000) to get married. He said if he could meet with a woman willing to share half the expenses, he would have married. My interviews with a few female minimalists confirm that they seek partners who can afford an apartment and marriage expenses.

Given such poor prospects, many male minimalists have decided to withdraw from marriage and childbearing so as to avoid the stress—at least at this stage of life. Although their parents might help a bit, they feel they cannot afford marital costs, especially those who have a brother, because their families need to distribute resources between the boys. Tony explained his withdrawal from dating and marriage:

> Two days ago, a colleague wanted to introduce me to a girl. I told him I was busy fixing bugs. Of course, if I wanted, I could squeeze in some time. My cousins in the countryside got married in their twenties. This is impossible for young people in the cities, where all kinds of stress refrains people from getting married. If you get married, you must take a mortgage loan. You'll also have to be responsible for old people on both sides and your child. If you are "lucky" to have a second child, you'll be doomed.

The few minimalists who are married and work in nontop firms told me they are *dingke* (DINK), and do not plan to have a child because they cannot afford one or the anxiety that would come with it.[49]

Unlike optimists and strivers, many minimalists cannot buy a housing property because they cannot pool enough resources for a down payment. Instead, most rent an apartment. Also, because most minimalists do not live in the most expensive cities, rents are relatively more affordable as long as they do not have other obligations. The few minimalists from working-class families in large cities live with their parents. Like optimists and strivers, the few minimalists who do have a property received help from their parents, but they tend to buy properties in a cheaper, nearby city while renting an apartment in the city where they live. Don, for instance, works and lives in Xi'an, but his family could only afford to buy an apartment in Xianyang. Don thus leases out his property in Xianyang and rents an apartment in Xi'an.

Recognizing and responding to their structural disadvantages, minimalists minimize their social reproduction aspirations.[50] Mark exemplified such thinking:

> I try not to care about the expectations that my parents, society, and the government impose on me because people who live according to those expectations live a life of slavery. . . . I want to live a life that makes me feel good. People should decide their lives. When I have low desire and "lie flat" [*tangping*, meaning to reduce desire and stress], I become less stressed.

As Mark's comment reveals, minimalists feel they can exercise control over their lives by lowering their social reproduction aspirations and quitting the rat race.

Minimalists understand the meaning of overwork norms and work in general through the lens of deciding one's social reproduction aspirations and resisting mainstream social norms. For them, work is part of the package of choice. Since they believe people can make choices, they are not sympathetic to people who subscribe to mainstream norms and suffer from extremely long working hours. As Paul argued, "If people choose to stay in the rat race, they can get what others cannot have, but they must work like hell. In a way, they decide to enslave themselves, so they have to accept work hours like 996. Because I don't want to work like hell, I chose to remain single and not buy a housing property or car."

Nonetheless, despite lowering their social reproduction aspirations and avoiding jobs that require extremely long hours, many minimalists still feel somewhat exploited by employers and alienated at work. They do not work as much as optimalists and strivers, but most minimalists do work over fifty hours a week. Tony described the enervating effect of his workload:

> I already work less than many software engineers, but I still feel tired. I arrive at my office at 9 a.m. and leave the office around 7 p.m. Sometimes I stay until 8 p.m. to finish my work. The only leisure activities I have are playing video games at work and in the metro and watching live broadcasts before sleep. On the weekend, I only want to lie flat and sleep; I have no energy for other things.

Several minimalists complained about how unrealistic task assignments, pressure from their managers to achieve KPIs, and competition between companies contribute to unnecessary and unproductive overwork. For instance, according to Andy, his manager did not know how to respond to market competition other than to encourage employers to "work harder and stay longer."

Many minimalists also bemoaned the repetitive nature of work. As mentioned above, most minimalists do not work for top tech firms but rather for smaller ones that handle outsourced work for top tech firms or local governments. Don portrayed his work: "Big techs outsource noncore business activities to us. Because tasks are modularized, I do things repeatedly and don't learn new things. What I do is not too different from what workers do on assembly lines because we all do very dull things." In fact, minimalist's complaints about the nature of their work often resemble those of factory workers (chapter 4), noting the repetitive, boring nature of tasks.

To address their dissatisfaction, minimalists develop some strategies. Rather than confronting the management and risking their employment, they cope with overwork norms by passing as having embraced workplace rules and overwork norms.[51] Many told me they pretend they are working in the offices when in fact they are playing video games or working on their personal business. Mark said,

> My colleagues and I try to spend as much time playing video games as we can at work. As engineers, we still have some skills to disguise ourselves to our dumb managers. They [the managers] do not completely know what we are doing and how much time we need to complete a task. Although I complain a lot, my situation is still better than delivery workers. I have skills, but they don't. Because their jobs are so easy, platform companies can use apps to monitor them automatically. But our companies cannot do this to us. . . . My skills allow me to pretend I'm working when I'm not.

In so doing, Mark and his colleagues attempted to reduce their working hours and "raise hourly wages." Mark's quote reveals the uneven application of instrumental power on workers too. Those without skills, like food delivery workers in chapter 7, tend to be subject to the most intensified instrumental control based on technology because supervision of work can be automated easily. In the interviews, several minimalists also mentioned wanting to regain freedom by becoming an entrepreneur; as such, they use their work time to try to plan their own small business. Such dreams resemble those of factory and platform workers.

Minimalists are mostly indifferent or, at most, only somewhat sympathetic to labor activism. Like optimalists and strivers, they think individual choices can better address overwork problems than activism. The most important choice for them is to lower their own aspirations for marriage, housing, and childbearing, and then match their job choices and workplace strategies accordingly. In general, they feel their income is sufficient to have a low-desire lifestyle and accumulate some savings. Their experiences make them believe that other software engineers should similarly be able to have a "less stressful" life. Unexpectedly, some minimalists described software engineers involved in labor activism as losers and expressed their contempt for the latter's failure to sustain their lives. Several minimalists said only "peasants workers" (*nongmin gong*), who tend to be low-skilled workers, would appeal to collective action because those workers do not have skills valued in society. In the interviews, minimalists distinguished themselves from these peasant workers by emphasizing their possession of skills. They believe only incompetent software engineers would need to confront their employers as low-skilled workers.

Minimalists somewhat sympathetic to labor activism are those who encountered difficulties finding a job with shorter working hours. Although there is plentiful information about top firms, little information is available about work conditions in nontop firms because of the huge number of such firms. Therefore engineers not in the major leagues often did not realize their mistake until already accepting a job at a lower-ranked firm and discovering the extensive hours. Other minimalists visited websites and social media sites established by activists in order to find information about companies' working hours and management practices. These minimalists are sympathetic to labor activism to the extent that it facilitates information exchange.

The Disillusioned

The disillusioned category has two subtypes: the first and largest is characterized by their difficulty in maintaining a basic level of social reproduction. Like minimalists, this group of the disillusioned are from working-class families in rural areas or small towns. They mostly attended nonselective universities; some also joined a coding boot camp. Most of them work for nontop firms. By contrast, the first subtype of the disillusioned differs from most minimalists by living in first-tier cities such as Beijing, Shenzhen, and Shanghai, where problems associated with housing and local citizenship are the most severe.[52] When I asked why they lived in such cities, interviewees in this group said they saw better job opportunities there. In social media groups, many discussed the pros and cons of working in the largest cities compared with other places. They complained that internet and IT companies outside the largest cities only do outsourced work or are on the brink of bankruptcy.

Due to high living expenses along with their humble salaries and family backgrounds, most of the first-type disillusioned see survival in the big cities as extremely difficult. Like minimalists, they are mostly single and have withdrawn from marriage, childbearing, and buying housing properties, at least at this stage of life. But although they have lowered their aspirations, they still experience enormous difficulties sustaining their daily lives, mostly because of housing problems. The state-led gentrification and growth of the real estate industry as a new bird decreased the availability of affordable rental housing.[53] Many expressed their frustration with trying to negotiate between commuting time, rent, and the quality of housing. Bill described his experiences:

> My monthly salary is around 8,000 RMB (US$1,239). I rent a one-bedroom apartment in an urban village in Shenzhen. My rent is 2,500 RMB (US$387). My previous landlords did not renew the leases because of the urban renewal project. I've moved several times. It becomes tough to find a place to stay. . . . My parents bought an apartment in a town. They used their savings for my brother's wedding, so I have to send remittance back home. I don't spend money except for rents, meals, and occasional medical expenses, but I still don't have savings, and the situation will worsen because rents will only increase.

In social media groups, many engineers share that their incomes are only slightly higher than food delivery workers, which is factually accurate. Ultimately, the first-type disillusioned who work for nontop firms have not only withdrawn from marriage, childbearing, and housing purchase but also are having difficulty securing even rental housing or accumulating enough savings to deal with any unexpected expenses.

Most of the first-type disillusioned who work for top firms have a stable relationship with a partner, but hesitate to marry given the dual obstacles of obtaining local citizenship and housing. Edward's experience helps illuminate the experience of these engineers. After graduating from a university in Chongqing, he first worked for Baidu in Beijing. He then moved to Alibaba in Hangzhou and Tencent in Shenzhen, hoping to settle down in Shenzhen. His girlfriend also works in Shenzhen. Yet unexpected policy changes and rocketing housing prices disrupted their plan. Despite their high incomes (700,000 RMB or US$108,299 jointly), they have still failed to realize their social reproduction goals of marrying, having a child, and owning property. When asked why they haven't simply lowered their aspirations, Edward explained,

> If I were single, it would be OK not to have a housing property. But my girlfriend and I have been together since college. We want to get married and have a baby. Without a housing property and hukou, our child will have difficulty going to school. Most of our colleagues solved their problems because of their parents. It's sad that you need to have rich parents to get married and form a family.

Edward's quote shows his frustration at not being able to secure what he considers the humblest social reproduction aims. Others voice similar criticisms in social media groups, complaining about rising social inequality and living costs, such as, "Now, only the rich can have a child; poor people will be childless. This is how China will get richer and richer."

Due to insurmountable challenges in matching their personal and family resources with social reproduction needs, many of the first-type disillusioned consider themselves as doing worse than their parents. As Phil put it, "Although my parents were peasant workers, and I have a college degree and white-collar job, my social status is as low as theirs. We are all wage slaves, but my parents have three children and a house. I'm spouseless, childless, and propertyless. My life is worse than theirs."

Differentiated from the first-type disillusioned by a sense of financial freedom, the second-type disillusioned are the minority. They come from upper-class families and work for top firms. They typically have one or two children and own two or three housing properties in Beijing, Hangzhou, or Shanghai, all without the burden of mortgage loans. Not surprisingly, they have received tremendous financial support from their parents. Ted, for example, an engineer at ByteDance, has two apartments in Shanghai's Jingan District, where some of the country's best public schools are located. His father worked for an SOE in the 1990s and became the owner of the enterprise later. To help Ted settle down in Shanghai, Ted's father bought him two apartments and paid the mortgage loans. Zack, an engineer at Alibaba, likewise owns three apartments in Hangzhou because of his parents' investment. Indeed, their financial assistance enabled Zack to declare, "I can sustain my family without working for at least ten years"—truly a minority status within the sample.

Unlike the first-type disillusioned, the second type are winners in the marriage and housing market, and well positioned in the labor market. They do better than optimists and strivers as they do not have to repay mortgage loans or worry about access to excellent schools. Nonetheless, the second-type disillusioned are deeply unsatisfied with their child-rearing arrangements. Ted, for instance, was emotional when he talked about his daughter. His happiest moments every day are the thirty minutes he can play with his daughter. Ted told me, "I have everything except for time for my family. Can you imagine I only have thirty minutes for my daughter on my workdays? I work six days a week. What kind of inhumane life is it? I often question myself about the purpose of life." In fact, when I asked engineers with children how much time they interact with their children on weekdays, most engineers in top firms who live with their children told me thirty minutes per day. Despite their abundant economic, cultural, and social capital, the second-type disillusioned feel desperate about not having time—a resource even more valuable than money— to interact with their children.

The first-type disillusioned who work for nontop firms feel alienated from work. Like manual workers and minimalists, they complained about having to work like a robot. Although they have less intense work schedules than top-firm employees, they still have to work fifty to sixty hours per week. Asked whether they could at least leave their offices earlier, most of them responded no. As Lucas shared, "Managers didn't say we have to stay because they would have to pay for overtime work, but everyone knows we have to stay 'voluntarily.' The fact that we're not able to finish our tasks or we're not in the office means we'd have poor performance evaluations. A former colleague was fired after he confronted managers about working hours."

Like minimalists, the first-type disillusioned in nontop firms fear retribution, and cope with overwork norms by passing as having embraced the workplace rules and "raising hourly wages." Both subtypes of the disillusioned who work for top firms describe themselves as a "human flesh battery" (*renrou dianchi*). They feel burned out and chronically overwhelmed. Frank became emotional as he described his life:

> My company often has sales events. If our platforms have problems, I have to solve the issues because we have hundreds of millions of users. I could rest only between 2 a.m. to 8 a.m. for two years, and I worked for fifteen to sixteen hours every day. Eventually I collapsed and transferred to another team. Now the situation is better, but I still work between eleven to thirteen hours on weekdays, and I must work on the weekends if the company has any event. I wish I have one hour belonging to myself. I often feel I'm a human flesh battery. I am not a human. I'm a battery. The intensity of the rat race [*neijuan*] is unbearable.

Frank and others who work for top firms also said their companies do not explicitly require them to work for such a long time, but they know that unless they do so, they cannot finish their tasks, and thus must worry about their performance evaluation and promotion.

There are differences in how engineers deal with overwork norms among the disillusioned who work for top firms. The first-type disillusioned worry that if they do not conform to the norms, they will not receive bonuses, stocks, and stock options, which can constitute over 50 percent of their remunerations. Therefore they feel forced to follow the workplace rules and overwork norms. The second-type disillusioned are the only group who dare to reveal their reluctance to comply with overwork norms.[54] Ted, for example, told his manager that he would like to spend more time with his daughter. He is always the first person to leave the office. Not surprisingly, he failed to get a major promotion recently, but Ted said he does not care about the promotion because he works not for subsistence but rather for self-realization.

The disillusioned have a strong sense of being exploited and having no choices. The first-type disillusioned feel that they work for long hours in exchange for remuneration, but their pay is inadequate to sustain the most basic standard of living. Lucas asserted that

> capitalists are like parasites. They suck laborer's blood. Now engineers have to rely on parents' savings and work like dogs to buy an apartment and raise their children. Companies take advantage of people's financial dependence and parasite on familial support. A fair wage should be enough for people to live a basic level of life without the need to rely on parents or harm their health.

Indeed, the impossibility for the first-type disillusioned to secure what they perceive as the lowest social reproduction goals despite their long work hours makes them feel profoundly disenchanted about work. Comparing their lives with those of their parents only strengthens their sense of disillusionment.

The second-type disillusioned focus not so much on the fair exchange of labor for wages as the effects of exploitation and commodification.[55] They believe there should be a limit to commodification so that they can have time to rest and stay with their families. The second-type disillusioned feel exploited because they feel forced to work. As Zack said, "I want to work to the extent that I can still be a human, but my company forces me to work for long hours even though I don't need that much money."

Unlike the other types, the disillusioned do not feel they have meaningful choices, nor do they believe they can "vote with feet" to bridge the chasm between their resources and what would be needed to achieve their social reproductive aspirations. Even the choices they do have are largely illusory and make little qualitative difference to their daily lives. The first-type disillusioned in nontop firms saw all firms as more or less the same. They pointed out the difficulty of changing jobs too. As Phil noted,

> Companies require higher and higher academic credentials. There are also more and more computer science students and people who go to boot camps. Finding a better job isn't that easy. Also, not everyone can afford rents if there is a gap between two jobs. Changing jobs might also require paying moving and other expenses. Who knows if the next job would be better?

As for the first-type disillusioned in top firms, they feel they have already exhausted their choices by moving between top firms and cities. The only remaining option is immigration out of China, but most of them consider immigration beyond their reach. The strong sense of exploitation and a lack of choice among the first-type disillusioned is revealed by their recurrent reference to the idea of flight. For example, Bill told me, "I often think about how I can escape from my job and terrible life, but I haven't found a solution."

Despite their financial freedom, the second-type disillusioned feel they have only limited options. Ted explained,

> I would immediately quit my job if I could find a company that has promising business prospects and technological capacity, and that allows me to go back home at 6 p.m., but such a company does not exist. All top tech firms are more or less the same. [As for foreign companies,] their development is quite restricted in China, and they don't recruit many people.

Like Ted, other interviewees expressed the simple desire for a job that would allow them to both pursue their ambition and have a family life.

Given their sense of exploitation and the absence of choice, the disillusioned are supportive of labor activism, although they are dubious that it could change their work conditions in the short term. The first-type disillusioned in nontop firms are the most likely group to join activism. They discuss and share information in social media groups. Some help build and maintain databases where engineers can search for information about work conditions in different companies. Research shows the growth of Marxism in China.[56] Indeed, the first-type disillusioned in nontop firms do frequently mobilize Marxist discourse to critique companies. Richard, for example, described the situation in these terms: "Instead of increasing workers' welfare, tech capitalists in China have given money to the government. In a country that is supposed to be led by peasants and workers, peasants and workers don't have rights." Justin told me he often feels he is "whipped by capitalists." The online sites and groups where the disillusioned exchange information and views are full of Marxist conversation.

Despite their support for and involvement in activism, the first-type disillusioned in nontop firms had few ideas beyond venting and exchanging information. Also, they emphasized they are not in opposition to the government or interested in strikes and offline protests, citing the state's crackdowns on lawyers, petitioners, workers, and labor organizations. That is why most of the anti-996 movement has remained online. As I wrote in chapter 4, some of the factory workers I interviewed (mostly women) protested in front of government buildings to demand access to local schools for their children. In chapter 7, I showed that food delivery workers went on strikes and protests, notwithstanding the potential state repression. Compared with factory and platform workers, software engineers involved in labor activism were too afraid of state repression and thus refrained from taking offline action.

Software engineers also saw internal divisions among engineers. As Justin reasoned, "Engineers' long working hours show the trend of proletarianization, but the trend hasn't become a reality. Since many software engineers belong to the petite bourgeoisie, they will follow the bourgeoisie rather than the proletariat." Even though they support activism, the disillusioned in top firms said they have no time for it. Some spend their valuable personal time with family, while others prepare for immigration.

In general, the disillusioned think labor activism will not improve engineers' work conditions, given China's political regime and the Chinese state's emphasis on development. But while they remain pessimistic about the efficacy of activism, the disillusioned still support it because they want dissenting voices to be heard and hope people will not have to overwork in the long term. I summarize the characteristics of the optimalists, strivers, minimalists, and disillusioned in table 8.2.

The State, Nation, and Development

Since most software engineers think overwork norms and practices violate China's labor law, questions arise as to the role of the Chinese state in protecting labor rights and its relationship with tech capital and labor. Despite their differences in class origin and perspectives on capital-labor relationships, most software engineers—except for the disillusioned along with a few optimalists who work for foreign companies—express similar views on the Chinese state. Although engineers might disagree with some of the state's policies, few are critical of the Chinese state for its inaction to protect labor; all is forgiven in the pursuit of national development.

This acceptance of overwork endures, even when it negatively impacts individuals. Mark, a minimalist, said, "Why can China have achieved so much since the reform and opening up? It is because of the hard work of China's 1.4 billion population. If Chinese people worked from 9 a.m. to 5 p.m. as people in developed countries, we would not have such accomplishment." An engineer at ByteDance told me, "Internet companies compete globally. If we had the same work hours as companies in Silicon Valley, we would not have rapid success abroad, especially when we haven't accumulated enough technologies. I think it makes sense for the government to postpone dealing with the labor-capital relationship before the country achieves a higher level of development." Similarly, a software engineer at Huawei said that not every Huawei engineer is more intelligent or efficient than engineers at Huawei's competitors in the world; Huawei has become a globally leading company only because its engineers work more than those of its competitors.

My interviewees believe labor conditions vis-à-vis overwork will only improve when the government chooses to change the legal and administrative environment—something they do not see the techno-developmental state as likely to do now. As Adam put it, "China remains a developing country. Since Western countries have already gone through the process, their people don't

TABLE 8.2. Comparison of Optimalists, Strivers, Minimalists, and the Disillusioned

	Optimalist (n = 20)	Striver (n = 12)	Minimalist (n = 16)	Disillusioned (n = 16) Type 1 (n = 11), type 2 (n = 5)
Class origin and family background	Middle-class families in cities; the only child	Working-class families in rural areas or small towns	Mostly from working-class families in rural areas or small towns; some from working-class families in cities	Type 1: mostly from working-class families in rural areas or small towns; type 2: upper-class families in cities
Education	211 or 985 universities; postgraduate education in China or abroad	211 or 985 universities; postgraduate education in China	Mostly nontop universities; coding boot camps	Type 1: mostly nontop universities, coding boot camps, only some top universities; type 2: top universities
Labor market	Top firms	Top firms	Mostly nontop firms	Type 1: mostly nontop firms, some top firms; type 2: top firms
Social reproduction				
Marriage	Married or in a stable relationship toward marriage	Married or in a stable relationship toward marriage	Withdrawing from marriage	Type 1: withdrawing from marriage; type 2: married
Housing	Significant parental help with the down payment	Some parental help with the down payment	Mostly unable to afford to buy a housing property; rental in less expensive cities or staying with parents (some urbanites)	Type 1: having difficulty securing affordable rental housing in first-tier cities; type 2: own at least two housing properties due to parental help
Childbearing/ child-rearing	Have or plan to have a child; parental help with childrearing; some access to great schools	Second-generation left-behind children; parental help with childrearing; intergenerational frictions about parenting	Not planning to have a child	Type 1: not planning to have a child; type 2: have one or two children and access to great schools, desperate about inadequate time for childrearing

Local citizenship	Problems mostly solved	Problems mostly solved	Mostly no problems except for those living in tier-one cities	Type 1: problems getting local citizenship; type 2: no problems
Social reproduction aspirations	Meeting mainstream standards	Meeting mainstream standards except for childrearing	Lowering social reproduction aspirations	Experiencing enormous gap between resources and social reproduction needs
Workplace				
Understanding of overwork	Personal choice	Personal choice	Personal choice	Exploitation
Meaning of choice	Calculated and informed decisions to find an optimal job	Opportunities to transform one's fate	Deciding social reproduction standards	Options that can bridge the chasm between available resources and social reproduction needs
Relationship with workplace rules and norms	Follow rules and norms somewhat reluctantly	Follow rules and norms gratefully	Covert noncompliance with rules and norms	Type 1 in nontop firms: covert noncompliance with rules and norms; type 1 in top firms: follow rules and norms reluctantly; type 2: challenge rules and norms
Response to overwork	Exit a nonmatching job	Loyal	Exit the mainstream lifestyle	Voice resistance
Attitude toward labor activism	Indifferent or somewhat sympathetic	Hostile	Indifferent or somewhat sympathetic	Supportive

have to work so much. Before they achieved development, people in Western countries worked for long hours. I don't think firms or the government can do anything if we want to catch up with developed countries." They all agree that the government prioritizes the country's developmental agenda over other things. Many point out that the government has no other choices, but engineers have some options. As Alice, an optimist, remarked, "If you are a government official in charge of economic development, you'll think in that way [neglecting labor issues or talking about labor rights in symbolic ways]. Given that we are born in such an era, we have to make our own decisions. There are many different kinds of jobs available. We have choices." Her quote reveals the immunity from blame accorded to the state because it has the mandate to advance national development. Two minimalists also reminded me that I might have little knowledge about China's progress because I live in the United States and US media depict China negatively. They told me life has improved a lot, and the Chinese nation has been getting stronger; as long as one works hard, everyone has opportunities to prosper in China. I asked what it means to them when the nation is getting more powerful. They replied that when the nation is strong, Chinese people, including those at the bottom of society, will have better lives than people in other countries. One minimalist told me, "The rise of China means that China can grab resources from other countries to improve Chinese people's lives."

But a few optimists who work for foreign companies did question whether long work time is a sustainable solution to China's development, and were more critical of the relationship between individuals, the nation, and development. For example, Ethan, a Microsoft engineer, emphasizes that it does not make sense for everyone to overdraft health to exchange for money and national development. He explained,

You don't know how long it will take for the country to develop. It could be five years, ten years, fifty years, or even a hundred years. But one's life is finite, right? As individuals and a nation, I think we should pursue a sustainable developmental path. We should try to balance work and life, and not overdraft health. We shouldn't work at the expense of abandoning our families. Many engineers in China treat their homes as hotels and stay with their families as strangers. They go back to sleep at night and go to work in the morning. They only have time to say one sentence to their family on the weekend. We only live once. We don't know how long it takes for China to develop. If the government doesn't change the developmental model, generations of Chinese will be sacrificed. Our national development has already sacrificed peasants, migrant workers, and their children. Now the sacrifice extends to software engineers because of the importance of technology to national development. I think national developmental policy based on sacrifice is wrong. When many people are unhealthy and unhappy, is our nation strong? If one has to separate from their family or has no time to enjoy life, what is the purpose of development?

Katheryn, another engineer who works for a foreign company, shared her observation from interacting with engineers in India. She was surprised to find that software engineers there do not work as much as Chinese engineers, nor do Indian engineers relate their work to their country or national development, although India is also an economically developing country. At the end of the interview, Katheryn lamented,

Sometimes, I feel bewildered about development. I think we Chinese should think for ourselves. Everyone works tremendously hard, but for what and for whom? You consider the nation's prosperity and appreciate the government, but does our country or government love you as much as you love them? Do you really enjoy the benefit of development when you lose your health and family lives?

Katheryn's quote demonstrates the work involved in making sense of one's relationship with the nation, the state, and national development.

Among my interviewees, the first-type disillusioned are the most critical of the Chinese state and its developmental policy. They complained about the state's implicit permission for internet and IT firms to exploit software engineers. Many pointed out that although they want to free themselves from exploitation through creating small firms, it is challenging to do so because the market is dominated by big techs, their affiliates, and local companies connected to the government. Many of the self-help web pages and social media groups established by the first-type disillusioned were censored by the government and tech companies. From the state's censorship and crackdowns on labor activism, this group sees the capitalist nature of the Chinese state, the alliance of the state and tech capital, and their exclusion from the techno-nation. Many pointed out the ironic fact that the internet or IT companies without overwork norms and practices in China are all operated by "foreign capitalists," but not "national capitalists."

"Not Our Fault"

Finally, although many of my interviewees complained about KPIs, long work hours, and exploitation, they could also be complicit in exploiting others in digital and surveillance capitalism.[57] In fact, some of my interviewees are involved in developing platforms and algorithms that enable technological control of workers, while others work on recommendation algorithms that could promote certain influencers' videos, including those that help specific platforms to recruit potential workers. As I described in chapter 7, many factory workers decided to work as food delivery platform workers after watching videos on platforms like Kuaishou or Douyin. I was curious about how software engineers view the plight of platform workers. Most of them expressed sympathy for platform workers, but insisted that software engineers were innocent and should not take the blame.

First, they reasoned that internet and IT firms, not software engineers, decide optimization goals according to the companies' values. In the process, engineers usually do not know whether their algorithms will lead to difficulties for specific social groups. An engineer at Meituan observed,

> This is absolutely not the engineers' responsibility. Indeed, it is likely that algorithms would harm underprivileged groups. Some recommendation algorithms could increase volumes for certain groups but undermine other groups. Oftentimes, the goals of optimization are clear, but the optimization methods tend to be black boxed. You don't know whether the goals you set and the models you train would harm certain groups and bring challenges to them. For example, Meituan's platforms aim to increase operational efficiency and the company's revenues through AI, so engineers optimize the system based on these goals. The company does not tell you to protect underprivileged groups or platform couriers because that's not part of the company's values and priorities. From the perspective of engineers, we can only optimize the goals according to the company's values to get better KPIs for ourselves.

Other engineers share similar views. All clarified that they do not have the authority to decide tech firms' values and optimization goals, and are glad that public concerns might change companies' values. In other words, they follow instructions from the management and have some autonomy only in terms of deciding technical choices to achieve the goals set by the management. As several engineers mentioned to me, they are "cogs in the machine" and not the boss. Some stressed that engineers did not intend to exploit others through their work, and that engineers themselves are victims of exploitation.

Secondly, similar to how they perceive overwork and exploitation in their occupation through the lens of choice, many engineers think that platform workers should be responsible for their choices. An optimalist who works at NetEase said,

> Job selection is always a two-way choice. Why do more and more people decide to work as food delivery workers? It is because they can make more

money. This rationale is similar to why many software engineers accept 996. You can choose not to do it, and you have many choices; not every engineer or platform worker has a miserable life. Platform workers can decide not to take so many orders or work for platforms. They make their choices.

Essentially, my interviewees think they should not be scapegoats for internet or IT firms, or responsible for platform workers' unwise personal decisions.

Conclusion

In the 1970s, Bell predicted that algorithms would substitute intuitive judgments for decision-making in the postindustrial society, and that software engineers would become part of the power elites thanks to their knowledge and expertise about the new intellectual technology.[58] As I have shown, notwithstanding the important role of software engineers in digital capitalism, it is crucial to distinguish tech CEOs and rank-and-file software engineers. Indeed, some CEOs of tech giants in China worked as software engineers and became powerful economic as well as political elites who can influence the country's policy, law, governance, and economic development. And yet rank-and-file software engineers are elites only to the extent that those who work for top firms have higher wages than the majority of the population in China. At their work, they follow their companies' values, instructions, and optimization goals. Software engineers in China also suffer from the instrumental power of tech firms and the state, as evidenced in their struggles with the rules and metric systems set by the Chinese state and tech firms.

This chapter offers a more nuanced picture of software engineers by uncovering the heterogeneity among them, and delving into their diverse relationships with tech capital, the techno-developmental state, the nation, and the cybertariat. Consistent with literature on intraoccupational inequalities, I find variations among software engineers in terms of their class origin and current position in the labor market.[59] It is true that those who work for top firms earn high remuneration, but engineers coming from middle- and upper-class families are more likely to enter top firms than their counterparts from working-class families. In addition, there are only slight differences in salaries and a sense of accomplishment between software engineers in the lower echelon of the labor market and platform food delivery workers—a typical example of the cybertariat—even given their divergent forms and levels of human capital. Accordingly, viewing software engineers as part of an elite occupational group can overlook their heterogeneity.

Furthermore, I show that engineers' expertise does not necessarily protect them from tech capital's exploitation due to their difficulties in social reproduction, which largely results from the rise of the real estate industry as a de facto new bird under China's techno-developmental regime. Suffering from intense labor control and overwork norms, software engineers' dreams to realize themselves or transform their fate are compromised, and at times, reduced to the humble hope of living more like humans instead of human flesh batteries. The ability of software engineers to deal with harsh work conditions varies by class origin. Engineers from upper-class families are the only group that dares to openly confront labor control and management along with overwork norms in the workplace. Middle-class-origin engineers are better positioned to vote with their feet while meeting their social reproduction aspirations.

In comparison, the most successful working-class-origin engineers in the labor market (i.e., strivers) totally submit themselves to tech capital. Less successful working-class-origin engineers either give up critical aspects of life in exchange for slightly better work conditions or find no solutions to their conundrum. Both minimalists and disillusioned engineers from working-class backgrounds often choose to forgo marriage and parenthood. This observation aligns with the broader trend in China, where marriage rates have been steadily declining since 2013, reaching a record low in 2022. Furthermore, in the same year, China experienced a population decline for the first time in six decades. Additionally, as I mentioned, the disillusioned, working-class-origin engineers often referred to the idea of hoping to escape from their jobs and lives in the interviews as if they lived in a birdcage. While middle-class-origin engineers can move to a better cage, the disillusioned, working-class-origin engineers feel unbearably trapped.

The heterogeneity among software engineers has implications for labor activism. Although recent literature on labor movements in China suggests hope that more software engineers might mobilize, my findings lend more support to work that highlights the difficulty of organizing professionals given intragroup divisions.[60] Optimalists and minimalists are mostly indifferent about activism, and think complaints about overwork can be addressed by the exit option or mitigated through covert noncompliance with overwork norms.[61] Surprisingly, strivers see themselves in conflict not with capital but instead with labor movement participants. As for the disillusioned, they support labor activism, but those who work for top firms have no time for it. Ultimately, only engineers situated at the bottom of both the labor market and sphere of social production are involved in activism. Like labor movements organized by tech workers in the United States, labor activism organized by Chinese software engineers primarily provides a venue for venting and information exchange.[62] As a whole, the evidence shows more division than solidarity among software engineers.

Despite the heterogeneity and division among software engineers, however, most do share similarities in terms of how they understand their work and life in relation to the nation and state. Except for the disillusioned and a few optimalists who work for foreign companies, most engineers see national techno-development as the mandate of the Chinese state. Although some question the rat race at the individual level, they take competition at the national level for granted. From this perspective, although engineers suffer from overwork, they see it as a necessary evil for China to advance techno-development and catch up with high-income countries. They hardly blame the Chinese state for failing to protect their labor rights as the Chinese state is choiceless in finding other ways to fulfill its mandate. Ultimately, most of my interviewees recognize that—whether they like it or not—labor rights are subsumed to the larger cause of national development. Such thinking also prevents software engineers from participating in labor activism. Essentially, when they consider their relationship with the nation, most engineers become sort of strivers at the national level, pursuing China's upward mobility on the global developmental ladder, although they still exercise their choices at individual levels to address their work and life problems.

Finally, software engineers are similar in terms of how they consider their relationship with the cybertariat.[63] They do not think that they should be responsible for the exploitation of the cybertariat since they have no autonomy as to the use of the digital means of production. They feel their hands are tied by tech capital. Although scholars consider them as part of the power elites in the postindustrial society or digital capitalism, the rank-and-file coding elites are subject to tech capital and the state under China's techno-developmental regime. Indeed, in the next chapter, I will show how the Chinese state—the ultimate power holder in China—exercises its power to reshape China's techno-state capitalism.

9

Rewiring Techno-State Capitalism

AS I DISCUSSED in the previous chapters, the Chinese state has created an arsenal of technological and legal instruments based on the bird/cage logic to pursue techno-development. According to this logic, the Chinese state evaluates industries and businesses, or birds, in terms of their contribution (or lack thereof) to the nation's techno-development. Those birds deemed deserving are allocated resources and rewards, including regulatory tolerance and exemption. The cage provided by the state for such birds, in other words, allows a fair amount of freedom and encourages growth. By contrast, the state uses all the technical and legal tools at its disposal to cage and punish those birds seen as either failing to contribute to or even harming techno-development. In doing so, the Chinese state has created a bifurcated regulatory environment.

The Chinese state has been harsh and unpredictable to low-end capital but benevolent and supportive to high-end capital. China's tech giants had been privileged in the amiable environment of political economy before the Chinese state initiated a crackdown on the tech sector in 2020. They had not only enjoyed the state's support but also had no supervision from independent trade unions or powerful civil society actors. In fact, the incredible growth of China's tech companies coincides with the relentless suppression and decline of civil society and the public sphere in China. Before the recent regulation tightening of the tech sector starting in 2020, regulations of tech companies focused on censorship.[1] That means that as long as tech companies fulfilled their jobs in implementing censorship, they could enjoy unparalleled business opportunities.

In such an environment, tech giants in China have achieved tremendous gains: accessing global capital and a protected domestic market of 1.4 billion people; partnering with the Chinese government in its global expansion initiatives; influencing law and policy making; establishing a cogovernance relationship with local states; and exercising enormous market, legal, and technological power over other actors, from platform workers to software engineers, providers, small and medium-sized internet and IT firms, and users of platforms. Outside China, similarly powerful private businesses do not receive as much support from the state and are not completely free from the oversight of civil society or trade union actors. It is thus not surprising that until the recent crackdown, tech firms based in China had been the darling of global capitalists like BlackRock, Citigroup, Deutsche Bank, Goldman Sachs, J. P. Morgan, Morgan Stanley, and SoftBank.[2]

At the same time, techno-development and the application of the bird/cage logic are dynamic processes. The state–tech capital relationship in China's techno-state capitalism is not static but instead constantly being recalibrated. When Chen Yun advocated for the birdcage economy in the 1980s, he emphasized the need to adjust the size of the cage dynamically.[3] Indeed, as I wrote in chapter 6, the unprecedented boundary-spanning instrumental and infrastructural power of tech giants in China has raised the urgent question of how the Chinese state should attempt regulation. Since October 2020, the Chinese central state has initiated a series of unexpected crackdowns on China's big tech companies and internet-related sectors. This chapter will explain those crackdowns as well as explore the efforts of the Chinese state to cage China's tech giants and rewire China's techno-state capitalism.

The Redlines

As I mentioned in chapter 6, Premier Li Keqiang formulated the regulatory principle of being tolerant and prudent in his Report on the Work of the Government in March 2017. This regulatory approach was promoted as creating space for new business forms and models to prosper, thereby facilitating industrial upgrading and transformation, generating employment opportunities, and helping China to achieve its developmental goals.[4] Even then, however, Li cautioned that the government would seek out necessary safety valves and redlines to deal with unacceptable risks.[5]

Over time, it has become clear that there *are* limits to the Chinese state's support for techno-development—the prudent side of the tolerant and prudent principle, if you will. Since President Xi Jinping's ascent to power, he has repeatedly underscored the importance of preventing and preparing for worst-case scenarios (*dixian siwei*). Put another way, the party-state should not tolerate certain risks to national security and the CCP's leadership.[6] Scenarios in which different kinds of risks overlap or escalate—for example, the escalation of international, socioeconomic, and specific risks into domestic, political, and systemic risks, respectively—must be avoided.[7] Indeed, political scientists have argued that Xi's governance centers around the imperatives of risk management and the CCP's political survival.[8]

What, then, are the possible redlines or unacceptable risks in the internet sector that could trigger the safety valves of the tolerant and prudent principle? There are no clear answers, but policy documents and the speeches of top leaders suggest three interconnected redlines or unacceptable risks. The first is systemic financial risk. Guidelines and policies concerning the platform economy or Internet Plus initiative tend to single out fintech and the problem of financial risks. Despite its initial support of fintech in 2015, the State Council kicked off a campaign to clamp down on fintech platforms in 2016 because of problems and protests generated by P2P lending platforms. Rather than keeping regulation decentralized, the State Council mandated coordination across state agencies and localities to implement a crackdown campaign.[9] In his speeches at the politburo in 2016 and 2017, Xi emphasized the importance of financial security while framing financial security as part of *national security*. He further pointed out the existence of some financial risks in China and how imperative it was to prevent systematic financial risks.[10] In 2019, Xi directed the enhancement of the governmental oversight of financial risks.[11]

The second redline is widespread social instability, which has been a long-standing concern for the CCP and contributed to changes in developmental agendas during Hu Jingtao's reign. With the rise of the platform economy, social protests that target platforms and internet companies have also emerged. Thus far, I have discussed protests organized by food delivery drivers (chapter 7), software engineers (chapter 8), Didi drivers, and P2P lending platform users. In June 2018, truck drivers in several provinces, including Chongqing, Sichuan, Shanghai, Jiangxi, Shandong, Hubei, Guizhou, and Zhejiang, organized strikes to protest rising fuel costs, numerous government fines and levies, and cutthroat rates in the platform economy. The truck drivers argued that they were being exploited by both business and the government. Manbang, the corporation that operates and monopolizes the platform or app for truck drivers to bid for jobs, was the focus of particular resentment when it made changes to the app, essentially forcing the drivers to compete with one another by offering increasingly lower rates. Following the strikes, which took place in several cities and lasted for about three days, Manbang changed the app's design.[12]

Significant differences exist between grievances and collective action in conventional sectors, such as manufacturing, and the platform sector due to the frequently centralized and monopolized market structure as well as murky legal relationship in the platform economy.[13] As I showed in chapter 7, since labor relations in the platform sector often fall outside labor laws, few gig workers can access institutionalized channels to solve their problems, and thus turn to protests or strikes as their only option. Collective action also tends to be more localized in terms of targets in the conventional sectors; workers organize strikes or protests against their employers in specific localities. In comparison, in the platform sector, grievants in different localities target the same platform companies that operate across localities in China, such as Meituan, Ele.me, Didi, and Manbang. Moreover, many participants in the platform economy are always on the road due to the nature of their work as delivery couriers, Didi drivers, and truck drivers. This gives them means and opportunities to obstruct traffic and public order. In chapter 7, I discussed cross-cutting solidarities too—the participation in collective action of small businesses and workers who work for different gig platforms. For the above reasons, grievance and collective action in the platform sector could lead to significant social instability.

Indeed, grievance and collective action in the platform economy triggered reactions from the Chinese party-state. To address protests organized by taxi and ride-hailing drivers, the Ministry of Transport instructed its local agencies to work with local party-states and institutionalize "social stability maintenance mechanisms" in 2018.[14] In addition, the ACFTU enacted a plan to incorporate platform workers. The ACFTU is an organ of and subordinate to the party-state, although it claims that it represents all Chinese workers.[15] In 2018, the ACFTU announced that it would accelerate building trade unions for eight targeted social groups: truck drivers, delivery workers, health care workers, domestic workers, mall workers, food delivery platform couriers, real estate agents, and safety guards. According to the ACFTU, each of these groups has seen growth with the rise of the platform economy.[16] But as I mentioned in chapter 7, none of my interviewees saw the implementation of the plan before the recent crackdown on China's tech giants. To address grievances and problems in internet-related sectors, the SAMR published the draft amendments of the Antimonopoly Law in January 2020.

The third redline is national security. After Xi rose to power, he elevated the importance of national security in response to the growth of China's public sphere and civil society during the Hu-Wen leadership. To counter such development, the Xi leadership cracked down on the internet and social media, while enacting the National Security Law (2015), Foreign Nongovernmental Organization Management Law (2016), and Cybersecurity Law (2017) to protect China's national security.[17] The National Security Law defines national security as "the relative absence of international or domestic threats to the state's power to govern, sovereignty, unity and territorial integrity, the welfare of the people, sustainable economic and social development, and other major national interests."[18] This definition reveals the relationship between systematic financial risk and widespread social instability (i.e., threats to sustainable socioeconomic development), on the one hand, and national security, on the other hand. Notably, the National Security Law incorporates data security as part of cyberspace and information security.[19] The Cybersecurity Law stipulates that critical information infrastructure operators that gather or produce personal information or important data shall store the information and data within China; these operators cannot store data outside China, or share their data with entities or actors outside China, unless they undertake a risk assessment process according to the relevant laws and regulations.[20] Here we can see the state's concern about tech firms' infrastructural power and its attempt to control such power. Xi specifically called for the protection of national data security through lawmaking at the politburo in 2017.[21] In addition, concerns have increased regarding the meaning of state secrecy and risk of cross-border data transfer in the age of big data.[22] Officials in the National Administration of State Secret Protection argue that data in many industries and areas are not state secrets per se, yet the aggregation of data across different areas of life or industries could become national secrets.[23] In summer 2020, the Standing Committee of the National People's Congress announced a draft of the Data Security Law, which emphasized the role of data in safeguarding national sovereignty, national security, and national interests.[24]

The Crackdown

Despite problems resulting from the internet sector along with the risk that companies therein might trigger safety valves or cross the above redlines, the Chinese state's stance vis-à-vis the digital economy was decidedly tolerant before October 2020, except for the crackdown on P2P lending platforms in 2016. Angela Zhang points out the bureaucratic inertia of China's regulatory agencies. For example, as I mentioned in chapter 6, internet companies headquartered in China, such as Tencent and Alibaba, often adopt a VIE structure to utilize foreign capital and circumvent regulatory restrictions on foreign investment in the internet sector. Due to VIEs' legally ambiguous status, the Chinese antitrust authority was reluctant to regulate VIEs for fear of legitimizing them. Paradoxically, this enabled tech giants to make numerous acquisitions and build their ecosystems without reporting to the authority.[25]

From Tolerance to Curbing the Excessive Expansion of Capital

The regulatory environment, however, shifted dramatically in 2020 before Ant Group's US$37 billion IPO on the Shanghai Stock Exchange and the Stock Exchange of Hong Kong, which was scheduled for November 5, 2020. Ant is an affiliate company of Alibaba and owns China's largest digital payment platform, Alipay. On November 2, 2021, the People's Bank of China (PBOC), China Banking and Insurance Regulatory Commission, China Securities

Regulatory Commission, and State Administration of Foreign Exchange summoned Ant's founder, Jack Ma, and its chair and CEO.[26] The next day, the Shanghai Stock Exchange abruptly suspended Ant's IPO based on the reasons that the evolving regulations on fintech might disqualify Ant's IPO.[27] The suspension was only the first in a series of law enforcement campaigns targeting tech capital. Scholars agree that the sudden and unexpected regulatory changes were decided by the top leadership.[28] Indeed, indirect evidence—policy documents, speeches, and scripts of press conferences—suggests that central state agencies and key technocrats in charge of financial stability convinced the highest leadership to shift the regulatory environment, thereby triggering a process of administrative centralization. As I mentioned in chapter 6, after Li became the premier in 2013, he immediately promoted decentralizing administrative power to reduce the state's intervention in the economy and invigorate market activities, but here we see a reversal of that development.

There were overt disagreements, if not clashes, between Ma and the central state agencies in charge of financial stability and fintech regulation. One significant difference between Chinese and US tech giants is that Chinese tech giants like Alibaba and Tencent profit tremendously from credit and other financial businesses. This shows the Chinese tech firms' boundary-spanning power across sectors, including finance. Under the previously supportive policy environment, big tech companies in China, from Alibaba (through Ant) to Tencent, JD, Meituan, Didi, ByteDance, Suning.com, and Xiaomi, provided microlending services starting in the mid-2010s, while using their apps, ecosystems, and microtargeting advertising to promote their credit and other financial businesses (e.g., investment and insurance). App users could apply for microloans using apps easily and swiftly. Big tech companies automatically approve a microloan within minutes by relying on big data, digital footprints, AI, and machine learning to gauge risks for lenders. Unlike getting a mortgage, borrowers of microloans do not need to provide collateral. In addition, although microlending services function like credit card services, the former do not require a credit history and are more convenient to use because they are embedded in many apps. Ant's revenues demonstrate the lucrativeness of microlending services. In 2020, 39.4 percent of Ant revenues came from its credit business, surpassing revenues from its digital payment services (35.9 percent of the revenues).[29]

Here I would like to present interview data to show how microlending and the tech giants' involvement in finance operate in and influence everyday life. Many factory managers and platform workers whom I interviewed mentioned microlending when we talked. Before the growth of microlending services, workers chose to work for more prominent and creditable manufacturers such as Foxconn, in part because employment there helped workers to get a credit card. Access to a credit card became unimportant, however, with easy access to microlending. I also discovered that many food delivery workers continue to work as gig workers despite the exploitative environment due partly to their obligations to repay numerous microloans that they borrowed using apps. The lives of food delivery platform workers are connected to tech companies and subject to the instrumental power of tech giants in complicated ways: they make decisions about consumption and work under the influence of platform live streaming; they shop and finance their purchases through apps under the influence of microtargeting advertising; and they work under platforms to repay their microloans.

More than half the platform workers I interviewed told me that they used apps like Taobao for online shopping, and while shopping, they frequently saw advertisements for microlending. Seeing such advertisements, the workers felt encouraged to purchase more than they could afford, and not surprisingly, over time many accumulated considerable debt. In fact, around one-third of my gig worker interviewees reported having to repay microloans; some were even actively dodging phone calls from the microlending platforms as they could not repay the debts. I interviewed a manager who worked for Alipay in order to better understand microlending. According to the manager, the interest rates of microlending are higher than those of credit cards and bank loans. People who use microlending also tend to be the working class or young adults like college students. He explained, "People who borrow microloans through apps are mostly poor people. Many didn't know the interest rates of microlending are very high. . . . Rich people don't need microlending." His quote shows the class dimension of the instrumental apparatus created by China's tech giants. In my interviewees, I found that although it is common for platform delivery workers to borrow microloans, most software engineers I interviewed did not have microloans. The only group of software engineers that borrowed microloans was the first type of the disillusioned—those whose salaries were slightly higher than the earnings of food delivery platform workers.

The rapid growth of microloans and extensive involvement of tech firms in the finance sector eventually became a concern for the Chinese state. In September 2020, the China Banking and Insurance Regulatory Commission issued a document outlining measures to strengthen the regulation of microlending.[30] In fact, the commission had already announced its plan to enact a new regulation on microlending in 2019, but it did not unveil the draft (together with the PBOC) until November 2020.[31] Furthermore, in September 2020, the State Council and PBOC issued new rules that regulate financial holding companies based on the draft rules they published in 2019.[32] According to Pan Gongsheng, the PBOC's deputy governor, the central state decided to strengthen financial regulation at the Fifth National Financial Work Conference in 2017.

One of the main purposes of the new rules was to incorporate nonfinancial firms involved in financial business into the financial regulatory framework as nonfinancial firms were not subject to the same stringent regulations as financial enterprises.

In the news conference that announced the new rules, Pan further used Ant to illustrate how internet companies, as examples of nonfinancial firms, became involved in financial business. He pointed out that more regulations would be on the way too. By mandating that nonfinancial firms involved in finance form financial holding companies, the new rules aim to set up a firewall between the industrial and financial sectors, and "prevent cross-institution, cross-market, and cross-sector contagion risks." Pan explained that such regulation would ensure that finance serves the "real" economy—meaning the production, transaction, and circulation of goods and services within an economy.[33] At the 2017 National Financial Work Conference, President Xi said, "Finance is the blood of the real economy. Serving the real economy is the duty of finance, the purpose of finance, and the fundamental way to prevent financial risks."[34]

On October 24, 2020, Ma delivered a provocative speech at the Bund Finance Summit in Shanghai, in front of China's financial regulators and senior government officials. Feeling held back by financial regulations, Ma abruptly criticized both international and domestic financial regulations as obstacles to development and innovation. Ma argued that there are no systematic financial risks in China. "To make risk-free innovation is to stifle innovation, and there is no risk-free innovation in the world. Oftentimes, managing risk down to zero is the biggest risk," he said. Challenging what he termed the "pawnshop mentality" of China's traditional financial institutions, Ma suggested replacing such an outdated mentality with cutting-edge fintech that builds on and integrates big data, risk control technologies, and credit systems. In his speech, he also congratulated himself for Ant's upcoming IPO pricing. He remarked, "This is the largest listing ever priced in the history of the entire human race, and the pricing happened in a place other than New York City. This was unthinkable five years ago, even three years ago, but miracles happen."[35] The fact that Ma criticized Chinese regulators in such a high-profile way and the context of China's highly repressive political environment revealed the power of tech giants in China—at least until then. Still, Ma did not expect that the miracles he described would turn into nightmares.

One week after Ma's open criticism, the State Council's Financial Stability and Development Committee (FSDC), presided over by Liu He, expressed the central state's view on financial risks in a special meeting on October 31, 2020. Liu was then a member of the politburo, vice premier of the State Council, and director of the FSDC. The meeting document stated that China is in a critical period to realize the great rejuvenation of the Chinese nation. The CCP's one-hundred-year anniversary in 2021 was cited as particularly significant to the party, especially during the COVID pandemic coupled with the rise in geopolitical tensions between the United States and China. The meeting reached a consensus that although the central state supports financial inclusiveness, the development of fintech, and innovation and entrepreneurship, financial activities should be regulated to ensure financial stability and security. Whereas Ma criticized international financial institutions like the Basel Accords, the FSDA meeting note emphasized that China respects international consensus and rules. Rather than invoking the tolerant and prudent principle, however, the meeting adopted a "zero tolerance" principle, announcing that the government would "resolutely rectify all kinds of financial chaos, have zero tolerance for any violations of laws and regulations, actively and prudently prevent and defuse financial risks, unwaveringly maintain financial stability, and firmly uphold the redline to prevent systemic financial risks."[36] Such language is frequently used in political and law enforcement campaigns, but its application to the tech sector was unprecedented. The meeting concluded by outlining how the central state would prevent financial risks—namely by establishing a delisting mechanism, ensuring that market entities operate in compliance with laws and regulations, enhancing the comprehensiveness and transparency of business information disclosure, protecting the legitimate rights and interests of consumers, strengthening antimonopoly and anti-unfair competition law enforcement, establishing basic systems for data resource property rights and data sharing, and strengthening the protection of personal information. Three days after the meeting, Ma was summoned by the central state, and Ant's IPO was suspended.

Party leaders discussed the issue of tech giants at the politburo on December 11, 2020, and the Central Economic Work Conference on December 16–18, 2020. Xi attended both meetings, at which the agenda of "strengthening antitrust regulation and preventing the excessive expansion of capital" was announced.[37] From the discussions at the two meetings, it is clear that the party-state was specifically focused on disciplining tech capital. For the first time since China's Antimonopoly Law took effect in 2008, the highest leadership talked about strengthening antitrust regulation. The document of the Central Economic Work Conference stated that although China supports platform companies in strengthening their global competitiveness and innovating, they should be regulated according to law. As such, the party-state would enhance laws and regulations concerning platform monopolies, management of data collection and use, and protection of consumers' rights and interests. The conference concluded that financial innovation could unfold only under "prudent" regulations. Notably, the tolerant part of the previous tolerant and prudent principle was dropped. Both meetings sent clear signals to state agencies that they should immediately act and coordinate to regulate tech companies. It did not take long for law enforcement campaigns as well as new lawmaking and policy-making activities to unfold.

Understanding the Regulatory Blitz

How, then, are we to make sense of this abrupt shift in the central state's regulatory principle vis-à-vis China's tech giants? I argue that changes in both domestic and international contexts since 2019 likely impacted how the central leadership understood the nature of the tech beasts it had nurtured along with the risks they precipitated. The Chinese state had set itself the task of transforming the nation into a techno-developmental leviathan, but few apprehended or could have predicted all the different implications or outcomes of that process, or the exacerbation of its associated risks with the rise in US-China tensions. Furthermore, as I have established in previous chapters, the prevalence and power of techno-developmentalist discourse in China had fostered a tendency to disregard risks and problems among state officials. In my fieldwork and interactions with various types of interviewees and informants, I often heard people, including government officials, expressing pride that other countries do not have the same convenient or powerful technologies as China. Commitment to the idea of "China Number One" seemingly trumps all other considerations, even among those whose lives have been profoundly and negatively impacted by the country's transformation. Almost none of my informants or interviewees seemed to consider that people and governments in other countries might have *chosen* not to pursue certain aspects of tech development precisely given the associated risks and potential consequences. Some local officials in Guangdong familiar with industrial policy specifically pointed to China's laxer regulatory environment as helping the country to compete and even surpass advanced economies. They call this strategy "overtaking on a bend" (*wandao chaoche*). Ma's controversial speech at the Bund Finance Summit in 2020 exemplified such thinking when he contended that Europe was falling behind in financial innovation due to its outdated stringent regulations.[38]

As circumstances have changed in both the domestic and international contexts, however, so has the central leadership's understanding of and concern regarding the risks associated with China's powerful tech giants. In chapter 6, I showed that the supportive and tolerant state as well as the state-tech partnership created new birds that straddle the boundaries between different industries and sectors, between the private and public, and between the local, national, and global. The government initially considered such boundary-spanning instrumental and infrastructural power as beneficial to China's techno-development, but eventually came to see that power in the hands of tech giants as a risk.

The Chinese state formed the FSDC under the State Council in November 2017 to safeguard financial security and prevent financial risks.[39] One of its most crucial tasks was to reduce the rapidly growing debt of SOEs, the so-called "deleveraging program."[40] In July 2018, the FSDC finalized its members and announced that it would be chaired by the vice premier of the State Council, Liu, who then coordinated with seven other key central government or party agencies (e.g., the PBOC, China Banking and Insurance Regulatory Commission, China Securities Regulatory Commission, State Administration of Foreign Exchange, and National Development and Reform Commission) to tackle the financial risks.[41] The establishment of the FSDC and incorporation of various top regulators into its ranks demonstrated the central leadership's growing desire to address and prevent financial risks.

Around the same time, many financial scandals emerged. Several prominent business conglomerates that operated across industries, sectors, and regions fell into crisis. The case of HNA Group is emblematic. Between 1998 and 2018, the company expanded rapidly from aviation to other industries like real estate, financial services, tourism, logistics, and technology. By 2018, though, HNA Group could no longer manage its enormous debt. In 2020, the Hainan provincial government seized control of the company and put it into bankruptcy proceedings. The Chinese state was particularly concerned about the complicated ownership structures of HNA Group's numerous subsidiaries as well as the potential cross-organizational and sector risks.[42] Instances like this made clear to the central government the downside of its strategy of unconditionally supporting large conglomerates operating across regions, industries, sectors, and ownership types. Such situations revealed the deep involvement of nonfinancial firms in finance industries.

In 2019, the PBOC's financial stability report and plan for regulation suggested the central bank had become highly concerned about tech capital's rapid encroachment into the financial sector along with the threats to data security in 2019. The report criticized tech companies for overcollecting information from consumers, monopolizing big data, and taking advantage of regulatory loopholes to pursue high financial returns instead of serving the "real" economy—all of which, combined with the risk of cyberattacks, could threaten national data security.[43] Although the FSDC was not originally created to tackle tech giants, its focus shifted there as regulators argued that the Chinese state should prevent cross-institution, cross-market, and cross-sector contagion risks, and seriously reexamine the role of tech giants in generating those risks. In addition to FSDC-affiliated state agencies, the CAC was concerned about the threats of tech firms to national data security, and in 2019, drafted a new regulation to restrict the cross-border transfer of personal information to protect personal information and national security.[44] Essentially, the Chinese state became concerned about tech firms' cross-sectoral power as such power could lead to boundary-crossing financial instability; the Chinese state also began to see data as part of the national infrastructure, which increased concern regarding tech firms' private, cross-border infrastructural power.

On top of domestic factors, transnational factors contributed to the Chinese state's regulatory shift. Previously, the Chinese state had seen China's tech giants as the country's national champions despite their private legal status and intimate connection with global financial capital. As global conditions changed, however, the Chinese state began to question whether the infrastructural power of the firms threatened China's national interests. The US-China trade war and deteriorating US-China bilateral relations brought national security—and importantly, the relationship between tech companies and national security—to the forefront in both countries. President Xi's tightening political control after taking power in 2012 had the unintended effect of escalating regulation in both China and the United States as relations between the two countries turned sour. US-China tensions have fueled a mutually reinforcing process by which regulatory scrutiny in one country sets in motion regulatory tightening in the other one. And as a result, both governments have increased their scrutiny of tech companies' transnational connections.[45] Let me elaborate on these processes.

After Xi took power in 2012, he elevated many social stability issues related to the internet to national security issues in an effort to suppress China's growing civil society and public sphere.[46] Prior to the onset of the US-China trade war in 2018, China had already enacted the National Security Law in 2015 and Cybersecurity Law in 2016. In 2018, China then started to draft the Data Security Law, which eventually passed in 2021. The Data Security Law restricts the cross-border transfer of important data for national security reasons.[47] All of these laws strengthen the CCP's political control of tech giants, whose central role in digital infrastructure building and vast data collection make their actions a concern for the central government. Under Xi's rule, the CCP has strengthened its control over all kinds of organizations too, including private businesses and FIEs, by asking them to establish internal party branches and imposing on those branches new regulations, such as the 2018 Regulations on the Work of Branches of the CCP.[48] Numerous tech companies in China likewise formed party branches in the mid- and late 2010s, prompting the CCP to brag about its penetration into tech giants and platform companies in general.[49] As political scientists Margaret Pearson, Meg

Rithmire, and Kellee Tsai convincingly argue, the CCP under Xi's leadership has essentially transformed China's state capitalism into party-state capitalism and developed a variety of means—including but not limited to state ownership—to discipline private capital. Such political controls upends capitalism's traditional public-private binary.[50]

The CCP's tightening political control had an unintended effect on US-China trade relations, however, making China-based multinational tech companies appear suspicious to US politicians and regulators, as demonstrated by the United States' sanction of Huawei and the Trump administration's attempt to ban TikTok. Many tech companies headquartered in China operate in the United States and are listed on the US stock market, such as Alibaba, JD, Baidu, and NetEase. Notwithstanding political polarization in the United States, China policy under the Trump and Biden administrations has been notably similar and has received strong bipartisan support. The Clean Network program announced in August 2020 under the Trump administration, for example, aims to address "the long-term threat to data privacy, security, human rights and principled collaboration posed to the free world from authoritarian malign actors." To do this, the program attempts to establish "clean carrier, clean store, clean apps, clean cloud, clean cable, and clean path."[51] Not surprisingly, US state agencies do not see Chinese tech companies along with their products and services as adequately clean.[52] Despite China's long-standing restrictions of FDI in IT areas, the Chinese state responded to the Clean Network program by criticizing the US government for attempting to maintain its digital hegemony and discriminating against Chinese tech companies.[53]

Beginning in 2019, legislators in the United States sought to increase the accountability of auditors of US-listed foreign companies currently not subject to oversight by the US Securities and Exchange Commission. The commission complained that Chinese authorities and Chinese laws had blocked US regulators from effectively overseeing audit firms based in China and Hong Kong. US regulators pointed out risks posed by China-based issuers (i.e., companies entirely or mostly based in China) to US investors due to fraudulent financial reporting, the Chinese state's restriction of information to and obstruction of US regulatory oversights, and opaque and legally uncertain VIE arrangements.[54] The Holding Foreign Companies Accountable Act was duly enacted in 2020. The act requires a foreign issuer on the US stock exchanges to establish that it is not owned or controlled by a governmental entity, and disclose the percentage of its shares owned by governmental entities. The act further requires that all China-based issuers disclose the names of all CCP officials who are members of the company's board of directors and whether the issuer's articles of incorporation contain any charter of the CCP.[55] Companies found in violation of the act can be delisted from US stock exchanges.[56] The Chinese state responded to this development by criticizing the United States' "politicization of securities regulation."[57] Immediately after the passage of the act, the Chinese state announced the Measures for the Security Review of Foreign Investment to strengthen its own scrutiny of foreign investment in China, citing national security concerns.[58]

These changes in the domestic and international contexts help contextualize relations between Ma and the Chinese state as well as the latter's swift regulatory tightening after Ma's controversial speech. Ultimately Ma overestimated his, Ant, and Alibaba's power, particularly as circumstances continued to change both within and outside China. He wrongly assumed he would continue to enjoy the power and space to negotiate with China's regulators, and failed to recognize the redlines he crossed in his 2020 speech. Indeed, Ma's speech gave the Chinese state precisely the justification it needed to tame the unruly new bird of tech giants that government policies had, until then, allowed so much freedom. In December 2020, the central leadership launched new measures to safeguard national security, prevent excessive capital expansion, and strengthen antitrust regulation. As the Chinese saying goes, it was necessary to "kill the chicken to scare the monkey." The state's swift response to Ma would serve as a warning to other big tech companies—a strategy of deterrence the Chinese state has long used in a variety of law enforcement campaigns.[59] The message was clear: Ma is wrong and the CCP is the only "master" of tech capital.

Remaking the Cage

The central leadership's signal immediately mobilized different branches of the government to strengthen the cage and put the tech capital back in its place. The new birds came dangerously close to escaping the cage. The current crackdown on tech companies seeks to rewire the relationship between tech capital, technology and data, the techno-developmental state, the nation, and labor. I use the word *crackdown* deliberately here to capture the state's efforts. Xueguang Zhou characterizes the action of the Chinese state as a form of governance that emphasizes mobilization. According to Zhou, the Chinese state frequently oscillates between a mundane and fragmented state, on one hand, and a mobilized and centralized state, on the other.[60] As I have asserted, there was a swing from decentralization to centralization as the Chinese central leadership detected unacceptable risks arising with the rapidly growing power of tech giants. Due to the existence of the rule by law instead of the rule of law in China, people or entities adversely impacted by the state's political campaigns have no meaningful legal channels to address their grievances. In the end, the regulatory environment depends on the highest leadership to shape and change institutions. Also, given the hierarchical structure of the party-state, each level is accountable to that above it and thus strives to demonstrate its conformity with the central leadership. In comparison, in democratic contexts, there are attempts to regulate tech firms, and that regulation does not take the form of orchestrated, centralized, and unchecked political campaigns that span the executive, legislative, and judiciary branches of the government. Essentially, the Chinese state's crackdown on China's tech giants is an instance of unchecked state power attempting to exert control over an increasingly unruly group of rival power holders—whose power came into existence and grew to such worrisome levels, ironically, in part due to the former's cultivation and tolerance.

Within the state, the executive branch has played the most crucial role in leading this campaign to discipline tech capital, followed by the legislative branch. State agencies in the executive branch, especially the SAMR, CAC, and PBOC, have enacted numerous departmental rules and administrative guidelines, summoning tech companies for punishment and overseeing their correction. The National People's Congress passed two important laws in 2021—the Data Security Law and Personal Information Protection Law—both of which regulate data localization and data export, while stipulating data protection requirements to protect data security and privacy.

The judiciary branch, in contrast, has been the least involved in the government crackdown. This is mainly because no tech companies dare to challenge executive agencies' decisions, even though tech firms technically have the legal right to do so.[61] Instead, tech firms have responded to recent administrative decisions in a way that, ironically, resembles the defeatism I saw among interviewees deemed obsolete in the state's earlier techno-developmental campaign (chapter 4). Such responses show the almost absolute power of executive agencies in China when they mobilize resources to implement political campaigns. In comparison, in other jurisdictions, such as the United States and European Union, the judicial systems play a critical role in checking and ensuring the legality of administrative decisions.[62] In the following sections, I discuss in turn the specific ways the crackdown has addressed issues related to antitrust, financial risks, data security and algorithms, and labor.

Antitrust

The SAMR is the most crucial state agency dealing with antitrust issues. The politicized nature of its operation is demonstrated by the fact that prior to December 2020, China's antitrust authorities had yet to penalize a single internet company under the Antimonopoly Law that took effect in 2008.[63] But in December 2020, only three days after the central leadership ordered the strengthening of antitrust regulation and a crackdown on excessive capital expansion, the SAMR hit Alibaba with a 500,000 RMB (US$76,500) fine for a 2014 failure to file a notification of investment (i.e., in legal language, "concentration of undertaking")—the maximum fine possible for such a violation.[64] In fact, whether companies with a VIE structure had a legal filing obligation was unclear. Some internet companies with a VIE structure filed a notification of investment, but their filings were not accepted by the antitrust authorities.[65] As a result, few other similarly structured companies bothered. In December 2020, though, such common practices in the legal gray area became illegal overnight and punished by the SAMR. The law itself did not change, but its enforcement did as the central leadership changed its policy. Since then, the SAMR has punished many more internet companies (including all the most prominent ones) for the same reason—often in waves of several companies at a time, whose names are publicly listed by the SAMR.[66]

Statistics make it clear how the central leadership's stance influenced the interpretation and enforcement of the same law. From 2008, when the Antimonopoly Law took effect, to November 2020, China's antitrust authority publicized only fifty-nine cases of violating the filing obligation, and none of them involved internet companies. In stark contrast, in 2021 alone, the SAMR announced 118 cases of violation, over three-quarters of which involved internet companies.[67] In addition to punishing past behavior, the SAMR barred a merger of internet companies coordinated by Tencent in July 2021—an unprecedented intervention by the state in an internet-related sector.[68] The SAMR's decisions have impacted Chinese tech giants' investment strategies. For example, as JD's largest shareholder, Tencent announced in December 2021 that it would distribute about 457 million shares of JD.com, worth around US$16.4 billion, in the form of a special dividend to Tencent's shareholders. The distribution decreased Tencent's stake in JD.com from 17 to 2.3 percent.[69] Similarly, as Meituan's largest shareholder, Tencent announced it would distribute most of its stake in Meituan (around US$20.3 billion) to shareholders as a dividend in November 2022. This move would decrease Tencent's stake in Meituan from 17 to less than 2 percent.[70]

The SAMR further made two landmark administrative decisions involving huge fines. In April 2021, it imposed yet another fine on Alibaba—this time, a record-breaking 18 billion RMB (US$2.8 billion), which was 4 percent of Alibaba's 2019 revenues in China. The SAMR accused Alibaba of forcing merchants not to operate on its rival platforms (i.e., "choosing one from two" [er xuan yi]) through a carrot-and-stick approach. Merchants that operated exclusively on Alibaba's platform got preferential treatment. But Alibaba monitored, both manually and automatically, whether merchants on its platform also operated on other platforms. Moreover, it used its vast market and instrumental powers based on platform rules, data, and algorithms to punish those who did so. The penalties imposed by Alibaba included disqualifying merchants from participating in Alibaba's sale events and making them less visible on Alibaba's platform by manipulating search results. In addition to penalizing such antitrust behavior by Alibaba, the SAMR provided the company with nonlegally binding administrative "guidance" on how to rectify its behavior. Specifically, the SAMR urged Alibaba to use algorithms and data impartially, respect merchants' choices, and facilitate cross-platform connections and operations rather than building a wall around its ecosystem.[71] Two days after the decision against Alibaba was announced, the SAMR, CAC, and State Taxation Administration jointly asked thirty-four other internet companies to attend an administrative guidance meeting, at which the state agencies instructed the companies to learn from Alibaba's case and promise not to cross the policy and legal redlines.[72] The SAMR publicized documents that these companies signed to guarantee their promises as well.[73]

After the SAMR's severe punishment of Alibaba, tech giants were waiting to see which companies would be next. They found out in October 2021, when Meituan received a 3.44 billion RMB (US$530 million) fine for violating the Antimonopoly Law. The penalty was 3 percent of Meituan's revenues in 2020 in China. Like Alibaba, Meituan was penalized for forcing restaurants to enter exclusive agreements and punishing restaurants that refused to do so. As I showed in chapter 7, some restaurants complained about Meituan's practices and joined gig workers' collective actions. Although the SAMR only identified one type of illegal behavior (i.e., choosing one from two), it similarly provided Meituan with nonlegally binding administrative guidance on how the company should rectify its actions. Specifically, the SAMR mandated that Meituan improve how it charges commissions to better protect restaurants' legal interests, and work with other state agencies to better protect couriers' legal rights and interests.[74]

In addition to disciplining tech capital through administrative decisions, the SAMR submitted a draft amendment of its thirteen-year-old Antimonopoly Law to the Standing Committee of the National People's Congress in 2021. The amendment was passed in June 2022. It focuses on tech companies' practice of using data, algorithms, technologies, platform rules, and capital advantages to engage in monopolistic practices or abuse their dominant market positions.[75] In November 2022, the SAMR announced a draft revision to the Anti-Unfair Competition Law. The draft aims to improve the anti-unfair competition rules for the digital economy, prohibiting firms from engaging in unfair competition using data, algorithms, and platform rules.[76] The SAMR has also enacted many departmental rules and administrative guidelines concerning antitrust and unfair competition in the platform economy, online transactions, classifications and responsibilities of internet companies, and protection of food delivery couriers.[77] All of this political mobilization led to the elevation of the SAMR's antimonopoly department to the State Antimonopoly Bureau in November 2021.[78] Such bureaucratic reorganization endowed the antitrust authority with more administrative power and resources to carry out its task.

Financial Risks

The PBOC has taken the lead in cracking down on financial risks. In December 2020, two weeks after the politburo indicated the policy shift, the PBOC, China Banking and Insurance Regulatory Commission, China Securities Regulatory Commission, and State Administration of Foreign Exchange jointly summoned Ant. Pan Gongsheng, the PBOC's deputy governor, gave the company a clear admonishment: Ant flouted (*mieshi*) regulatory requirements and had little legal consciousness. Pang deliberately chose the word *flouting* in reference to Ma's controversial speech and defiant attitudes. According to Pan, "As an enterprise with significant influence in fintech and the platform economy, Ant Group shall consciously abide by national laws and regulations, integrate its business development into the overall national development, and earnestly assume corporate social responsibility."[79] Pan's quote demonstrates how the central leadership would like to reconfigure the relationship between tech capital, the state, and the nation: tech giants should submit themselves to the law and serve the techno-nation's development. Responding to the PBOC's guidance, Ant immediately formed a working group to rectify its practices.

The PBOC and other state agencies have been sure to follow up, checking on Ant's progress again in April 2021. The PBOC communicated that it wanted Ant to give consumers more choices in online payments as well as cut the improper linkage between Ant's payments service Alipay, virtual credit card business Jiebei, and consumer loan services Huabei. It also asked Ant to break its "monopoly on information" to protect personal information and national data security. According to the state's plan, Ant would become a financial holding company, rectify illegal financial activities in credit, insurance, and wealth management, and control its leverage and product risks. For its part, the PBOC emphasized that it would adhere to the principle of fair and strict oversight. But it was essential that fintech would start serving the real economy and prevent financial risks rather than using technology as a "camouflage" for illegal behavior.[80]

The PBOC also expanded its oversight of other internet companies and made new departmental rules. Insisting on a zero tolerance approach, the

PBOC and other state agencies summoned thirteen other internet companies involved in fintech, including Tencent, JD, ByteDance, Meituan, Didi, Qihoo360, Sina, Suning.com, Gome, Trip.com, and others. According to the PBOC, these companies were chosen because of their significant influence and problematic practices. The companies were provided with rectification plans similar to Ant's, but the new wave of oversight revealed that the government is now strengthening its regulation of overseas listings too.[81] In addition to regulating specific internet companies, the PBOC, like the SAMR, has enacted new rules to regulate nonbank payments, and created a regulatory framework for collaboration between financial regulators and antitrust authorities.[82]

Data and Algorithms

Because data and algorithms are so integral to tech firms' instrumental and infrastructural power, controlling them is a crucial component of the government's political campaign against tech companies. In 2019, with the rise of the digital economy, the Chinese central state began to characterize data as one of the factors of production, along with land, capital, labor, and technology.[83] The significance of data and algorithms also manifests in their role in antitrust practices, as demonstrated by the SAMR's decisions against Alibaba and Meituan. Furthermore, as previously discussed, the escalation in US-China tensions and tightening of the US regulation of China-based firms heightened the issue of data security, especially in terms of cross-border data transfer. The main state agency in charge of issues related to data and algorithms, the CAC, has been responsible for regulating internet companies since 2011. Since President Xi took power and tightened political control, the CAC has launched numerous censorship campaigns to keep China's online space "pure." Foreign media often call the CAC's directors China's "internet czars," and their power has only expanded.[84]

The CAC started to review and publicize apps that illegally collect or use personal information in 2019, but it did not make such data collection an issue of cybersecurity until the central state shifted its regulatory gaze to tech firms in 2020. Since the onset of the crackdown, the CAC, like the SAMR, has been almost hyperactive in making administrative decisions and rules. The identification and publicizing of illegal apps violating the Cybersecurity Law increased steadily over time, with the naming of 33, 84, 105, and 129 apps on May 1, May 10, May 21, and June 11, 2021, respectively.[85]

Up to this point, only one of Didi's apps, Didi Finance, was included on such a list. Even though the Measures for Cybersecurity Review were announced in June 2020, the CAC did not—to the best of my knowledge—conduct or publicize any cybersecurity review cases against any internet companies until it announced that Didi was under investigation in July 2021. Also, the measures focused on reviewing the purchase of network products and services by "critical information infrastructure operators," and did not previously cover platform operators and cross-border data transfer. Didi, however, was to serve as another "chicken" that the state could "kill to scare the monkeys"—with the monkeys in this case being tech firms seeking to hold an IPO in the United States and thus subject themselves to US laws. On June 30, 2021, Didi raised US$4.4 billion in a New York Stock Exchange IPO. Two days later, the CAC launched a cybersecurity review of the company, which led to the CAC suddenly suspending new downloads of 26 Didi apps, including its ride-hailing app, for allegedly illegally collecting and using personal information.[86] In June 2022, Didi delisted from the New York Stock Exchange.[87] The next month, the CAC imposed a US$1.2 billion fine on Didi for its supposed violations in cybersecurity, data security, and personal information protection. Didi CEO Cheng Wei and president Jean Liu were each fined US$150,000 by the CAC too.[88] Unsurprisingly, in a public statement, Didi said, "We sincerely thank the relevant authorities for their inspection and guidance, and the public for their criticism and supervision."[89]

After Didi, the CAC went after Manbang's two apps for Uber-like truck services and Boss Zhipin's job recruitment app.[90] Both Manbang and Boss Zhipin had IPOs in the United States in June 2021.[91] According to the CAC, the reviews were necessary to prevent national data security risks, maintain national security, and protect public interests.[92] Later, the CAC amended the Measures for Cybersecurity Review, requiring companies holding data on more than a million users to apply for a cybersecurity approval when seeking listings in other countries due to national security concerns.[93]

If Ant's downfall was meant to teach tech firms never to challenge their master, the Chinese state, Didi's case specified that the master's reach extends well beyond China, and that wherever China-based tech companies are, the Chinese state still has sovereignty over them, their data, and their technologies, unless those companies want to surrender their business in China.

The CAC's hyperactivity manifests in its rule-making behavior as well, especially concerning algorithms. In fact, the CAC began to regulate algorithms in 2019 as part of its efforts to carry out a censorship campaign. At that time, the CAC already stipulated that when internet content providers use algorithms to recommend information to users, the recommendation models must manifest "mainstream values."[94] In September 2021, the CAC announced new administrative guidance on algorithms. The agency pointed out the challenges that algorithms have brought to the market order, social order, ideological security, social justice and fairness, and internet users' legal rights and interests. Hence it announced it would set up governance rules in three years to ensure that internet companies would not use algorithms to manipulate public opinion, disturb social order, suppress market competition, or infringe the rights and interests of internet users.[95]

The CAC issued yet another new regulation in November 2021, this time calling on algorithmic recommendation service providers to not only promote mainstream values but also "spread positive energy." It prohibits algorithmic recommendation service providers from being involved in antitrust or anti-competition practices. The regulation further imposes obligations to protect minors, senior citizens, laborers, and consumers, though the language regarding these obligations and the legal consequences of failing to meet them is vague.[96] For instance, according to Article 20 of the regulation, "When algorithm recommendation service providers provide workers with job scheduling services, they shall protect workers' legitimate rights and interests, such as labor remuneration, rest, and vacation, and establish and improve relevant algorithms in areas like task allocation, remuneration, working hours, and rewards and punishments." As such, Article 20 does not provide specific information about how algorithms can be viewed as legally adequate. When one violates such an obligation, Article 32 states that the CAC and other relevant agencies "shall handle it according to their duties and in accordance with the provisions of relevant laws, administrative regulations, and departmental rules." There is no clear information about the type and scope of punishment that the CAC and other state agencies could impose on algorithmic recommendation service providers. In a political and legal environment where one does not have the de facto right to challenge state agencies, such legal vagueness can endow state agencies with tremendous discretionary space and power.

Labor

The central state's political campaign has also dealt with labor issues, though these are apparently less significant or urgent than other concerns in the eyes of the central leadership. For one thing, the central state has not severely punished any tech companies due to labor issues, unlike its multiple regulatory actions related to antitrust, financial risks, and national data security. The central state has thus far enacted only two major administrative guidelines on labor protection as part of the recent crackdown. In July 2021, the Ministry of Human Resources and Social Security, along with seven other party-state agencies, issued a guideline on protecting the rights and interests of workers in the platform economy (hereafter the platform worker guideline), while the SAMR, along with six other party-state agencies, announced a guideline on protecting the rights and interests of food delivery workers (hereafter the food delivery worker guideline).[97] A careful reading of the two documents reveals that their main purpose is to "stabilize employment" and "stabilize workers," as written in the first case, and "effectively resolve conflicts" and "resolutely maintain social stability," as written in the second instance. In March 2021, President Xi chaired a meeting at the Central Financial and Economic Affairs Commission. One of the conclusions of the meeting was that the development of the platform economy should maintain social stability.[98] To wit, in its attempt to adjust capital-labor relations, the Chinese state wants to ensure that internet-related sectors, especially the platform economy, will continue to absorb surplus labor, but without generating widespread social instability. Both tech capital and labor are therefore obliged to maintain social stability in pursuing their respective interests.

The above two administrative guidelines provide instructions on how platform companies and their partners or contractors should prevent and address labor grievances. Many instructions are not specific or feasible. The platform worker guideline instructs companies to pay minimum wages for platform workers who do not have a labor contract. Yet the guideline does not specify how to calculate minimum wages in nonstandard work relations where workers have the flexibility to decide how many tasks they would like to do. Also, according to my analysis, the monthly earnings of full-time gig workers tend to be higher than the minimum wages in their cities. In addition, the platform worker guideline mandates that platform companies should listen to labor unions and labor representatives' suggestions regarding platform rules and algorithms, while tasking the ACFTU to actively absorb platform workers and negotiate with tech companies. At the same time, the Chinese state does not allow independent trade unions, and it is unclear what "labor representatives" mean, and to what extent the ACFTU has expertise on platform rules or algorithms. Similarly, the food delivery worker guideline stipulates that platform companies should not use the "strictest algorithms" to evaluate work performance and should relax delivery time, but it does not define what strictest algorithms means and who has the authority to decide this matter.

Despite their vagueness and questionable feasibility, these guidelines are part of the Chinese state's effort to showcase its responsiveness and benevolence, and in doing so, shape state-labor relations in the state's favor. In addition to demonstrating their response to platform workers' grievances, the central state has responded to software engineers' problems. Specifically, in August 2021, the Ministry of Human Resources and Social Security, along with the Supreme People's Court, issued a set of model cases on overtime labor disputes as a central-level institutional response to overwork problems in the tech sector (chapter 8).[99] Such actions are in keeping with scholars' arguments that the Chinese party-state's durability is linked to its "responsiveness," meaning that it takes into account the demands of societal actors just enough to strengthen the party's legitimacy with the mass public, but without sharing its monopoly on political power.[100]

To get a sense of how workers actually view the state's response to labor issues in the tech sector, I followed up with some of the platform workers and software engineers whom I interviewed. Most of the platform workers reported feeling positive about the government's effort to discipline platform companies, although they were unsure whether such intervention would significantly enhance their work conditions. Thus far they have not observed significant improvement. The only difference is that they now receive small gifts from the ACFTU on holidays. A few platform workers, however, expressed criticism of the state's continuing restriction on labor unions and suppression of labor activism. They told me that it had become increasingly difficult for couriers to form social media groups to discuss their work issues. Indeed, many of the groups that I joined in 2019 or 2020 were ultimately dissolved by WeChat in 2021. My interviewees also mentioned that the government arrested Chen Guojiang, a well-known labor activist in Beijing who was a food delivery worker and spoke for workers. They told me their work conditions would be improved only when the state allowed bottom-up organization and mobilization for workers.

The responses of software engineers, by contrast, were mixed. On the one hand, they appreciated the state's attention to their overwork issues. Several tech companies have changed their work policies thanks to governmental intervention. Also, software engineers who work in small or medium-sized companies applauded the state's effort to tackle antitrust issues. On the other hand, most software engineers were experiencing adverse consequences of the state's crackdown on the internet sector. They worried about being laid off and not being able to repay their mortgage loans because of the relentless and unpredictable crackdown. Some even told me that having a 996 work schedule is better than not having a job.[101] They agreed with the government that tech companies must be regulated, but they did not support what they saw as the state's overzealous regulatory approach. They described feeling extremely uncertain about the futures of their companies, China's tech sector in general, and their own lives as individuals under such a drastically and rapidly changing institutional, political, and legal environment. They told me that the best era of the internet sector in China had already passed. In follow-up interviews, two optimists (see chapter 8) asked me detailed questions about immigration to the United States and Canada because they were seriously considering that possibility.

Interestingly, President Xi himself responded to work and life problems faced by Chinese people in an essay on common prosperity published in October 2021 in *Qiushi*, the CCP's leading official theoretical journal. Here I quote from *Qiushi's* official English translation. Xi acknowledges the relationship between techno-development and economic inequality, although he clarifies that inequality is a global problem and hints that it is even worse in other countries. He writes, "The latest round of scientific and technological revolution and industrial transformation has not only given a strong push to economic development, but also exerted a profound impact on employment and income distribution. This includes certain negative impacts that we must take effective steps to address."[102]

As I mentioned in chapter 2, the official discourse on techno-development tends to downplay issues of domestic inequality except when the central leadership sees growing threats to social stability. Xi's writing shows that he saw such threats. For example, he noted, "We are now living in a world in which income inequality is a glaring problem. Some countries have witnessed the growth of a huge gulf between rich and poor and the collapse of the middle class, which has led to social division, political polarization, and a surge of populism. This is a profound lesson. We in China must make resolute efforts to prevent polarization and promote common prosperity in order to safeguard social harmony and stability."[103]

One of his strategies to address inequality is to regulate high income. According to Xi, "We must firmly oppose disorderly expansion of capital, establish negative lists for access to sensitive fields, and intensify anti-monopoly oversight. Meanwhile, we must energize entrepreneurs, and promote sound and well-regulated development of all types of capital." He also promises that "we will . . . improve preferential tax policies in order to encourage high-income groups and enterprises to give more back to society."[104] Following Xi's call, China's tech giants along with their CEOs and founders have poured billions into Xi's common prosperity agenda.[105]

Despite the rising social inequality and other problems that have resulted from China's techno-developmental regime, Xi urges everyone to take responsibility for national development. "We are now marching toward the Second Centenary Goal of building China into a great modern socialist country," and "the gap between China and developed countries in terms of level of development remains large." In other words, the existence of social inequality and other problems does not excuse people for slacking off. He encourages Chinese people to pursue common prosperity through innovation and of course hard work. "Just as a happy life is achieved through hard work, common prosperity can only be created with ingenuity and effort." To advance national development, he proposes strengthening education on patriotism and collectivism, while preventing people "from getting lost in the ideas of 'lying flat' and 'involution.'"[106] As I mentioned in chapter 8, *lying flat* refers to reducing desire and stress instead of working diligently. It is a strategy for software engineers to cope with overwork norms. *Involution* refers to participating in the rat race.

The above quote shows that although Xi discourages undue competition at work amid China's demographic crisis, he reminds everyone to work as hard as possible for individual and national prosperity.[107] For this reason, Xi qualifies the state's responsibility to provide social welfare, despite growing social inequality: "The government cannot take on everything. Instead, its main responsibility should be . . . meeting basic needs. Even in the future when we have reached a higher level of development . . . we still must not aim too high or go overboard with social security, and steer clear of the idleness-breeding trap of welfarism."[108] Ultimately Xi sends laborers in China a clear message: the state recognizes your work and life problems, but it is still most important that you work hard to advance the development of the Chinese nation under the wise leadership of the party-state.

When I first read Xi's essay, I thought of my interviewee Ethan, a software engineer who works for Microsoft. He is one of the few engineers who expressed skepticism about China's national developmental agenda. In chapter 8, I shared this memorable quote: "You don't know how long it will take for the country to develop. It could be five years, ten years, fifty years, or even a hundred years. But one's life is finite, right?" Now President Xi's essay provides some clues about China's national development timeline. As the nation marches toward its second centenary goal of building China into a great nation, Chinese laborers might need to work hard for decades, if not a century.

Cultivating the Next New Birds

One might well wonder whether the Chinese state's experiences with China's tech giants have undermined its determination to pursue techno-development. Absolutely not. In December 2021, Xi and other leaders attended the Central Economic Working Conference to discuss the country's priorities for economic development in 2022. The leadership pointed out the critical challenges facing China domestically and internationally. Domestically, China's economic development is facing pressure from demand contraction, supply shocks, and weakening expectations. Internationally, the geopolitical environment has become even more complicated and grim. According to the conference note, there are "unprecedented global changes and a once-in-a-century pandemic." Globalization contributed to China's ascendence, but growing geopolitical tensions have now undermined this progress. To overcome the crisis and rejuvenate the Chinese nation, the central leadership still views techno-development as the solution. The meeting called for more scientific and technological innovation, high-quality development, and multilateralism.[109]

As Xi pointed out in a meeting at the politburo in 2021, he has had the same view since he worked as Fujian's governor in 2000.[110] But now Xi has identified some candidates as the next new birds in the digital economy. This time, the new birds are firms that can promote the integration of the digital and real economy, and facilitate the digital upgrading and transformation of traditional industries. Instead of betting on tech giants that span across boundaries, the Chinese state has shifted its efforts to cultivate specialized or smaller new birds that integrate the digital and real economy, especially globally influential large software enterprises, technologically advanced "little giant" enterprises, and enterprises leading in an individual field of the manufacturing industry.[111] The Chinese state has already established new metrics as well as targets, announced new subsidies, and classified new talent to cultivate the newest birds and pursue the ongoing project of national rejuvenation.[112]

As the Chinese state and Xi have emphasized national security, some readers might wonder whether the pursuit of national security means the sidelining of techno-development. I do not think so. Indeed, techno-development could become even more central as it is perceived by the Chinese state as a national security issue. As I have mentioned earlier, the National Security Law defines national security in relation to economic power and security (sustainable socioeconomic development).[113] Article 24 of the National Security Law stipulates that the state shall strengthen the building of the capability of independent innovation and accelerate the development of strategic new and high technologies along with core technologies in important fields. Barry Naughton and his colleagues point out that since 2020, China's industrial and technology policies have shifted to self-sufficiency and self-empowerment in S&T. The Chinese state might think consumer-focused big tech firms should not be deserving birds anymore in China's techno-developmental regime, but the bird/cage logic for techno-development remains. The question for the Chinese state is how to scientifically select and cultivate the right new birds in order to continue techno-development in increasingly hostile global conditions for China.

In fact, the simultaneous pursuit of multiple goals is nothing new for the Chinese state. Since the late 1970s, the Chinese party-state has aimed to advance economic development while maintaining its political monopoly. During the Hu-Wen era, since the global conditions were favorable to China, national security was not a severe concern for the Chinese state; the Chinese state focused on pursuing the kind of economic development that did not threaten social stability. But with intensified geographic tensions, the Chinese state will chase the type of techno-development and cultivate the kind of new birds that align with its national security priorities.

Conclusion

This chapter has described and sought to explain the Chinese state's seemingly sudden turn against the new birds that it once cultivated and held dear. Before the crackdown, the state adopted a tolerant and prudent approach to regulating internet-related sectors. Despite the existence of relevant laws and regulations as well as widely known problematic practices, China's state agencies did not actively enforce the rules, enabling questionable practices to flourish in legal gray areas. This regulatory approach was meant to nurture tech firms. Ironically, however, in its campaign to cultivate new birds to solve the overcapacity problem of old birds in obsolete sectors, the Chinese state facilitated the excessive expansion of capital and created unruly new birds in internet-related sectors. As if realizing such problems only belatedly, the central state abruptly shifted to a zero tolerance regulatory approach in late 2020 and started to mobilize various state agencies to curb the very tech giants it had given such free rein.

I argue that a combination of domestic and international factors led to this regulatory shift and crackdown. Domestically, China's financial regulators detected the crossing of two redlines: systematic financial risks and national security. Internationally, the geopolitical tensions between China and the United States have further amplified national security issues. And whereas previously the Chinese state encouraged and valued the boundary-spanning operation of China's tech firms because it meant innovation and the global ascendence of China's national champions, as domestic and international contexts have changed, boundary crossing now threatens financial stability, market order, social stability, and national security. The Chinese state appears to be questioning whether tech giants are indeed national champions and whether they serve the interests of the Chinese nation.

Since the onset of the crackdown, tech firms have experienced a rude awakening, suddenly being subjected to harsh and unpredictable government scrutiny and regulation similar to that first directed toward the low-end manufacturers displaced by techno-development (chapter 4). Scholars are interested in the relationship between institutionalization and state-led political mobilization in China since cyclic top-down political campaigns remain in China, despite the Chinese state's efforts in institution building.[114] As the crackdown on China's tech firms shows, state-led political campaigns are still highly viable and effective instruments through which the Chinese state can seek to prevent threats and solve all kinds of crises. Institutionalization, specifically hyperactive rule making, is a critical part of state-led political campaigns.[115] Yet such rule making does not guarantee predictability or prevent politicization for several reasons. First, as I have shown in my analysis, rules are often vague and unspecific. This gives executive agencies adequate space to interpret rules as they wish. Second, the central leadership's policy can easily influence rule making and enforcement. Third, firms do not have de facto rights to challenge executive agencies through any channels, such as the court system, in political campaigns. Fourth, hyperactive rule making results in a rapidly changing legal and regulatory environment. Hence institutionalization does not increase predictability for firms when the central state decides to launch a political campaign.

I have also shown that the Chinese state has intervened in tech capital–labor relations to ensure that the platform sector can continue to absorb surplus labor without creating widespread social instability. On the one hand, if platform companies fail to do so, they risk severe punishment. On the other hand, the central state expects workers to work hard and refrain from causing any social instability. All actors, large and small, must contribute to the prosperity of the techno-nation.

The most intriguing and unexpected findings to me are some ironic similarities between the power of the Chinese state and that of China's tech giants. State-led political campaigns and severe punishment allow the Chinese state to control its tech companies. Arguably, what the Chinese state has done to China's tech giants resembles what those tech giants are frequently criticized as having done to workers, merchants, and platform users. The Chinese state has a political monopoly over tech firms in China, while China's tech giants have economic monopolistic power over those who want to use their platforms. The SAMR punished Alibaba and Meituan for effectively prohibiting other businesses from operating on rival platforms (i.e., choosing one from two). And when the Chinese state sabotages China-based tech firms' IPOs in the United States, it likewise demands that those firms choose one from two. Despite their enormous instrumental and infrastructural power over other actors, China's tech giants, like their obsolete counterparts, remain birds in the cages made by the Chinese state and are subject to the state's unchecked instrumental power. As China's techno-development continues to evolve, we are likely to see the cultivation of new deserving birds and possibly the clipping of their wings too.

10

Conclusion

DEVELOPING AND WRITING *The Gilded Cage* was a process of connecting and understanding two seemingly distinct stories. Beginning in the early 2010s, I observed a number of developments signaling significant transformations in China. Foxconn announced its plan to build a one-million robot army as its workforce. Local governments in coastal China similarly sought to replace human workers with robots and started to zealously crack down on the labor-intensive manufacturers they had previously tried to attract to the region. These developments revealed the seemingly sudden fall from grace of labor-intensive manufacturing and turn to automation. Over roughly the same period, I also witnessed the rapid rise of the digital economy, and speaking to people in China between 2017 and 2019, discovered near-universal pride, regardless of social class or political orientation, in China's technological progress. "China's four great new inventions"—Alipay, online shopping, high-speed rail, and bike-sharing applications—were singled out for particular praise, with three of the four seen as evidence of China's successful digital economy. But when the Chinese government suddenly clamped down on China's large tech firms in 2020, members of the general public struggled to make sense of yet another apparent fall from grace as tech entrepreneurs once lauded as national heroes were quickly rebranded as evil capitalists.

Investigating these two stories in China could easily have taken the form of two separate books—one about China's shift to robotization or automation, and another about the digital economy. Indeed, I have been encouraged at various points in the book-writing process to separate these analyses, or focus on only one or the other, as a considerable literature exists examining each phenomenon on its own. Shoshana Zuboff, for example, has published two groundbreaking books—*In the Age of the Smart Machine* (1988) and *The Age of Surveillance Capitalism* (2019)—documenting these transitions in the US context, where the longer timeline and slower pacing of events made such elongated analysis appropriate.[1] But the developments in China differ from the two ages written about by Zuboff in two crucial respects. First, in the Chinese context, the enthusiastic pursuit of automation in manufacturing (i.e., the old sectors) and rise of the digital economy (i.e., the new internet-related sectors) occurred around the same time, reflecting China's time-compressed development.[2] Second, the Chinese state has played a significant role in orchestrating the changes in both the old and new sectors, and has done so according to an overarching logic of and commitment to techno-development. Understanding the profound transformations within China in recent decades thus requires combining these two, only seemingly distinct stories.

Order and Contradictions in *The Gilded Cage*

In this book, I have developed the theoretical concept of techno-developmental regime to refer to the ensemble of state and nonstate actors, institutions, ideas, cultural norms, forms of materiality, and practices that foreground the role of S&T in socioeconomic development.[3] As I mentioned in the introduction, components of the ensemble can be linked and configured in a variety of ways across time and place, comprising different types of techno-developmental regimes. I have explained the emergence of a techno-development regime in China at the local level as the local states in coastal provinces became determined to pursue techno-development. I have also shown the rise and expansion of such a regime nationwide in the aftermath of the 2008 financial crisis, with President Xi Jinping's ascendency to the highest power along with the rise of digital technology and big data.

The Gilded Cage aims to uncover the order and contradictions that have emerged in the process of China's compressed techno-development. Throughout the book, I have shown that the techno-developmental regime in China is characterized by the proliferation of technical and legal instruments established by the state and large tech companies to regulate work and life, and enhance legibility, valuation, efficiency, and behavior modification; the legal, cultural, and economic subordination of workers and forms of capital deemed low-end to those valorized as high-end; and the intensified subjection of both low- and high-end workers and capital to the precarious and despotic rule by instruments. I use the metaphor of the *gilded cage* to capture China's success in building techno-state capitalism, on the one hand, and the enormous expansion of enhanced instrumental power based on technology and law, on the other hand, as the country shifted to techno-development. China currently epitomizes a society marked by heightened instrumental power based on technology and law.

I have also demonstrated that despite its extraordinary success, China's techno-developmental regime has generated contradictions between appearance and reality, the state and capital, the state and citizens, and capital and labor. And I contend that the characteristics of and contradictions generated by China's techno-developmental regime can be explained by China's hyper-instrumentally rational developmental state, authoritarian political regime, and amalgamated ideology of high modernism, techno-nationalism, techno-logical fetishism, and meritocracy.

That China's techno-developmental regime has generated multiple con-tradictions should not be that surprising from a Weberian perspective. As Max Weber so effectively established, rationality (in the strictly Weberian sense) taken to extremes generates its own forms of irrationality.[4] In China, the first contradiction exists between the efforts to maximize calculability, legibility, and efficiency, and the disconnect between such efforts and their outcomes in reality. Local governments and businesses have worked fever-ishly to calculate and increase the numbers of industrial robots, laborers replaced by robots, patents, high- and new-tech companies, workers with certificates, business incubators, and so on. Notwithstanding the rules pur-portedly ensuring the objectivity of this process, though, state and nonstate actors regularly mobilize personal networks as well as collude to produce desirable metric values and classification outcomes. These results often di-verge from reality, but nonetheless are disseminated through media propa-ganda as evidence of local governments' accomplishments. This disparity was clear to many of my interviewees, who described public expenditures to this end as wasted given the fraudulent practices used to reap rewards and avoid punishments. Meanwhile, there have been few efforts to resolve this discon-nect from reality. Sincere attempts to overcome the limits of rationality often fail because such suggestions do not fit the metrics of the official evaluation systems. This contradiction does not produce specific grievants per se but rather impacts the public interest by influencing how and where public re-sources are used—an issue of particular relevance for workers with low "human" or economic capital and their children.

A second kind of contradiction exists between the state and capital in terms of (un)predictability. With this proliferation of metrics, classification schemes, and administrative and regulatory rules, the Chinese state aims to create a predictable economic and legal environment for state and nonstate actors, while allowing the state to exercise its continued control of capital. But as I have demonstrated throughout the preceding chapters, the Chinese state tends to oscillate between not regulating certain forms of capital as a form of reward, or being exceedingly harsh to capital in ways that seem arbitrary and unpredictable, thereby fostering extreme outcomes, from excessive capital expansion to a seemingly chaotic legal environment.[5] In a supportive policy environment, we see rare implementation of existing laws or regulations, and few attempts to address potential problems or risks. Under such circumstances, it is difficult for nonstate actors to demand that the state implement its own laws or regulations. With the shift to a harsh regulatory environment, as I have shown in chapters 4 and 9, we see hyperactive, campaign-style rule making and enforcement, which makes it extremely difficult, if not impossible, for business actors to calculate risks and costs. Furthermore, businesses have no effective legal or other institutional channels to address complaints to the politically mobilized state. The Chinese state's policies and signals have thus created a bifurcated regulatory environment. The fundamental problem stems from the Chinese state's reliance on performance, as opposed to elections and the rule of law, as its major source of legitimacy and impetus to sustain a political monopoly.[6] Despite its effort to rationalize the bureaucracy and the country's legal system, the party-state as the highest authority still has arbitrary power.[7] And in order to sustain its legitimacy and political monopoly, the central leadership seems willing to ride the wave of economic crises, cycles, and risks as it changes policies and signals as needed.

The third contradiction emerges from the government's stated commitment to socialist egalitarian values along with the real conditions and possibilities for different groups of citizens.[8] Embracing a capitalist logic of facilitating techno-development, local governments, especially those in the most prosperous areas or postindustrial frontiers, have enacted metrics and classifications that systematically discriminate against people with less human and economic capital, specifically the working class and people without local housing properties.[9] Children of these groups have much less chance to access local public education. As I discussed in chapter 4, this has triggered social protests among migrant parents angry that their children do not have equal opportunities to accumulate human capital in a knowledge-oriented economy. Similar dissatisfaction with official rhetoric versus people's lived reality can be seen in the online protests organized by software engineers. Faced with overwork norms and difficulties in social reproduction, disillusioned tech workers complain that only the rich can afford to have children in today's China. This contradiction between formal rationality based on economic calculations and substantive rationality based on egalitarian values has generated conflict between citizens and the state. As I pointed out in chapter 9, President Xi responded to rising social inequality with the so-called common prosperity agenda. But his agenda does not include systematic institutional reforms that could solve fundamental issues (e.g., fiscal and tax reforms that can help local governments to build a more inclusive welfare state). Instead, he reminds Chinese people that China should not strive for high social security standards and should avoid falling into the trap of welfarism.

Tensions between tech capital and labor have emerged too. They reflect the contradiction between formal rationality to optimize productivity and efficiency, on the one hand, and substantive rationality based on freedom from exploitation, on the other hand. As I have shown, the state's goal of achieving techno-development contributed to tech giants' monopolistic power, and provided the unfettered regulatory conditions that enabled them to impose meticulously calculated technological and legal control on platform workers. This intensified control has, in turn, triggered protests and strikes as platform workers have come to realize that algorithms and technology as well as law in general serve as instruments for platform companies to control workers instead of liberating the latter from unfree and tedious lives in factories. Capital-labor tensions have likewise emerged between tech companies and software engineers, who are viewed by the state and tech firms as the techno-nation's talent. Though it is their technical expertise that helps tech firms to optimize revenues and efficiency, and aids the Chinese state in advancing digital governance and economy, software engineers' human capital does not necessarily protect them from tech capital's exploitation because they are still vulnerable to "being optimized" (laid off or asked to resign). Engineers' vulnerability to exploitation is partly due to their difficulties in social reproduction, which largely results from the state's policy on real estate. As I have noted in chapter 5, the real estate industry emerged as a de facto new bird in China's techno-developmental regime, despite its absence in China's techno-developmental policy and its tenuous relationship with high technology. Feeling exploited and choiceless, some software engineers have turned to labor activism.

Despite these frictions between the state, capital, and labor, my analysis reveals that the state has been able to use certain elements of China's techno-developmentalism to mitigate the very tensions and discontent it generates—most important, by diverting blame from the state. As I demonstrated in chapter 2, the official discourse of techno-developmentalism emphasizes the central role of S&T in rejuvenating the Chinese nation while downplaying issues related to domestic social inequality and class tensions.[10] Also, notwithstanding their criticism of the state and tech capital as well as their work and life problems, most of my interviewees still appreciated the Chinese state, which they credit with building a strong and prosperous nation. It is crucial to recognize that my interviewees and their parents experienced improving material conditions over the course of their lives and witnessed the ascendance of China into a leading global power. Many interviewees talked about the Chinese state heroically taking on the historic responsibility of national development. From this perspective, sacrifice is inevitable and necessary for China's global ascendancy, and the state should not be blamed for carrying out its duties.

Moreover, a nonnegligible proportion of my working-class interviewees have not only accepted but also adopted the framework classifying countries, industries, companies, and individuals as high-end or advanced and low-end or backward, despite the fact that it is this very framework that has devalued them and defined them as obsolete. In light of such a view, tech sectors are high-end, while people with a higher level of human capital, especially S&T expertise, are more deserving because they make more significant contributions to the economy and society. Such thinking is a kind of meritocracy based on one's contribution to national socioeconomic development. This framework mirrors the numerous metrics and classifications enacted by many local governments and the dominant discourse of techno-developmentalism. It trumps egalitarian values, pardons the unequal treatment of citizens, and justifies the legally questionable punishment of capital deemed obsolete by the state.

Finally, as Michael Burawoy's work suggests, playing the game or engaging with instrumental rule to better position oneself in the gilded cage can manufacture consent.[11] China's techno-developmental regime has been characterized by the state-led pursuit of formal rationality and means-end rational action, seemingly above all else. Such rationalization at the macrolevel has led to a similar valorization of means-ends rational action at the individual level as well. I find that individuals across classes and sectors use means-end rational thinking—first, to believe that they *have* choices with regard to their work and other life decisions, and second, to seek the best strategies in light of those options. Such thinking and the practice of engaging with instrumental rule serve to mitigate many of the tensions that have emerged through the process of techno-development. Only when people feel they do not have any meaningful options do they act to express or address their grievances.

Techno-Developmental Regimes in Comparative Perspective

Although *The Gilded Cage* is about China's techno-developmental regime, my analysis is inherently comparative. While developing the project, I continually compared China and other contexts as doing so helps me to understand precisely what characterizes and differentiates the Chinese case. I was encouraged by many scholars to think from a comparative perspective too. Indeed, an important motivation for developing the concept of techno-developmental regime was to facilitate future comparisions of techno-development—by myself and others—across contexts. Now that we have learned about the Chinese case, we can situate China's techno-developmental regime in relation to other regimes, specifically the South Korean, Taiwanese, and US cases (see table 10.1). The South Korean, Taiwanese, and Chinese cases are worth comparison because despite similarly featuring a developmental state seeking to

TABLE 10.1. Comparison of Techno-Developmental Regimes

	Developmental state	Political regime	Ideas and beliefs about S&T	Techno-development
South Korea and Taiwan	Classical developmental states Cultivating specific new sectors	Democratization The building of the rule of law The building of an inclusive welfare state	Techno-nationalism	Strong IT industries No globally leading internet companies
United States	A "hidden" or "disguised" developmental state State's involvement limited to R&D in technology at an early stage	Liberal democracy A strong separation of powers between the executive, legislature, and judiciary A strong separation of powers between the federal, state, and local levels A weak welfare state A weak organized labor force	The Californian Ideology: the mixing of counterculture with a faith in the emancipatory potential of new ITs, social liberalism, and economic liberalism	Globally dominating digital capitalism system Internet companies gain enormous instrumental and infrastructure power "Politics of lawlessness" and self-regulation
China	A hyper-instrumentally rational developmental state that continually uses performance evaluation systems to measure, classify, and evaluate capital, labor, technology, and industry Dealing with both old and new sectors	Authoritarian regime Performance legitimacy and political monopoly Rule by law Intensified control of the public sphere and civil society since the mid-2010s A weak welfare state The absence of independent trade unions	An amalgamated ideology of high modernism, techno-nationalism, technological fetishism, and meritocracy	Globally leading digital capitalism system (techno-state capitalism) Internet companies gain enormous instrumental and infrastructure power Asymmetrically symbiotic relationship between the state and internet companies

advance economic development, the three countries have different types and trajectories of techno-development.

First, as classical examples of developmental states, the developmental states in South Korea and Taiwan cultivated and intervened in only very specific new sectors, using conventional instruments for intervention (e.g., subsidies, interest rates, tax breaks, and state procurement).[12] In comparison, the Chinese state has been involved in the process of "destroying the old and creating the new" through enacting and using numerous instruments for evaluation and classification. I use the term *hyper-instrumentally rational* to describe the Chinese state because it endeavors to measure the worth and worthiness of everything from capital to labor, technology, business, and industry in order to *scientifically* allocate resources, rewards, and punishments. Chinese governments have also reoriented their performance evaluation systems in light of the new goal of techno-development. The hyper-instrumental rationality of the state can be attributed to the prevailing ideology in China's techno-developmental regime. Such ideology often leads to the dissolution of ends, concentration on means alone, and justification of social inequality.[13]

Second, in the Korean and Taiwanese cases, despite their success in the IT-related sectors, the two countries do not have world-leading internet companies under US-dominated global digital capitalism. In contrast, China has developed a globally leading digital capitalist system in which China's large tech firms have developed boundary-spanning infrastructural and instrumental power. One critical condition that gave rise to China's digital capitalism is neoliberal globalization. As I mentioned in chapter 2, the Chinese state was able to retain its control of the economy as it integrated China into neoliberal globalization.[14] On the one hand, neoliberal globalization allowed China's tech firms to access global financial capital. On the other hand, China's integration into neoliberal globalization did not prevent the Chinese state from using the Great Firewall and industrial policy protectionism to shield the country's homegrown tech companies from external competition.[15] US politicians, such as Bill Clinton, and multinational corporations based in the United States did not anticipate such state capacity when they zealously integrated China into the neoliberal global order.

Third, South Korea and Taiwan's turn to techno-development was accompanied by the process of democratization, which further contributed to the building of the rule of law and an increasingly inclusive welfare state (chapter 3).[16] Democratization freed the two authoritarian states from having to rely on economic performance as a major source of legitimacy. Democratic institutions constrain how the government can enact and use legal and technical instruments. For example, as I discussed in chapter 3, certain practices of the Chinese state might well be considered unconstitutional or in violation of fundamental legal principles in Taiwan. The democratic regime, rule of law, and inclusive welfare state in Taiwan help prevent as well as address contradictions in techno-development. In comparison, in the Chinese context, there are few restrictions on how the Chinese state can enact and use legal and technical instruments to foster techno-development under the rule by law. This is demonstrated by the official metric and classification systems that are systematically biased against the working class and contribute to the exacerbation of social inequality. Also, in a tolerant regulatory environment and with support from the state, China's tech giants developed instrumental and infrastructural power over a vast number of people. As a result, people are subject to the tremendous power of both the state and tech capital. Furthermore, there is little external pressure from civil society on the ability of the state and tech giants to construct the rules of games between persons, especially after the Chinese state's intensified control of the public sphere and civil society since the mid-2010s. Due to the absence of the rule of law and institutionalized channels for political participation, contradictions in China's techno-developmental regime to a great extent can only be addressed by the state, which largely neglects them (e.g., contradictions between appearance and reality). To the degree that the state does act to address some contradictions, its action tends to have limited efficacy (e.g., contradictions between labor and tech capital) or only exacerbates a chaotic situation (e.g., contradictions between the state and tech capital).

It is also meaningful to compare China's techno-developmental regime with its US counterpart. The similarities between China and the United States are often overlooked. China and the United States are the only two countries whose techno-development has led to a globally leading digital capitalist system. Prior to China's recent crackdown on its tech sector, both countries had a tech sector that was loosely regulated. Additionally, both countries exhibit a weak welfare state, high levels of social inequality, and a labor force that is poorly organized. Despite these similarities, China and the United States have created two very different forms of digital capitalism. China's hyper-instrumentally rational developmental state, authoritarian political regime, and dominant ideology have led to what I call techno-state capitalism, in which major internet companies have enormous instrumental and infrastructural power, and the Chinese state can exercise instrumental power over them and even appropriate their infrastructural power. While prioritizing techno-development over regulations, the Chinese state enabled the country's major internet companies to amass considerable power. As discussed in chapter 9, however, the unchecked power of the state has caused uncertainty and turmoil in China's digital capitalism as the Chinese state has struggled to contain the very tech giants it fostered.

In comparison, the United States had a hidden or disguised developmental state along with a dominant ideology (the Californian Ideology) that blends counterculture with a belief in the transformative power of new ITs, social liberalism, and economic liberalism. The US state's role in techno-development was mostly restricted to R&D in technology during the initial stages.[17] The unrestricted instrumental power of large tech companies in the United States can be attributed to the fragmented political and legal environment rather than a potent developmental state such as that found in China. Like the Chinese techno-developmental regime, the US regime has generated some contradictions, exemplified by emergent battles between regulatory agencies, tech companies, workers, and civil society organizations—battles fought in the courts and legislative forums.[18] But unlike the Chinese case, these contradictions are not handled by an unchecked and centralized political power.

The concept of techno-development regime also allows us to compare techno-development across time. Developmental studies scholars argue that the historical period in which development takes place and evolves matters since the geopolitical, institutional, technological, and ideological context for development changes over time.[19] When we think about techno-developmental regimes from a *temporal* and *relational* perspective, we have to consider the decline of neoliberal globalization and "Chimerica."[20] Although this book is about China, I have emphasized that the rise of postreform China unfolded under neoliberal globalization. As beneficiaries of neoliberal globalization, US politicians, capitalists, and corporations were among the most enthusiastic and powerful advocates for the neoliberal global order. I opened the book with President Clinton's ambitious, future-looking visit to China in 1998 amid domestic criticisms at home. I included Clinton's optimistic remark on the ample collaborative opportunities for US and Chinese companies in the internet sector as well as for the United States and China in S&T. Ironically, the Clinton administration's endeavor to use China to invigorate US capitalism is not unlike the Chinese state's effort to use Chinese internet companies to facilitate techno-development. Both decisions inadvertently created new birds that ultimately burst the cage—the neoliberal global order shaped by the United States and the domestic political and economic order engineered by the Chinese state. Now the United States and China both struggle with caging their respective new birds again.

In the era of post-neoliberal globalization, as geopolitical tensions have intensified, techno-nationalism has been rising and techno-development has become even more crucial. On the Chinese side, the Chinese state will pursue the type of techno-development and cultivate the kind of new birds that align with its national security priorities. On the US side, as geopolitical conditions have shifted, the US developmental state is no longer hidden or disguised and is now actively pursuing technological self-reliance.[21] It will be important to see how the techno-developmental regimes in China and the United States continue to evolve under the changing global conditions. As the two countries reassess their respective national sociotechnical imaginaries, it will be crucial to observe which stakeholders are included or excluded both domestically and transnationally.

Revisiting the Scholarly Landscape

Situating China's techno-developmental regime comparatively helps in discussing how *The Gilded Cage* contributes to the scholarly work that has informed and motivated it, beginning with the literature on the developmental state.

The Developmental State

I have added to the existing literature on developmental states by showing the importance of analyzing the cage created by developmental states and their partners under certain material conditions (e.g., digital technology and big data), cultural forms (e.g., high modernism, technological fetishism, and meritocracy), and political regimes (e.g., authoritarian rule), and the lives of both old and new birds. Classical East Asian developmental states are characterized by Weberian bureaucracies, controlled relations between the state and capital, and the subordination of labor.[22] In the Chinese case, hyper-instrumental rationality, the rise of digital technology and big data, and authoritarianism led to a developmental state that along with China's tech giants, has built, enhanced, and expanded cages that aim to control bureaucrats, capital, and labor. As I have demonstrated, cages built by both the Chinese state and China's tech giants have enormous and uneven impacts on different kinds of capital and labor, and shape the action and interaction of state and nonstate actors. And yet such control can be ineffective from time to time and even lead to out-of-control situations.

Like capital and labor, government officials are constrained by the instruments that constitute the expanding cage. The analysis of Weberian bureaucracies in the literature tends to focus on the role of bureaucrats along with their selection, professionalization, and promotion.[23] In the Chinese case, bureaucrats are subject to evaluation systems. In the past, such evaluation systems focused on GDP.[24] As China's techno-developmental regime consolidates, however, bureaucrats, especially those in local states, have to contend with numerous metrics that evaluate their performance and aim to foster techno-development. These metric systems do not generally come directly from the central state, but they do aim to support the central state's policy. Local states emulate their peers, particularly those in coastal areas, enacting similar metrics to make themselves look more scientific. Put another way, although such metrics are often not mandated by the central state, similar systems of supervision and evaluation proliferate as different localities compete to be seen as valuable in China's techno-developmental regime.

A more specific understanding of the bureaucracy in China helps explain the limits of the cage. As I showed in chapter 5, the metrics set by higher-level local states channel bureaucratic energy and public resources away from considering the *substance* of techno-development to coping with metrics and pursuing *formal* rationality. The state and business actors have a symbiotic relationship at the local level. Bureaucrats and business actors are embedded in social networks, but their interactions are frequently collusive collaborations to meet their respective needs—getting better metric values, classification outcomes, and rewards while avoiding punishments. The metric and reward/punishment systems further disincentivize bureaucrats from taking feedback and suggestions from business actors and other stakeholders.

Through its technical and legal instruments, the Chinese state offers rewards to some selected deserving business actors. In so doing, the Chinese state plays the role of what Peter Evans calls "midwifery": state efforts to promote private capital. Rewards offered by the state, though, are not always appreciated by business actors, such as manufacturers that have upgraded themselves but do not want to get involved in collusion or corruption.[25] In fact, most manufacturers that I interviewed do not want the state to put so much emphasis on technological fads. Instead, they want the state to focus on "old-fashioned" goals like building the rule of law along with giving private enterprises fair access to land and bank credit—resources firmly controlled by the state. But such hopes have not been realized.

Evans also points out that a "custodian" role—policing private actors through regulations—is the conventional role of the state in the economy and not a unique feature of developmental states.[26] The analysis of such a role nevertheless helps understand China's developmental regime. As I have discussed, the Chinese state is a fickle, Janus-faced custodian, being either extremely severe and unpredictable, or tremendously tolerant and supportive, depending on policy priorities. To be sure, the Chinese state has placed ever-increasing emphasis on the *form* of formalized rules.[27] The problem is that it can change its rule making and implementation swiftly without constraints. On the one hand, the state can put businesses in a relatively free cage. The uncritical, tolerant face of the custodian state ignores the negative side effects of technology, leading to accumulating risks and problems as well as the unconstrained expansion of tech capital. The material characteristics of the internet also mean that such risks and problems span multiple sectoral and geographic boundaries and social groups. On the other hand, the state can suddenly throw businesses in a cage with terrifying conditions. The harsh and unpredictable face of the custodian state undermines the business conditions for techno-development. For example, even those manufacturers with the potential to upgrade themselves chose not to given the unpredictable legal environment. For China's tech firms, the legal unpredictability has dramatically influenced their ability to receive capital investment.[28]

My analysis of the lives of both old and new birds responds to the call from Evans and Patrick Heller for scholarship on the developmental state in the twenty-first century to analyze ties between the state and a wider range of social groups, especially disadvantaged ones.[29] Indeed, most literature on classical developmental states does not tell us what happens to old birds. By analyzing techno-development in different sectors, I show the multidimensional relationship between the state and Chinese people. The relations between the Chinese state and its citizens increasingly depend on the perceived values of different groups of individuals in contributing to techno-development. Human and economic capital can be converted into privileged access to social welfare, public resources, and local citizenship, with their human value resting on their economic value as a high-skilled laborer or property owner. Such social class-based discrimination conflicts with China's socialist egalitarian principles and the common practice of prioritizing disadvantaged groups in social welfare provisions in most countries. Eli Friedman accordingly describes the Chinese approach as an inverted means test.[30] The economic-centric state-citizen relationship has significant consequences in the already highly unequal society. On the one hand, local states in first- and second-tier cities vie for tech talent by giving them preferential treatment. Large cities in coastal areas—where the first-tier tech companies are located—have received a net inflow of talent. On the other hand, citizens without high human and economic capital and their children are deemed worthy only to live in places with inferior educational and employment opportunities unless they happen to have local citizenship in high-end cities. China's large tech firms help the Chinese state to keep undeserving populations in third- and fourth-tier cities through the creation of platform jobs that do not provide social protection. Such a state-citizen relationship aggravates the already highly unequal regional development.[31]

Like the classical East Asian developmental states, China's techno-development is characterized by the subordination of labor, but there are differences in terms of how and what kind of labor is subordinated across the cases. In the classical cases, developmental states repressed labor rights and movements to suppress the wages of the working class.[32] Under China's techno-developmental regime, it is not just the working class but also tech professionals that are subordinated by the state and tech capital. Tech capital has aided the state to absorb surplus labor, while for its part, the Chinese state has provided tech capital with a tolerant regulatory environment, at least until the recent crackdown. This environment has enabled tech capital to exercise monopolistic and disciplinary power over platform workers through relentless algorithms, platform rules, and contract clauses. Furthermore, the Chinese state has contributed to the exploitation of tech professionals through weak labor protection and its real estate policy that has enriched local governments but indebted Chinese people. As demonstrated in chapter 8, although the central state has responded to some grievances of platform workers and tech professionals by asking tech firms to rectify themselves and their algorithms, it remains hostile to bottom-up labor organizing efforts and independent trade unions. President Xi has even instructed Chinese laborers that they should remember their obligation to achieve individual and common prosperity through hard work.[33]

Instrumentality in Postindustrial Society and Digital Capitalism

Bell's work on postindustrial society and scholarship on digital capitalism predicts and shows, respectively, the rise of a society characterized by enhanced instrumental power based on technology over people.[34] *The Gilded Cage* contributes to literature in these areas by highlighting the intricate entanglements between technology and law, adding a critical case to the literature, and analyzing class relations in such a society.

Despite its focus on instruments, Bell's work and scholarship on digital capitalism tends to neglect, or does not adequately theorize, the relationship between technology and law, specifically how law enables and facilities instrumental power based on technology. Indeed, when I first began to work on this book project, I did not expect themes related to law, such as despotic rule, despotic clauses, and critiques of the arbitrary and unliterary nature of legal instruments to be so salient; it was my interviews that proved otherwise. Then I found that the Chinese state and China's tech giants have relied on both legal and technical instruments to impose instrumental rule over people, and used the two types of instruments to complement each other.

Specifically, the Chinese state employs technical instruments to evaluate and classify labor, technologies, businesses, and industries, while using legal instruments to stipulate the allocation of rewards and punishments according to the classification outcomes and metric values, as illustrated by legal campaigns against obsolete capital under the rule by law. In other words, legal instruments give teeth to technical instruments. Furthermore, China's tech giants can use harsh legal and technical instruments due largely to the tolerant regulatory environment created by the Chinese state. As I have shown in chapter 7, with the freedom to reign over their respective digital kingdoms, China's two food delivery platforms built legal and technological instruments to control and manage workers and suppliers. For example, they use meticulously designed, asymmetrical contracts to impose and change platform rules unilaterally. As a result, many platform workers and suppliers complained about despotic rules and clauses in the interviews.

As I mentioned in the book's introduction, there are differences between law and technology. One of the major differences is that law can be more than an instrument for extracting obedience from its subjects under certain political conditions. Jürgen Habermas argues that democratic deliberation can prevent law from being unduly used as means for control and domination.[35] Under such circumstances, law can instead be used to keep technology in check. But the realities in the United States and China both deviate from this ideal scenario. In the United States, the politically and legally fragmented institutional environment allows tech giants to use their legal and technical instruments with few constraints.[36] In the Chinese case, the authoritarian regime and rule by law allow the Chinese state and tech firms to use law and technology synergistically for control and domination.

The Gilded Cage has added a critical case to scholarship on digital captialism too. Thanks to the global impact of China, understanding China's techno-development and digital capitalism is not only critical in its own right but has far-reaching implications as well. Zuboff has pointed out that disappointed by the turmoil of market democracy, some commentators in liberal democracies look to emulate China. Political leaders in developing countries are also keen to learn from China.[37] My analysis can clarify writings about and understandings of the Chinese case. In *The Age of Surveillance Capitalism*, Zuboff compares the United States with China. She suggests that tech firms and the state aim to create behavioral certainty in the United States and China, respectively, through instruments that shape people's behavior. She writes that in the United States, tech firms have power over the state in the politics of lawlessness; in comparison, in China, "the state will run the show and own it, not as a market project but as a political one, a machine solution that shapes a new society of automated behavior for guaranteed political and social outcomes: certainty without terror." As such, she characterizes the Chinese case as "a utopia of certainty."[38]

Such an understanding of China's digital capitalist system overlooks the Chinese state's economic project and its dependency on China's tech firms, overestimates the Chinese state's capacity, and neglects how instruments work in reality. As I have emphasized, the Chinese state relies on economic performance as a major source of its political legitimacy. Techno-development, including building a digital economy and cultivating China's tech firms, is a crucial means through which the Chinese state maintains its political legitimacy. As such, techno-development is simultaneously a political and economic project. Also, in spite of its enormous power over tech capital, the Chinese state has had to rely on China's tech firms to advance digital governance and the digital economy. As shown in chapter 6, despite their private legal status and intimate connection with global financial capital, China's private tech giants exist as China's national champions, straddling the boundaries between the private and public. Furthermore, although the Chinese state aims to control and engineer political, economic, and social outcomes through numerous legal and technical instruments, it has difficulty controlling how various actors engage with and respond to its instrumental rule, as exemplified by the disconnect between appearance and reality that obfuscates legibility, the excessive expansion of tech capital, and resistance to its instrumental rules. In other words, although the Chinese state tends to have a utopian view of the efficacy of technical and legal instruments for social engineering, this view does not accord with reality.

Finally, the findings of the book reveal class relations in a society characterized by enhanced instrumental power based on technology over people. Bell expected technological advances would bring about material abundance and decrease social inequality, but he later regretted not predicting the persistence of an impoverished underclass in the postindustrial society to come.[39] Manuel Castells contends that although technological innovation enables unprecedented fluidity, it makes redundant whole areas and populations bypassed by informational networks.[40] More recently, Burrell and Fourcade suggest that the coding elite, consisting of entrepreneurs and tech professionals, have gained economic power by controlling digital means of production and exploiting labor from marginalized workers.[41]

I have shown that rather than being bypassed by informational networks and living in the "black holes of informational capitalism" as Castells's work suggests, disadvantaged groups in China are incorporated into digital capitalism in many ways.[42] While considered undeserving factors of production by the Chinese state, low-skilled workers are subjected by tech capital to the most intensive and extensive instrumental rule. In chapter 7, I demonstrated how tech firms use algorithms, platform rules, and asymmetrical contracts to manage and control platform workers. Those without skills, like food delivery workers, tend to be subject to the harshest instrumental control based on technology because the supervision of work can be automated easily. Moreover, the relationship between tech firms and disadvantaged groups goes beyond exploitation. Tech firms have also attempted to shape the behavior of disadvantaged groups regarding job seeking, consumption, and finance. Specifically, China's tech giants use live streaming apps to influence and recruit potential platform workers, while employing microtargeting advertising to encourage online shopping and microlending for disadvantaged groups. In my fieldwork, I found that many food delivery workers continue to work as gig workers despite the exploitative environment due in part to their obligations to repay the numerous microloans they have borrowed using apps.

Although tech professionals occupy a much better position than those in the working class, their lives are not entirely rosy. On the one hand, they are subject to the discipline of capital. On the other hand, they too have suffered from the state's economic-centric policies that aim to boost GDP and local states' revenues through the real estate market. The latter condition puts engineers—especially those from working-class families—in a vulnerable situation to resist exploitation as they are enslaved by mortgages. Finally, in China's techno-developmental regime, even high-end capital and labor are subject to the precarious and despotic rule by instruments. The state's recent harsh and unpredictable crackdown on the tech sector has put the employment of software engineers in danger. As the situation of Alibaba's founder Jack Ma shows, tech CEOs in China are at risk of being persecuted as well, and their assets are at risk of being confiscated under the agenda of common prosperity. Ultimately, they are also birds in the cage of China's techno-developmental regime, despite their wealth and power.

Ideas and Beliefs about Instruments

I turn next to China's techno-developmental regime in relation to scholarship on ideas and beliefs about instruments. In an insightful article, David Harvey cautions against the fetishism of technology.[43] Harvey warns of the consequences when social actors, from corporations to the state, invest in the belief that technology can and will solve all of their problems. Indeed, in China's story of techno-development, we see numerous instances of technological fetishism, such as beliefs in the power of robots, the internet, platforms, metrics, algorithms, and scientific methods to solve all China's economic problems as well as the state's governance problems.

In the preceding chapters, I have traced how technological fetishism has been produced and reproduced in China's techno-developmental regime. Both business and state actors tend to endow technologies with more power than they have in reality. The Chinese state, however, has an even higher tendency to do this than business actors given the former's organizational and institutional characteristics. As shown in chapter 5, following widespread implementation of new technologies, most business actors became cognizant of such technologies' limitations and problems. They adjusted their business decisions accordingly, but almost never shared their insights and lessons learned with other actors. Even as local state actors became aware of problems on the ground, they were not motivated to inform higher-level state actors or suggest that the latter change industrial policies. This is because local officials are evaluated according to how they meet policy targets, and business actors receive material and symbolic benefits when they conform to state policy and disseminate success stories of technological progress. This incentive structure sustains top-down national sociotechnical imaginaries that fetishize technology.[44] Moreover, when such technologies do not work as expected, or have certain risks or problems, media stories focus only on success stories. The fetishism of technology also manifests in how the state responds to disappointment. As discussed in chapter 9, even when the state cannot tolerate the problems or risks associated with certain technologies, it quickly turns its attention to cultivating the next new birds and endowing them, like their predecessors, with exaggerated power. And so the cycle of technological fetishism continues.

Technological fetishism has significant social consequences. As noted above, the state's fetishism of technology has made it reluctant to acknowledge any associated problems or risks. This, in turn, has informed the state's (initially) extremely tolerant regulatory approach, leading to intractable problems in the long term. In addition to ignoring problems in the tech sector, the Chinese state has overinvested in technological fads, leading to a tremendous waste of public resources, with local officials not held accountable for failed investments and subsidies. And at the most basic level, technological fetishism not only dehumanizes and devalues people but convinces them of their own low human capital too.

Understanding the fetishism of technology also helps us better appreciate the capacity of the Chinese state—and its limits. With the rapid development of AI, machine learning, and data science, scholars have pointed out the emergence of dataism and the dataist state as well as new statecraft in the digital age.[45] China is often cited as an example to show how new technologies and the abundance of data can strengthen the state's capacity. It is true that the Chinese state is an avid supporter and user of technologies and data. And to be sure, certain technologies do strengthen the state's capacity in some ways. For instance, online monitoring systems in factories help local governments monitor pollution (chapter 4). But my analyses suggest we should distinguish subjective rationality from objective rationality. As seen in chapter 3, for example, experts whom local governments contracted to design quantitative indicators were unsure about whether their indicators would achieve policy goals because their design rested on shaky assumptions. Throughout the book, I have shown as well that the institutional structure and behavioral approach adopted by the

Chinese state incentivize state and nonstate actors to manipulate all kinds of data that the state collects. Although local states contract companies to build various data platforms, to what extent platforms based on problematic data can increase the state's capacity is unknown. In short, we should be wary of simply assuming the power of technologies and data to enhance statecraft.

Finally, I want to return to Gabrielle Hecht's *The Radiance of France*, as I drew on her insightful work to develop the concept of the techno-developmental regime.[46] In the process of writing this book, I revisited *The Radiance of France* from time to time and was always attracted by the similarities as well as differences between it and my study. The dream of becoming a powerful techno-nation and the belief in planning are common themes in both studies. After World War II, France's technical experts and the government turned to technological prowess to restore the country's national glory. Similarly, the Chinese state became determined to pursue techno-development in the mid-2000s as it saw the limitation of economic development based on labor-intensive manufacturing.

But there are critical differences between the two stories, many of which relate to the problems and limits of rationality. Tensions resulting from rationalization processes and the limits of rationality are fundamental problems that have long occupied sociologists, philosophers, and political theorists. In his attempt to address such problems, Habermas suggests communicative action or deliberation as a potential solution.[47] There are no shortage of critiques of Habermas's work, such as those pointing out the problem of inequality and various forms of exclusion, but I deeply appreciate his work nonetheless because he so clearly identifies a fundamental human problem and then suggests a solution.[48] In a similar vein, Amartya Sen argues that the viability of development and human flourishing depends on the process of public reasoning.[49] Patrick Heller and Vijayendra Rao show the importance of deliberation, voice, and collective action to development.[50]

Reading Hecht's *The Radiance of France*, I was struck by the frequency and intensity of disagreements, debates, and discussions among a variety of actors, from experts to officials, engineers, union leaders, workers, artists, writers, and the general public. For instance, union members debated about whether and why certain technologies were "inhumane," and whether a state in the service of technology would "govern men as though they were things" and negate the existence of class conflicts. Technologists and experts needed to persuade the nation to choose their proposed solution amid a range of alternatives. As Hecht points out, the very multiplicity of visions for a "technological France" made the notion contested terrain, making it possible for ideas about the nation to divide as well as unite.[51]

In China's story of techno-development, disagreements and discussions about China's development models did emerge to some extent, until the state under Xi's leadership clamped down on the country's emergent public sphere (chapter 3). Some critical voices of platform workers and software engineers emerged and entered the public sphere only after these laborers could no longer bear the exploitation and stress. But many of these voices are still censored and silenced. In my interviews, interviewees frequently expressed disbelief that anyone would want to listen to them or be sympathetic to their voices. I vividly remember the reaction of factory workers when I inquired about their children's education. They were surprised that I was interested in their lives and told me I was the first person to ask about their difficulties. They were so eager to share their stories. Yet despite experiencing harsh and legally questionable crackdowns, executives and managers who worked for obsolete manufacturers told me they did not want to voice their grievances. When I asked why, it became clear that they already knew they would receive no moral or discursive support in the dominant official narrative and sociotechnical imaginaries. Within the Chinese state, the metrics and classification systems disincentivize officials from discussing anything but targets and the means to achieve them. Unlike in Hecht's story, in China, ideas about the nation only unite. They are not permitted to divide given the singular vision of the nation—one designed by the Chinese state.

The Future of the Gilded Cage

China's techno-development is a case in which instrumental rationality has expanded tremendously, but what Habermas calls communicative or discursive rationality is largely absent.[52] It is also essentially a story about the contested and variegated relationship between instruments (the cage) and different groups of humans (the bird) during a period of rapid transformation. Starting in 2003, then President Hu Jintao sought to reconfigure development from a unidimensional, GDP-centered project to a multidimensional, *human-centered* approach that would prioritize people's well-being over economic growth at all costs. He named this, as mentioned earlier, the scientific concept of development, and emphasized its promise to improve the quality, efficiency, and sustainability of development. Over time, however, as Hu's notion was mobilized to advance techno-development, government officials in China focused on building and using instruments to "scientifically" evaluate and classify humans—as factors of production—and other factors of productions so that the government could allocate rewards and punishments accordingly. Through this process, the scientific or instrumental aspects of the scientific concept of development have come to overshadow and even erode the "human" aspects of Hu's vision.

In China's story of techno-development, the state has the last say about who can use what instruments—technologies, techniques, or formalized rules—and for the benefit of which groups, all in the name of national development. People now seen as having low economic and human capital have little say in this system, despite being the ones most likely to be controlled or replaced by the above instruments. Instead, the instruments themselves are often worshipped at the expense of human existence, values, and problems. And though Chinese people are proud of the nation's progress, they are frequently uncritical of the techno-developmental discourse that rationalizes all hardship as necessary, and only rarely voice their discontent or grievances in the shrinking public sphere. Meanwhile, human suffering and difficulties continue. Is this the inevitable end of the story? Alternately, what other futures might there be for the gilded cage?

In recent years, as China's economic growth has slowed, the gilded facade of China's techno-developmental regime has begun to fade somewhat, revealing the weakness of such a regime and the limited efficacy of instruments that constitute the regime. Notwithstanding the Chinese state's ambition to foster techno-development and cultivate all kinds of new birds, the internet sector remains the most important new bird that significantly contributes to China's economy. As the government again cages the internet sector under the rule by law, however, this critical pillar of the economy has been shaken. Even the toxic but irresistible new bird of the real estate sector has encountered serious problems as China's top developers have been embroiled in a debt crisis. Since many problems in China's economy are fundamental and have only been exacerbated, but not caused by, the COVID-19 pandemic or Chinese state's zero-COVID policy, I do not put much weight on issues related to the pandemic. All things considered, China is entering a new era in which most Chinese people are not going to experience "stage-skipping" improvements in their material lives and upward social mobility. As the gilded facade of China's techno-development fades, the limits, downsides, contradictions, and exclusions of China's techno-developmental regime could become increasingly clear to a wider number of people. And yet in the current highly centralized authoritarian regime under Xi, it is quite unlikely that the Chinese state would allow public discussions and deliberation on what kind of technological *and* human future Chinese people would like to pursue and prioritize.

What might be the social consequences of the fading gilded cage? On the one hand, I believe scattered, localized covert and overt resistance to the hyper-rational instrumental rule will continue to exist, but I do not expect such resistance will lead to large-scale conflicts that cut across different social groups and threaten political stability. On the other hand, more people might find it meaningless to play the games set up by the Chinese state and tech firms. In *Exit, Voice, and Loyalty*, economist Albert O. Hirschman wrote about ways of reacting to deterioration in organizations.[53] Building on Hirschman's work, some scholars have added a fourth possibility: neglect or passive response.[54] From a Hirschmanian perspective, I would expect exit (e.g., immigration) for some business elites and highly educated professionals, scattered voice for some disadvantaged groups, and neglect or passive response for the majority.

The final question is to what extent the Chinese state will be able to cultivate new birds (e.g., advanced semiconductor manufacturing) capable of solving its economic and national security problems. I speculate that changing global conditions and the cage that the Chinese state has built would make such a task daunting. Global conditions have changed enormously. When Bell published *The Coming of Post-Industrial Society* in 1973, few people would have been able to predict the rise of neoliberal globalization. And when Clinton visited China in 1998 amid the heyday of neoliberal globalization, few would have been able to anticipate the waning of neoliberal globalization in just two decades. With rising US-China tensions, the conditions that aided China's global ascendence and techno-development have ceased to exist. Even worse, China must now contend with a United States that actively seeks, through measures like export controls, to prevent China from cultivating strategic new birds. I also have doubts about whether the Chinese state will be able to achieve its goals with the instruments that it has created thus far. For one thing, the Chinese state's hyper-instrumental rationality and absence of space for public reasoning could ironically cage the Chinese state itself, preventing it from enhancing legibility, efficacy, and efficiency.

I finished writing this book at the beginning of a new era. President Xi has centralized power to such a degree that it is difficult to foresee how his rule might come to an end and what might follow. Meanwhile, neoliberal globalization, once the condition that aided China's global ascendence and techno-development, has significantly declined. I grapple with an unknown future at both the domestic and global level while trying to offer a sociological understanding of an emergent, still-unfolding phenomenon. My hope is that the analytic tools that I have developed in this book provide insight at least into how we have arrived at this historic moment, and what questions we must ask of the future, particularly on behalf of those who stand to suffer most from what it holds. For if there is one thing I expect of future techno-development in China with certainty, it is that it will be as unequal in its effects as it will seem inexorable.

METHODOLOGICAL APPENDIX

Chapters 2–3

These two chapters are based on an analysis of secondary literature, newspaper articles, policy documents, and in-depth interviews with two retired central government officials, four local officials in Jiangsu and Guangdong, three economists, five managers and executives of export-oriented companies, and two executives of IT companies.

Chapter 4

This chapter is based on my analysis of interviews and ethnographic data. Between 2016 and 2019, I visited the factories of about twenty manufacturing companies deemed obsolete by the local governments in the Pearl River Delta in Guangdong Province. During my visits, I interviewed thirty executives and managers. In addition, I conducted interviews with five Didi drivers who were former executives or managers. Furthermore, I conducted three phone interviews with current or former executives and managers of manufacturing companies in Zhejiang Province regarding the same topics. The interview questions related to interviewees' experiences with campaigns against obsolete businesses and their views on China's industrial policy. I also interviewed three township- and street-level officials in the Pearl River Delta to understand how they implemented campaigns against obsolete businesses.

I received permission to conduct weeklong observations and interviews in two factories in 2019: Diligence in Dongguan and Jade in Shenzhen. This allowed me to develop a deeper understanding of the concerns of workers, managers, and engineers by listening to and joining in their daily conversations. Since campaigns against obsolete businesses frequently occurred in 2019, I was able to observe how management interacted with local officials and mobilized resources to address their problems. During these research trips, I conducted interviews with two managers and executives along with fifteen workers at Diligence as well as interviews with three managers and executives along with fifteen workers at Jade.

Chapter 5

I examined the perceptions and practices of local states, manufacturers, and workers regarding automation in electronics manufacturing between 2017 and 2019, based on analysis of ninety-two interviews. All the names of cities, manufacturers, and individual subjects are anonymized. In-depth interviewing was, arguably, the most effective research method to understand how actors responded to techno-developmentalism, and how they viewed the value of robots and employment security. I interviewed executives, managers, and low-skilled workers currently or previously employed by one of the six manufacturers studied in this chapter. The distribution of interviewees is shown in table 5.1. I also interviewed two government officials.

There were three interview protocols; the first was designed for executives and managers. Questions included the employment history of interviewees, why and how manufacturers implemented automation, how robotization influenced employment, and how industrial policies influenced manufacturers. The second protocol was designed for low-skilled workers, technicians, and engineers, and asked about interviewees' employment history, whether and how they knew about the use of robots in and beyond their factories, whether and how they knew about any human-robot substitution initiative, and how they viewed automation. The final interview protocol was used to interview the two government officials about industrial policies and implementation. Each interview lasted from one to two hours.

In addition to formal interviews, I had casual conversations with executives, managers, and workers. I also had lunch with workers in factory cafeterias and talked with them about their work, families, and views on automation. The subjects were all informed that these conversations would be part of research data and gave informed consent.

The interview data and field notes have been analyzed at three levels: policy contexts, decision-making at the firm level, and worker responses. First, I analyzed policies mentioned by the interviewees, and triangulated the data by comparing different interviews as well as interviews with policy documents. Then I coded interview data about policy implementation. Second, I coded interview data with managers and executives as well as my field notes to analyze how manufacturers constructed the value of robots, and how the state's policies influenced this process. Finally, I coded low-skilled workers' views about automation.

Chapter 6

This chapter is mainly based on newspaper articles, policy documents, and six in-depth interviews with engineers and managers in China's leading internet companies.

Chapter 7

I draw on multiple qualitative methods to collect and analyze data. First, I conducted in-depth interviews with thirty SPCs and thirty GPCs in seven cities between 2018 and 2019. I recruited people who were couriers at the time of the interview or in the preceding twelve months. At the beginning of the study, I attempted to diversify the interviewee pool according to location, given the possibility of variation across cities in terms of how platforms operate and couriers work. When it became clear there was no significant difference across cities, I did most of my interviews in Chongqing, a municipality in southwest China, given my access to research support there.

The interview questions included basic demographic information, employment history, work situation, interactions with other workers and supervisors, and experiences of strikes and protests. Many couriers shared their photos, videos, and social media communications with me, thereby helping me to reconstruct collective action. Existing literature tends to neglect management's role, so I interviewed six people with management positions (four at service platforms, and two at gig platforms). I also interviewed a system development engineer and in-house lawyer to understand the technological and legal aspects of control and management. In addition, I interviewed two government affairs professionals who worked for Meituan and Ele.me to understand their strategies for interacting with government agencies. Finally, I interviewed an official in charge of market regulations in a city in order to gain an understanding of how the government regulates the food delivery platform economy.

Second, I conducted online ethnography between 2018 and 2019. I joined four nationwide discussion boards used by food delivery couriers in Baidu Tieba, one of the largest online communities in China. I joined ten social media groups formed by couriers too. I examined the Weibo content of certain couriers who organized or participated in strikes or protests. Online ethnography enabled me to reach out to participants in collective action. I read discussions, listened to couriers' voice messages, and took notes and screenshots.

Third, I conducted on-the-ground ethnography in Chongqing. I began to conduct online ethnography with couriers in Chongqing two months before GPCs there organized a series of strikes and protests in May 2018. As figure 7.6 shows, Chongqing is one of the many cities in which platform couriers staged collective action. I went to Chongqing in June 2018 to conduct fieldwork. When I arrived in Chongqing, many GPCs still had fresh memories of the collective action. I stayed in a plaza where gig couriers hung out and joined their conversations. One service platform station allowed me to observe their couriers' and supervisors' routines, and a gig platform manager allowed me to visit his office. After I left Chongqing, I continued to observe the situation through follow-up interviews.

I analyzed and collected interview and ethnographic data iteratively, moving between data and theories. Initially, I designed my interview questions based on literature on algorithmic control. After conducting the first twenty interviews and some online ethnography, I began to analyze data. As a number of the emerging themes and codes did not appear in the literature on algorithmic control, my preliminary empirical analysis prompted me to develop a broader theoretical framework. I then revised my interview protocols based on the newly included literature. I did supplemental interviews with the first twenty interviewees and then conducted forty-eight more interviews.

Fourth, I compiled a data set that contains eighty-seven cases of strikes or protests organized by food delivery couriers between 2017 and 2018 in China. I compiled the list from a professional news database (WiseNews), search engines, online communities, Weibo, WeChat, and the China Labour Bulletin. The China Labour Bulletin is a labor nongovernmental organization in Hong Kong that provides the most comprehensive data about labor disputes in China. The data I collected include texts describing strikes and protests along with photos and videos. I documented slogans written on banners and signs. For each collective action, I coded the data in terms of type of platform, platform company, location, content of the complaint, and couriers' actions. The data set is limited in terms of its exhaustiveness, so I use these data to complement my interviews and ethnography data rather than trying to subject them to rigorous quantitative analysis.

Fifth, I collected the texts of contracts between different actors involved in food delivery. I also compiled the texts of rules enacted by the two platform companies and their franchisees and local offices. In addition, I read sixty court decisions made by the Basic People's Courts or Intermediate People's Courts that listed either Meituan or Ele.me as one of the parties in the case. Most of the decisions concerned compensation following deaths or injuries of platform couriers or other parties due to traffic incidents. The disputes in these cases are not central to collective contention, but the court decisions provide detailed information about the legal and organizational design of the service and gig platforms.

Finally, I collected and analyzed public corporate documents, including IPO documents and corporate annual reports.

Chapter 8

The data for this chapter come from in-depth interviews and online ethnography. All the interviewees have a four-year college degree or above. Most of them are male as the profession is predominantly male. The male-to-female ratio is often higher than nine to one in teams where my interviewees worked, except in the case of foreign firms. The sample is restricted to software engineers without a managerial position because professionals with and without a managerial position have different interests. According to my informants, most software engineers without managerial positions are between twenty-five and thirty-five, so I restricted my sample to this age range. In order to capture the heterogeneity among software engineers, I recruited engineers with various class origins. Table 8.1 shows the distribution of these software engineers.

Interview questions included several components. The first one collected data about their parents' education, occupation, and property along with their parent's role in their upbringing. Next I asked about their housing, dating, marriage, and childbearing/child-rearing situation. I then transitioned to interviewees' employment history, experiences on the job market, work situation, health, stress, interaction with other employees and supervisors, and work-life balance. This component included questions about their experiences with, views on, and reaction to overwork and labor activism. Each interview lasted about 1 to 1.5 hours. Most of the interviews were conducted through phone calls. I took notes during all the interviews, but taped them if I received permission too.

In addition, I conducted online ethnography between 2019 and 2021, and reached out to participants of labor activism. Since activism organized by software engineers has been primarily online, online ethnography is a crucial method to understand such activism and its participants. I observed discussions and interactions on GitHub, WeChat, Discord, and Telegram. Although labor activism among engineers initially received much public attention, the level of activity on these sites plummeted soon after. I read discussions and took notes and screenshots regularly. I also reached out to participants in those online spaces. Only two of them agreed to accept my interviews. Although declining my interview request, eleven filled out a questionnaire based on my interview protocol.

I collected and analyzed data iteratively, using subsequent interviews to investigate and understand themes that emerged earlier as well as improve my interview protocol. I repeatedly read interview transcripts, interview notes, online ethnography notes, and questionnaire responses, while writing case profiles for each interviewee, and recording emerging themes and patterns in analytic memos. Using these profiles and memos, I developed a list of analytic themes and reread each transcript, note, and questionnaire response to code specifically for those themes. The analytic process allowed me to develop four ideal types of engineers that I term optimalists, strivers, minimalists, and the disillusioned.

Chapter 9

This chapter is mainly based on analyses of laws, regulations, official documents, and news. I also conducted followed-up interviews with ten platform workers and ten software engineers to understand how they viewed the government's crackdown on tech companies.

NOTES

Chapter 1. Introduction

1. https://www.iatp.org/sites/default/files/Full_Text_of_Clintons_Speech_on_China _Trade_Bi.htm, accessed September 18, 2022.

2. https://www.latimes.com/archives/la-xpm-1998-jun-26-mn-63808-story.html, accessed July 20, 2022; https://archive.nytimes.com/www.nytimes.com/library/world/asia/063098 china-summit.html, accessed July 20, 2022.

3. https://www.presidency.ucsb.edu/documents/remarks-roundtable-discussion-shaping -china-for-the-21st-century-shanghai-china, accessed July 11, 2022.

4. Whittaker et al. 2020.

5. Bell 1999, lxxxvii, lxxxv.

6. Bell 1999, lxxxv.

7. Duff 1998.

8. Bell 1999, cii, xciv.

9. Bell 1999, xcix, 116. For Bell, intellectual technology relies on mathematics, linguistics, computing, data, algorithms, programming, and modeling. It allows people to model "games between persons," substitutes algorithms for intuitive judgments, and helps to "chart more efficient, 'rational' solution[s] to economic and engineering, if not social problems" (Bell 1999, xciv).

10. Bell 1999, xvii, lxxxv.

11. For example, in his speech on China's WTO accession in 2000, Clinton said the Chinese government's effort to crack down on the internet was like "trying to nail jello to the wall," and that "in the knowledge economy, economic innovation and political empowerment, whether anyone likes it or not, will inevitably go hand in hand." https://www.iatp.org/sites/default/files /Full_Text_of_Clintons_Speech_on_China_Trade_Bi.htm, accessed July 23, 2022.

12. Whittaker et al. 2020.

13. International institutions like the WTO were established to remove state-imposed barriers to international trade under neoliberal globalization.

14. Whittaker et al. 2020.

15. Huang 2008.

16. Wu 2019; Gallagher 2005.

17. *Nikkei Weekly*, October 1, 2001.

18. Rozelle et al. 2020.

19. Tang 2020.

20. Tang 2020.

21. https://www.statista.com/statistics/277483/market-value-of-the-largest-internet
-companies-worldwide/, accessed July 24, 2022.

22. https://news.cgtn.com/news/2022-07-09/China-s-digital-economy-grows-rapidly-in
-2021-1bwyYStbus8/index.html, accessed July 29, 2022.

23. Hao and Cao 2019; Hu 2017; Li and Cui 2020.

24. Ang 2020.

25. https://www.youtube.com/watch?v=_eFQsiLm-EE, accessed July 24, 2022.

26. https://www.eurasiareview.com/05072022-china-opens-its-first-political-party-school
-in-africa/, accessed July 30, 2022.

27. https://www.nile1.com/mwalimu-julius-nyerere-leadership-school-holds-inauguration
-ceremony/, accessed July 30, 2022.

28. Woo 1999.

29. Schumpeter 2008, 83.

30. Bell 1999, 35.

31. Ampuja and Koivisto 2014.

32. Castells 2010a.

33. Castells 2010b, 166.

34. Rowthorn and Ramaswamy 1997; Brick 1992.

35. Baccini and Weymouth 2021; Broz, Frieden, and Weymouth 2021.

36. Bell and Graubard 1997.

37. Lei 2022.

38. Bell 1999, xcix.

39. Ampuja and Koivisto 2014; Bell 1999, xviii.

40. Bell 1999.

41. Mau 2019; Burrell and Fourcade 2021; Srnicek 2017; Zuboff 2019; Deterding 2019; Griesbach et al. 2019.

42. Zuboff 2019, 432, 437.

43. http://news.sohu.com/20161121/n473686289.shtml, accessed July 27, 2022.

44. https://www.ft.com/content/6250e4ec-8e68-11e7-9084-d0c17942ba93, accessed September 15, 2022.

45. http://news.sohu.com/20161121/n473686289.shtml, accessed July 27, 2022.

46. Binbin and Xiaoyan 2017.

47. Hecht 1998, 16–17.

48. Schiller 1999.

49. Barbrook and Cameron 1996.

50. Bell 1999.

51. Haggard 2018; Evans and Heller 2015.

52. Evans 1995.

53. Caldentey 2008.

54. Block 2008.

55. Barbrook and Cameron 1996; Wade 2014.

56. Mann 1984, 189.

57. Bell 1999.

58. Habermas 1971.

59. Brubaker 1984.

60. Zuboff 2019; Mau 2019; Burrell and Fourcade 2021.

61. Hildebrandt 2015; Brownsword 2019.

62. Hildebrandt 2015; Brownsword 2019; Lessig 1999.

63. https://www.lexico.com/en/definition/technology, accessed August 20, 2022.

64. https://www.lexico.com/en/definition/power, accessed August 21, 2022; Zuboff 2019.

65. Lee 2017, 423.

66. Bell 1999.

67. Lessig 1999; Brownsword 2019; Hildebrandt 2015.

68. Lee 2017.

69. https://www.whitehouse.gov/briefing-room/statements-releases/2022/08/09/fact
-sheet-chips-and-science-act-will-lower-costs-create-jobs-strengthen-supply-chains-and
-counter-china/, accessed August 20, 2022.

70. Lessig 1999; Brownsword 2019; Hildebrandt 2015.

71. Lessig 1999.

72. Zysman and Kenney 2018, 62.

73. Lessig 1999.

74. Habermas 1996.

75. Schumpeter 2008; Castells 2010b, 166.

76. Bell 1999.

77. Burrell and Fourcade 2021, 1.

78. Lilkov 2020.

79. Dai and Hao 2018.

80. Dai and Hao 2018.

81. Barbrook and Cameron 1996; O'Mara 2021.

82. Barbrook and Cameron 1996; Turner 2006.

83. Schor 2020; Zuboff 2019.

84. Scott 1998, 4.

85. https://nottspolitics.org/wp-content/uploads/2013/06/Labours-Plan-for-science.pdf,
accessed September 11, 2021.

86. Hecht 1998.

87. Greenhalgh 2020, 1.

88. Jasanoff and Kim 2009, 120.

89. Jasanoff 2015.

90. Scott 1998, 4.

91. Harvey 2003, 3.

92. Bell 1999.

93. Weber 1956.

94. Mejia 2015, 291.

95. Marcuse 1964.

96. Horkheimer and Adorno 1979.

97. Habermas 1971, 1984. In 1986, when Habermas gave the Tanner Lectures at Harvard
University, Bell praised Habermas's "heroic effort to re-think, in a critical way, the legacy of the
Enlightenment, to re-assert the standpoint of Reason in an irrational world. He has taken from

his forebears, as [Johann Wolfgang von] Goethe would say, and made it his own" (Daniel Bell's personal archive in the Harvard Library).

98. Freedom in the World is an annual global report on political rights and civil liberties, composed of numerical ratings and descriptive texts for each country and a select group of territories. It is the most widely read and cited report of its kind, tracking global trends in political rights and civil liberties for almost fifty years.

99. Slater and Wong 2022.

100. Zhao 2004, 22.

101. Lei 2018a.

102. Pearson, Rithmire, and Tsai 2021.

103. Hay 1999.

104. Zhou 2017.

105. Hildebrandt 2015, 164.

106. Sen 2000.

107. Heller and Rao 2015.

108. Harvey 2014, 1.

109. Brubaker 1984.

110. Pearson, Rithmire, and Tsai 2021.

111. Brubaker 1984; Kalberg 1980.

112. Brubaker 1984.

113. Scott 1998; Harvey 2003.

114. Brick 1992, 357.

115. Burawoy 1982; Marcuse 1964.

116. Scott 1998, 2008.

117. Ang 2020.

118. Ang 2016.

119. Harvey 2014.

120. One exception is workers who critique the system on behalf of and out of concern for their children. I will elaborate on this in chapter 4.

121. Vogel 1990.

122. http://www.gov.cn/zhengce/content/2014-06/27/content_8913.htm, accessed September 18, 2022.

Chapter 2. From Labor to Land and Technology

1. Schumpeter 2008; Harvey 2014; Srnicek 2017.

2. Hsing 2010; Liu, Oi, and Zhang 2022.

3. Greenhalgh 2020, 1; http://scitech.people.com.cn/GB/25509/56813/57267/57268/4001431.html, accessed October 18, 2021.

4. Weber 2020.

5. Oi 1992.

6. Rozelle et al. 2020.

7. Chan, Pun, and Selden 2013; Aguiar de Medeiros and Trebat 2017.

8. Chan, Pun, and Selden 2013.

9. Aguiar de Medeiros and Trebat 2017.

10. Rozelle et al. 2020.

11. http://zgsn.ahu.edu.cn/2011/1228/c17129a233124/page.htm, accessed October 10, 2022.

12. Wu 2011.

13. http://www.jyb.cn/rmtzcg/xwy/wzxw/202112/t20211213_670142.html, accessed October 11, 2022.

14. Gallagher 2020.

15. Wu 2011.

16. Fan and Wan 2017.

17. Liu, Oi, and Zhang 2022.

18. Liu, Oi, and Zhang 2022.

19. Fan and Wan 2017; Liu, Oi, and Zhang 2022.

20. Ji and Zhang 2020.

21. Local government financing vehicles are companies capitalized and owned by local governments. These companies sell bonds in the bond market for the purpose of financing real estate development and municipal infrastructure construction. Liu, Oi, and Zhang 2022.

22. Liu, Oi, and Zhang 2022.

23. Ji and Zhang 2020.

24. Yi, Peng, and Zu 2018.

25. Cao, Feng, and Tao 2008.

26. Ji and Zhang 2020.

27. http://mil.news.sina.com.cn/2005-10-01/0650323207.html, accessed October 12, 2022.

28. http://english.www.gov.cn/archive/publications/2014/08/23/content_2814749829 87826.htm, accessed October 12, 2022.

29. Gallagher 2020.

30. Yi, Peng, and Zu 2018.

31. Gallagher 2020.

32. Fan and Wan 2017.

33. Liu, Oi, and Zhang 2022; Fan and Wan 2017.

34. Gallagher 2020.

35. Swider 2015a, 2015b; Chuang 2020.

36. Fan and Wan 2017.

37. Swidler 1986.

38. Shen and Williams 2005.

39. Huang 1997.

40. Edgerton 2007.

41. Zhang 2012.

42. Chambers 1984; Shen and Williams 2005; Kwok 1965.

43. http://cpc.people.com.cn/n1/2018/0807/c69113-30213273.html, accessed October 18, 2021.

44. Oi 1999; Huang 2008.

45. He 2018.

46. Wang 2015.

47. Y. Wang 2018; He 2018.

48. Wu 2018.

49. He 2018; Li 1995.

50. Y. Wang 2018.

51. Yuan 2008.

52. Ye 2012; Wu 2018.

53. Quoted in *People's Daily*, March 25, 1978.

54. Wu 2018.

55. http://scitech.people.com.cn/GB/25509/56813/57267/57268/4001431.html, accessed October 18, 2021.

56. Bell 1999.

57. Quoted in *People's Daily*, March 8, 1985.

58. Deng 1993, 378.

59. Jiang 2009, 143.

60. Zhao 2004.

61. Jiang 2006.

62. Jiang 2006.

63. Halpern 1989.

64. See Zhao's report on economic reforms and practical problems during China's seventh five-year plan in 1986, and his report at the Thirteenth National Congress of the CCP in 1987.

65. Greenhalgh 2008.

66. Quoted in *People's Daily*, July 18, 1986.

67. *People's Daily*, August 12, 1987; *People's Daily*, September 23, 1988.

68. *People's Daily*, October 15, 1992.

69. Decision on Several Major Issues concerning Strengthening the Building of the Party.

70. Porter 1995; Davis, Kingsbury, and Merry 2012; Mau 2019.

71. Henshel 1982; Bell 1999.

72. Lei 2022.

73. Japanese economist Akamatsu Kaname's theory of flying geese paradigm was not cited by Chinese scholars in the debates in the 1980s and 1990s.

74. Li and Zhao 2008.

75. Liu 1986.

76. Zhang 1986.

77. See Jiang's report at the Fourteenth National Congress of the CCP in 1992.

78. Jiang 2006.

79. Export-processing enterprises are export-oriented enterprises invested in by foreign individuals or entities. Foreign investors were in charge of investing in facilities, such as plants and machines, importing raw materials, providing designs and managerial assistance, and exporting final products. Such enterprises relied on the cheap and abundant supply of land and labor in China.

80. Jiang 2006. Jiang's view in the early 1990s is consistent with his talks and the State Council's development plans for eastern, inner, and western China in the early 2000s. The policies that formed in the 2000s include the Great Western Development Strategy for western China; promoting agricultural industrialization, transforming traditional industries, and accelerating industrialization and urbanization for inner China; and accelerating the upgrading of industrial

structure while developing high-tech industries and high value-added processing and manufacturing for eastern China.

81. Scott 1998.

82. Wang, Rothwell, and Sun 2009.

83. Dickson 2003.

84. https://www.fmprc.gov.cn/web/ziliao_674904/zyjh_674906/t10855.shtml, accessed April 9, 2020.

85. Dickson 2003.

86. *People's Daily*, June 26, 2007.

87. See the Decision of the Central Committee of the CCP on Strengthening the Construction of the Party's Ruling Capability in 2004, http://www.gov.cn/test/2008-08/20/content_1075279.htm, accessed April 9, 2020; *People's Daily*, September 27, 2004.

88. Holbig 2009.

89. *People's Daily*, March 10, 1999.

90. *People's Daily*, July 28, 2003.

91. Howell and Duckett 2018.

92. Howell and Duckett 2018; Huang 2008.

93. In 2006, the State Council also passed the Outline of National Medium- and Long-Term Science and Technology Development Plan (2006–20) as a blueprint to strengthen China's capabilities for indigenous innovation and build an innovative nation. http://www.gov.cn/ldhd/2006-01/09/content_152487.htm, accessed March 12, 2023.

94. http://www.gov.cn/gongbao/content/2006/content_240241.htm, accessed April 9, 2020.

95. http://www.cas.cn/zt/hyzt/zgkxydswcysdh/yw/201006/t20100607_2874812.html, accessed April 9, 2020.

96. Greenhalgh 2020.

97. Shen and Williams 2005.

98. Shen and Williams 2005.

99. Freedom in the World is a yearly survey and report by the US-based nongovernmental Organization Freedom House that measures the degree of civil liberties and political rights in every nation along with significant related and disputed territories around the world.

100. For readers' interest, the average scores of respondents in the United States to the four questions are all below the average scores of the fifty-four countries/territories, showing relatively lukewarm attitudes toward S&T.

101. Lan 2009.

102. Kostka 2019; Su, Xu, and Cao 2021.

103. Xie 2016.

104. As defined in the *Oxford English Dictionary, scientize* means "to make scientific; to give a scientific character or appearance to; to organize on a scientific basis," while *scientization* means "the action of making scientific." In applying this term to refer to how the Chinese state reconfigured both its very conception of development and its statecraft, I am using scientize descriptively—that is, to capture how the state itself understood what it was doing according to *its* understanding of science—not analytically—that is, to reflect my own evaluation of these processes as indeed scientific.

105. Davis, Kingsbury, and Merry 2012; Kurunmäki and Miller 2006.

106. In general, there are two types of performance evaluation. The first evaluates individual cadres, officials, or collective leadership. The second type evaluates local governments or specific government agencies.

107. https://www.chinanews.com/gn/2021/01-19/9390762.shtml, accessed October 17, 2021.

108. Porter 1995; Mau 2019.

109. Zhao 2004, 22.

110. See the article published by the Huxin Cement Factory in *China Building Materials*, July 1962, 7–8.

111. Zhao 2005.

112. Zhao 1983.

113. Wang and Wang 2009; Huang 2014.

114. Tian 1987.

115. Zhou 2007.

116. 1995 关于加强和完善县(市)党委、政府领导班子工作实绩考核的通知.

117. *People's Daily*, April 9, 1997.

118. *People's Daily*, December 16, 1999.

119. *People's Daily*, December 16, 1999.

120. Edin 2003.

121. The Decision of the Central Committee of the CCP on Strengthening the Construction of the Party's Ruling Capability in 2004, http://www.gov.cn/test/2008-08/20/content_1075279.htm, accessed April 9, 2020.

122. Hu 2005.

123. http://www.reformdata.org/2004/0310/4952.shtml, accessed March 12, 2023.

124. Tian and Tian 2011.

125. Wu 2004.

126. Zheng 2009.

127. *People's Daily*, April 13, 2004.

128. *People's Daily*, June 24, 2004.

129. *People's Daily*, March 11, 2004.

130. *People's Daily*, June 6, 2004.

131. 2006 体现科学发观要求的地方党政领导班子和领导干部综合考核评价试行办法, http://www.gov.cn/zwhd/2006-07/09/content_331301.htm; http://www.gov.cn/jrzg/2006-07/07/content_329499.htm, accessed April 9, 2020.

132. 2009 中共中央办公厅关于建立促进科学发展的党政领导班子和领导干部考核评价机制的意见.

133. 2005 云南省县(市、区)党政领导班子和成员政绩考核评价办法(试行); *People's Daily*, June 6, 2005.

134. Shang 2018.

135. Mau 2019.

136. Zuo 2017.

137. Scott 1998.

138. Huang 2008; Holbig 2009; Chen 2009.

139. Shen and Williams 2005.

140. Chang 2012.

141. Mau 2019.

142. Tsai, Wang, and Lin 2021.

143. http://www.gov.cn/zhengce/content/2014-06/27/content_8913.htm, accessed October 19, 2021.

144. Power 2004.

Chapter 3. The Turn to Techno-Development

1. Oi 1992.

2. http://www.yanfufoundation.org/who-is-yan-fu/, accessed October 28, 2021; Wang 2017.

3. Xi 2001a, i.

4. https://www.bbc.com/zhongwen/simp/press_review/2013/08/130811_press_xi_degree, accessed October 24, 2021.

5. Xi 2001c.

6. https://www.bbc.com/news/business-58784315, accessed October 19, 2022.

7. Xi 2001b.

8. Quoted in *People's Daily*, December 25, 2005; *People's Daily*, March 3, 2006.

9. Kojima 2000.

10. Rozelle and Hell 2020.

11. *People's Daily*, April 9, 2007; *21st Century Business Herald*, October 1, 2007.

12. Wu 2019.

13. *People's Daily*, August 25, 2005.

14. *People's Daily*, August 9, 2006; *People's Daily*, November 30, 2006.

15. *People's Daily*, July 18, 2005; *People's Daily*, August 8, 2005.

16. *People's Daily*, January 23, 2007; Ang 2018.

17. Quoted in *Southern Daily*, April 8, 2008.

18. Quoted in *Southern Daily*, April 8, 2008.

19. Lei 2018a.

20. *Private Economy News*, November 9, 2006; *Southern Daily*, June 19, 2008.

21. Quoted in *Oriental Daily News*, November 12, 2005.

22. Quoted in *Southern Metropolis Daily*, July 26, 2006.

23. *China Business Times*, December 11, 2003; *Jiefang Daily*, March 19, 2004.

24. Quoted in *Southern Metropolis Daily*, July 26, 2006.

25. Ang 2018.

26. Quoted in *Southern Metropolis Daily*, July 26, 2006.

27. Quoted in *People's Daily*, October 17, 2008.

28. Liu 2009.

29. *People's Daily*, March 20, 2010; Lim 2016; Jia and Li 2014; 2008 广东省产业转移和劳动力转移目标责任考核评价试行办法.

30. *People's Daily*, August 9, 2006; *People's Daily*, November 30, 2006.

31. Zhao 2004.

32. *People's Daily*, November 17, 2008; Lim 2016.

33. *People's Daily*, December 25, 2008.

34. Quoted in *People's Daily*, December 28, 2008.

35. *People's Daily*, December 28, 2008.

36. Quoted in *Southern Metropolis Daily*, August 18, 2009.

37. Bell 1999.

38. Kojima 2000.

39. *Southern Metropolis Daily*, September 24, 2008.

40. *Securities Times*, October 30, 2008.

41. http://school.nseac.com/a/10559/10559021.html, accessed October 28, 2021; Zhu 2009.

42. Lei 2020.

43. *People's Daily*, February 5, 2010.

44. *People's Daily*, March 30, 2010.

45. *People's Daily*, June 30, 2010.

46. Nee and Opper 2012.

47. Wang and Chen 2014.

48. Zhang 2015.

49. Jia and Li 2014.

50. Zeng, Zhou, and Guo 2015.

51. Lim and Horesh 2017; Chen and Dickson 2018.

52. Whittaker et al. 2020.

53. *People's Daily*, August 23, 2013; *People's Daily*, December 20, 2013; *People's Daily*, March 25, 2014.

54. *People's Daily*, August 23, 2013; *People's Daily*, December 20, 2013.

55. *People's Daily*, April 12, 2017.

56. Quoted in *People's Daily*, October 17, 2013.

57. *People's Daily*, March 15, 2015; *People's Daily*, August 11, 2015.

58. Naughton 2016.

59. *People's Daily*, May 22, 2019.

60. Huang and Sharif 2017.

61. Wade 2012.

62. Wang 2020.

63. http://money.hexun.com/2010-05-26/123801451.html, accessed October 31, 2021; https://finance.qq.com/a/20100520/001963.htm, accessed October 31, 2021.

64. http://czt.gd.gov.cn/gkmlpt/content/0/184/post_184143.html#3525, accessed October 31, 2021; https://finance.qq.com/a/20110125/000442.htm, accessed October 31, 2021.

65. http://www.gd.gov.cn/gdywdt/tzdt/content/post_66792.html, accessed October 31, 2021.

66. http://www.mofcom.gov.cn/article/swfg/swfgbl/gfxwj/201304/20130400105884.shtml, accessed October 31, 2021.

67. http://money.hexun.com/2010-05-26/123801451.html, accessed October 31, 2021.

68. http://money.hexun.com/2010-05-26/123801451.html, accessed October 31, 2021.

69. 2008 广东省市厅级党政领导班子和领导干部落实科学发展观评价指标体系及考核评价办法(试行).

70. 2008 广州市区(县级市)局级党政领导班子和领导干部落实科学发展观评价指标体系年度考核评价办法 (试行).

71. http://www.huarong.gov.cn/33816/content_1447386.html, accessed November 4, 2021.

72. https://www2.deloitte.com/tw/tc/pages/tax/articles/newsletter16-02-16.html, accessed November 2, 2021.

73. 2008 高新技术企业认定管理办法; 2016 高新技术企业认定管理办法.

74. 2008 深圳人才引进实施办法; 2010 广州市高层次人才认定评定办法.

75. Swider 2015a; Wang 2020.

76. *Southern Daily*, October 20, 2008.

77. *Southern Daily*, December 1, 2009.

78. *Southern Daily*, November 14, 2010.

79. *Southern Daily*, December 30, 2010.

80. Wang 2020; Friedman 2018.

81. https://zj.zjol.com.cn/news.html?id=1502347, accessed November 3, 2021.

82. http://www.hbsddz.com/a/product/business/gongye.html, accessed October 31, 2021; http://www.xinhuanet.com//politics/2017-04/20/c_1120840352.htm/, accessed November 3, 2021.

83. https://zj.zjol.com.cn/news.html?id=1502347, accessed November 3, 2021.

84. http://www.xinhuanet.com//politics/2017-04/20/c_1120840352.htm, accessed November 3, 2021.

85. https://www.smartcity.team/news/yugangaodawanquidc/, accessed November 3, 2021.

86. A smart city presents a new city pattern that integrates resources in a way that can provide better urban services based on the use of ICTs. Shen et al. 2018.

87. Evans 1995.

88. Slater and Wong 2022.

89. Aspalter 2002; Slater and Wong 2022; Holliday 2000.

90. Slater and Wong 2022.

91. Kim 2009.

92. Slater and Wong 2022.

93. Campbell 2012.

94. Slater and Wong 2022.

95. Holliday 2000.

96. Lindtner 2020.

97. Friedman 2018.

98. Gallagher 2017; Rozelle and Hell 2020.

99. Ringen and Ngok 2017.

100. Block and Somers 2014.

101. Bell 1999.

102. Lamont 2012.

Chapter 4. Obsolete Capital and Labor

1. http://sz.people.com.cn/BIG5/n2/2021/0517/c202846-34728535.html, accessed November 11, 2021; http://tjj.dg.gov.cn/pczl/rkpc7/content/post_3524622.html, accessed November 11, 2021.

2. Loh and Remick 2015.

3. Lee 1995, 1998.

4. Hsiung 1991; Lim 1981; Fernández-Kelly 1983; Ong 2010; Wolf 1992.

5. In contrast to Guangdong, Jilin, Liaoning, and Heilongjiang had the lowest level of gender ratio in 2020. Jilin and Liaoning had more female than male residents. The three provinces of northeast China were once the pride of the country's planned industrial economy but have been seen as China's rust belt since the 1990s. http://www.stats.gov.cn/tjsj/tjgb/rkpcgb/qgrkpcgb/202106/t20210628_1818823.html, accessed November 13, 2021.

6. http://www.jwview.com/jingwei/html/08-29/424535.shtml, accessed November 13, 2021.

7. Few executives of the manufacturers are Taiwanese, but the companies are registered as local resident companies instead of FIEs. As I have mentioned in chapter 3, the Chinese government canceled tax benefits for FIEs. Therefore holders of Taiwanese capital do not see benefits from registering a company as an FIE.

8. Kan 2019.

9. Kostka and Zhang 2018.

10. http://epaper.southcn.com/nfdaily/html/2018-08/10/content_7743706.htm, accessed November 14, 2021.

11. Wedeman 2003.

12. Zhou 2012, 2017.

13. Trevaskes 2006.

14. Van Rooij 2016.

15. https://www.sohu.com/a/239680479_465088, accessed November 14, 2021; https://www.sohu.com/a/339921420_198937, accessed November 14, 2021.

16. I got this information from the executives of the company and did not witness the process.

17. Barak 2012.

18. Liu 2021; 国家安全监管总局《关于进一步深化安全生产行政执法工作的意见》.

19. https://www.mee.gov.cn/gkml/sthjbgw/qt/201805/t20180528_441554.htm, accessed November 14, 2021.

20. Van der Kamp 2021; Trevaskes 2006.

21. Kostka and Zhang 2018.

22. Wu 2019.

23. http://app.www.gov.cn/govdata/gov/201704/15/402974/article.html, accessed November 27, 2021.

24. Lei 2018a; Gallagher 2006, 2017.

25. Deng 2017; Wang 2019.

26. Foxconn is the largest contract electronics manufacturer in the world.

27. Deng 2017.

28. Huawei is a leading global provider of ICT infrastructure and smart devices.

29. Burawoy 1982, 1983; Lee 1995; Ngai and Koo 2015.

30. Li 2015.

31. Li 2015; Pun and Koo 2019.

32. Pun and Koo 2019.

33. Woronov 2011; Ling 2019; Lan 2014.

34. Pun and Koo 2019.

35. Ngai and Koo 2015; Pun and Koo 2019; Smith and Chan 2015. Many government agencies in China, including public security agencies, hire contract-based service workers.

36. Koo 2016; Pun and Koo 2019.

37. Shieh 1989.

38. Pun and Koo 2019.

39. Pun and Koo 2019; Hansen 2013.

40. Evans 1995; Haggard 2018.

41. Bell 1999.

42. Zhou 2012, 2017; Kostka and Zhang 2018; Van der Kamp 2021.

43. Zhang and Ginsburg 2019; Minzner 2011, 2018.

44. Habermas 1996.

45. Zhang and Ginsburg 2019; Zhao 2004; A. Wang 2018.

46. Kostka and Zhang 2018; Ang 2020.

47. Evans 1995, 12.

48. Ang 2020; Wu 2019; Wedeman 2003, 2012.

49. Li 2015; Lee 2007.

50. Zhao 1998.

51. Research also shows growing protests asking for access to public education organized by migrant parents in Zhejiang. Zhu 2021.

52. Bell 1999.

Chapter 5. Robotization

1. Nof 2009, 17.

2. Bell 1999.

3. Grint and Woolgar 1997.

4. Marx 1973, 693–94.

5. National Commission on Technology, Automation, and Economic Progress 1966.

6. http://www.lbjlibrary.net/collections/on-this-day-in-history/august.html, accessed September 7, 2021.

7. Lei 2022.

8. Autor 2015; Autor, Dorn, and Hanson 2015; Acemoglu and Restrepo 2017; Brynjolfsson and McAfee 2014.

9. McClure 2018.

10. Mulas-Granados et al. 2019.

11. Daniel and Hogarth 1990.

12. Mulas-Granados et al. 2019.

13. Katz and Murphy 1992.

14. Adler 1992; Attewell 1992.

15. Goos and Manning 2007; Autor, Levy, and Murnane 2003.

16. Dahlin 2019.

17. Acemoglu and Restrepo 2017; Autor and Salomons 2017.

18. Chen and Naughton 2016.

19. Naughton, Xiao, and Xu 2022.

20. https://www.jonesday.com/en/insights/2008/05/china-high--and-new-technology-enterprises, accessed October 29, 2022.

21. http://www.mofcom.gov.cn/aarticle/bh/200805/20080505534363.html, accessed October 29, 2022.

22. 工业和信息化部《关于推进工业机器人产业发展的指导意见》.

23. Ernst 2018.

24. Butollo and Lüthje 2017.

25. https://china.zjol.com.cn/system/2014/01/17/019816145.shtml, accessed December 3, 2021.

26. 浙经信投资（2013），519号，浙江省经信委关于印发《发展工业设计与"机器换人"专项行动方案》的通知.

27. http://www.budgetofchina.com/show-3538.html, accessed December 4, 2021.

28. Cheng et al. 2019.

29. According to Dieter Ernst (2018), Chinese policy makers have largely neglected employment effects and other labor market issues when designing their industrial policy.

30. Davis 2014.

31. http://www.stats.gov.cn/tjsj/zxfb/201405/t20140512_551585.html, accessed October 30, 2021.

32. Ernst 2018.

33. Huang and Sharif 2017.

34. Cheng et al. 2019.

35. Cheng et al. 2019.

36. Autor 2015.

37. Swider 2015b.

38. "Enterprises above a designated size" refers to industrial enterprises with an annual main business revenue of twenty million yuan or more.

39. Harvey 2003.

40. Sharif and Huang 2019a, 2019b, 2019c; Cheng et al. 2019.

41. Cheng et al. 2019.

42. Lüthje and Butollo 2017.

43. Goos and Manning 2007.

44. Adler 1992.

45. Butollo and Lüthje 2017.

46. Xu and Gui 2019.

47. Autor 2015; Autor, Dorn, and Hanson 2015; Acemoglu and Restrepo 2017; Brynjolfsson and McAfee 2014.

48. Chen, Long, and Qin 2020; Wrenn, Yi, and Zhang 2019.

49. https://www.lincolninst.edu/sites/default/files/pubfiles/sun_wp20ls1.pdf, accessed December 6, 2021.

50. Chen, Long, and Qin 2020.

51. Chen et al. 2016.

52. Chen, Long, and Qin 2020.

53. Chen et al. 2017.

54. Chen, Long, and Qin 2020.

55. Chen et al. 2016.

56. Wu et al. 2020.

57. http://gdii.gd.gov.cn/2015n3261/content/post_924485.html, accessed December 9, 2021.

58. Autor 2015.

59. Sharif and Huang 2019a.

60. Cheng et al. 2019.

61. Goos and Manning 2007.

62. Goos and Manning 2007; Dahlin 2019; Cheng et al. 2019.

63. Mulas-Granados et al. 2019.

64. Cheng et al. 2019; Huang and Sharif 2017; Sharif and Huang 2019a.

65. Chen et al. 2017.

Chapter 6. The Rise of Big Tech

1. Tirole 2017.

2. Kenney and Zysman 2016; Rahman and Thelen 2019.

3. Quoted in *People's Daily*, November 21, 2014.

4. http://www.caict.ac.cn/english/research/whitepapers/202007/P020200728343679920779.pdf, accessed November 2, 2022.

5. Bukht and Heeks 2017.

6. Tang 2020.

7. https://www.markinblog.com/largest-internet-companies/, accessed December 15, 2021.

8. https://www.statista.com/statistics/277483/market-value-of-the-largest-internet-companies-worldwide/, accessed July 24, 2022. Market capitalization refers to the total dollar market value of a company's outstanding shares of stock.

9. Lei 2018a.

10. Tang 2020.

11. Shen 2022; Tang 2020; Hong 2017a, 2017b.

12. http://www.gov.cn/2011lh/content_1825838_4.htm, accessed December 16, 2021.

13. http://www.stats.gov.cn/english/PressRelease/202007/t20200708_1772805.html, accessed December 16, 2021; *People's Daily*, November 21, 2014; *People's Daily*, May 21, 2016.

14. Hong 2017b.

15. Lei 2018a.

16. Shen 2022.

17. Naughton 2020, 29.

18. Su and Flew 2021.

19. Wu 2019.

20. Hsueh 2011, 2016.

21. Lei 2018a; Qiao 2022.

22. Hsueh 2011, 2016; Shen 2022; Tang 2020.

23. https://corpgov.law.harvard.edu/2018/09/09/reporting-obligations-of-variable-interest-entities/, accessed December 17, 2021.

24. Shen 2012.

25. Qiao 2022.

26. Shen 2012.

27. Pearson, Rithmire, and Tsai 2021.

28. http://efaidnbmnnnibpcajpcglclefindmkaj/https://www.mayerbrown.com/-/media /files/news/2012/08/rising-tide/files/alb-china/fileattachment/alb-china.pdf, accessed November 5, 2023; Dong 2011.

29. Zhang 2021a.

30. *People's Daily*, June 7, 2013; *People's Daily*, September 26, 2013.

31. Hu and Kong 2021.

32. Didi's 2021 global prospectus.

33. https://money.163.com/photoview/251H0025/22519.html?from=tj_xytj, accessed January 17, 2022; https://baike.baidu.com/item/1%C2%B74%E6%B2%88%E9%98%B3%E5 %87%BA%E7%A7%9F%E8%BD%A6%E7%BD%A2%E5%B7%A5%E4%BA%8B%E4%B B%B6/16528240, accessed January 17, 2022; https://www.rfa.org/mandarin/yataibaodao /renquanfazhi/yf1-06012016102134.html, accessed January 17, 2022; https://www.hkcd.com /content/2016-01/05/content_978728.html, accessed January 17, 2022.

34. 2016 国务院《关于深化改革推进出租汽车行业健康发展的指导意见》.

35. http://english.www.gov.cn/premier/news/2017/03/16/content_281475597911192 .htm, accessed January 17, 2022.

36. http://www.gov.cn/guowuyuan/2017-04/18/content_5186934.htm, accessed January 17, 2022.

37. 2017 发展改革委等《关于促进分享经济发展的指导性意见》; 2018 发展改革委办公厅等《关于做好引导和规范共享经济健康良性发展有关工作的通知》; 2019 国务院办公厅《关于促进平台经济规范健康发展的指导意见》.

38. http://cdxjj.chengdu.gov.cn/xjjfzw/c002005/2020-06/04/content_e5bf88ab1c7e45f 2b8d0119316b60d5c.shtml, accessed January 21, 2022; http://www.km.gov.cn/c/2019-01-07 /3723042.shtml, accessed January 21, 2022.

39. 2018 发展改革委办公厅等《关于做好引导和规范共享经济健康良性发展有关工作的通知》.

40. 2017 发展改革委等《关于促进分享经济发展的指导性意见》; 2018 发展改革委办公厅等《关于做好引导和规范共享经济健康良性发展有关工作的通知》; 2019 国务院办公厅《关于促进平台经济规范健康发展的指导意见》.

41. http://www.jwview.com/jingwei/html/03-02/137912.shtml, accessed December 16, 2021.

42. http://theory.people.com.cn/n1/2015/1217/c49154-27939669.html, accessed December 16, 2021.

43. Zhang 2021a.

44. Deng and Liu 2017.

45. Zhang 2021a.

46. http://www.aliresearch.com/cn/index/expertOpinion?type=%E8%A7%82%E7 %82%B9&expert=%E5%AE%89%E7%AD%B1%E9%B9%8F, accessed December 16, 2021; http://amcorg.com/zjtdshow.php?id=129, accessed December 16, 2021; https://m.ebrun.com /personage/gaohongbing.html, accessed December 16, 2021.

47. Interview with a tech firm employee who works on government affairs.

48. Tirole 2017; interview with a tech firm employee who works on government affairs.

49. Liu, Yang, and Zheng 2020.

50. He and Ma 2020.

51. http://finance.people.com.cn/n/2015/1102/c1004-27764002.html, accessed November 6, 2022.

52. Liu, Yang, and Zheng 2020.

53. https://www.yicai.com/news/4618566.html, accessed November 6, 2022.

54. Große-Bley and Kostka 2021.

55. Naughton 2020.

56. http://www.xinhuanet.com/techpro/2021-05/17/c_1127454407.htm, accessed November 6, 2022.

57. http://www.gov.cn/guowuyuan/2016-03/17/content_5054901.htm, accessed November 8, 2022.

58. http://www.xinhuanet.com/politics/2018lh/2018-03/22/c_1122575588.htm, accessed November 8, 2022.

59. http://www.rmlt.com.cn/2016/1026/443367.shtml, accessed November 8, 2022.

60. Shen 2018.

61. Naughton 2020; Su and Flew 2021.

62. https://www.cfr.org/china-digital-silk-road/, accessed November 8, 2022.

63. Naughton 2020.

64. https://www.alibabacloud.com/blog/city-brain-now-in-23-cities-in-asia _595479#:~:text=Alibaba%20Cloud's%20ET%20City%20Brain,living%20just%20that%20 much%20better, accessed November 8, 2022.

65. Su and Flew 2021.

66. https://www.alibabacloud.com/global-locations#J_5392902970, accessed November 8, 2022.

67. Scholars had already expressed concerns about the consequences of such a strategy on market competition in the late 1990s and suggested the government enact antitrust laws. *People's Daily*, April 25, 1998.

68. *People's Daily*, February 8, 1994; *People's Daily*, January 22, 1996; *People's Daily*, November 20, 1997.

69. *People's Daily*, February 25, 1999; Zhao 2000.

70. 2021 浙江省发展改革委 省商务厅关于印发《浙江省国内贸易发展"十四五"规划》; *People's Daily*, May 13, 2021.

71. Steinberg, Mukherjee, and Punathambekar 2022, 1047.

72. The term *network effect* refers to any situation in which the value of a product, service, or platform depends on the number of buyers, sellers, or users who leverage it. https://online.hbs .edu/blog/post/what-are-network-effects, accessed December 17, 2021.

73. For instance, market surveys show that as of 2020, 89, 69, and and 63 percent of mobile users in China installed Tencent's social networking app WeChat, Alibaba's online payment app Alipay, and Alibaba's online shopping app Taobao, respectively. https://www.jiguang.cn/reports /513, accessed December 18, 2021.

74. Jia, Nieborg, and Poell 2022.

75. Plantin et al. 2016.

76. https://new.qq.com/omn/20210522/20210522A056G400.html, accessed December 18, 2021.

77. Jia, Nieborg, and Poell 2022.

78. Tirole 2017.

79. Wright et al. 2021, 2.

80. Tsai 2015.

81. Haley and Haley 2013, 24.

82. Lin and Milhaupt 2013.

83. http://en.sasac.gov.cn/2021/08/03/c_7528.htm, accessed November 9, 2022.

84. Milhaupt and Zheng 2015.

85. Haley and Haley 2013.

86. Melnik 2019.

87. Liu, Yang, and Zheng 2020.

88. Bell 1999, 174, 42.

89. He and Ma 2020.

90. https://www.investopedia.com/articles/investing/111114/top-five-alibaba-shareholders.asp, accessed January 24, 2022.

91. Shen 2022; Tang 2020.

92. Plantin et al. 2016; Shen 2022.

93. Zuboff 2019, 352. *Instrumentation* refers to "the ubiquitous connected material architecture of sensate computation that renders, interprets, and actuates human experience." *Instrumentalization* denotes the social relations that transform us into "means to others' market ends."

94. Zuboff 2019, ix.

95. https://j.eastday.com/p/1642154020034798, accessed November 11, 2022.

96. Griesbach et al. 2019; Lei 2021; Rosenblat and Stark 2016.

97. Wood et al. 2019; Yao 2020.

98. Schor et al. 2020.

99. Deng and Liu 2017.

100. Zuboff 2019.

101. Mann 1984, 188, 189.

102. Plantin et al. 2016, 306–7.

103. https://www.tencent.com/zh-cn/business/health-code.html, accessed November 12, 2022.

104. According to Oxford Languages, an *influencer* is "a person with the ability to influence potential buyers of a product or service by promoting or recommending the items on social media."

105. 国家税务总局《网络直播行业税收检查指引》.

106. Whittaker et al. 2020.

107. Perez 2010.

108. Perez 2002.

109. Miller 2022.

110. Srnicek 2017.

111. Miller 2022.

112. Wu 2019.

113. Shen 2022.

114. Wade 2014; Soskice 2022b.

115. Soskice 2022a, 2022b; Rahman and Thelen 2019.

116. Vallas and Schor 2020.

117. Zuboff 2019, 443.

118. Zuboff 2019, 326.

Chapter 7. From Factories to Platforms

1. http://www.gov.cn/guowuyuan/2016-03/17/content_5054901.htm, accessed November 8, 2022.

2. http://www.xinhuanet.com/politics/2018lh/2018-03/22/c_1122575588.htm, accessed November 8, 2022.

3. http://en.people.cn/n3/2022/0211/c90000-9956524.html, accessed November 22, 2022.

4. The tier system refers to an unofficial hierarchical classification of cities in China according to indicators like population size, GDP, and administrative hierarchy. First-tier cities represent the most economically developed areas with the most affluent residents.

5. https://www.csis.org/features/how-inequality-undermining-chinas-prosperity, accessed November 22, 2022; Rozelle et al. 2020.

6. https://www.ilo.org/global/topics/wages/minimum-wages/beneficiaries/WCMS _436492/lang--en/index.htm, accessed November 16, 2022.

7. https://www.csis.org/features/how-inequality-undermining-chinas-prosperity, accessed November 22, 2022; Rozelle et al. 2020.

8. Schor et al. 2020.

9. https://n2.sinaimg.cn/finance/a2d36afe/20210827/FuJian1.pdf, accessed December 21, 2021.

10. https://n2.sinaimg.cn/finance/a2d36afe/20210827/FuJian1.pdf, accessed December 21, 2021.

11. http://www.ceweekly.cn/2020/0910/312331.shtml, accessed December 21, 2021; https:// fengniao.ele.me/?spm=a2f95.17632747.0.0.501a32bd60WEjs, accessed December 21, 2021; http://www.d-long.com/eWebEditor/uploadfile/2020080116534843821408.pdf, accessed December 21, 2021.

12. http://www.gov.cn/zhengce/2019-07/12/content_5408550.htm, accessed December 21, 2021; http://www.gov.cn/zhengce/content/2020-07/31/content_5531613.htm, accessed December 21, 2021.

13. http://www.xinhuanet.com/2020-03/02/c_1125652147.htm, accessed December 21, 2021.

14. https://mp.ofweek.com/hr/a245693828916, accessed December 21, 2021.

15. Tirole 2017.

16. Meituan IPO prospectus.

17. https://www.reuters.com/article/us-meituan-ipo/tencent-backed-meituan-raises-4-2 -billion-in-ipo-priced-near-range-top-sources-idUSKCN1LT05D, accessed December 21, 2021.

18. Responding to the Chinese state's crackdown on the tech sector, in November 2022, Tencent announced it would distribute most of its 159.4 billion Hong Kong dollar (US$20.3 billion) stake in Meituan to shareholders as a dividend. Currently, Tencent owns a 17 percent stake in Meituan, but it will hold a less than 2 percent stake in Meituan after the distribution.

https://asia.nikkei.com/Business/China-tech/Tencent-cuts-stake-in-food-delivery-app -Meituan-as-Q3-sales-drop, accessed November 18, 2022.

19. Meituan's annual reports in 2018–20.

20. Meituan IPO prospectus.

21. Meituan IPO prospectus; https://pianshen.com/article/23471354884/, accessed December 21, 2021; https://tech.meituan.com/2020/02/20/meituan-delivery-operations -research.html, accessed December 21, 2021; https://new.qq.com/omn/20210609/20210609 A042XO00.html, accessed December 21, 2021.

22. Meituan IPO prospectus.

23. http://www.weihai.gov.cn/art/2019/7/27/art_60663_2107219.html, accessed December 21, 2021; https://www.sohu.com/a/479960164_571524, accessed December 21, 2021.

24. Meituan IPO prospectus; http://it.people.com.cn/n1/2018/1205/c1009-30445225 .html, accessed December 21, 2021.

25. Ele.me's 2017 corporate social responsibility report.

26. https://new.qq.com/omn/20191202/20191202A0DYWS00.html, accessed December 22, 2021; https://www.thepaper.cn/newsDetail_forward_2092003, accessed December 22, 2021; Ele.me's 2017 corporate social responsibility report.

27. http://www.xinhuanet.com/tech/2020-10/17/c_1126623270.htm, accessed December 22, 2021.

28. https://finance.sina.cn/stock/ssgs/2021-07-02/detail-ikqcfnca4578164.d.html, accessed December 22, 2021.

29. http://www.sheitc.sh.gov.cn/zxxx/20200930/54ff46581ce74a11a384590ac76804df .html, accessed December 22, 2021.

30. A reserve price means a minimum amount that a seller would be willing to accept from a buyer.

31. https://www.sohu.com/a/433243826_118622, accessed December 23, 2021.

32. http://www.199it.com/archives/823693.html, accessed December 23, 2021; http://www .199it.com/archives/1039390.html, accessed December 23, 2021; https://s3plus.meituan.net /v1/mss_531b5a3906864f438395a28a5baec011/official-website/ed3e2bb5-13dd-46ca-93ba -30808a1ca852, accessed December 23, 2021.

33. Friedman 2018.

34. http://www.199it.com/archives/823693.html, accessed December 23, 2021; http://www .199it.com/archives/1039390.html, accessed December 23, 2021; https://s3plus.meituan.net /v1/mss_531b5a3906864f438395a28a5baec011/official-website/ed3e2bb5-13dd-46ca-93ba -30808a1ca852, accessed December 23, 2021.

35. https://www.dsb.cn/147326.html, accessed December 24, 2021.

36. Meituan 2020 annual report; https://www.linkedin.com/company/%E9%A5%BF% E4%BA%86%E4%B9%88/?originalSubdomain=cn, accessed December 26, 2021.

37. Vallas 2017.

38. Meituan IPO prospectus, 220.

39. Hyman 1987, 52.

40. *Standard employment* refers to a work arrangement between an employer and employee that is both full-time and permanent. *Nonstandard forms of employment* is an umbrella term for different employment arrangements that deviate from standard employment. They include tem-

porary employment, part-time and on-call work, temporary agency work and other multiparty employment relationships, disguised employment, and dependent self-employment. https://www.ilo.org/global/topics/non-standard-employment/lang--en/index.htm, retrievaccessed December 25, 2021.

41. Kalleberg 2009.

42. Meituan IPO prospectus.

43. In some situations, Meituan and Ele.me's delivery partners employ part-time SPCs or have SPCs as individual contractors.

44. Schor et al. 2020.

45. https://www.sohu.com/a/456078451_349247, accessed December 25, 2021.

46. http://www.stats.gov.cn/tjsj/zxfb/202005/t20200515_1745763.html, accessed December 25, 2021.

47. Lei 2021.

48. Hecht 1998, 11.

49. Griesbach et al. 2019; Goods, Veen, and Barratt 2019; Moore and Joyce 2019; Rosenblat and Stark 2016; Rosenblat 2018; Wood et al. 2019.

50. Rosenblat and Stark 2016.

51. Roppo 2009.

52. Collier, Dubal, and Carter 2017.

53. Pollert and Charlwood 2009.

54. Rosenblat and Stark 2016.

55. Huang 2019.

56. Collier, Dubal, and Carter 2017; Liu and Friedman 2021; Lei 2021.

57. Burawoy 1982; Deterding 2019.

58. A labor contract can be formed in an oral or written format. Sixty percent of my service platform interviewees signed a contract with their employers. Even among interviewees who signed a contract, one-third of them did not receive a copy of their contract.

59. Thompson and van Den Broek 2010; Hochschild 1983.

60. Burawoy 1982; Deterding 2019.

61. Veen, Barratt, and Goods 2019.

62. Kalleberg 2009.

63. Stewart and Stanford 2017.

64. Liu and Friedman 2021.

65. Webster 2016.

66. Rosenblat and Stark 2016.

67. Gallagher 2017.

68. Tassinari and Maccarrone 2017, 2020.

69. Rosenblat and Stark 2016.

70. This is similar to Rosenblat and Stark's (2016) study of how Uber constrains its drivers' freedom to reject a request.

71. Atzeni 2009; Fantasia 1988.

72. Vallas 2017; Veen, Barratt, and Goods 2019.

73. Rosenblat and Stark 2016.

74. Polletta and Kretschmer 2013; Tassinari and Maccarrone 2020.

75. Vallas and Schor 2020.

76. Burawoy 1985; Collier, Dubal, and Carter 2017.

77. Bell 1999.

Chapter 8. Coding Elites

1. Meituan IPO prospectus.

2. Zhou and Yue 2020.

3. https://www.shyp.gov.cn/shypq/yqyw-wb-rsjzl-rsxx/20210322/376800.html, accessed January 2, 2022.

4. Bell 1999, 344.

5. Zuboff 2019.

6. Burrell and Fourcade 2021, 1.

7. Zuboff 2019.

8. Dorschel 2022.

9. http://www.jwview.com/jingwei/html/03-02/137912.shtml, accessed December 16, 2021.

10. Pun and Koo 2019; Hansen 2013.

11. Zuboff 2019.

12. Cha 2010.

13. Li 2019; Lin 2020.

14. Tencent 2020 annual report.

15. Most female software engineers work on front-end development and quality assurance. Front-end engineers work on the development of the graphical user interface. Quality-assurance engineers oversee the testing and quality management of software.

16. Friedman, Laurison, and Miles 2015; Laurison and Friedman 2016.

17. Zhou and Yue 2019.

18. Burawoy 1985.

19. Wu and Li 2018.

20. Wang, Li, and Deng 2017.

21. Cui, Huang, and Wang 2020.

22. Lamont 2019; Cooper 2014.

23. According to the National Bureau of Statistics, first-tier cities refer to Beijing, Shanghai, Guangzhou, and Shenzhen; second-tier cities refer to Tianjin, Shijiazhuang, Taiyuan, Hohhot, Shenyang, Dalian, Changchun, Harbin, Nanjing, Hangzhou, Ningbo, Hefei, Fuzhou, Xiamen, Nanchang, Jinan, Qingdao, Zhengzhou, Wuhan, Changsha, Nanning, Haikou, Chongqing, Chengdu, Guiyang, Kunming, Xi'an, Lanzhou, Xining, Yinchuan, and Urumqi. http://ligboy .cc/xinwen/2021-11/15/content_5650938.htm, accessed January 2, 2022.

24. Lei 2018b.

25. Laurison and Friedman 2016.

26. Zhou and Yue 2019.

27. Lupu and Empson 2015; Reid 2015.

28. Bell 1999.

29. Lareau 2015.

30. Friedman, Laurison, and Miles 2015; Friedman, O'Brien, and Laurison 2017; Laurison and Friedman 2016; Cooper 2014; Hamilton and Armstrong 2021.

31. Lamont 2019; Cooper 2014.

32. Blossfeld and Buchholz 2009.

33. Brinton and Oh 2019.

34. Schwarz 2018.

35. Streib 2015.

36. Zhou, Murphy, and Tao 2014.

37. Murphy 2020.

38. Zhou 2019.

39. Blossfeld and Buchholz 2009.

40. Zhou, Murphy, and Tao 2014.

41. Lupu and Empson 2015.

42. Zhou and Yue 2019.

43. Thayer and Ko 2017.

44. Friedman, Laurison, and Miles 2015; Laurison and Friedman 2016.

45. Blossfeld and Buchholz 2009.

46. Zhao et al. 2017.

47. Zhou 2019.

48. Cui 2020. A *bride price* is money paid by a groom or his family to the woman or the family of the woman he will be married to.

49. The term *dingke* comes from the English term *DINK*, meaning "dual income, no kids."

50. Cooper 2014.

51. Reid 2015; Costas et al. 2018.

52. Wang, Li, and Deng 2017.

53. He 2019.

54. Reid 2015.

55. Burawoy 2008.

56. Pun 2020.

57. Burrell and Fourcade 2021.

58. Bell 1999.

59. Friedman, Laurison, and Miles 2015; Friedman, O'Brien, and Laurison 2017; Laurison and Friedman 2016.

60. Lin 2020; Li 2019.

61. Hirschman 1970; Scott 2008; Reid 2015.

62. Van Jaarsveld 2004.

63. Burrell and Fourcade 2021, 1.

Chapter 9. Rewiring Techno-State Capitalism

1. Lei 2018a.

2. Tang 2020; Shen 2022.

3. Woo 1999.

4. http://english.www.gov.cn/premier/news/2017/03/16/content_281475597911192.htm, accessed January 17, 2022.

5. http://www.gov.cn/guowuyuan/2017-04/18/content_5186934.htm, accessed January 17, 2022.

6. *People's Daily*, July 31, 2013.

7. *People's Daily*, August 9, 2019; *People's Daily*, October 1, 2020.

8. Pearson, Rithmire, and Tsai 2021.

9. 2016 国务院办公厅《互联网金融风险专项整治工作实施方案》.

10. *People's Daily*, December 10, 2016; *People's Daily*, April 27, 2017; *People's Daily*, November 22, 2017.

11. *People's Daily*, January 15, 2019.

12. Lei 2018b.

13. Tirole 2017.

14. http://www.gov.cn/zhengce/zhengceku/2018-12/31/content_5444678.htm, accessed January 17, 2022.

15. Taylor and Li 2007.

16. 2018 中华全国总工会办公厅《推进货车司机等群体入会工作方案》的通知.

17. Lei 2018a.

18. Article 2 of the National Security Law.

19. Article 25 of the National Security Law.

20. Article 37 of the Cybersecurity Law.

21. *People's Daily*, July 10, 2018.

22. *People's Daily*, March 5, 2017.

23. *People's Daily*, October 29, 2018.

24. *People's Daily*, June 29, 2020.

25. Zhang 2021a.

26. https://www.pymnts.com/news/ipo/2020/jack-ma-summoned-for-questioning-about-ant-ipo/, accessed January 22, 2022.

27. http://www.sse.com.cn/disclosure/announcement/general/c/c_20201103_5253315.shtml, accessed January 22, 2022.

28. Zhang 2021a; Pearson, Rithmire, and Tsai 2021.

29. 2020 Ant Group global prospectus.

30. 2020 银保监会《关于加强小额贷款公司监督管理的通知》; http://stock.finance.sina.com.cn/stock/go.php/vReport_Show/kind/search/rptid/653652904601/index.phtml, accessed January 23, 2022.

31. http://epaper.bjnews.com.cn/html/2019-07/17/content_760063.htm?div=0, accessed January 26, 2022; 2020 中国银保监会 中国人民银行关于《网络小额贷款业务管理暂行办法 (征求意见稿)》.

32. 2020 国务院《国务院关于实施金融控股公司准入管理的决定》; 2020 中国人民银行《金融控股公司监督管理试行办法》.

33. http://www.gov.cn/xinwen/2020zccfh/28/sjbb.htm#hygqmd, accessed January 23, 2022; Menkhoff and Tolksdorf 2000.

34. http://www.qstheory.cn/dukan/hqwg/2018-10/12/c_1123550892.htm, accessed January 23, 2022.

35. https://interconnected.blog/jack-ma-bund-finance-summit-speech/, accessed January 23, 2022.

36. http://www.gov.cn/guowuyuan/2020-10/31/content_5556394.htm, accessed January 24, 2022.

37. *People's Daily*, December 11, 2020; *People's Daily*, December 19, 2020.

38. https://interconnected.blog/jack-ma-bund-finance-summit-speech/, accessed January 23, 2022.

39. http://www.gov.cn/guowuyuan/2017-11/08/content_5238161.htm, accessed January 26, 2022.

40. http://www.xinhuanet.com//politics/2017-07/15/c_1121324747.htm, accessed January 26, 2022.

41. https://www.chinabankingnews.com/2018/07/04/members-chinas-financial-stability-development-committee-revealed/, accessed January 26, 2022.

42. https://www.forbes.com/sites/russellflannery/2021/10/07/hna-evergrande-woes-underscore-how-china-paradigm-for-business-success-is-being-swept-away/?sh=3fd4535394c8, accessed January 26, 2022.

43. 2019 中国人民银行《2019 年规章制定工作计划》; http://www.gov.cn/xinwen/2019-11/26/5455673/files/8d8e5b3e9ffd40cc934f585c1fc1de8a.pdf, accessed January 26, 2022.

44. 2019 国家互联网信息办公室关于《个人信息出境安全评估办法(征求意见稿)》.

45. Zhang 2021b.

46. Lei 2018a.

47. http://www.npc.gov.cn/npc/c30834/202106/2ecfc806d9f1419ebb03921ae72f217a.shtml, accessed January 27, 2022.

48. Lei 2018a.

49. http://dangjian.people.com.cn/n1/2018/0326/c117092-29889441.html, accessed January 27, 2022.

50. Pearson, Rithmire, and Tsai 2021.

51. https://2017-2021.state.gov/the-clean-network/index.html, accessed January 27, 2022.

52. https://2017-2021.state.gov/the-clean-network/index.html, accessed January 27, 2022.

53. *People's Daily*, August 16, 2020.

54. https://spartz.house.gov/media/press-releases/spartz-sherman-and-barr-introduce-bill-accelerate-holding-foreign-companies, accessed January 27, 2022.

55. https://www.federalregister.gov/documents/2021/04/05/2021-06292/holding-foreign-companies-accountable-act-disclosure, accessed January 27, 2022.

56. https://www.marketwatch.com/story/senate-could-vote-on-bill-that-could-delist-chinese-companies-from-us-stock-exchanges-2020-05-19, accessed January 27, 2022.

57. https://www.financialnews.com.cn/jg/dt/202012/t20201204_207015.html, accessed January 27, 2022.

58. https://www.chinanews.com.cn/cj/2020/12-19/9366581.shtml, accessed January 27, 2022.

59. Lei 2018a.

60. Zhou 2017.

61. Zhang 2021b.

62. Zhang 2021a.

63. https://news.stcn.com/sd/202103/t20210313_2907892.html, accessed January 29, 2022.

64. https://www.samr.gov.cn/fldj/tzgg/xzcf/202012/t20201214_324334.html, accessed January 29, 2022.

65. 2021 Baidu prospectus.

66. http://www.legaldaily.com.cn/index/content/2021-12/31/content_8651443.htm, accessed January 29, 2022; https://www.samr.gov.cn/xw/zj/202107/t20210707_332396.html, accessed January 30, 2022.

67. https://www.sohu.com/a/510623473_114988, accessed January 30, 2022.

68. https://www.scmp.com/tech/policy/article/3140625/chinas-antitrust-regulator-blocks-tencents-us53-billion-merger-game, accessed January 30, 2022.

69. https://www.wsj.com/articles/tencent-slashes-jd-com-stake-with-16-billion-dividend-to-shareholders-11640235329, accessed November 24, 2022.

70. https://asia.nikkei.com/Business/China-tech/Tencent-cuts-stake-in-food-delivery-app-Meituan-as-Q3-sales-drop, accessed November 18, 2022.

71. https://www.samr.gov.cn/xw/zj/202104/t20210410_327702.html, accessed January 30, 2022.

72. http://www.cac.gov.cn/2021-04/13/c_1619894556494868.htm, accessed January 31, 2022.

73. http://www.xhby.net/index/202104/t20210415_7048254.shtml, accessed January 31, 2022.

74. https://www.samr.gov.cn/xw/zj/202110/t20211008_335364.html, accessed January 30, 2022.

75. https://www.chinalawtranslate.com/en/anti-monopoly-law-2022/, accessed November 24, 2022.

76. https://www.globaltimes.cn/page/202211/1280195.shtml#:~:text=The%20draft%20revision%20of%20China's,data%2C%20algorithms%20and%20platform%20rules, accessed November 24, 2022.

77. 2021《国务院反垄断委员会关于平台经济领域的反垄断指南》; 2021《网络交易监督管理办法》; 2021《关于禁止网络不正当竞争行为规定(公开征求意见稿)的说明》; 2021《互联网平台分类分级指南(征求意见稿)》; 2021《互联网平台落实主体责任指南(征求意见稿)》; 2021《关于落实网络餐饮平台责任,切实维护外卖送餐员权益的指导意见》.

78. http://www.gov.cn/guowuyuan/2021-11/18/content_5651790.htm, accessed January 30, 2022.

79. http://www.pbc.gov.cn/goutongjiaoliu/113456/113469/4153479/index.html, accessed January 30, 2022.

80. http://www.pbc.gov.cn/goutongjiaoliu/113456/113469/4229432/index.html, accessed January 31, 2022.

81. http://www.pbc.gov.cn/goutongjiaoliu/113456/113469/4241211/index.html, accessed January 31, 2022.

82. 2021《支付机构客户备付金存管办法》; 2021《非银行支付机构条例(征求意见稿)》.

83. https://www.sohu.com/a/350987753_161795, accessed January 31, 2022.

84. Lei 2018a.

85. http://www.cac.gov.cn/2021-05/20/c_1623091083320667.htm, accessed January 31, 2022; http://www.cac.gov.cn/2021-06/11/c_1624994586637626.htm, accessed January 31, 2022; http://www.cac.gov.cn/2021-04/30/c_1621370239178608.htm, accessed January 31, 2022; http://www.cac.gov.cn/2020-11/17/c_1607178245870454.htm, accessed January 31, 2022.

86. http://www.cac.gov.cn/2021-07/02/c_1626811521011934.htm, accessed January 31, 2022; http://www.cac.gov.cn/2021-07/04/c_1627016782176163.htm, accessed January 31, 2022; http://www.cac.gov.cn/2021-07/09/c_1627415870012872.htm, accessed January 31, 2022.

87. https://technode.com/2022/06/13/chinese-ride-hailing-giant-didi-delisted-from-nyse/, accessed November 24, 2022.

88. https://technode.com/2022/07/22/a-timeline-of-didi-and-its-year-long-cybersecurity -investigation/, accessed November 24, 2022.

89. https://www.nytimes.com/2022/07/21/business/china-fines-didi.html?_ga=2 .154742456.182377638.1669298923-1798091788.1572594259, accessed November 24, 2022.

90. http://www.cac.gov.cn/2021-07/05/c_1627071328950274.htm, accessed January 31, 2022.

91. https://www.thepaper.cn/newsDetail_forward_13128799, accessed January 31, 2022; https://www.bloomberg.com/news/articles/2021-06-22/china-trucking-startup-raises-1-6 -billion-in-u-s-ipo, accessed January 31, 2022.

92. http://www.xinhuanet.com/legal/2021-07/05/c_1127623122.htm, accessed January 31, 2022.

93. 2022《网络安全审查办法》.

94. 2019 互联网信息办公室关于《网络生态治理规定(征求意见稿)》.

95. 2021《关于加强互联网信息服务算法综合治理的指导意见》.

96. 2021《互联网信息服务算法推荐管理规定》.

97. 2021《关于维护新就业形态劳动者劳动保障权益的指导意见》; 2021《关于落实网络餐饮平台责任切实维护外卖送餐员权益的指导意见》.

98. http://www.xinhuanet.com/politics/leaders/2021-03/15/c_1127214324.htm, accessed February 2, 2022.

99. https://www.court.gov.cn/zixun-xiangqing-319151.html, accessed February 2, 2022.

100. Nathan 2003; Qiaoan and Teets 2020.

101. As mentioned earlier, 996 refers to working from 9 a.m. to 9 p.m. for six days a week.

102. http://en.qstheory.cn/2022-01/18/c_699346.htm, accessed February 2, 2022.

103. http://en.qstheory.cn/2022-01/18/c_699346.htm, accessed February 2, 2022.

104. http://en.qstheory.cn/2022-01/18/c_699346.htm, accessed February 2, 2022.

105. https://www.scmp.com/news/china/politics/article/3155367/chinas-path-common -prosperity-puts-pressure-private-enterprise, accessed February 3, 2022.

106. http://en.qstheory.cn/2022-01/18/c_699346.htm, accessed February 2, 2022.

107. As I wrote in chapter 7, many software engineers gave up on the idea of marriage and reproduction because of various kinds of stress in work and life.

108. http://en.qstheory.cn/2022-01/18/c_699025.htm, accessed February 2, 2022.

109. https://www.12371.cn/2021/12/10/ARTI1639136209677195.shtml, accessed February 2, 2022.

110. http://www.qstheory.cn/dukan/qs/2022-01/15/c_1128261632.htm, accessed February 2, 2022.

111. http://www.qstheory.cn/dukan/qs/2022-01/15/c_1128261632.htm, accessed February 2, 2022. Technologically advanced little giant enterprises refers to small and medium-sized enterprises that are refined, specialized, and novel.

112. https://sme.miit.gov.cn/xwzx/jdxw/art/2021/art_e6ff258b305b4dcc9548066198cac 521.html, accessed February 2, 2022; https://www.sohu.com/a/519276597_120348080, accessed February 2, 2022.

113. Article 2 of the National Security Law.

114. Zhang 2021a; Zhou 2012, 2017.

115. Zhou 2012.

Chapter 10. Conclusion

1. Zuboff 1988, 2019.

2. Whittaker et al. 2020.

3. Hecht 1998, 16–17.

4. Brubaker 1984.

5. Zhang 2021a.

6. Zhao 2004.

7. Zhou 2017.

8. Brubaker 1984.

9. Friedman 2018.

10. Greenhalgh 2020.

11. Burawoy 1982.

12. Naughton, Xiao, and Xu 2022.

13. Xie 2016.

14. Weber 2020.

15. Naughton 2020, 29.

16. Slater and Wong 2022.

17. Wade 2014; Soskice 2022b; Schrank and Whitford 2009.

18. Srnicek 2017; Vallas 2017; Zuboff 2019; Vallas and Schor 2020.

19. Whittaker et al. 2020.

20. Hung 2022.

21. Wade 2014.

22. Haggard 2018.

23. Chibber 2002, 2003.

24. Zhou 2007; Jing, Cui, and Li 2015.

25. Evans 1995.

26. Evans 1995.

27. Zhang and Ginsburg 2019.

28. Zhang 2021a.

29. Evans and Heller 2015.

30. Friedman 2018.

31. Zhou, Guo, and Liu 2018.

32. Haggard 2018.

33. http://www.qstheory.cn/dukan/qs/2021-10/15/c_1127959365.htm, accessed February 19, 2022.

34. Bell 1999; Zuboff 2019; Srnicek 2017; Burrell and Fourcade 2021.

35. Habermas 1996.

36. Zuboff 2019; Rahman and Thelen 2019.

37. https://www.eurasiareview.com/05072022-china-opens-its-first-political-party-school
-in-africa/, accessed July 30, 2022.

38. Zuboff 2019, 394, 398.

39. Bell 1999.

40. Castells 2010a.

41. Burrell and Fourcade 2021, 1.

42. Castells 2010b, 166.

43. Harvey 2003, 3.

44. Jasanoff 2015.

45. Fourcade and Gordon 2020; Zuboff 2019; Harari 2016, 2017, 2018.

46. Hecht 1998, 16–17.

47. Habermas 1971, 1984, 1991, 1996.

48. Fraser 1990.

49. Sen 2000.

50. Heller and Rao 2015.

51. Hecht 1998, 30.

52. Habermas 1971, 1984.

53. Hirschman 1970.

54. Rusbult and Lowery 1985.

REFERENCES

Acemoglu, Daron, and Pascual Restrepo. 2017. "Robots and Jobs: Evidence from US Labor Markets." NBER Working Paper No. w23285. https://ssrn.com/abstract=2941263.

Adler, Paul S. 1992. Introduction to *Technology and the Future of Work*, edited by Paul S. Adler, 3–14. New York: Oxford University Press.

Aguiar de Medeiros, Carlos, and Nicholas Trebat. 2017. "Inequality and Income Distribution in Global Value Chains." *Journal of Economic Issues* 51 (2): 401–8.

Ampuja, Marko, and Juha Koivisto. 2014. "From 'Post-Industrial' to 'Network Society' and Beyond: The Political Conjunctures and Current Crisis of Information Society Theory." *TripleC* 12 (2): 447–63.

Ang, Yuen Yuen. 2016. *How China Escaped the Poverty Trap*. Ithaca, NY: Cornell University Press.

———. 2018. "Domestic Flying Geese: Industrial Transfer and Delayed Policy Diffusion in China." *China Quarterly* 234:420–43.

———. 2020. *China's Gilded Age: The Paradox of Economic Boom and Vast Corruption*. Cambridge: Cambridge University Press.

Aspalter, Christian. 2002. *Democratization and Welfare State Development in Taiwan*. New York: Routledge.

Attewell, Paul. 1992. "Skill and Occupational Changes in US Manufacturing." In *Technology and the Future of Work*, edited by Paul S. Adler, 46–88. New York: Oxford University Press.

Atzeni, Maurizio. 2009. "Searching for Injustice and Finding Solidarity? A Contribution to Mobilisation Theory." *Industrial Relations Journal* 40 (1): 5–16.

Autor, David H. 2015. "Why Are There Still So Many Jobs? The History and Future of Workplace Automation." *Journal of Economic Perspectives* 29 (3): 3–30.

Autor, David H., David Dorn, and Gordon H. Hanson. 2015. "Untangling Trade and Technology: Evidence from Local Labour Markets." *Economic Journal* 125 (584): 621–46.

Autor, David H., Frank Levy, and Richard J. Murnane. 2003. "The Skill Content of Recent Technological Change: An Empirical Exploration." *Quarterly Journal of Economics* 118 (4): 1279–333.

Autor, David, and Anna Salomons. 2017. "Does Productivity Growth Threaten Employment?" Paper presented at the Investment and Growth in Advanced Economies conference, Sintra, Portugal, June 26–28.

Baccini, Leonardo, and Stephen Weymouth. 2021. "Gone for Good: Deindustrialization, White Voter Backlash, and US Presidential Voting." *American Political Science Review* 115 (2): 550–67.

Barak, Aharon. 2012. *Proportionality: Constitutional Rights and Their Limitations*. Cambridge: Cambridge University Press.

Barbrook, Richard, and Andy Cameron. 1996. "The Californian Ideology." *Science as Culture* 6 (1): 44–72.

Bell, Daniel. 1999. *The Coming of Post-Industrial Society: A Venture in Social Forecasting*. New York: Basic Books.

Bell, Daniel, and Stephen Richards Graubard. 1997. "Preface to the MIT Press Edition." In *Toward the Year 2000: Work in Progress*, edited by Daniel Bell and Stephen Richards Graubard, ix–xix. Cambridge, MA: MIT Press.

Binbin, Wang, and Li Xiaoyan. 2017. "Big Data, Platform Economy and Market Competition: A Preliminary Construction of Plan-Oriented Market Economy System in the Information Era." *World Review of Political Economy* 8 (2): 138–61.

Block, Fred. 2008. "Swimming against the Current: The Rise of a Hidden Developmental State in the United States." *Politics and Society* 36 (2): 169–206.

Block, Fred, and Margaret R. Somers. 2014. *The Power of Market Fundamentalism: Karl Polanyi's Critique*. Cambridge, MA: Harvard University Press.

Blossfeld, Hans-Peter, and Sandra Buchholz. 2009. "Increasing Resource Inequality among Families in Modern Societies: The Mechanisms of Growing Educational Homogamy, Changes in the Division of Work in the Family and the Decline of the Male Breadwinner Model." *Journal of Comparative Family Studies* 40 (4): 603–15.

Brick, Howard. 1992. "Optimism of the Mind: Imagining Postindustrial Society in the 1960s and 1970s." *American Quarterly* 44 (3): 348–80.

Brinton, Mary C., and Eunsil Oh. 2019. "Babies, Work, or Both? Highly Educated Women's Employment and Fertility in East Asia." *American Journal of Sociology* 125 (1): 105–40.

Brownsword, Roger. 2019. *Law, Technology and Society: Re-Imagining the Regulatory Environment*. New York: Routledge.

Broz, J. Lawrence, Jeffry Frieden, and Stephen Weymouth. 2021. "Populism in Place: The Economic Geography of the Globalization Backlash." *International Organization* 75 (2): 464–94.

Brubaker, Rogers. 1984. *The Limits of Rationality: An Essay on the Social and Moral Thought of Max Weber*. London: Allen and Unwin.

Brynjolfsson, Erik, and Andrew McAfee. 2014. *The Second Machine Age: Work, Progress, and Prosperity in a Time of Brilliant Technologies*. New York: W. W. Norton and Company.

Bukht, Rumana, and Richard Heeks. 2017. "Defining, Conceptualising and Measuring the Digital Economy." Development Informatics Working Paper. https://ssrn.com/abstract=3431732.

Burawoy, Michael. 1982. *Manufacturing Consent: Changes in the Labor Process under Monopoly Capitalism*. Chicago: University of Chicago Press.

———. 1983. "Between the Labor Process and the State: The Changing Face of Factory Regimes under Advanced Capitalism." *American Sociological Review* 48 (5): 587–605.

———. 1985. *The Politics of Production: Factory Regimes under Capitalism and Socialism*. London: Verso.

———. 2008. "The Public Turn: From Labor Process to Labor Movement." *Work and Occupations* 35 (4): 371–87.

Burrell, Jenna, and Marion Fourcade. 2021. "The Society of Algorithms." *Annual Review of Sociology* 47 (1): 213–37.

Butollo, Florian, and Boy Lüthje. 2017. "'Made in China 2025': Intelligent Manufacturing and Work." In *The New Digital Workplace: How New Technologies Revolutionise Work*, edited by Kendra Briken, Shiona Chillas, Martin Krzywdzinski, and Abigail Marks, 42–61. London: Palgrave.

Caldentey, Esteban Pérez. 2008. "The Concept and Evolution of the Developmental State." *International Journal of Political Economy* 37 (3): 27–53.

Campbell, Joel. 2012. "Building an IT Economy: South Korean Science and Technology Policy." *Issues in Technolog Innovation* 19:1–9.

Cao, Guangzhong, Changchun Feng, and Ran Tao. 2008. "Local 'Land Finance' in China's Urban Expansion: Challenges and Solutions." *China and World Economy* 16 (2): 19–30.

Castells, Manuel. 2010a. *The Information Age: Economy, Society and Culture, Vol. 1, The Rise of the Network Society*. Malden, MA: Wiley-Blackwell.

———. 2010b. *The Information Age: Economy, Society and Culture, Vol. 3, End of Millennium*. Malden, MA: Wiley-Blackwell.

Cha, Youngjoo. 2010. "Reinforcing Separate Spheres: The Effect of Spousal Overwork on Men's and Women's Employment in Dual-Earner Households." *American Sociological Review* 75 (2): 303–29.

Chambers, David Wade. 1984. *Red and Expert: A Case Study of Chinese Science in the Cultural Revolution*. Victoria, Australia: Deakin University.

Chan, Jenny, Ngai Pun, and Mark Selden. 2013. "The Politics of Global Production: Apple, Foxconn and China's New Working Class." *New Technology, Work and Employment* 28 (2): 100–115.

Chang, Ssu-ming. 2012. *Research on Government Performance Management System*. Taipei: Research, Development and Evaluation Commission.

Chen, Chih-jou Jay. 2009. "Growing Social Unrest in China: Rising Social Discontents and Popular Protests." In *Socialist China, Capitalist China*, edited by Guoguang Wu and Helen Lansdowne, 24–42. London: Routledge.

Chen, Chunhua, and Bruce Dickson. 2018. "Coping with Growth in China: Comparing Models of Development in Guangdong and Chongqing." *Journal of Chinese Governance* 3 (2): 197–222.

Chen, Kaiji, Patrick Higgins, Daniel F. Waggoner, and Tao Zha. 2016. "Impacts of Monetary Stimulus on Credit Allocation and the Macroeconomy: Evidence from China." National Bureau of Economic Research. https://doi.org/10.3386/w22650.

Chen, Kunqiu, Hualou Long, and Chenrong Qin. 2020. "The Impacts of Capital Deepening on Urban Housing Prices: Empirical Evidence from 285 Prefecture-Level or above Cities in China." *Habitat International* 99:102–73.

Chen, Ling, and Barry Naughton. 2016. "An Institutionalized Policy-Making Mechanism: China's Return to Techno-Industrial Policy." *Research Policy* 45 (10): 2138–52.

Chen, Ting, Laura Liu, Wei Xiong, and Li-An Zhou. 2017. "Real Estate Boom and Misallocation of Capital in China." Working Paper, Princeton University. https://economics.princeton.edu/working-papers/real-estate-boom-and-misallocation-of-capital-in-china/.

Cheng, Hong, Ruixue Jia, Dandan Li, and Hongbin Li. 2019. "The Rise of Robots in China." *Journal of Economic Perspectives* 33 (2): 71–88.

Chibber, Vivek. 2002. "Bureaucratic Rationality and the Developmental State." *American Journal of Sociology* 107 (4): 951–89.

———. 2003. *Locked in Place: State-Building and Late Industrialization in India*. Princeton, NJ: Princeton University Press.

Chuang, Julia. 2020. *Beneath the China Boom: Labor, Citizenship, and the Making of a Rural Land Market*. Berkeley: University of California Press.

Collier, Ruth, Veena Dubal, and Christopher Carter. 2017. "The Regulation of Labor Platforms: The Politics of the Uber Economy." Kauffman Foundation. https://brie.berkeley.edu/sites /default/files/reg-of-labor-platforms.pdf.

Cooper, Marianne. 2014. *Cut Adrift: Families in Insecure Times*. Berkeley: University of California Press.

Costas, Jana, Susanne Ekman, Laura Empson, Dan Kärreman, and Sara Louise Muhr. 2018. "Working Time Regimes: A Panel Discussion on Continuing Problems." *German Journal of Human Resource Management* 32 (3–4): 271–82.

Cui, Can. 2020. "Housing Career Disparities in Urban China: A Comparison between Skilled Migrants and Locals in Nanjing." *Urban Studies* 57 (3): 546–62.

Cui, Can, Youqin Huang, and Fenglong Wang. 2020. "A Relay Race: Intergenerational Transmission of Housing Inequality in Urban China." *Housing Studies* 35 (6): 1088–109.

Dahlin, Eric. 2019. "Are Robots Stealing Our Jobs?" *Socius* 5:1–14.

Dai, Yu-Xiao, and Su-Tong Hao. 2018. "Transcending the Opposition between Techno-Utopianism and Techno-Dystopianism." *Technology in Society* 53:9–13.

Daniel, W. W., and Terence Hogarth. 1990. "Worker Support for Technical Change." *New Technology, Work and Employment* 5 (2): 85–93.

Davis, Deborah S. 2014. "Demographic Challenges for a Rising China." *Daedalus* 143 (2): 26–38.

Davis, Kevin E., Benedict Kingsbury, and Sally Engle Merry. 2012. "Introduction: Global Governance by Indicators." In *Governance by Indicators: Global Power through Quantification and Rankings*, edited by Kevin E. Davis, Angelina Fisher, Benedict Kingsbury, and Sally Engle Merry, 3–28. New York: Oxford University Press.

Deng, Jian-bang. 2017. "A Place-Bound Factory: Changing Labor Regimes in Taiwanese Manufacturers to Inland China." *Taiwanese Sociology* 33:63–112.

Deng, Jinting, and Pinxin Liu. 2017. "Consultative Authoritarianism: The Drafting of China's Internet Security Law and E-Commerce Law." *Journal of Contemporary China* 26 (107): 679–95.

Deng, Xiaoping. 1993. *Selected Works of Deng Xiaoping (Vol. 3)*. Beijing: People's Publishing House.

Deterding, Sebastian. 2019. "Gamification in Management: Between Choice Architecture and Humanistic Design." *Journal of Management Inquiry* 28 (2): 131–36.

Dickson, Bruce J. 2003. "Whom Does the Party Represent? From 'Three Revolutionary Classes' to 'Three Represents.'" *American Asian Review* 21 (1): 1–24.

Dong, Huijuan. 2011. "Reconsidering the First Antitrust Case in China." *Hebei Law Science* 1:23–30.

Dorschel, Robert. 2022. "Reconsidering Digital Labour: Bringing Tech Workers into the Debate." *New Technology, Work and Employment*, 1–20.

Duff, A. S. 1998. "Daniel Bell's Theory of the Information Society." *Journal of Information Science* 24 (6): 373–93.

Edgerton, David E. H. 2007. "The Contradictions of Techno-Nationalism and Techno-Globalism: A Historical Perspective." *New Global Studies* 1 (1): 1–31.

Edin, Maria. 2003. "State Capacity and Local Agent Control in China: CCP Cadre Management from a Township Perspective." *China Quarterly* 173:35–52.

Ernst, Dieter. 2018. "Advanced Manufacturing and China's Future for Jobs." In *Confronting Dystopia: The New Technological Revolution and the Future of Work*, edited by Eva Paus, 181–206. Ithaca, NY: Cornell University Press.

Evans, Peter. 1995. *Embedded Autonomy: States and Industrial Transformation*. Princeton, NJ: Princeton University Press.

Evans, Peter, and Patrick Heller. 2015. "Human Development, State Transformation, and the Politics of the Developmental State." In *The Oxford Handbook of Transformations of the State*, edited by Stephan Leibfried, Evelyne Huber, Matthew Lange, Jonah D. Levy, and John D. Stephens, 691–713. Oxford: Oxford University Press.

Fan, Ziying, and Guanghua Wan. 2017. "The Fiscal Risk of Local Government Revenue in the People's Republic of China." In *Central and Local Government Relations in Asia*, edited by Naoyuki Yoshino and Peter J. Morgan, 223–49. Northampton, MA: Edward Elgar Publishing.

Fantasia, Rick. 1988. *Cultures of Solidarity: Consciousness, Action, and Contemporary American Workers*. Berkeley: University of California Press.

Fernández-Kelly, María Patricia. 1983. *For We Are Sold, I and My People: Women and Industry in Mexico's Frontier*. Albany: SUNY Press.

Fourcade, Marion, and Jeffrey Gordon. 2020. "Learning Like a State: Statecraft in the Digital Age." *Journal of Law and Political Economy* 1 (1): 78–108.

Fraser, Nancy. 1990. "Rethinking the Public Sphere: A Contribution to the Critique of Actually Existing Democracy." *Social Text* 25–26:56–80.

Friedman, Eli. 2018. "Just-in-Time Urbanization? Managing Migration, Citizenship, and Schooling in the Chinese City." *Critical Sociology* 44 (3): 503–18.

Friedman, Sam, Daniel Laurison, and Andrew Miles. 2015. "Breaking the 'Class' Ceiling? Social Mobility into Britain's Elite Occupations." *Sociological Review* 63 (2): 259–89.

Friedman, Sam, Dave O'Brien, and Daniel Laurison. 2017. " 'Like Skydiving without a Parachute': How Class Origin Shapes Occupational Trajectories in British Acting." *Sociology* 51 (5): 992–1010.

Gallagher, Mary E. 2005. *Contagious Capitalism: Globalization and the Politics of Labor in China*. Princeton, NJ: Princeton University Press.

———. 2006. "Mobilizing the Law in China: 'Informed Disenchantment' and the Development of Legal Consciousness." *Law and Society Review* 40 (4): 783–816.

———. 2017. *Authoritarian Legality in China: Law, Workers, and the State*. New York: Cambridge University Press.

———. 2020. "Can China Achieve Inclusive Urbanization?" In *Fateful Decisions: Choices That Will Shape China's Future*, edited by Thomas Fingar and Jean C. Oi, 180–99. Stanford, CA: Stanford University Press.

Goods, Caleb, Alex Veen, and Tom Barratt. 2019. "'Is Your Gig Any Good?' Analysing Job Quality in the Australian Platform-Based Food-Delivery Sector." *Journal of Industrial Relations* 61 (4): 502–27.

Goos, Maarten, and Alan Manning. 2007. "Lousy and Lovely Jobs: The Rising Polarization of Work in Britain." *Review of Economics and Statistics* 89 (1): 118–33.

Greenhalgh, Susan. 2008. *Just One Child: Science and Policy in Deng's China*. Berkeley: University of California Press.

———. 2020. "Introduction: Governing through Science: The Anthropology of Science and Technology in Contemporary China." In *Can Science and Technology Save China?*, edited by Susan Greenhalgh and Li Zhang, 1–24. Ithaca, NY: Cornell University Press.

Griesbach, Kathleen, Adam Reich, Luke Elliott-Negri, and Ruth Milkman. 2019. "Algorithmic Control in Platform Food Delivery Work." *Socius* 5:1–13.

Grint, Keith, and Steve Woolgar. 1997. *The Machine at Work: Technology, Work, and Organization*. Malden, MA: Polity.

Große-Bley, Jelena, and Genia Kostka. 2021. "Big Data Dreams and Reality in Shenzhen: An Investigation of Smart City Implementation in China." *Big Data and Society* 8 (2): 1–14.

Habermas, Jürgen. 1971. "Technology and Science as Ideology." In *Toward a Rational Society: Student Protest, Science, and Politics*, 81–122. Boston: Beacon Press.

———. 1984. *The Theory of Communicative Action*. Boston: Beacon Press.

———. 1991. *The Structural Transformation of the Public Sphere: An Inquiry into a Category of Bourgeois Society*. Cambridge, MA: MIT Press.

———. 1996. *Between Facts and Norms: Contributions to a Discourse Theory of Law and Democracy*. Cambridge, MA: MIT Press.

Haggard, Stephan. 2018. *Developmental States*. New York: Cambridge University Press.

Haley, Usha C. V., and George T. Haley. 2013. *Subsidies to Chinese Industry: State Capitalism, Business Strategy, and Trade Policy*. New York: Oxford University Press.

Halpern, Nina P. 1989. "Scientific Decision Making: The Organization of Expert Advice in Post-Mao China." In *Science and Technology in Post-Mao China*, edited by Denis Fred Simon and Merle Goldman, 167–74. Cambridge, MA: Harvard University Press.

Hamilton, Laura T., and Elizabeth A. Armstrong. 2021. "Parents, Partners, and Professions: Reproduction and Mobility in a Cohort of College Women." *American Journal of Sociology* 127 (1): 102–51.

Hansen, Mette Halskov. 2013. "Learning Individualism: Hesse, Confucius, and Pep-Rallies in a Chinese Rural High School." *China Quarterly* 213:60–77.

Hao, Shouyi, and Qingfeng Cao. 2019. "The Primary Stage of Post-Industrialization and China's Economic Transformation in the New Era." *Economic Perspectives* 9:26–38.

Harari, Yuval Noah. 2016. *Homo Deus: A Brief History of Tomorrow*. New York: Random House.

———. 2017. "Dataism Is Our New God." *New Perspectives Quarterly* 34 (2): 36–43.

———. 2018. "Why Technology Favors Tyranny." *Atlantic Monthly*. https://www.theatlantic.com/magazine/archive/2018/10/yuval-noah-harari-technology-tyranny/568330/.

Harvey, David. 2003. "The Fetish of Technology: Causes and Consequences." *Macalester International* 13 (1): 3–30.

———. 2014. *Seventeen Contradictions and the End of Capitalism*. New York: Oxford University Press.

Hay, Colin. 1999. "Crisis and the Structural Transformation of the State: Interrogating the Process of Change." *British Journal of Politics and International Relations* 1 (3): 317–44.

He, Alex Jingwei, and Liang Ma. 2020. "Corporate Policy Entrepreneurship and Cross-Boundary Strategies: How a Private Corporation Champions Mobile Healthcare Payment Innovation in China." *Public Administration and Development* 40 (1): 76–86.

He, Shenjing. 2019. "Three Waves of State-Led Gentrification in China." *Tijdschrift voor economische en sociale geografie* 110 (1): 26–34.

He, Zhuoma. 2018. "Recalling the Spring of Science in 1978." *Bulletin of the Chinese Academy of Sciences* 33 (4): 409–15.

Hecht, Gabrielle. 1998. *The Radiance of France: Nuclear Power and National Identity after World War II*. Cambridge, MA: MIT Press.

Heller, Patrick, and Vijayendra Rao. 2015. "Deliberation and Development." In *Deliberation and Development: Rethinking the Role of Voice and Collective Action in Unequal Societies*, edited by Patrick Heller and Vijayendra Rao, 1–26. Washington, DC: World Bank Publications.

Henshel, Richard L. 1982. "Sociology and Social Forecasting." *Annual Review of Sociology* 8 (1): 57–79.

Hildebrandt, Mireille. 2015. *Smart Technologies and the End(s) of Law: Novel Entanglements of Law and Technology*. Cheltenham, UK: Edward Elgar Publishing.

Hirschman, Albert O. 1970. *Exit, Voice, and Loyalty: Responses to Decline in Firms, Organizations, and States*. Cambridge, MA: Harvard University Press.

Hochschild, Arlie. 1983. *The Managed Heart*. Berkeley: University of California Press.

Holbig, Heike. 2009. "Remaking the CCP's Ideology: Determinants, Progress, and Limits under Hu Jintao." *Journal of Current Chinese Affairs* 3:35–61.

Holliday, Ian. 2000. "Productivist Welfare Capitalism: Social Policy in East Asia." *Political Studies* 48 (4): 706–23.

Hong, Yu. 2017a. *Networking China: The Digital Transformation of the Chinese Economy*. Urbana: University of Illinois Press.

———. 2017b. "Pivot to Internet Plus: Molding China's Digital Economy for Economic Restructuring?" *International Journal of Communication* 11:1486–506.

Horkheimer, Max, and Theodor W. Adorno. 1979. *Dialectic of Enlightenment*. London: Verso.

Howell, Jude, and Jane Duckett. 2018. "Reassessing the Hu-Wen Era: A Golden Age or Lost Decade for Social Policy in China?" *China Quarterly* 237:1–14.

Hsing, You-tien. 2010. *The Great Urban Transformation: Politics of Land and Property in China*. Oxford: Oxford University Press.

Hsiung, Ping-chun. 1991. "Class, Gender, and the Satellite Factory System in Taiwan." PhD diss., University of California at Los Angeles.

Hsueh, Roselyn. 2011. *China's Regulatory State*. Ithaca, NY: Cornell University Press.

———. 2016. "State Capitalism, Chinese-Style: Strategic Value of Sectors, Sectoral Characteristics, and Globalization." *Governance* 29 (1): 85–102.

Hu, Angang. 2017. "China Entering Post-Industrial Era." *Journal of Beijing Jiaotong University (Social Science Edition)* 16 (1): 1–16.

Hu, Jintao. 2006. "Implementing the Scientific Outlook on Development." *Qiushi* 1:9.

Hu, Xiaobo, and Fanbin Kong. 2021. "Policy Innovation of Local Officials in China: The Administrative Choice." *Journal of Chinese Political Science* 26 (4): 695–721.

Huang, Junyao. 2014. *Government Performance Evaluation, Public Participation and Bureaucratic Autonomy: Hangzhou's Practice to Control Bureaucracy*. Beijing: China Social Sciences Press.

Huang, Ray. 1997. *China: A Macro History*. Armonk, NY: Routledge.

Huang, Yasheng. 2008. *Capitalism with Chinese Characteristics: Entrepreneurship and the State*. New York: Cambridge University Press.

Huang, Yi. 2019. "Monopoly and Anti-Monopoly in China Today." *American Journal of Economics and Sociology* 78 (5): 1101–34.

Huang, Yu, and Naubahar Sharif. 2017. "From 'Labour Dividend' to 'Robot Dividend': Technological Change and Workers' Power in South China." *Agrarian South: Journal of Political Economy* 6 (1): 53–78.

Hung, Ho-fung. 2022. *Clash of Empires: From "Chimerica" to the "New Cold War."* New York: Cambridge University Press.

Hyman, Richard. 1987. "Strategy or Structure? Capital, Labour and Control." *Work, Employment and Society* 1 (1): 25–55.

Jasanoff, Sheila. 2015. "Future Imperfect: Science, Technology, and the Imaginations of Modernity." In *Dreamscapes of Modernity: Sociotechnical Imaginaries and the Fabrication of Power*, edited by Sheila Jasanoff and Sang-Hyun Kim, 1–33. Chicago: University of Chicago Press.

Jasanoff, Sheila, and Sang-Hyun Kim. 2009. "Containing the Atom: Sociotechnical Imaginaries and Nuclear Power in the United States and Korea." *Minerva* 47 (2): 119–46.

Ji, Li, and Wei Zhang. 2020. "Fiscal Incentives and Sustainable Urbanization: Evidence from China." *Sustainability* 12 (1): 1–12.

Jia, Lianrui, David B. Nieborg, and Thomas Poell. 2022. "On Super Apps and App Stores: Digital Media Logics in China's App Economy." *Media, Culture and Society* 44 (8): 1437–53.

Jia, Weili, and Puliang Li. 2014. "The Dilemma and Countermeasures of Undertaking the Upgrading of Local Industries in the 'Dual Transfer' Strategy." *Economic Reform* 1:63–67.

Jiang, Zemin. 2006. *Selected Works of Jiang Zemin (Vol. 1)*. Beijing: People's Publishing House.

———. 2009. *On the Development of China's Information Technology Industry*. Boston: Academic Press.

Jing, Yijia, Yangyang Cui, and Danyao Li. 2015. "The Politics of Performance Measurement in China." *Policy and Society* 34 (1): 49–61.

Kalberg, Stephen. 1980. "Max Weber's Types of Rationality: Cornerstones for the Analysis of Rationalization Processes in History." *American Journal of Sociology* 85 (5): 1145–79.

Kalleberg, Arne L. 2009. "Precarious Work, Insecure Workers: Employment Relations in Transition." *American Sociological Review* 74 (1): 1–22.

Kan, Karita. 2019. "Accumulation without Dispossession? Land Commodification and Rent Extraction in Peri-Urban China." *International Journal of Urban and Regional Research* 43 (4): 633–48.

Katz, Lawrence F., and Kevin M. Murphy. 1992. "Changes in Relative Wages, 1963–1987: Supply and Demand Factors." *Quarterly Journal of Economics* 107 (1): 35–78.

Kenney, Martin, and John Zysman. 2016. "The Rise of the Platform Economy." *Issues in Science and Technology* 32 (3): 61–69.

Kim, Ho-Yeon. 2009. "The Making of a Science Town: The Case of Daedeok, Korea." *Journal of the Economic Geographical Society of Korea* 12 (1): 83–95.

Kojima, Kiyoshi. 2000. "The 'Flying Geese' Model of Asian Economic Development: Origin, Theoretical Extensions, and Regional Policy Implications." *Journal of Asian Economics* 11 (4): 375–401.

Koo, Anita. 2016. "Expansion of Vocational Education in Neoliberal China: Hope and Despair among Rural Youth." *Journal of Education Policy* 31 (1): 46–59.

Kostka, Genia. 2019. "China's Social Credit Systems and Public Opinion: Explaining High Levels of Approval." *New Media and Society* 21 (7): 1565–93.

Kostka, Genia, and Chunman Zhang. 2018. "Tightening the Grip: Environmental Governance under Xi Jinping." *Environmental Politics* 27 (5): 769–81.

Kurunmäki, Liisa, and Peter Miller. 2006. "Modernising Government: The Calculating Self, Hybridisation and Performance Measurement." *Financial Accountability and Management* 22 (1): 87–106.

Kwok, D.W.Y. 1965. *Scientism in Chinese Thought, 1900–1950.* New Haven, CT: Yale University Press.

Lamont, Michèle. 2012. "Toward a Comparative Sociology of Valuation and Evaluation." *Annual Review of Sociology* 38 (1): 201–21.

———. 2019. "From 'Having' to 'Being': Self-Worth and the Current Crisis of American Society." *British Journal of Sociology* 70 (3): 660–707.

Lan, Lü. 2009. "The Value of the Use of Biotechnology: Public Views in China and Europe." *Public Understanding of Science* 18 (4): 481–92.

Lan, Pei-chia. 2014. "Segmented Incorporation: The Second Generation of Rural Migrants in Shanghai." *China Quarterly* 217:243–65.

Lareau, Annette. 2015. "Cultural Knowledge and Social Inequality." *American Sociological Review* 80 (1): 1–27.

Laurison, Daniel, and Sam Friedman. 2016. "The Class Pay Gap in Higher Professional and Managerial Occupations." *American Sociological Review* 81 (4): 668–95.

Lee, Ching Kwan. 1995. "Engendering the Worlds of Labor: Women Workers, Labor Markets, and Production Politics in the South China Economic Miracle." *American Sociological Review* 60 (3): 378–97.

———. 1998. *Gender and the South China Miracle: Two Worlds of Factory Women.* Berkeley: University of California Press.

———. 2007. *Against the Law: Labor Protests in China's Rustbelt and Sunbelt.* Berkeley: University of California Press.

Lee, Yong-Shik. 2017. "General Theory of Law and Development." *Cornell International Law Journal* 50:415–71.

Lei, Ya-Wen. 2018a. *The Contentious Public Sphere: Law, Media, and Authoritarian Rule in China.* Princeton, NJ: Princeton University Press.

———. 2018b. "Social Protest under Hard Authoritarianism." *China Leadership Monitor* 58 (4): 1–9.

———. 2020. "Revisiting China's Social Volcano: Attitudes toward Inequality and Political Trust in China." *Socius* 6:1–21.

———. 2021. "Delivering Solidarity: Platform Architecture and Collective Contention in China's Platform Economy." *American Sociological Review* 86 (2): 279–309.

———. 2022. "Upgrading China through Automation: Manufacturers, Workers and the Techno-Developmental State." *Work, Employment and Society* 36 (6): 1078–96.

Lessig, Lawrence. 1999. *Code and Other Laws of Cyberspace*. New York: Basic Books.

Li, Guoping, and Yongchao Zhao. 2008. "A Summary of the Gradient Development Theory." *Human Geography* 1:61–65.

Li, Ju. 2015. "From 'Master' to 'Loser': Changing Working-Class Cultural Identity in Contemporary China." *International Labor and Working Class History* 88:190–208.

Li, Kwok Sing. 1995. *A Glossary of Political Terms of the People's Republic of China*. Hong Kong: Chinese University Press.

Li, Peilin, and Yan Cui. 2020. "The Changes in Social Stratum Structure from 2008 to 2019 in China and the Economic and Social Impact." *Jiangsu Social Sciences* 4:51–60.

Li, Xiaotian. 2019. "The 996.ICU Movement in China: Changing Employment Relations and Labour Agency in the Tech Industry." *Made in China Journal*. https://madeinchinajournal.com/2019/06/18/the-996-icu-movement-in-china-changing-employment-relations-and-labour-agency-in-the-tech-industry/.

Lilkov, Dimitar. 2020. "Made in China: Tackling Digital Authoritarianism." *European View* 19 (1): 110.

Lim, Kean Fan. 2016. "'Emptying the Cage, Changing the Birds': State Rescaling, Path-Dependency and the Politics of Economic Restructuring in Post-Crisis Guangdong." *New Political Economy* 21 (4): 1–22.

Lim, Kean Fan, and Niv Horesh. 2017. "The Chongqing vs. Guangdong Developmental 'Models' in Post-Mao China: Regional and Historical Perspectives on the Dynamics of Socioeconomic Change." *Journal of the Asia Pacific Economy* 22 (3): 372–95.

Lim, Linda. 1981. "Women's Work in Multinational Electronics Factories." In *Women in Technological Change in Developing Countries*, edited by Roslyn Dauber and Melinda Cain, 181–90. Boulder, CO: Westview Press.

Lin, Kevin. 2020. "Tech Worker Organizing in China: A New Model for Workers Battling a Repressive State." *New Labor Forum* 29 (2): 52–59.

Lin, Li-Wen, and Curtis J. Milhaupt. 2013. "We Are the (National) Champions: Understanding the Mechanisms of State Capitalism in China." *Stanford Law Review* 65 (4): 697–759.

Lindtner, Silvia M. 2020. *Prototype Nation: China and the Contested Promise of Innovation*. Princeton, NJ: Princeton University Press.

Ling, Minhua. 2019. *The Inconvenient Generation: Migrant Youth Coming of Age on Shanghai's Edge*. Stanford, CA: Stanford University Press.

Liu, Adam Y., Jean C. Oi, and Yi Zhang. 2022. "China's Local Government Debt: The Grand Bargain." *China Journal* 87 (1): 40–71.

Liu, Chuxuan, and Eli Friedman. 2021. "Resistance under the Radar: Organization of Work and Collective Action in China's Food Delivery Industry." *China Journal* 86 (1): 68–89.

Liu, Li. 2009. "The 'Double Transfer' Strategy of Regional Industrial Structure Synergy: Evidence from Guangdong Province." *Industrial Economics* 8:62–67.

Liu, Quan. 2021. "A New Interpretation of the Constitutional Basis for Proportionality Principle in China." *Political Science and Law* 4:68–78.

Liu, Te, Xuemin Yang, and Yueping Zheng. 2020. "Understanding the Evolution of Public-Private Partnerships in Chinese E-Government: Four Stages of Development." *Asia Pacific Journal of Public Administration* 42 (4): 222–47.

Liu, Zaixin. 1986. "Theoretical Understanding of Several Issues in the Study of Economic Development Strategy in Central China." *Academic Journal of Zhongzhou* 5:16–19.

Loh, Charis, and Elizabeth J. Remick. 2015. "China's Skewed Sex Ratio and the One-Child Policy." *China Quarterly* 222:295–319.

Lupu, Ioana, and Laura Empson. 2015. "Illusion and Overwork: Playing the Game in the Accounting Field." *Accounting, Auditing and Accountability Journal* 28 (8): 1310–40.

Lüthje, Boy, and Florian Butollo. 2017. "Why the Foxconn Model Does Not Die: Production Networks and Labour Relations in the IT Industry in South China." *Globalizations* 14 (2): 216–31.

Mann, Michael. 1984. "The Autonomous Power of the State: Its Origins, Mechanisms and Results." *European Journal of Sociology* 25 (2): 185–213.

Marcuse, Herbert. 1964. *One-Dimensional Man: Studies in the Ideology of Advanced Industrial Society*. Boston: Beacon Press.

Marx, Karl. 1973. *Grundrisse: Foundations of the Critique of Political Economy*. New York: Vintage Books.

Mau, Steffen. 2019. *The Metric Society: On the Quantification of the Social*. Medford, MA: Polity Press.

McClure, Paul K. 2018. "'You're Fired,' Says the Robot: The Rise of Automation in the Workplace, Technophobes, and Fears of Unemployment." *Social Science Computer Review* 36 (2): 139–56.

Mejia, Robert. 2015. "A Pressure Chamber of Innovation: Google Fiber and Flexible Capital." *Communication and Critical/Cultural Studies* 12 (3): 289–308.

Melnik, Jeffrey. 2019. "China's 'National Champions' Alibaba, Tencent, and Huawei." *Education about Asia* 24 (2): 28–33.

Menkhoff, Lukas, and Norbert Tolksdorf. 2000. *Financial Market Drift: Decoupling of the Financial Sector from the Real Economy?* Berlin: Springer Science and Business Media.

Milhaupt, Curtis J., and Wentong Zheng. 2015. "Beyond Ownership: State Capitalism and the Chinese Firm." *Georgetown Law Journal* 103 (3): 665–722.

Miller, Chris. 2022. *Chip War: The Fight for the World's Most Critical Technology*. New York: Simon and Schuster.

Minzner, Carl. 2011. "China's Turn against Law." *American Journal of Comparative Law* 59 (4): 935–84.

———. 2018. *End of an Era: How China's Authoritarian Revival Is Undermining Its Rise*. New York: Oxford University Press.

Moore, Phoebe V., and Simon Joyce. 2019. "Black Box or Hidden Abode? The Expansion and Exposure of Platform Work Managerialism." *Review of International Political Economy*, 1–23.

Mulas-Granados, Carlos, Richard Varghese, Judith Wallenstein, Vizhdan Boranova, and Alice deChalendar. 2019. "Automation, Skills and the Future of Work: What Do Workers Think?" IMF Working Papers. https://www.imf.org/en/Publications/WP/Issues/2019/12/20/Automation-Skills-and-the-Future-of-Work-What-do-Workers-Think-48791.

Murphy, Rachel. 2020. *The Children of China's Great Migration*. New York: Cambridge University Press.

Nathan, Andrew J. 2003. "China's Changing of the Guard: Authoritarian Resilience." *Journal of Democracy* 14 (1): 6–17.

National Commission on Technology, Automation, and Economic Progress. 1966. *Automation and Economic Progress*. Edited by Howard Rothmann Bowen and Garth L. Mangum. Englewood Cliffs, NJ: Prentice Hall.

Naughton, Barry. 2016. "Supply-Side Structural Reform: Policy-Makers Look for a Way Out." *China Leadership Monitor* 49 (1): 1–13.

———. 2020. "Chinese Industrial Policy and the Digital Silk Road: The Case of Alibaba in Malaysia." *Asia Policy* 27 (1): 23–39.

Naughton, Barry, Siwen Xiao, and Yaosheng Xu. 2022. "The Trajectory of China's Industrial Policies." Paper presented at China's Industrial Policy: Sectors and Resources conference, San Diego, CA, September 30–October 2.

Nee, Victor, and Sonja Opper. 2012. *Capitalism from Below: Markets and Institutional Change in China*. Cambridge, MA: Harvard University Press.

Ngai, Pun, and Anita Koo. 2015. "A 'World-Class' (Labor) Camp/us: Foxconn and China's New Generation of Labor Migrants." *Positions* 23 (3): 411–35.

Nof, Shimon Y. 2009. "Automation: What It Means to Us around the World." In *Springer Handbook of Automation*, edited by Shimon Y. Nof, 13–52. New York: Springer Science and Business Media.

O'Mara, Margaret. 2021. "Assessing Daniel Bell in the Age of Big Tech." In *Defining the Age: Daniel Bell, His Time and Ours*, edited by Paul Starr and Julian E. Zelizer, 195–215. New York: Columbia University Press.

Oi, Jean C. 1992. "Fiscal Reform and the Economic Foundations of Local State Corporatism in China." *World Politics* 45 (1): 99–126.

———. 1999. "Two Decades of Rural Reform in China: An Overview and Assessment." *China Quarterly* 159:616–28.

Ong, Aihwa. 2010. *Spirits of Resistance and Capitalist Discipline: Factory Women in Malaysia*. Albany: SUNY Press.

Pearson, Margaret, Meg Rithmire, and Kellee S. Tsai. 2021. "Party-State Capitalism in China." *Current History* 120 (827): 207–13.

Perez, Carlota. 2002. *Technological Revolutions and Financial Capital: The Dynamics of Bubbles and Golden Ages*. Cheltenham, UK: Edward Elgar Publishing.

———. 2010. "Technological Revolutions and Techno-Economic Paradigms." *Cambridge Journal of Economics* 34 (1): 185–202.

Plantin, Jean-Christophe, Carl Lagoze, Paul N. Edwards, and Christian Sandvig. 2016. "Infrastructure Studies Meet Platform Studies in the Age of Google and Facebook." *New Media and Society* 20 (1): 293–310.

Pollert, Anna, and Andy Charlwood. 2009. "The Vulnerable Worker in Britain and Problems at Work." *Work, Employment and Society* 23 (2): 343–62.

Polletta, Francesca, and Kelsy Kretschmer. 2013. "Free Spaces." In *The Wiley-Blackwell Encyclopedia of Social and Political Movements*, edited by David A. Snow, Donatella della Porta, Bert Klandermans, and Doug McAdam. Malden, MA: Wiley-Blackwell. https://onlinelibrary.wiley.com/doi/abs/10.1002/9780470674871.wbespm094.

Porter, Theodore M. 1995. *Trust in Numbers*. Princeton, NJ: Princeton University Press.

Power, Michael. 2004. "Counting, Control and Calculation: Reflections on Measuring and Management." *Human Relations* 57 (6): 765–83.

Pun, Ngai. 2020. "The New Chinese Working Class in Struggle." *Dialectical Anthropology* 44 (4): 319–29.

Pun, Ngai, and Anita Koo. 2019. "Double Contradiction of Schooling: Class Reproduction and Working-Class Agency at Vocational Schools in China." *British Journal of Sociology of Education* 40 (1): 50–64.

Qiao, Shitong. 2022. "Finance without Law: The Case of China." *Harvard International Law Journal.* https://ssrn.com/abstract=4179436.

Qiaoan, Runya, and Jessica C. Teets. 2020. "Responsive Authoritarianism in China: Review of Responsiveness in Xi and Hu Administrations." *Journal of Chinese Political Science* 25 (1): 139–53.

Rahman, K. Sabeel, and Kathleen Thelen. 2019. "The Rise of the Platform Business Model and the Transformation of Twenty-First-Century Capitalism." *Politics and Society* 47 (2): 177–204.

Reid, Erin. 2015. "Embracing, Passing, Revealing, and the Ideal Worker Image: How People Navigate Expected and Experienced Professional Identities." *Organization Science* 26 (4): 997–1017.

Ringen, Stein, and Kinglun Ngok. 2017. "What Kind of Welfare State Is Emerging in China?" In *Towards Universal Health Care in Emerging Economies*, edited by Icheong Yi, 213–37. London: Palgrave Macmillan.

Roppo, Vincenzo. 2009. "From Consumer Contracts to Asymmetric Contracts: A Trend in European Contract Law?" *European Review of Contract Law* 5 (3): 304–49.

Rosenblat, Alex. 2018. *Uberland: How Algorithms Are Rewriting the Rules of Work.* Berkeley: University of California Press.

Rosenblat, Alex, and Luke Stark. 2016. "Algorithmic Labor and Information Asymmetries: A Case Study of Uber's Drivers." *International Journal of Communication* 10:3758–84.

Rowthorn, Robert, and Ramana Ramaswamy. 1997. *Deindustrialization: Its Causes and Implications.* Vol. 10. Washington, DC: International Monetary Fund.

Rozelle, Scott, and Natalie Hell. 2020. *Invisible China: How the Urban-Rural Divide Threatens China's Rise.* Chicago: University of Chicago Press.

Rozelle, Scott, Yiran Xia, Dimitris Friesen, Bronson Vanderjack, and Nourya Cohen. 2020. "Moving beyond Lewis: Employment and Wage Trends in China's High- and Low-Skilled Industries and the Emergence of an Era of Polarization." *Comparative Economic Studies* 62 (4): 555–89.

Rusbult, Caryl, and David Lowery. 1985. "When Bureaucrats Get the Blues: Responses to Dissatisfaction among Federal Employees." *Journal of Applied Social Psychology* 15 (1): 80–103.

Schiller, Dan. 1999. *Digital Capitalism: Networking the Global Market System.* Cambridge, MA: MIT Press.

Schor, Juliet B. 2020. *After the Gig: How the Sharing Economy Got Hijacked and How to Win It Back.* Berkeley: University of California Press.

Schor, Juliet B., William Attwood-Charles, Mehmet Cansoy, Isak Ladegaard, and Robert Wengronowitz. 2020. "Dependence and Precarity in the Platform Economy." *Theory and Society* 49 (5): 833–61.

Schrank, Andrew, and Josh Whitford. 2009. "Industrial Policy in the United States: A Neo-Polanyian Interpretation." *Politics and Society* 37 (4): 521–53.

Schumpeter, Joseph A. 2008. *Capitalism, Socialism and Democracy*. New York: Harper Perennial.

Schwarz, Ori. 2018. "Cultures of Choice: Towards a Sociology of Choice as a Cultural Phenomenon." *British Journal of Sociology* 69 (3): 845–64.

Scott, James C. 1998. *Seeing Like a State: How Certain Schemes to Improve the Human Condition Have Failed*. New Haven, CT: Yale University Press.

———. 2008. *Weapons of the Weak: Everyday Forms of Peasant Resistance*. New Haven, CT: Yale University Press.

Sen, Amartya. 2000. *Development as Freedom*. New York: Anchor Books.

Shang, Huping. 2018. "Paths to Motivations and Accountabilities—A Review of China's Forty-Year Government Performance Evaluation Reform." *Chinese Public Administration* 8:85–92.

Sharif, Naubahar, and Yu Huang. 2019a. "Achieving Industrial Upgrading through Automation in Dongguan, China." *Science, Technology and Society* 24 (2): 237–53.

———. 2019b. "Industrial Automation in China's 'Workshop of the World.'" *China Journal* 81 (1): 1–22.

———. 2019c. "Introduction: Innovation and Work in East Asia." *Science, Technology and Society* 24 (2): 193–98.

Shen, Hong. 2018. "Building a Digital Silk Road? Situating the Internet in China's Belt and Road Initiative." *International Journal of Communication* 12:2683–701.

———. 2022. *Alibaba: Infrastructuring Global China*. New York: Routledge.

Shen, Liyin, Zhenhua Huang, Siu Wai Wong, Shiju Liao, and Yingli Lou. 2018. "A Holistic Evaluation of Smart City Performance in the Context of China." *Journal of Cleaner Production* 200:667–79.

Shen, Wei. 2012. "Deconstructing the Myth of Alipay Drama—Repoliticizing Foreign Investment in the Telecommunications Sector in China." *Telecommunications Policy* 36 (10): 929–42.

Shen, Xiaobai, and Robn Williams. 2005. "A Critique of China's Utilitarian View of Science and Technology." *Science, Technology and Society* 10 (2): 197–223.

Shieh, Gwo-Shyong. 1989. "'Black-Hands Becoming Their Own Bosses': Class Mobility in Taiwan's Manufacturing Sectors." *Taiwan: A Radical Quarterly in Social Studies* 2 (2): 11–54.

Slater, Dan, and Joseph Wong. 2022. *From Development to Democracy: The Transformations of Modern Asia*. Princeton, NJ: Princeton University Press.

Smith, Chris, and Jenny Chan. 2015. "Working for Two Bosses: Student Interns as Constrained Labour in China." *Human Relations* 68 (2): 305–26.

Soskice, David. 2022a. "The American Political Economy: Macroeconomics and Electoral Politics." In *The American Political Economy: Macroeconomics and Electoral Politics*, edited by Jacob S. Hacker, Alexander Hertel-Fernandez, Paul Pierson, and Kathleen Thelen, 323–50. Cambridge, MA: Harvard University Press.

———. 2022b. "Rethinking Varieties of Capitalism and Growth Theory in the ICT Era." *Review of Keynesian Economics* 10 (2): 222–41.

Srnicek, Nick. 2017. *Platform Capitalism*. Oxford: Polity Press.

Steinberg, Marc, Rahul Mukherjee, and Aswin Punathambekar. 2022. "Media Power in Digital Asia: Super Apps and Megacorps." *Media, Culture and Society* 44 (8): 1405–19.

Stewart, Andrew, and Jim Stanford. 2017. "Regulating Work in the Gig Economy: What Are the Options?" *Economic and Labour Relations Review* 28 (3): 420–37.

Streib, Jessi. 2015. *The Power of the Past: Understanding Cross-Class Marriages.* New York: Oxford University Press.

Su, Chunmeizi, and Terry Flew. 2021. "The Rise of Baidu, Alibaba and Tencent (BAT) and Their Role in China's Belt and Road Initiative (BRI)." *Global Media and Communication* 17 (1): 67–86.

Su, Zheng, Xu Xu, and Xun Cao. 2021. "What Explains Popular Support for Government Monitoring in China?" *Journal of Information Technology and Politics* 19 (4): 377–92.

Swider, Sarah. 2015a. *Building China: Informal Work and the New Precariat.* Ithaca, NY: Cornell University Press.

———. 2015b. "Building China: Precarious Employment among Migrant Construction Workers." *Work, Employment and Society* 29 (1): 41–59.

Swidler, Ann. 1986. "Culture in Action: Symbols and Strategies." *American Sociological Review* 51 (2): 273–86.

Tang, Min. 2020. *Tencent: China's Surging Internet Giant and Its Political Economy.* New York: Routledge.

Tassinari, Arianna, and Vincenzo Maccarrone. 2017. "The Mobilisation of Gig Economy Couriers in Italy: Some Lessons for the Trade Union Movement." *Transfer* 23 (3): 353–57.

———. 2020. "Riders on the Storm: Workplace Solidarity among Gig Economy Couriers in Italy and the UK." *Work, Employment and Society* 34 (1): 35–54.

Taylor, Bill, and Qi Li. 2007. "Is the ACFTU a Union and Does It Matter?" *Journal of Industrial Relations* 49 (5): 701–15.

Thayer, Kyle, and Andrew J. Ko. 2017. "Barriers Faced by Coding Bootcamp Students." *Proceedings of the 2017 ACM Conference on International Computing Education Research.* New York: Association for Computing Machinery.

Thompson, Paul, and Diane van Den Broek. 2010. "Managerial Control and Workplace Regimes: An Introduction." *Work, Employment and Society* 24 (3): 1–12.

Tian, Wei, and Hongyun Tian. 2011. "On the Pros and Cons of China's Target Responsibility Management." *Statistics and Decision* 5:44–47.

Tian, Xun. 1987. "Wuxi City Proposed to Expand Industry." *Economic Work Newsletter* 11:31.

Tirole, Jean. 2017. *Economics for the Common Good.* Princeton, NJ: Princeton University Press.

Trevaskes, Susan. 2006. "Severe and Swift Justice in China." *British Journal of Criminology* 47 (1): 23–41.

Tsai, Kellee S. 2015. "The Political Economy of State Capitalism and Shadow Banking in China." *Issues and Studies* 51 (1): 55–98.

Tsai, Wen-Hsuan, Hsin-Hsien Wang, and Ruihua Lin. 2021. "Hobbling Big Brother: Top-Level Design and Local Discretion in China's Social Credit System." *China Journal* 86:1–20.

Turner, Fred. 2006. *From Counterculture to Cyberculture: Stewart Brand, the Whole Earth Network, and the Rise of Digital Utopianism.* Chicago: University of Chicago Press.

Vallas, Steven P. 2017. "Platform Capitalism: What Is at Stake for Workers?" *New Labor Forum,* 1–11.

Vallas, Steven, and Juliet B. Schor. 2020. "What Do Platforms Do? Understanding the Gig Economy." *Annual Review of Sociology* 46 (1): 273–94.

Van der Kamp, Denise S. 2021. "Blunt Force Regulation and Bureaucratic Control: Understanding China's War on Pollution." *Governance* 34 (1): 191–209.

Van Jaarsveld, Danielle D. 2004. "Collective Representation among High-Tech Workers at Microsoft and Beyond: Lessons from WashTech/CWA." *Industrial Relations: A Journal of Economy and Society* 43 (2): 364–85.

Van Rooij, Benjamin. 2016. "The Campaign Enforcement Style: Chinese Practice in Context and Comparison." In *Comparative Law and Regulation*, edited by Francesca Bignami and David Zaring, 217–37. Cheltenham, UK: Edward Elgar Publishing.

Veen, Alex, Tom Barratt, and Caleb Goods. 2019. "Platform-Capital's 'App-etite' for Control: A Labour Process Analysis of Food-Delivery Work in Australia." *Work, Employment and Society* 34 (3): 388–406.

Vogel, Ezra F. 1990. *One Step Ahead in China: Guangdong under Reform*. Cambridge, MA: Harvard University Press.

Wade, Robert H. 2012. "Return of Industrial Policy?" *International Review of Applied Economics* 26 (2): 223–39.

———. 2014. "The Paradox of US Industrial Policy: The Developmental State in Disguise." In *Transforming Economies: Making Industrial Policy Work for Growth, Jobs and Development*, edited by José M. Salazar-Xirinachs, Irmgard Nübler, and Richard Kozul-Wright, 379–400. Geneva: International Labour Organization.

Wang, Alex L. 2018. "Symbolic Legitimacy and Chinese Environmental Reform." *Environmental Law* 48:699–760.

Wang, Greg G., William J. Rothwell, and Judy Y. Sun. 2009. "Management Development in China: A Policy Analysis." *International Journal of Training and Development* 13 (4): 205–20.

Wang, Hansheng, and Yige Wang. 2009. "Target Management Responsibility System: The Practical Logic of Local Party-State in Rural China." *Sociological Studies* 2:61–92.

Wang, Hao, Wei Li, and Yu Deng. 2017. "Precarity among Highly Educated Migrants: College Graduates in Beijing, China." *Urban Geography* 38 (10): 1497–516.

Wang, Hong-Zen. 2019. *Under Global Production Pressure: Taiwan Capital, Vietnamese Workers and the State*. Taipei: National Taiwan University Press.

Wang, Jun. 2017. "Shizhe Shengcun (Survival of the Fittest): The Origin and Adaptation of Social Darwinist Concepts in Modern China." PhD diss., Queen's University at Kingston. https://qspace.library.queensu.ca/handle/1974/23756?show=full.

Wang, Xiang. 2020. "Permits, Points, and Permanent Household Registration: Recalibrating Hukou Policy under 'Top-Level Design.'" *Journal of Current Chinese Affairs* 49 (3): 269–90.

Wang, Yangzong. 2018. "Historical Transformation of Chinese Science and Technology— Revisiting National Science and Technology Conference in 1978." *Bulletin of the Chinese Academy of Sciences* 33 (4): 351–61.

Wang, Zhiyong, and Xuemei Chen. 2014. "Research on the Efficacy of Industrial Upgrading Policy—Taking Guangdong's 'Double Transfer' Strategy as an Example." *Urban Development Research* 21 (9): 69–76.

Wang, Zuoyue. 2015. "The Chinese Developmental State during the Cold War: The Making of the 1956 Twelve-Year Science and Technology Plan." *History and Technology* 31 (3): 180–205.

Weber, Isabella. 2020. "Origins of China's Contested Relation with Neoliberalism: Economics, the World Bank, and Milton Friedman at the Dawn of Reform." *Global Perspectives* 1 (1): 1–14.

Weber, Max. 1956. *The Protestant Ethic and the Spirit of Capitalism*. New York: Charles Scribner's Sons.

Webster, Juliet. 2016. "Microworkers of the Gig Economy: Separate and Precarious." *New Labor Forum* 25 (3): 56–64.

Wedeman, Andrew H. 2003. *From Mao to Market: Rent Seeking, Local Protectionism, and Marketization in China*. Cambridge: Cambridge University Press.

———. 2012. *Double Paradox: Rapid Growth and Rising Corruption in China*. Ithaca, NY: Cornell University Press.

Whittaker, D. Hugh, Timothy Sturgeon, Toshie Okita, and Tianbiao Zhu. 2020. *Compressed Development: Time and Timing in Economic and Social Development*. Oxford: Oxford University Press.

Wolf, Diane L. 1992. *Factory Daughters: Gender, Household Dynamics, and Rural Industrialization in Java*. Berkeley: University of California Press.

Wong, Christine. 2011. "The Fiscal Stimulus Programme and Public Governance Issues in China." *OECD Journal on Budgeting* 11 (3): 1–22.

Woo, Wing Thye. 1999. "The Real Reasons for China's Growth." *China Journal* 41:115–37.

Wood, Alex J., Mark Graham, Vili Lehdonvirta, and Isis Hjorth. 2019. "Good Gig, Bad Gig: Autonomy and Algorithmic Control in the Global Gig Economy." *Work, Employment and Society* 33 (1): 56–75.

Woronov, Terry E. 2011. "Learning to Serve: Urban Youth, Vocational Schools and New Class Formations in China." *China Journal* 66:77–99.

Wrenn, Douglas H., Junjian Yi, and Bo Zhang. 2019. "House Prices and Marriage Entry in China." *Regional Science and Urban Economics* 74:118–30.

Wright, Mike, Geoffrey Wood, Aldo Musacchio, Ilya Okhmatovskiy, Anna Grosman, and Jonathan P. Doh. 2021. "State Capitalism in International Context: Varieties and Variations." *Journal of World Business* 56 (2): 1–16.

Wu, Fulong, Jie Chen, Fenghua Pan, Nick Gallent, and Fangzhu Zhang. 2020. "Assetization: The Chinese Path to Housing Financialization." *Annals of the American Association of Geographers* 110 (5): 1483–99.

Wu, Haiyan. 2004. "Evaluation of Political Performance under the Scientific Outlook on Development." *Contemporary Chinese Politics Review* 1:322–33.

Wu, Jieh-min. 2011. "Strangers Forever? Differential Citizenship and China Rural Migrant Workers." *Taiwanese Sociology* (21): 51–99.

———. 2019. *Rent-Seeking Developmental State in China: Taishang, Guangdong Model and Global Capitalism*. Taipei: National Taiwan University Press.

Wu, Mingyu. 2018. "Drafting Deng Xiaoping's Speech for the 1978 National Science and Technology Conference " *Bulletin of the Chinese Academy of Sciences* 33 (4): 419–22.

Wu, Yi, and Yunong Li. 2018. "Impact of Government Intervention in the Housing Market: Evidence from the Housing Purchase Restriction Policy in China." *Applied Economics* 50 (6): 691–705.

Xi, Jinping. 2001a. Preface to *Science and Patriotism*, i–ii. Beijing: Tsinghua University Press.

Xi, Jinping. 2001b. "Speeding up Structural Adjustment and Promoting Economic Development." *Qiushi* 4:4–5.

———. 2001c. "A Tentative Study on China's Rural Marketization." PhD diss., Tsinghua University.

Xie, Yu. 2016. "Understanding Inequality in China." *Chinese Journal of Sociology* 2 (3): 327–47.

Xu, Guangdong, and Binwei Gui. 2019. "From Financial Expression to Financial Crisis? The Case of China." *Asian-Pacific Economic Literature* 33 (1): 48–63.

Yao, Yao. 2020. "Uberizing the Legal Profession? Lawyer Autonomy and Status in the Digital Legal Market." *British Journal of Industrial Relations* 58 (3): 483–506.

Ye, Yonglie. 2012. *Deng Xiaoping Changed China*. Nanchang: Jiangxi Peoples Publishing House.

Yi, Wang, Zhan Peng, and Jiang Zu. 2018. "The Income Gap between Land-Lost Farmers and Non-Land-Lost Residents in the Process of Urbanization: Based on Survey Data in Beijing." *Chinese Rural Economy* 2018 (4): 121–39.

Yuan, Zhendong. 2008. "1978 National Science Conference: The Landmark in China's History of Technology." *Science and Culture Review* 5 (2): 37–57.

Zeng, Guang, Guolan Zhou, and Yuan Guo. 2015. "Research on Industrial Transfer from Yangtze River Delta, Pearl River Delta, and Fujian to Jiangxi." *Regional Economic Review* 1:123–26.

Zhang, Angela Huyue. 2021a. "Agility over Stability: China's Great Reversal in Regulating the Platform Economy." University of Hong Kong Faculty of Law Research Paper No. 2021/36. https://doi.org/http://dx.doi.org/10.2139/ssrn.3892642.

———. 2021b. *Chinese Antitrust Exceptionalism: How the Rise of China Challenges Global Regulation*. Oxford: Oxford University Press.

Zhang, Haoran. 2015. "Can 'Emptying the Cage and Changing the Bird' Improve the Economic Efficiency of the Host City?" *Exploring Economic Problems* 6:126–29.

Zhang, Li. 2012. "Soviet Experts in Chinese Academy of Sciences: Historical Review of Sino-Soviet Cooperation and Exchange between Two Academies of Sciences in 1950s." *Science and Culture Review* 9 (2): 54–71.

Zhang, Mingzhong. 1986. "Different Views on the Gradient Development Theory." *Researches in Science Management* 4 (8): 62–64.

Zhang, Taisu, and Tom Ginsburg. 2019. "China's Turn toward Law." *Virginia Journal of International Law* 59:306–89.

Zhao, Bo. 2005. "On Mu Ouchu's Scientific Management Thoughts and Practices." *Commercial Research* 310:98–99.

Zhao, Dingxin. 2004. *The Power of Tiananmen: State-Society Relations and the 1989 Beijing Student Movement*. Chicago: University of Chicago Press.

Zhao, Guochang, Jingjing Ye, Zhengyang Li, and Sen Xue. 2017. "How and Why Do Chinese Urban Students Outperform Their Rural Counterparts?" *China Economic Review* 45:103–23.

Zhao, Keman. 1983. "Two Pathways to Improve Economic Efficiency." *Journal of Hubei University of Economics* 1:49–53.

Zhao, Suisheng. 1998. "A State-Led Nationalism: The Patriotic Education Campaign in Post-Tiananmen China." *Communist and Post-Communist Studies* 31 (3): 287–302.

Zhao, Yuezhi. 2000. "From Commercialization to Conglomeration: The Transformation of the Chinese Press within the Orbit of the Party State." *Journal of Communication* 50 (2): 3–26.

Zheng, Zhilong. 2009. "Government Performance Evaluation in Local Governance." *Chinese Public Administration* 1:49–54.

Zhou, Li-An. 2007. "Governing China's Local Officials: An Analysis of Promotion Tournament Model." *Economic Research Journal* 7:36–50.

Zhou, Liping, and Changjun Yue. 2019. "From Entry to Exit: Research on the Impact of Family Background on Equity in Higher Education." *Jiangsu Higher Education* (8): 47–58.

Zhou, Liping, and Changjun Yue. 2020. "Does Occupation Choice Matter?" *Review of Higher Education* 56 (1): 44–57.

Zhou, Minhui, Rachel Murphy, and Ran Tao. 2014. "Effects of Parents' Migration on the Education of Children Left Behind in Rural China." *Population and Development Review* 40 (2): 273–92.

Zhou, Xueguang. 2012. "Mobilizational State: Further Exploration of the Institutional Logic of State Governance in China." *Open Times* 9:105–25.

———. 2017. *The Institutional Logic of Governance in China: An Organizational Approach*. Beijing: SDX Joint Publishing.

Zhou, Yang, Yuanzhi Guo, and Yansui Liu. 2018. "High-Level Talent Flow and Its Influence on Regional Unbalanced Development in China." *Applied Geograph* 91:89–98.

Zhou, Yun. 2019. "Economic Resources, Cultural Matching, and the Rural-Urban Boundary in China's Marriage Market." *Journal of Marriage and Family* 81 (3): 567–83.

Zhu, Fangsheng. 2021. "Empowered by Procedures: The Emergence of School Admissions Protests in China." Unpublished manuscript.

Zhu, Weiping. 2009 "'Emptying the Cage and Changing the Bird' Benefits Economic Growth." *Informatization in China's Manufacturing Industry* 3:76.

Zuboff, Shoshana. 1988. *In the Age of the Smart Machine: The Future of Work and Power*. New York: Basic Books.

———. 2019. *The Age of Surveillance Capitalism: The Fight for a Human Future at the New Frontier of Power*. New York: PublicAffairs.

Zuo, Cai. 2017. "Operation and Efficacy of Local Cadre Evaluation System." *Academia Bimestrie* 3:137–45.

Zysman, John, and Martin Kenney. 2018. "The Next Phase in the Digital Revolution: Intelligent Tools, Platforms, Growth, Employment." *Communications of the ACM* 61 (2): 54–63.

INDEX

A page number in *italics* refers to a figure or table.

financial crisis of 2008 (*continued*)
central and Guangdong governments
about, 77–78; dominant narrative on
handling of, 80–83; export-oriented
enterprises and, 82, 169; Hu on transforming the development model after, 51;
platform capitalism in US following, 188;
postindustrial society in period following,
8; promotion of S&T to save China and,
63; stimulus package and, 81, 82, 159–60;
techno-developmental regime in aftermath of, 301; urbanization and, 37; Wang
on solution to, 79

financial risks: concerns leading to the crackdown and, 274, 275, 276–81; cracking
down on, 289–90

financial scandals, 282

Financial Stability and Development Committee (FSDC), 282

financial technology (fintech), 178, 181, 240,
274, 277, 280; crackdown on, 289–90

first-tier cities, 203, 240, 241, 347n4, 350n23

fiscal expenditures, of local governments, 35

fiscal reforms, 32, 33, 35, 63

fiscal revenue, and land urbanization, 36, 37

five coordination, 49, 50, 60

fixed-asset investment: in real estate vs.
manufacturing, 161–64, *162, 163, 164*; in
Shenzhen, 161–62, *162, 163*

flexible employment, 179, 193, 196, 197

Flora, 141, *142*, 145, 150, 154

flying geese paradigm, 71, 334n73

food delivery couriers, 200–206; as escape
from manufacturing jobs, 206; in France,
206, 212, 214, 231; interviewees' characteristics, 201, *202*; number of couriers, 197;
performance metrics of, 208; research
methodology with, 325–26. See also gig
platform couriers (GPCs); service platform couriers (SPCs)

food delivery platforms, 28, 197–200; absorbing low-skilled labor, 197; architecture
for control and management in, 206–14,
213, 222, 314; delivery partners (franchisees)

of, 203–5, 207, 210; factories losing workers
to, 127, 194; food safety–related technology of, 199; as labor-intensive services,
196; local governments and, 199–200;
supported by the central state, 229. See also
food delivery couriers

food delivery worker guideline, 292–93

foreign direct investment (FDI): allowed in
nonstrategic sectors, 172; export-oriented
manufacturing and, 4; restricted in IT
areas, 284; from Taiwan, 188

foreign-invested enterprises (FIEs): alliances
between local governments and, 190;
CCP's strengthened control over, 283;
cheap labor for manufacturing by, 33;
Jiang on management technicians of, 49;
mobility from workers to factory owners
in, 126; moving elsewhere, 120; preferential treatment of, 74–75; removal of tax
benefits for, 88, 340n7

Fourcade, Marion, 15, 234, 315

fourth technological revolution, 4

fourth world, 7, 15

Foxconn: disciplinary rules at, 125; as largest
contract electronics manufacturer, 340n26;
local governments and, 190; low on
global value chain, 33; robotization and,
7, 146, 300

France: food delivery couriers in, 206, 212,
214, 231; postwar technological visions
for, 17, 318

Frankfurt school, 18–19, 331n97

Friedman, Eli, 101, 312

games between persons, 8, 14–15, 16, 22, 25,
190, 308

gamification of food delivery platforms,
208, 210

gaming the point systems, 128–29, 132

GDP: criticisms of focus on, 58–59, 60;
digital economy as share of, 169, *169*;
in evaluation systems, 58, 60, 61, 310;
Guangdong as largest province by, 77,
79; local governments' focus on, 115; of

rural population. *See* migrant workers; peasants
rural targeted poverty alleviation, 102

Schumpeter, Joseph, 6–7, 12, 15
science and technology (S&T): Bell on role of, 2, 8; Chinese attitudes toward, 52, 53–55, 56; Clinton on US-China partnership in, 1; enthusiasm in Chinese society for, 52; fetishization of, 26; Marcuse on political power and, 18; saving China with, 39, 63, 69, 78; technical rationalization and, 13; techno-developmentalism and, 32–33, 38–39; techno-developmental regime and, 10; technology fundamentalism and, 102; techno-nationalism and, 17; US attitudes toward, 335n100; world attitudes toward, 52, 53–55, 56, 335n100. *See also* techno-development; techno-developmentalism; technology
science and technology studies, 17, 52
scientific concept of development, 49–51; bias against working class and, 73–74; bird/cage logic and, 67; erosion of Hu's vision for, 319; evaluation systems based on, 59–60, 64; Wang's application to Guangdong, 78; Xi's use of, 71
scientific decision-making, 44–45, 48, 177, 178
scientific management: Jiang on, 48; performance evaluation systems in, 57–58, 62, 64
scientific ruling, 49–50
scientism, 51–52, 69
scientization: of birdcage economy, 67–76; of statecraft, 56–62, 64–65, 86, 132, 177, 199, 335n104
Scott, James C., 16–18, 22, 63
second-tier cities, 240, 241, 350n23
self-strengthening movement, 38
semiconductor industry, 12, 14, 28, 41, 98–99, 187–89
Sen, Amartya, 21, 318
service platform couriers (SPCs), 203–5; communication between, 208, 209;

grievances of, 214–19, 215, 218; performance metrics of, 207–9. *See also* food delivery couriers
service platforms, 207–9, 213
service sector: growth of employment in, 195, 195; low-skilled jobs in, 138; manufacturing workers wanting to move to, 153, 154; workers disappointed with, 127. *See also* platform economy
Shandong, 34, 68
Shanghai: bird/cage logic and, 68, 72; collaboration agreement with Meituan, 200, 233–34; cooperation agreements with Alibaba and Tencent, 178; difficulty obtaining local citizenship in, 239; shortage of land for manufacturing, 66; tech companies concentrated in, 240
shanzhai, 27, 29
sharing economy, 175–76
Shen, Xiaobai, 52, 63–64
Shenzhen: access to factory in, 29, 323; conversion of closed factories in, 121; demography of, 104–7, 105, 106; difficulty of obtaining local citizenship in, 239; evaluation instruments in, 87, 92; factory worker becoming platform courier in, 228; faking a high- and new-tech certificate in, 119; fixed-asset investment in, 161–62, 162, 163; high real estate prices in, 121; Household Registration Scheme, 92, 94, 95–97; housing prices in, 158, 159; industrial transformation and, 72; land value in, 161, 162; low-end population in, 73; real estate investment in, 161, 161, 162, 163; robotization in, 7; special status and resources of, 104; tech companies in, 240; workers at Jade in, 121–22
Silicon Valley, 169, 187–88, 189, 263
Singapore, 5
skill-intensive services, 195, 195, 197. *See also* software engineers
small and medium-sized enterprises (SMEs): development policy criticized in, 74–75, 80; financial crisis of 2008 and, 77–78, 81;

Printed in the USA
CPSIA information can be obtained
at www.ICGtesting.com
JSHW020012270923
49160JS00002B/3